The Time Machine

The War of the Worlds

H.G.

THE TIME MACHINE

A Critical Edition

NEW YORK OXFORD

WELLS

THE WAR OF THE WORLDS

EDITED BY

FRANK D. McCONNELL
Northwestern University

UNIVERSITY PRESS ⚜ 1977

ACKNOWLEDGMENTS

A number of friends have given information and encouragement that have made the preparation of this edition not only possible, but a pleasure. I am happy to thank Edward Espenshade, Elizabeth Dipple, A. Robert Lee, and Robert Mayo for kindnesses rendered. And my students in English B-12 at Northwestern University, "Science Fiction," have contributed more by their enthusiasm for Wells than most of them will ever know.

My friends Alfred Appel, Jr., and Sam Hynes have been extraordinarily important to the completion of this book. The reader will find only a slight portion of their aid represented in Sam's collaboration with me on one of the essays, and in the illustrations, to the selection of which Alfred brought his wide knowledge and generosity. John Wright of Oxford University Press has, from the first conception of this book, been unflaggingly generous and encouraging, and he has brought to its organization a wit and an intelligence without which it would be the poorer. Martha Browne of Oxford University Press has also made important contributions to what I hope will be the usefulness and intelligibility of this edition.

My wife Carolyn, finally, has been the most indispensable of all. The idea of an edition of Wells was first suggested by her, and throughout all the stages of preparing it she has not only actively collaborated, but continually made this, like all other enterprises, joyful.

Frank D. McConnell

CONTENTS

H. G. WELLS

THE TIME MACHINE
THE WAR OF THE WORLDS

INTRODUCTION

This is the first annotated critical edition of *The Time Machine* and *The War of the Worlds,* and perhaps the most remarkable thing about it is that it *is* the first, more than three-quarters of a century after the appearance of these two brilliant and crucial modern novels. H. G. Wells was born September 21, 1866, seven years after Charles Darwin's *Origin of Species* began the demolition of traditional ideas of man's innate nobility, uniqueness, and importance to the universe at large. He died August 13, 1946—a year, almost to the day, after a different and more ominous demolition, the explosion of the atomic bomb over Hiroshima. Both events, furthermore, were to find their earliest and perhaps their best imaginative expression in his own work; for *The Time Machine* is, among many other things, a meditation on the implications of evolutionary theory and the vastness of geological time, and *The War of the Worlds* envisions, in part, weapons whose mystery and ferocity anticipate the age of nuclear fission. Indeed, by the time of his death, Wells had long been established as an analyst and prophet of the technological era, an interpreter of physics to the masses, and a pleader for the masses at the court of physics, the tribunal of a cold and inhospitable cosmos. Disturbing in his own work, he was the cause of disturbance in other men. His unflinching acceptance of the grimmest implications of modern science, his rejection of humanistic ideas of culture and art, and his final pessimism about the whole enterprise of human civilization, all made him the object of alternate ridicule and adulation, and a center of controversy throughout the twentieth century and well beyond his own death. Even his amazing gift for prediction (e.g., he was the first man to use the phrase "atomic bomb"; it appeared in his 1908 *The War in the Air*) could bear a double significance. To those who hated Wells and what he stood for, his predictive power could suggest—with almost medieval overtones—that he was too deeply in league with those soulless powers of abstraction, science, and technology that threaten to overrun and rule our age. But to those who admired and venerated him, the same uncanny power was proof that he, of all men, understood the tendency of thought in his age, had discovered both the perils and the possibilities of the future, and was the true father of science fiction—the epic literature of tomorrow, and of all our tomorrows.

What would have surprised and, perhaps, chagrined Wells himself is the fact that such debates and such variant images of the writer invariably center on a handful of stories and five novels written before the twentieth century had even begun. He came to regard them almost as juvenilia, but these writings of the 1890s were Wells's first purchase upon influence and fame, and they have remained his most definitive achievements: *The Time Machine,* his first novel, appeared in 1895, followed by *The Island of Dr. Moreau* in 1896, *The Invisible Man* in 1897, *The War of the Worlds* in 1898, and *The First Men in the Moon* in 1901. Other tales of science and anticipations of the future were to follow, almost to the end of his creative life, but it is to these early stories that Wells continued to owe his literary eminence, and to these that his critics and admirers alike returned for the central, the essential Wells. And of all that prodigious output of the nineties, the most widely celebrated and richly suggestive productions are the two novels reproduced in this volume.

Both *The Time Machine* and *The War of the Worlds* are, of

course, classics not only of English literature but of "science fiction": a curious fact, since they were written almost thirty years before the term "science fiction" was invented. And the phrase itself conjures up images and associations—bug-eyed monsters, cigar-shaped rocket ships, scantily-clad maidens in melodramatic perils—that distort Wells's own achievement, as well as the stature of science fiction as an important strain of modern literature. But the associations are there, and only recently have literary critics and cultural historians learned to recognize the enduring imaginative values such trappings express and, paradoxically, obscure. Science fiction, we have been in process of discovering for some years now, is *not* the tawdry, sensationalist literature of the half-educated inhabitants of a robotized society, but rather one of the few authentic mythologies of the twentieth century, a reexamination of the most ancient psychic dilemmas in the vocabulary of a distinctively contemporary world-view. To describe it as a mythology, moreover, is to imply that, at least at its best, science fiction bridges the gap—otherwise a widening one in our century—between so-called popular culture and so-called high culture. And in this respect as in so many others, these early Wells novels are a triumphant, perhaps *the* triumphant, example of the genre he fathered.

Wells himself was eminently suited for the role of arbitrator between levels of culture, *chargé d'affaires* between the humanistic past and the technological future. He was born at Bromley, Kent, in the most unpromising of working-class circumstances. His mother, a former maid, and his father, a former gardener, operated a china shop in his early years, but the shop was a failure. His mother soon returned to service—at Up Park in Sussex—and his father played for some years as a semiprofessional cricketeer, to make ends meet. The young Wells, however, showed early signs of the fierce independence and arrogant intelligence that were to mark his whole career. After a mediocre primary education, he was apprenticed to a draper's shop—a trade at which he failed miserably, returning not to the china shop but to Up Park to lick his wounds. There, privy not only to the downstairs kitchen but also to the upstairs library, he gorged himself on the classics of philosophy and of English literature, acquiring by himself the liberal education his social class had denied him.

After some desultory teaching in Sussex grammar schools, he won a scholarship in 1884 to the Normal School of Science in Kensington. It was probably the most important accomplishment of his life. For it took him out of the stulifying lower-class background of the housemaid's son at Up Park, and introduced him to the most exciting, most definitively "modern" intellectual society of his day. Darwin's ideas, published almost thirty years before, were still a matter of passionate argument and deep fear among the poets and thinkers of the day; and Wells's tutor at the Normal School was none other than T. H. Huxley, the most articulate and brilliant defender and exponent of the Darwinian view. Huxley, indeed, may be the unacknowledged genius behind Wells's great novels, written almost a decade after the two men first met. At any rate, Wells earned first honors in his first year at the Normal School. But it was not his fate to be a scientist. Early in his second year he became editor and chief contributor to the *Science Schools Journal,* an otherwise unremarkable publication, which nevertheless both whetted Wells's literary appetite and sufficiently distracted him from his proper studies to force him, by the end of his third year, to withdraw from their pursuit.

He was a very ill young man. Having married his cousin Isabel after leaving school, he embarked upon a writing and teaching career with a wife who seems to have satisfied none of his passionate (and lifelong) sexual expectations, and with a hemorrhage-prone condition that the doctors diagnosed as tubercular. In a famous and often-recorded moment in 1888 he had solved the latter problem to his own satisfaction by resolving to live whatever the predictions of the medical profession. The first, and perhaps more important, problem he resolved—temporarily—by eloping in 1894 with Amy Catharine Robbins, one of his science students in London, and thereby taking upon himself the responsibility of supporting two households, his own and that of the young and brilliant woman with whom, according to the morality of the time, he was living in sin. Of Catharine, ultimately Mrs. Wells, he was later to write: "She stuck to me so well that in the end I stuck to myself."

But in the early days, the days out of which *The Time Machine* and *The War of the Worlds* arose, such retrospective complacency was not so natural. Wells was literally not sure that he was not fated to die at an early age, and was saddled in the midst of that uncertainty with the maintenance of not one but two families. He was in his thirties and had irrevocably committed himself to making his way as a writer; but by 1894, he had published only a few sketches, startling indeed but essentially ephemeral, on the implications of modern science for the modern view of man in the universe. It is no surprise, given his straitened circumstances, that the discoveries of science should have suggested to him at the time more an outlook of universal pessimism than the measured optimism that characterized his work after this crucial and definitive period. But it is a surprise, and one of the biggest surprises in English literature, that this undereducated, disorganized, scruffy young Englishman should, with so many odds against him, have written as brilliantly as he did during those unpleasant years of the nineties.

A canny newspaper editor, William Ernest Henley, aided Wells in his first great escape from the trap into which his social class and his personal cantankerousness had led him. It was Henley who, first in the *National Observer* in 1893 and then in the *New Review* in 1894, published the serial sketches that evolved into *The Time Machine* of 1895. And with the publication of this, his first novel, Wells was celebrated enthusiastically as the new Dickens, the new Trollope, the new great novelist of the age. Wells consolidated his first success by publishing a flurry of novels over the next five years, each of which was avidly received by the public and most of which were reviewed with great favor by the reigning critical pundits. The "scientific romance"—Wells's own term for these productions—was not only a wholly novel kind of narrative, but apparently one that caught the attention, at the clearest and most popular levels, of the age. The serialization of *The War of the Worlds* in *Pearson's Weekly* in 1897 was not quite the end of this first period of unalloyed fame for Wells—*The First Men in the Moon* was to follow three years later—but it was certainly its height. Wells by this time had built himself an elegant house with the royalties from his earlier books, and was settling into a kind of peace with himself and with the cosmos that was to mark most of his later work as, if not contradictory to, at least differing significantly from the dark visions of these first productions. Throughout the century he helped initiate, he argued strenuously for the saving reign of reason and science against the destructive passions of the blood and the primitive psyche, and was often caricatured and often admired as a wealthy, exceptionally comfortable and self-important prophet of the age of technocracy and the ascendancy of the Scientific Brain. He also found himself, as the twentieth century progressed, increasingly opposed to ideas of self-conscious and self-celebrating art in fiction, and more and more ranged on the side of writing as proselytizing, of literature as the straightforward and unabashed presentation of ideas.

This last development of Wells's thought, particularly, gave rise to one of the more celebrated literary quarrels of the turn of the century. During the years of his first success, he had been greeted by many as a brilliant heir to the robust tradition of English fiction; and among those who so greeted him was Henry James, the writer who perhaps more than any other raised the art of fiction to its distinctively modern level of artistic self-consciousness and stylistic fastidiousness. Few literary friendships are more unlikely than that between the lower middle class, scientifically trained, desperately ambitious Wells and James, the mandarin, all but obsessively cultured, American expatriate. But friendship and mutual admiration there were at the beginning of Wells's career (the later and most complexly brilliant phase of James's own); indeed, one of the most famous and widely reproduced photographs of James was taken by

Wells, an enthusiastic and gifted amateur photographer, on a week-end visit of the older to the younger writer. But as Wells's fiction after 1900 became increasingly shrill and argumentative at the expense of narrative form, James expressed his disappointment, in both letters and essays, at Wells's apparent desertion of the vineyards of art for the soapboxes of public debate. And Wells, never a man to suffer criticism gladly, responded by hardening his own stance in favor of fiction as public education and against fiction as self-conscious, pure form, and by bitterly attacking James and the Jamesian novel. The friendship, probably, could not have lasted long under any circumstances. But it is ironic that Henry James may have been at least partly responsible for forcing H. G. Wells into the position he uneasily maintained for much of his creative life: the position that the novel must *choose* between artistic excellence and social utility, between formal beauty and intellectual responsibility.

But whatever his later development, it is undeniably the case that for those few years of the 1890s, desperately unhappy ones for Wells but fortunate ones for literature, he was the sole and powerful creator of a new mode of storytelling: a mode that has increasingly, in all its complexity and in all its crudity, become the distinctive mythology of our time.

After so many films and books deriving from or recapitulating the ideas of these two novels, it is perhaps easy to forget their own startling originality. And in a way, even their predictive power is a block to a fresh, wholly unprejudiced reading of them; for reading Wells today, recognizing his clear and sometimes cruel insight into the delusions and false comforts of the gaslight era, we are apt to ignore how firmly his imagination is grounded in the literature of his time, how strong a light gaslight does cast. Histories of science fiction that treat *The Time Machine* or *The War of the Worlds* only as paradigms for later explorations distort the genius of the books as surely as do histories of the English novel that treat them only as sports, as early expressions of a scientific or "Darwinian" consciousness. They are, both by themselves and in their influence on later forms of imagination, central fictions. The present edition is designed to indicate both how rich and controversial these two novels are, and how lasting has been their influence on later writing within and about the sphere of science fiction.

THE TIME MACHINE
An Invention[1]

1. The first edition carries the dedication "To William Ernest Henley." Henley (1849-1903) serialized two versions of *The Time Machine* in his newspapers (in the *National Observer* in 1894 and in the *New Review* in 1895); he also suggested some important revisions of the story to Wells (see Chapter X, Note 2).

I

The Time Traveller (for so it will be convenient to speak of him) was expounding a recondite matter to us. His grey eyes shone and twinkled, and his usually pale face was flushed and animated. The fire burned brightly, and the soft radiance of the incandescent lights[1] in the lilies of silver caught the bubbles that flashed and passed in our glasses. Our chairs, being his patents, embraced and caressed us rather than submitted to be sat upon, and there was that luxurious after-dinner atmosphere when thought runs gracefully free of the trammels[2] of precision. And he put it to us in this way—marking the points with a lean forefinger—as we sat and lazily admired his earnestness over this new paradox (as we thought it) and his fecundity.

'You must follow me carefully. I shall have to controvert one or two ideas that are almost universally accepted. The geometry, for instance, they taught you at school is founded on a misconception.'

'Is not that rather a large thing to expect us to begin upon?' said Filby, an argumentative person with red hair.

'I do not mean to ask you to accept anything without reasonable ground for it. You will soon admit as much as I need from you. You know of course that a mathematical line, a line of thickness *nil*,[3] has no real existence. They taught you that? Neither has a mathematical plane. These things are mere abstractions.'

'That is all right,' said the Psychologist.

'Nor, having only length, breadth, and thickness, can a cube have a real existence.'

'There I object,' said Filby. 'Of course a solid body may exist. All real things———'

1. Still a novelty in 1895. The late nineteenth century saw many attempts to perfect a cheap method of electric lighting. Edison's first lamp was exhibited in 1879, and first commercially installed in 1880 on the steamship Columbia.
2. Restraints.
3. Latin, "nothing" or "zero."

'So most people think. But wait a moment. Can an *instantaneous* cube exist?'

'Don't follow you,' said Filby.

'Can a cube that does not last for any time at all, have a real existence?'

Filby became pensive. 'Clearly,' the Time Traveller proceeded, 'any real body must have extension in *four* directions: it must have Length, Breadth, Thickness, and—Duration. But through a natural infirmity of the flesh, which I will explain to you in a moment, we incline to overlook this fact. There are really four dimensions, three which we call the three planes of Space, and a fourth, Time. There is, however, a tendency to draw an unreal distinction between the former three dimensions and the latter, because it happens that our consciousness moves intermittently[4] in one direction along the latter from the beginning to the end of our lives.'

'That,' said a very young man, making spasmodic efforts to re-light his cigar over the lamp; 'that . . . very clear indeed.'

'Now, it is very remarkable that this is so extensively over-looked,' continued the Time Traveller, with a slight accession of cheerfulness. 'Really this is what is meant by the Fourth Dimension, though some people who talk about the Fourth Dimension do not know they mean it. It is only another way of looking at Time. *There is no difference between Time and any of the three dimensions of Space except that our consciousness moves along it.* But some foolish people have got hold of the wrong side of that idea. You have all heard what they have to say about this Fourth Dimension?'

'*I* have not,' said the Provincial Mayor.

'It is simply this. That Space, as our mathematicians have it, is spoken of as having three dimensions, which one may call Length, Breadth, and Thickness, and is always definable by reference to three planes, each at right angles to the others. But some philosophical people have been asking why *three* dimensions particularly—why not another direction at right angles to the other three?—

4. At successive instants.

and have even tried to construct a Four-Dimensional geometry. Professor Simon Newcomb was expounding this to the New York Mathematical Society[5] only a month or so ago. You know how on a flat surface, which has only two dimensions, we can represent a figure of a three-dimensional solid, and similarly they think that by models of three dimensions they could represent one of four—if they could master the perspective of the thing. See?'

'I think so,' murmured the Provincial Mayor; and, knitting his brows, he lapsed into an introspective state, his lips moving as one who repeats mystic words. 'Yes, I think I see it now,' he said after some time, brightening in a quite transitory manner.

'Well, I do not mind telling you I have been at work upon this geometry of Four Dimensions for some time. Some of my results are curious. For instance, here is a portrait of a man at eight years old, another at fifteen, another at seventeen, another at twenty-three, and so on. All these are evidently sections, as it were, Three-Dimensional representations of his Four-Dimensioned being, which is a fixed and unalterable thing.

'Scientific people,' proceeded the Time Traveller, after the pause required for the proper assimilation of this, 'know very well that Time is only a kind of Space. Here is a popular scientific diagram, a weather record.[6] This line I trace with my finger shows the movement of the barometer. Yesterday it was so high, yesterday night it fell, then this morning it rose again, and so gently upward to here. Surely the mercury did not trace this line in any of the dimensions of Space generally recognized? But certainly it traced such a line, and that line, therefore, we must conclude was along the Time-Dimension.'

5. The New York Mathematical Society was founded in 1888; in 1894 it became the American Mathematical Society. Simon Newcomb (1835-1909) was a Professor of Mathematics and Astronomy at Johns Hopkins University, and one of America's most distinguished scientists. His paper on four-dimensional geometry was read in December, 1893.

6. This would have been a daily record of changes in barometric pressure, traced by a stylus on a revolving paper drum. The worldwide keeping and comparison of weather records had only begun around 1860, initiated by the Englishman Robert Fitzroy.

'But,' said the Medical Man, staring hard at a coal in the fire, 'if Time is really only a fourth dimension of Space, why is it, and why has it always been, regarded as something different? And why cannot we move in Time as we move about in the other dimensions of Space?'

The Time Traveller smiled. 'Are you so sure we can move freely in Space? Right and left we can go, backward and forward freely enough, and men always have done so. I admit we move freely in two dimensions. But how about up and down? Gravitation limits us there.'

'Not exactly,' said the Medical Man. 'There are balloons.'[7]

'But before the balloons, save for spasmodic jumping and the inequalities of the surface, man had no freedom of vertical movement.'

'Still they could move a little up and down,' said the Medical Man.

'Easier, far easier down than up.'

'And you cannot move at all in Time, you cannot get away from the present moment.'

'My dear sir, that is just where you are wrong. That is just where the whole world has gone wrong. We are always getting away from the present moment. Our mental existences, which are immaterial and have no dimensions, are passing along the Time-Dimension with a uniform velocity from the cradle to the grave. Just as we should travel *down* if we began our existence fifty miles above the earth's surface.'

'But the great difficulty is this,' interrupted the Psychologist. 'You *can* move about in all directions of Space, but you cannot move about in Time.'

'That is the germ of my great discovery. But you are wrong to say that we cannot move about in Time. For instance, if I am re-

7. Ballooning had originated in the late eighteenth century, and had been used for military purposes in the American Civil War. By the late nineteenth century it was a popular "daredevil" sport, with long-distance balloon races organized throughout America and Western Europe.

calling an incident very vividly I go back to the instant of its occur-
rence: I become absent-minded, as you say. I jump back for a moment. Of course we have no means of staying back for any length of
Time, any more than a savage or an animal has of staying six feet
above the ground. But a civilized man is better off than the savage
in this respect. He can go up against gravitation in a balloon, and
why should he not hope that ultimately he may be able to stop or
accelerate his drift along the Time-Dimension, or even turn about
and travel the other way?'

'Oh, *this,*' began Filby, 'is all————'

'Why not?' said the Time Traveller.

'It's against reason,' said Filby.

'What reason?' said the Time Traveller.

'You can show black is white by argument,' said Filby, 'but you
will never convince me.'

'Possibly not,' said the Time Traveller. 'But now you begin to see
the object of my investigations into the geometry of Four Dimensions. Long ago I had a vague inkling of a machine————'

'To travel through Time!' exclaimed the Very Young Man.

'That shall travel indifferently in any direction of Space and
Time, as the driver determines.'

Filby contented himself with laughter.

'But I have experimental verification,' said the Time Traveller.

'It would be remarkably convenient for the historian,' the Psychologist suggested. 'One might travel back and verify the accepted
account of the Battle of Hastings,[8] for instance!'

'Don't you think you would attract attention?' said the Medical
Man. 'Our ancestors had no great tolerance for anachronisms.'

'One might get one's Greek from the very lips of Homer and
Plato,' the Very Young Man thought.

'In which case they would certainly plough you for the Little-go.
The German scholars have improved Greek so much.'[9]

8. In 1066 the Norman invader, William the Conqueror, defeated King
   Harold of England at Hastings.
9. Throughout the nineteenth century, philologists—particularly in Germany

'Then there is the future,' said the Very Young Man. 'Just think! One might invest all one's money, leave it to accumulate at interest, and hurry on ahead!'

'To discover a society,' said I, 'erected on a strictly communistic basis.'[10]

'Of all the wild extravagant theories!' began the Psychologist.

'Yes, so it seemed to me, and so I never talked of it until————'

'Experimental verification!' cried I. 'You are going to verify *that*?'

'The experiment!' cried Filby, who was getting brain-weary.

'Let's see your experiment anyhow,' said the Psychologist, 'though it's all humbug, you know.'

The Time Traveller smiled round at us. Then, still smiling faintly, and with his hands deep in his trousers pockets, he walked slowly out of the room, and we heard his slippers shuffling down the long passage to his laboratory.

The Psychologist looked at us. 'I wonder what he's got?'

'Some sleight-of-hand trick or other,' said the Medical Man, and

---

—were concerned with finding scientific laws to explain the historical changes of classical and modern languages. The "Little-go" was the general examination in history, languages, and literature taken by a Cambridge undergraduate after his first two years. To "plough" someone, in English university slang, is to reject him—usually for failing an examination.

10. There is much speculation about communism in *The Time Machine,* and it is important to realize that in the 1890s communism was not limited to the Marxist variety. In fact, Marxist Communism had come to a temporary standstill in Europe and was under attack from a number of rivals. In England, the Fabian Society, which advocated a peaceful and gradual movement toward socialism, had been founded in 1884; Wells attended some Fabian lectures during his student days, and joined the movement for a brief and stormy time in 1903. In France, the revolutionary "syndicalism" or trade unionism of Georges Sorel violently opposed the too-conservative stance of the Marxists, calling for a massive general strike and giving rise to the first international trade union, the French General Confederation of Labor, in 1895, the year of *The Time Machine.*

Filby tried to tell us about a conjurer he had seen at Burslem;[11] but before he had finished his preface the Time Traveller came back, and Filby's anecdote collapsed.

The thing the Time Traveller held in his hand was a glittering metallic framework, scarcely larger than a small clock, and very delicately made. There was ivory in it, and some transparent crystalline substance. And now I must be explicit, for this that follows—unless his explanation is to be accepted—is an absolutely unaccountable thing. He took one of the small octagonal tables that were scattered about the room, and set it in front of the fire, with two legs on the hearthrug. On this table he placed the mechanism. Then he drew up a chair, and sat down. The only other object on the table was a small shaded lamp, the bright light of which fell full upon the model. There were also perhaps a dozen candles about, two in brass candlesticks upon the mantel and several in sconces,[12] so that the room was brilliantly illuminated. I sat in a low arm-chair nearest the fire, and I drew this forward so as to be almost between the Time Traveller and the fire-place. Filby sat behind him, looking over his shoulder. The Medical Man and the Provincial Mayor watched him in profile from the right, the Psychologist from the left. The Very Young Man stood behind the Psychologist. We were all on the alert. It appears incredible to me that any kind of trick, however subtly conceived and however adroitly done, could have been played upon us under these conditions.

The Time Traveller looked at us, and then at the mechanism. 'Well?' said the Psychologist.

'This little affair,' said the Time Traveller, resting his elbows upon the table and pressing his hands together above the apparatus, 'is only a model. It is my plan for a machine to travel through time. You will notice that it looks singularly askew, and that there is an odd twinkling appearance about this bar, as though it was in some

11. A town in Staffordshire well known for its porcelain factories and for an annual fair.
12. Wall brackets for candles.

way unreal.' He pointed to the part with his finger. 'Also, here is one little white lever, and here is another.'

The Medical Man got up out of his chair and peered into the thing. 'It's beautifully made,' he said.

'It took two years to make,' retorted the Time Traveller. Then, when we had all imitated the action of the Medical Man, he said: 'Now I want you clearly to understand that this lever, being pressed over, sends the machine gliding into the future, and this other reverses the motion. This saddle represents the seat of a time traveller. Presently I am going to press the lever, and off the machine will go. It will vanish, pass into future Time, and disappear. Have a good look at the thing. Look at the table too, and satisfy yourselves there is no trickery. I don't want to waste this model, and then be told I'm a quack.'

There was a minute's pause perhaps. The Psychologist seemed about to speak to me, but changed his mind. Then the Time Traveller put forth his finger towards the lever. 'No,' he said suddenly. 'Lend me your hand.' And turning to the Psychologist, he took that individual's hand in his own and told him to put out his forefinger. So that it was the Psychologist himself who sent forth the model Time Machine on its interminable voyage. We all saw the lever turn. I am absolutely certain there was no trickery. There was a breath of wind, and the lamp flame jumped. One of the candles on the mantel was blown out, and the little machine suddenly swung round, became indistinct, was seen as a ghost for a second perhaps, as an eddy of faintly glittering brass and ivory; and it was gone— vanished! Save for the lamp the table was bare.

Every one was silent for a minute. Then Filby said he was damned.

The Psychologist recovered from his stupor, and suddenly looked under the table. At that the Time Traveller laughed cheerfully. 'Well?' he said, with a reminiscence of the Psychologist. Then, getting up, he went to the tobacco jar on the mantel, and with his back to us began to fill his pipe.

We stared at each other. 'Look here,' said the Medical Man, 'are you in earnest about this? Do you seriously believe that that machine has travelled into time?'

'Certainly,' said the Time Traveller, stooping to light a spill[13] at the fire. Then he turned, lighting his pipe, to look at the Psychologist's face. (The Psychologist, to show that he was not unhinged, helped himself to a cigar and tried to light it uncut.) 'What is more, I have a big machine nearly finished in there'—he indicated the laboratory—'and when that is put together I mean to have a journey on my own account.'

'You mean to say that that machine has travelled into the future?' said Filby.

'Into the future or the past—I don't, for certain, know which.'

After an interval the Psychologist had an inspiration. 'It must have gone into the past if it has gone anywhere,' he said.

'Why?' said the Time Traveller.

'Because I presume that it has not moved in space, and if it travelled into the future it would still be here all this time, since it must have travelled through this time.'

'But,' said I, 'if it travelled into the past it would have been visible when we came first into this room; and last Thursday when we were here; and the Thursday before that; and so forth!'

'Serious objections,' remarked the Provincial Mayor, with an air of impartiality, turning towards the Time Traveller.

'Not a bit,' said the Time Traveller, and, to the Psychologist: 'You think. *You* can explain that. It's presentation below the threshold,[14] you know, diluted presentation.'

'Of course,' said the Psychologist, and reassured us. 'That's a simple point of psychology. I should have thought of it. It's plain enough, and helps the paradox delightfully. We cannot see it, nor

13. A splinter of wood or piece of twisted paper for lighting lamps, pipes, etc.

14. I.e., below the threshold of consciousness or, as we now say, subliminal. Interestingly, some early reviewers of the novel faulted it for the same objections raised by the Psychologist and the narrator. Apparently they failed to absorb or understand the Time Traveller's own explanation.

can we appreciate this machine, any more than we can the spoke of a wheel spinning, or a bullet flying through the air. If it is travelling through time fifty times or a hundred times faster than we are, if it gets through a minute while we get through a second, the impression it creates will of course be only one-fiftieth or one-hundreth of what it would make if it were not travelling in time. That's plain enough.' He passed his hand through the space in which the machine had been. 'You see?' he said, laughing.

We sat and stared at the vacant table for a minute or so. Then the Time Traveller asked us what we thought of it all.

'It sounds plausible enough to-night,' said the Medical Man; 'but wait until to-morrow. Wait for the common sense of the morning.'

'Would you like to see the Time Machine itself?' asked the Time Traveller. And therewith, taking the lamp in his hand, he led the way down the long, draughty corridor to his laboratory. I remember vividly the flickering light, his queer, broad head in silhouette, the dance of the shadows, how we all followed him, puzzled but incredulous, and how there in the laboratory we beheld a larger edition of the little mechanism which we had seen vanish from before our eyes. Parts were of nickel, parts of ivory, parts had certainly been filed or sawn out of rock crystal. The thing was generally complete, but the twisted crystalline bars lay unfinished upon the bench beside some sheets of drawings, and I took one up for a better look at it. Quartz it seemed to be.

'Look here,' said the Medical Man, 'are you perfectly serious? Or is this a trick—like that ghost you showed us last Christmas?'[15]

'Upon that machine,' said the Time Traveller, holding the lamp

15. The "ghost" presented at a Christmas party was one of a number of familiar tricks of parlor magic around the turn of the century. It would probably have involved the use of a "magic lantern," an ancestor of the film projector (the first public projection of photographic film was in Paris, by the brothers Pierre and Auguste Lumière, in the summer of 1895). The Time Traveller would have been interested in such gadgetry, and Wells himself came to be deeply interested in the possibilities of the new medium of film, long before it was regarded as an "art form." Albert Hopkins in his compendium of parlor tricks, *Magic* (1897), lists film as one of the tools to be used by an amateur magician.

aloft, 'I intend to explore time. Is that plain? I was never more serious in my life.'

None of us quite knew how to take it.

I caught Filby's eye over the shoulder of the Medical Man, and
he winked at me solemnly.

II

I think that at that time none of us quite believed in the Time Machine. The fact is, the Time Traveller was one of those men who
are too clever to be believed: you never felt that you saw all round
him; you always suspected some subtle reserve, some ingenuity in
ambush, behind his lucid frankness. Had Filby shown the model
and explained the matter in the Time Traveller's words, we should
have shown *him* far less scepticism. For we should have perceived
his motives; a pork butcher could understand Filby. But the Time
Traveller had more than a touch of whim among his elements, and
we distrusted him. Things that would have made the fame of a less
clever man seemed tricks in his hands. It is a mistake to do things
too easily. The serious people who took him seriously never felt
quite sure of his deportment; they were somehow aware that trust-
ing their reputations for judgment with him was like furnishing a
nursery with egg-shell china. So I don't think any of us said very
much about time travelling in the interval between that Thursday
and the next, though its odd potentialities ran, no doubt, in most of
our minds: its plausibility, that is, its practical incredibleness, the
curious possibilities of anachronism and of utter confusion it suggested. For my own part, I was particularly preoccupied with the
trick of the model. That I remember discussing with the Medical
Man, whom I met on Friday at the Linnaean.[1] He said he had seen

1. The Linnaean Society of London was founded in 1788 to preserve the
   specimen collections of the great taxonomist Linnaeus (1707-1788). But
   it rapidly became a center for discussion and debate among students of
   the natural sciences; and it was at the Linnaean Society in 1858 that
   Charles Darwin first presented his theory of evolution through natural
   selection.

a similar thing at Tübingen,[2] and laid considerable stress on the blowing out of the candle. But how the trick was done he could not explain.

The next Thursday I went again to Richmond[3]—I suppose I was one of the Time Traveller's most constant guests—and, arriving late, found four or five men already assembled in his drawing-room. The Medical Man was standing before the fire with a sheet of paper in one hand and his watch in the other. I looked round for the Time Traveller, and—'It's half-past seven now,' said the Medical Man. 'I suppose we'd better have dinner?'

'Where's ————?' said I, naming our host.

'You've just come? It's rather odd. He's unavoidably detained. He asks me in this note to lead off with dinner at seven if he's not back. Says he'll explain when he comes.'

'It seems a pity to let the dinner spoil,' said the Editor of a well-known daily paper; and thereupon the Doctor rang the bell.

The Psychologist was the only person besides the Doctor and myself who had attended the previous dinner. The other men were Blank, the Editor aforementioned, a certain journalist, and another—a quiet, shy man with a beard—whom I didn't know, and who, as far as my observation went, never opened his mouth all the evening. There was some speculation at the dinner-table about the Time Traveller's absence, and I suggested time travelling, in a half-jocular spirit. The Editor wanted that explained to him, and the Psychologist volunteered a wooden account of the 'ingenious paradox and trick' we had witnessed that day week. He was in the midst of his exposition when the door from the corridor opened slowly and without noise. I was facing the door, and saw it first. 'Hallo!' I said. 'At last!' And the door opened wider, and the Time Traveller stood before us. I gave a cry of surprise. 'Good heavens! man, what's the matter?' cried the Medical Man, who saw him next. And the whole tableful turned towards the door.

2. A town in Germany, near Stuttgart, and the site of a famous university founded in 1477.
3. The area southwest of London where the Time Traveller lives; see map.

He was in an amazing plight. His coat was dusty and dirty, and smeared with green down the sleeves; his hair disordered, and as it seemed to me greyer—either with dust and dirt or because its colour had actually faded. His face was ghastly pale; his chin had a brown cut on it—a cut half healed; his expression was haggard and drawn, as by intense suffering. For a moment he hesitated in the doorway, as if he had been dazzled by the light. Then he came into the room. He walked with just such a limp as I have seen in foot-sore tramps. We stared at him in silence, expecting him to speak.

He said not a word, but came painfully to the table, and made a motion towards the wine. The Editor filled a glass of champagne, and pushed it towards him. He drained it, and it seemed to do him good: for he looked round the table, and the ghost of his old smile flickered across his face. 'What on earth have you been up to, man?' said the Doctor. The Time Traveller did not seem to hear. 'Don't let me disturb you,' he said, with a certain faltering articula-tion. 'I'm all right.' He stopped, held out his glass for more, and took it off at a draught. 'That's good,' he said. His eyes grew brighter, and a faint colour came into his cheeks. His glance flick-ered over our faces with a certain dull approval, and then went round the warm and comfortable room. Then he spoke again, still as it were feeling his way among his words. 'I'm going to wash and dress, and then I'll come down and explain things. . . . Save me some of that mutton. I'm starving for a bit of meat.'

He looked across at the Editor, who was a rare visitor, and hoped he was all right. The Editor began a question. 'Tell you pres-ently,' said the Time Traveller. 'I'm—funny! Be all right in a minute.'

He put down his glass, and walked towards the staircase door. Again I remarked his lameness and the soft padding sound of his footfall, and standing up in my place, I saw his feet as he went out. He had nothing on them but a pair of tattered, bloodstained socks. Then the door closed upon him. I had half a mind to follow, till I remembered how he detested any fuss about himself. For a minute, perhaps, my mind was wool-gathering. Then, 'Remarkable

Behaviour of an Eminent Scientist,' I heard the Editor say, thinking (after his wont) in head-lines. And this brought my attention back to the bright dinner-table.

'What's the game?' said the Journalist. 'Has he been doing the Amateur Cadger?[4] I don't follow.' I met the eye of the Psychologist, and read my own interpretation in his face. I thought of the Time Traveller limping painfully upstairs. I don't think any one else had noticed his lameness.

The first to recover completely from this surprise was the Medical Man, who rang the bell—the Time Traveller hated to have servants waiting at dinner—for a hot plate. At that the Editor turned to his knife and fork with a grunt, and the Silent Man followed suit. The dinner was resumed. Conversation was exclamatory for a little while, with gaps of wonderment; and then the Editor got fervent in his curiosity. 'Does our friend eke out his modest income with a crossing? or has he his Nebuchadnezzar phases?'[5] he inquired. 'I feel assured it's this business of the Time Machine,' I said, and took up the Psychologist's account of our previous meeting. The new guests were frankly incredulous. The Editor raised objections. 'What *was* this time travelling? A man couldn't cover himself with dust by rolling in a paradox, could he?' And then, as the idea came home to him, he resorted to caricature. Hadn't they any clothes-brushes in the Future? The Journalist, too, would not believe at any price, and joined the Editor in the easy work of heaping ridicule on the whole thing. They were both the new kind of journalist—very joyous, irreverent young men. 'Our Special Correspondent in the Day after To-morrow reports,' the Journalist was saying—or rather shouting—when the Time Traveller came back. He was dressed in ordinary evening clothes, and nothing save his haggard look remained of the change that had startled me.

4. Amateur criminal.
5. "Crossing" is a term for a highwayman's obstruction of his victim's path. King Nebuchadnezzar of Babylon, in Daniel 4:1-37, is condemned by God to spend seven years transformed into a beast of the field. The implication of both remarks is that the Time Traveller must lead a criminal or bestial "other life."

'I say,' said the Editor hilariously, 'these chaps here say you have been travelling into the middle of next week!! Tell us all about little Rosebery,[6] will you? What will you take for the lot?'

The Time Traveller came to the place reserved for him without a word. He smiled quietly, in his old way. 'Where's my mutton?' he said. 'What a treat it is to stick a fork into meat again!'

'Story!' cried the Editor.

'Story be damned!' said the Time Traveller. 'I want something to eat. I won't say a word until I get some peptone[7] into my arteries. Thanks. And the salt.'

'One word,' said I. 'Have you been time travelling?'

'Yes,' said the Time Traveller, with his mouth full, nodding his head.

'I'd give a shilling a line[8] for a verbatim note,' said the Editor. The Time Traveller pushed his glass towards the Silent Man and rang it with his fingernail; at which the Silent Man, who had been staring at his face, started convulsively, and poured him wine. The rest of the dinner was uncomfortable. For my own part, sudden questions kept on rising to my lips, and I dare say it was the same with the others. The Journalist tried to relieve the tension by telling anecdotes of Hettie Potter.[9] The Time Traveller devoted his atten-

6. A horse named for its owner, Lord Rosebery, who was Prime Minister from March 1894 to June 1895. Rosebery, a racing enthusiast, is the only Prime Minister in history to have run winners in the Derby (1894 and 1895).

7. The substance into which protein is converted before entering the bloodstream.

8. In the monetary values of the time, this would have been equal to twenty-three cents per line; a good, though not an extravagant, rate for journalism. A "verbatim note" is a first-hand report.

9. Perhaps an oblique reference to Beatrice (Potter) Webb (1858-1943), cofounder with her husband Sidney of the Fabian Movement. Well known before her marriage as a successful London hostess and daughter of a wealthy industrialist, Mrs. Webb from the nineties on was a tireless campaigner for socialism and a frequent visitor of the worst London slums. She naturally became the object of pointless and insensitive jokes and anecdotes, such as the Journalist appears to be telling. But there was also a well-known family of music-hall entertainers named Potter, and this may be a reference to one of them.

tion to his dinner, and displayed the appetite of a tramp. The Medical Man smoked a cigarette, and watched the Time Traveller through his eyelashes. The Silent Man seemed even more clumsy than usual, and drank champagne with regularity and determination out of sheer nervousness. At last the Time Traveller pushed his plate away, and looked round us. 'I suppose I must apologize,' he said. 'I was simply starving. I've had a most amazing time.' He reached out his hand for a cigar, and cut the end. 'But come into the smoking-room. It's too long a story to tell over greasy plates.' And ringing the bell in passing, he led the way into the adjoining room.

'You have told Blank, and Dash, and Chose about the machine?' he said to me, leaning back in his easychair and naming the three new guests.

'But the thing's a mere paradox,' said the Editor.

'I can't argue to-night. I don't mind telling you the story, but I can't argue. I will,' he went on, 'tell you the story of what has happened to me, if you like, but you must refrain from interruptions. I want to tell it. Badly. Most of it will sound like lying. So be it! It's true—every word of it, all the same. I was in my laboratory at four o'clock, and since then . . . I've lived eight days . . . such days as no human being ever lived before! I'm nearly worn out, but I shan't sleep till I've told this thing over to you. Then I shall go to bed. But no interruptions! Is it agreed?'

'Agreed,' said the Editor, and the rest of us echoed 'Agreed.' And with that the Time Traveller began his story as I have set it forth. He sat back in his chair at first, and spoke like a weary man. Afterwards he got more animated. In writing it down I feel with only too much keenness the inadequacy of pen and ink—and, above all, my own inadequacy—to express its quality. You read, I will suppose, attentively enough; but you cannot see the speaker's white, sincere face in the bright circle of the little lamp, nor hear the intonation of his voice. You cannot know how his expression followed the turns of his story! Most of us hearers were in shadow, for the candles in the smoking-room had not been lighted, and only the face of the Journalist and the legs of the Silent Man from the knees downward were illuminated. At first we glanced now and again at each other. After a time we ceased to do that, and looked only at the Time Traveller's face.

III

'I told some of you last Thursday of the principles of the Time Machine, and showed you the actual thing itself, incomplete in the workshop. There it is now, a little travel-worn, truly; and one of the ivory bars is cracked, and a brass rail bent; but the rest of it's sound enough. I expected to finish it on Friday; but on Friday, when the putting together was nearly done, I found that one of the nickel bars was exactly one inch too short, and this I had to get remade; so that the thing was not complete until this morning. It was at ten o'clock to-day that the first of all Time Machines began its career. I gave it a last tap, tried all the screws again, put one more drop of oil on the quartz rod, and sat myself in the saddle. I suppose a suicide who holds a pistol to his skull feels much the same wonder at what will come next as I felt then. I took the starting lever in one hand and the stopping one in the other, pressed the first, and almost immediately the second. I seemed to reel; I felt a nightmare sensation of falling; and, looking round, I saw the laboratory exactly as before. Had anything happened? For a moment I suspected that my intellect had tricked me. Then I noted the clock. A moment before, as it seemed, it had stood at a minute or so past ten; now it was nearly half-past three!

'I drew a breath, set my teeth, gripped the starting lever with both hands, and went off with a thud. The laboratory got hazy and went dark. Mrs. Watchett[1] came in and walked, apparently without

1. The Time Traveller's housekeeper. The modern reader immediately recognizes in Mrs. Watchett's speeded-up movements a common, usually comic, device of filmmaking. But Wells anticipates technology here. Such tricks do not seem to have been employed in film exhibitions before 1896, though they were sometimes utilized in earlier Kinetoscope-machine sequences.

seeing me, towards the garden door. I suppose it took her a minute or so to traverse the place, but to me she seemed to shoot across the room like a rocket. I pressed the lever over to its extreme position. The night came like the turning out of a lamp, and in another moment came to-morrow. The laboratory grew faint and hazy, then fainter and ever fainter. To-morrow night came black, then day again, night again, day again, faster and faster still. An eddying murmur filled my ears, and a strange, dumb confusedness descended on my mind.

'I am afraid I cannot convey the peculiar sensations of time travelling. They are excessively unpleasant. There is a feeling exactly like that one has upon a switchback²—of a helpless headlong motion! I felt the same horrible anticipation, too, of an imminent smash. As I put on pace, night followed day like the flapping of a black wing. The dim suggestion of the laboratory seemed presently to fall away from me, and I saw the sun hopping swiftly across the sky, leaping it every minute, and every minute marking a day. I supposed the laboratory had been destroyed and I had come into the open air. I had a dim impression of scaffolding, but I was already going too fast to be conscious of any moving things. The slowest snail that ever crawled dashed by too fast for me. The twinkling succession of darkness and light was excessively painful to the eye. Then, in the intermittent darknesses, I saw the moon spinning swiftly through her quarters from new to full, and had a faint glimpse of the circling stars. Presently, as I went on, still gaining velocity, the palpitation of night and day merged into one continuous greyness; the sky took on a wonderful deepness of blue, a splendid luminous colour like that of early twilight; the jerking sun became a streak of fire, a brilliant arch, in space; the moon a fainter fluctuating band; and I could see nothing of the stars, save now and then a brighter circle flickering in the blue.

'The landscape was misty and vague. I was still on the hill-side upon which this house now stands, and the shoulder rose above me grey and dim. I saw trees growing and changing like puffs of va-

2. A zigzag path of railroad track, for ascending or descending steep hills.

pour, now brown, now green; they grew, spread, shivered, and passed away. I saw huge buildings rise up faint and fair, and pass like dreams. The whole surface of the earth seemed changed—melting and flowing under my eyes. The little hands upon the dials that registered my speed raced round faster and faster. Presently I noted that the sun belt swayed up and down, from solstice to solstice,[3] in a minute or less, and that consequently my pace was over a year a minute; and minute by minute the white snow flashed across the world, and vanished, and was followed by the bright, brief green of spring.

'The unpleasant sensations of the start were less poignant now. They merged at last into a kind of hysterical exhilaration. I remarked indeed a clumsy swaying of the machine, for which I was unable to account. But my mind was too confused to attend to it, so with a kind of madness growing upon me, I flung myself into futurity. At first I scarce thought of stopping, scarce thought of anything but these new sensations. But presently a fresh series of impressions grew up in my mind—a certain curiosity and therewith a certain dread—until at last they took complete possession of me. What strange developments of humanity, what wonderful advances upon our rudimentary civilization, I thought, might not appear when I came to look nearly into the dim elusive world that raced and fluctuated before my eyes! I saw great and splendid architecture rising about me, more massive than any buildings of our own time, and yet, as it seemed, built of glimmer and mist. I saw a richer green flow up the hill-side, and remain there without any wintry intermission. Even through the veil of my confusion the earth seemed very fair. And so my mind came round to the business of stopping.

'The peculiar risk lay in the possibility of my finding some substance in the space which I, or the machine, occupied. So long as I travelled at a high velocity through time, this scarcely mattered; I

3. One of the two points in the year when the sun is farthest from the celestial equator (about June 21 and December 22) and hence, to the Time Traveller's vision, the points when its arc is highest or lowest.

was, so to speak, attenuated—was slipping like a vapour through the interstices[4] of intervening substances! But to come to a stop involved the jamming of myself, molecule by molecule, into whatever lay in my way; meant bringing my atoms into such intimate contact with those of the obstacle that a profound chemical reaction—possibly a far-reaching explosion—would result, and blow myself and my apparatus out of all possible dimensions—into the Unknown. This possibility had occurred to me again and again while I was making the machine; but then I had cheerfully accepted it as an unavoidable risk—one of the risks a man has got to take! Now the risk was inevitable, I no longer saw it in the same cheerful light. The fact is that, insensibly, the absolute strangeness of everything, the sickly jarring and swaying of the machine, above all, the feeling of prolonged falling, had absolutely upset my nerve. I told myself that I could never stop, and with a gust of petulance I resolved to stop forthwith. Like an impatient fool, I lugged over the lever, and incontinently the thing went reeling over, and I was flung headlong through the air.

'There was the sound of a clap of thunder in my ears. I may have been stunned for a moment. A pitiless hail was hissing round me, and I was sitting on soft turf in front of the overset machine. Everything still seemed grey, but presently I remarked that the confusion in my ears was gone. I looked round me. I was on what seemed to be a little lawn in a garden, surrounded by rhododendron bushes, and I noticed that their mauve and purple blossoms were dropping in a shower under the beating of the hailstones. The rebounding, dancing hail hung in a cloud over the machine, and drove along the ground like smoke. In a moment I was wet to the skin. "Fine hospitality," said I, "to a man who has travelled innumerable years to see you."

'Presently I thought what a fool I was to get wet. I stood up and looked round me. A colossal figure, carved apparently in some white stone, loomed indistinctly beyond the rhododendrons through the hazy downpour. But all else of the world was invisible.

4. Small intervals.

'My sensations would be hard to describe. As the columns of hail grew thinner, I saw the white figure more distinctly. It was very large, for a silver birch-tree touched its shoulder. It was of white marble, in shape something like a winged sphinx, but the wings, instead of being carried vertically at the sides, were spread so that it seemed to hover. The pedestal, it appeared to me, was of bronze, and was thick with verdigris.[5] It chanced that the face was towards me; the sightless eyes seemed to watch me; there was the faint shadow of a smile on the lips. It was greatly weather-worn, and that imparted an unpleasant suggestion of disease. I stood looking at it for a little space—half a minute, perhaps, or half an hour. It seemed to advance and to recede as the hail drove before it denser or thinner. At last I tore my eyes from it for a moment, and saw that the hail curtain had worn threadbare, and that the sky was lightening with the promise of the sun.

'I looked up again at the crouching white shape, and the full temerity of my voyage came suddenly upon me. What might appear when that hazy curtain was altogether withdrawn? What might not have happened to men? What if cruelty had grown into a common passion? What if in this interval the race had lost its manliness, and had developed into something inhuman, unsympathetic, and overwhelmingly powerful? I might seem some old-world savage animal, only the more dreadful and disgusting for our common likeness—a foul creature to be incontinently slain.

'Already I saw other vast shapes—huge buildings with intricate parapets[6] and tall columns, with a wooded hill-side dimly creeping in upon me through the lessening storm. I was seized with a panic fear. I turned frantically to the Time Machine, and strove hard to readjust it. As I did so the shafts of the sun smote through the thunderstorm. The grey downpour was swept aside and vanished like the trailing garments of a ghost. Above me, in the intense blue of the summer sky, some faint brown shreds of cloud whirled into

5. The film or patina that forms on copper, brass, or bronze when exposed to air.
6. Fortified walls.

nothingness. The great buildings about me stood out clear and distinct, shining with the wet of the thunderstorm, and picked out in white by the unmelted hailstones piled along their courses. I felt naked in a strange world. I felt as perhaps a bird may feel in the clear air, knowing the hawk wings above and will swoop. My fear grew to frenzy. I took a breathing space, set my teeth, and again grappled fiercely, wrist and knee, with the machine. It gave under my desperate onset and turned over. It struck my chin violently. One hand on the saddle, the other on the lever, I stood panting heavily in attitude to mount again.

'But with this recovery of a prompt retreat my courage recovered. I looked more curiously and less fearfully at this world of the remote future. In a circular opening, high up in the wall of the nearer house, I saw a group of figures clad in rich soft robes. They had seen me, and their faces were directed towards me.

'Then I heard voices approaching me. Coming through the bushes by the White Sphinx were the heads and shoulders of men running. One of these emerged in a pathway leading straight to the little lawn upon which I stood with my machine. He was a slight creature—perhaps four feet high—clad in a purple tunic, girdled at the waist with a leather belt. Sandals or buskins[7]—I could not clearly distinguish which—were on his feet; his legs were bare to the knees, and his head was bare. Noticing that, I noticed for the first time how warm the air was.

'He struck me as being a very beautiful and graceful creature, but indescribably frail. His flushed face reminded me of the more beautiful kind of consumptive—that hectic beauty[8] of which we used

7. Sandals which lace up the leg to boot length.
8. "Consumptive, hectic beauty" is a phrase and concept closely associated with the controversial "decadent" artists and poets of the nineties (among them Aubrey Beardsley and Oscar Wilde) and with their journal, the famous and notorious *Yellow Book* (1894-97). In their obsessive, unorthodox eroticism and their defense of "pure" (i.e., non-functional, nonmechanical) art, the decadents are an important source for Wells's conception of the Eloi.

to hear so much. At the sight of him I suddenly regained confidence. I took my hands from the machine.

IV

'In another moment we were standing face to face, I and this fragile thing out of futurity. He came straight up to me and laughed into my eyes. The absence from his bearing of any sign of fear struck me at once. Then he turned to the two others who were following him and spoke to them in a strange and very sweet and liquid tongue.

'There were others coming, and presently a little group of perhaps eight or ten of these exquisite creatures were about me. One of them addressed me. It came into my head, oddly enough, that my voice was too harsh and deep for them. So I shook my head, and, pointing to my ears, shook it again. He came a step forward, hesitated, and then touched my hand. Then I felt other soft little tentacles upon my back and shoulders. They wanted to make sure I was real. There was nothing in this at all alarming. Indeed, there was something in these pretty little people that inspired confidence—a graceful gentleness, a certain childlike ease. And besides, they looked so frail that I could fancy myself flinging the whole dozen of them about like nine-pins. But I made a sudden motion to warn them when I saw their little pink hands feeling at the Time Machine. Happily then, when it was not too late, I thought of a danger I had hitherto forgotten, and reaching over the bars of the machine I unscrewed the little levers that would set it in motion, and put these in my pocket. Then I turned again to see what I could do in the way of communication.

'And then, looking more nearly into their features, I saw some further peculiarities in their Dresden-china type of prettiness. Their hair, which was uniformly curly, came to a sharp end at the neck and cheek; there was not the faintest suggestion of it on the face, and their ears were singularly minute. The mouths were small, with bright red, rather thin lips, and the little chins ran to a point. The

eyes were large and mild; and—this may seem egotism on my part—
I fancied even then that there was a certain lack of the interest I
might have expected in them.

'As they made no effort to communicate with me, but simply
stood round me smiling and speaking in soft cooing notes to each
other, I began the conversation. I pointed to the Time Machine and
to myself. Then hesitating for a moment how to express time, I
pointed to the sun. At once a quaintly pretty little figure in cheq-
uered purple and white followed my gesture, and then astonished
me by imitating the sound of thunder.

'For a moment I was staggered, though the import of his gesture
was plain enough. The question had come into my mind abruptly:
were these creatures fools? You may hardly understand how it took
me. You see I had always anticipated that the people of the year
Eight Hundred and Two Thousand odd would be incredibly in
front of us in knowledge, art, everything. Then one of them suddenly asked me a question that showed him to be on the intellectual
level of one of our five-year-old children—asked me, in fact, if I had
come from the sun in a thunderstorm! It let loose the judgment I
had suspended upon their clothes, their frail light limbs, and fragile
features. A flow of disappointment rushed across my mind. For a
moment I felt that I had built the Time Machine in vain.

'I nodded, pointed to the sun, and gave them such a vivid rendering of a thunderclap as startled them. They all withdrew a pace
or so and bowed. Then came one laughing towards me, carrying
a chain of beautiful flowers altogether new to me, and put it about
my neck. The idea was received with melodious applause; and presently they were all running to and fro for flowers, and laughingly
flinging them upon me until I was almost smothered with blossom.
You who have never seen the like can scarcely imagine what delicate and wonderful flowers countless years of culture had created.
Then someone suggested that their plaything should be exhibited in
the nearest building, and so I was led past the sphinx of white marble, which had seemed to watch me all the while with a smile at my
astonishment, towards a vast grey edifice of fretted stone. As I

went with them the memory of my confident anticipations of a profoundly grave and intellectual posterity came, with irresistible mer-
riment, to my mind.

'The building had a huge entry, and was altogether of colossal
dimensions. I was naturally most occupied with the growing crowd
of little people, and with the big open portals that yawned before
me shadowy and mysterious. My general impression of the world I
saw over their heads was of a tangled waste of beautiful bushes and
flowers, a long-neglected and yet weedless garden. I saw a number
of tall spikes of strange white flowers, measuring a foot perhaps
across the spread of the waxen petals. They grew scattered, as if
wild, among the variegated shrubs, but, as I say, I did not examine
them closely at this time. The Time Machine was left deserted on
the turf among the rhododendrons.

'The arch of the doorway was richly carved, but naturally I did
not observe the carving very narrowly, though I fancied I saw suggestions of old Phoenician decorations[1] as I passed through, and it
struck me that they were very badly broken and weather-worn.
Several more brightly clad people met me in the doorway, and so
we entered, I, dressed in dingy nineteenth-century garments, looking grotesque enough, garlanded with flowers, and surrounded by
an eddying mass of bright, soft-coloured robes and shining white
limbs, in a melodious whirl of laughter and laughing speech.

'The big doorway opened into a proportionately great hall hung
with brown. The roof was in shadow, and the windows, partially
glazed with coloured glass and partially unglazed, admitted a tem-
pered light. The floor was made up of huge blocks of some very
hard white metal, not plates nor slabs—blocks, and it was so much
worn, as I judged by the going to and fro of past generations, as to
be deeply channelled along the more frequented ways. Transverse[2]
to the length were innumerable tables made of slabs of polished

1. That is, the decorations resemble the figures of the complicated cuneiform
   alphabet developed by the Phoenicians, around the eleventh century B.C.,
   in what is now Syria.
2. Across the line of vision.

stone, raised perhaps a foot from the floor, and upon these were heaps of fruits. Some I recognized as a kind of hypertrophied[3] raspberry and orange, but for the most part they were strange.

'Between the tables was scattered a great number of cushions. Upon these my conductors seated themselves, signing for me to do likewise. With a pretty absence of ceremony they began to eat the fruit with their hands, flinging peel and stalks, and so forth, into the round openings in the sides of the tables. I was not loath to follow their example, for I felt thirsty and hungry. As I did so I surveyed the hall at my leisure.

'And perhaps the thing that struck me most was its dilapidated look. The stained-glass windows, which displayed only a geometrical pattern, were broken in many places, and the curtains that hung across the lower end were thick with dust. And it caught my eye that the corner of the marble table near me was fractured. Nevertheless, the general effect was extremely rich and picturesque. There were, perhaps, a couple of hundred people dining in the hall, and most of them, seated as near to me as they could come, were watching me with interest, their little eyes shining over the fruit they were eating. All were clad in the same soft, and yet strong, silky material.

'Fruit, by the by, was all their diet. These people of the remote future were strict vegetarians, and while I was with them, in spite of some carnal cravings, I had to be frugivorous[4] also. Indeed, I found afterwards that horses, cattle, sheep, dogs, had followed the Ichthyosaurus[5] into extinction. But the fruits were very delightful; one, in particular, that seemed to be in season all the time I was there—a floury thing in a three-sided husk—was especially good, and I made it my staple. At first I was puzzled by all these strange fruits, and by the strange flowers I saw, but later I began to perceive their import.

3. Overdeveloped, gigantically mutated.
4. Fruit-eating. There is a mild joke in the Time Traveller's "carnal cravings"—meaning cravings for meat, but also implying sexual desire.
5. An extinct, sharklike reptile of the Mesozoic Era (70,000,000 to 20,000,000 B.C.), approximately twenty-five feet long.

'However, I am telling you of my fruit dinner in the distant future now. So soon as my appetite was a little checked, I determined to make a resolute attempt to learn the speech of these new men of mine. Clearly that was the next thing to do. The fruits seemed a convenient thing to begin upon, and holding one of these up I began a series of interrogative sounds and gestures. I had some considerable difficulty in conveying my meaning. At first my efforts met with a stare of surprise or inextinguishable laughter, but presently a fair-haired little creature seemed to grasp my intention and repeated a name. They had to chatter and explain the business at great length to each other, and my first attempts to make the exquisite little sounds of their language caused an immense amount of amusement. However, I felt like a schoolmaster amidst children, and persisted, and presently I had a score of noun substantives at least at my command; and then I got to demonstrative pronouns, and even the verb "to eat." But it was slow work, and the little people soon tired and wanted to get away from my interrogations, so I determined, rather of necessity, to let them give their lessons in little doses when they felt inclined. And very little doses I found they were before long, for I never met people more indolent or more easily fatigued.

'A queer thing I soon discovered about my little hosts, and that was their lack of interest. They would come to me with eager cries of astonishment, like children, but like children they would soon stop examining me and wander away after some other toy. The dinner and my conversational beginnings ended, I noted for the first time that almost all those who had surrounded me at first were gone. It is odd, too, how speedily I came to disregard these little people. I went out through the portal into the sunlit world again so soon as my hunger was satisfied. I was continually meeting more of these men of the future, who would follow me a little distance, chatter and laugh about me, and, having smiled and gesticulated in a friendly way, leave me again to my own devices.

'The calm of evening was upon the world as I emerged from the great hall, and the scene was lit by the warm glow of the setting sun. At first things were very confusing. Everything was so entirely different from the world I had known—even the flowers. The big building I had left was situate on the slope of a broad river valley, but the Thames had shifted perhaps a mile from its present position. I resolved to mount to the summit of a crest, perhaps a mile and a half away, from which I could get a wider view of this our planet in the year Eight Hundred and Two Thousand Seven Hundred and One A.D.[6] For that, I should explain, was the date the little dials of my machine recorded.

'As I walked I was watchful for every impression that could possibly help to explain the condition of ruinous splendour in which I found the world—for ruinous it was. A little way up the hill, for instance, was a great heap of granite, bound together by masses of aluminium,[7] a vast labyrinth of precipitous walls and crumbled heaps, amidst which were thick heaps of very beautiful pagoda-like plants—nettles possibly—but wonderfully tinted with brown about the leaves, and incapable of stinging. It was evidently the derelict remains of some vast structure, to what end built I could not determine. It was here that I was destined, at a later date, to have a very strange experience—the first intimation of a still stranger discovery—but of that I will speak in its proper place.

'Looking round with a sudden thought, from a terrace on which I rested for a while, I realized that there were no small houses to be seen. Apparently the single house, and possibly even the household, had vanished. Here and there among the greenery were palace-like buildings, but the house and the cottage, which form such characteristic features of our own English landscape, had disappeared.

6. In this general parable of the decline of man, the date itself—802,701—suggests a kind of running-down in the decreasing order of its numerals.
7. Aluminum (or "aluminium," in British usage) was first isolated in 1825, but it was not until 1886 that an efficient method of producing it was developed, making possible the gigantic aluminum industry of modern times.

' "Communism," said I to myself.

'And on the heels of that came another thought. I looked at the half-dozen little figures that were following me. Then, in a flash, I perceived that all had the same form of costume, the same soft hairless visage, and the same girlish rotundity of limb. It may seem strange, perhaps, that I had not noticed this before. But everything was so strange. Now, I saw the fact plainly enough. In costume, and in all the differences of texture and bearing that now mark off the sexes from each other, these people of the future were alike. And the children seemed to my eyes to be but the miniatures of their parents. I judged, then, that the children of that time were extremely precocious, physically at least, and I found afterwards abundant verification of my opinion.

'Seeing the ease and security in which these people were living, I felt that this close resemblance of the sexes was after all what one would expect; for the strength of a man and the softness of a woman, the institution of the family, and the differentiation of occupations are mere militant necessities of an age of physical force. Where population is balanced and abundant, much child-bearing becomes an evil rather than a blessing to the State; where violence comes but rarely and offspring are secure, there is less necessity—indeed there is no necessity—for an efficient family, and the specialization of the sexes[8] with reference to their children's needs disappears. We see some beginnings of this even in our time, and in this future age it was complete. This, I must remind you, was my speculation at the time. Later, I was to appreciate how far it fell short of the reality.

8. This is not—or not only—a striking anticipation of the "unisex" phenomenon of the 1960s and 1970s. Along with other theories of social reform, the late nineteenth century produced many arguments favoring liberation from or abolition of traditional sexual roles, including the unselective eroticism of the *Yellow Book* aesthetes, the defenses of homosexuality of Edward Carpenter (1844-1929), and the origins of the Women's Suffrage movement, espoused by novelists like Grant Allen (see Note 10 to Chapter V).

'While I was musing upon these things, my attention was attracted by a pretty little structure, like a well under a cupola.[9] I thought in a transitory way of the oddness of wells still existing, and then resumed the thread of my speculations. There were no large buildings towards the top of the hill, and as my walking powers were evidently miraculous, I was presently left alone for the first time. With a strange sense of freedom and adventure I pushed on up to the crest.

'There I found a seat of some yellow metal that I did not recognize, corroded in places with a kind of pinkish rust and half smothered in soft moss, the armrests cast and filed into the resemblance of griffins' heads.[10] I sat down on it, and I surveyed the broad view of our old world under the sunset of that long day. It was as sweet and fair a view as I have ever seen. The sun had already gone below the horizon and the west was flaming gold, touched with some horizontal bars of purple and crimson. Below was the valley of the Thames, in which the river lay like a band of burnished steel. I have already spoken of the great palaces dotted about among the variegated greenery, some in ruins and some still occupied. Here and there rose a white or silvery figure in the waste garden of the earth, here and there came the sharp vertical line of some cupola or obelisk.[11] There were no hedges, no signs of proprietary rights, no evidences of agriculture; the whole earth had become a garden.

'So watching, I began to put my interpretation upon the things I had seen, and as it shaped itself to me that evening, my interpretation was something in this way. (Afterwards I found I had got only a half-truth—or only a glimpse of one facet of the truth.)

'It seemed to me that I had happened upon humanity upon the wane. The ruddy sunset set me thinking of the sunset of mankind. For the first time I began to realize an odd consequence of the social

9. A domelike roof.
10. The griffin is a mythical monster with the head and wings of an eagle and the body of a lion. Like the sphinx and the obelisk (see Note 11), it is associated with Egyptian and Mesopotamian mythology.
11. A four-sided shaft of stone, usually monolithic, with a pointed apex.

effort in which we are at present engaged. And yet, come to think, it is a logical consequence enough. Strength is the outcome of need;[12] security sets a premium on feebleness. The work of ameliorating the conditions of life—the true civilizing process that makes life more and more secure—had gone steadily on to a climax. One triumph of a united humanity over Nature had followed another. Things that are now mere dreams had become projects deliberately put in hand and carried forward. And the harvest was what I saw!

'After all, the sanitation and the agriculture of to-day are still in the rudimentary stage. The science of our time has attacked but a little department of the field of human disease, but, even so, it spreads its operations very steadily and persistently. Our agriculture and horticulture destroy a weed just here and there and cultivate perhaps a score or so of wholesome plants, leaving the greater number to fight out a balance as they can. We improve our favourite plants and animals—and how few they are—gradually by selective breeding; now a new and better peach, now a seedless grape, now a sweeter and larger flower, now a more convenient breed of cattle. We improve them gradually, because our ideals are vague and tentative, and our knowledge is very limited; because Nature, too, is shy and slow in our clumsy hands. Some day all this will be better organized, and still better. That is the drift of the current in spite of the eddies. The whole world will be intelligent, educated, and co-operating; things will move faster and faster towards the subjugation of Nature. In the end, wisely and carefully we shall readjust the balance of animal and vegetable life to suit our human needs.

'This adjustment, I say, must have been done, and done well; done indeed for all Time, in the space of Time across which my machine had leaped. The air was free from gnats, the earth from weeds or fungi; everywhere were fruits and sweet and delightful flowers; brilliant butterflies flew hither and thither. The ideal of preventive medicine was attained. Diseases had been stamped out. I saw no

---

12. These arguments are a fairly commonplace version of "social Darwinism," or the extension to the realm of human culture of Darwin's idea of the "survival of the fittest" in Nature.

evidence of any contagious diseases during all my stay. And I shall have to tell you later that even the processes of putrefaction and decay had been profoundly affected by these changes.

'Social triumphs, too, had been effected. I saw mankind housed in splendid shelters, gloriously clothed, and as yet I had found them engaged in no toil. There were no signs of struggle, neither social nor economical struggle. The shop, the advertisement, traffic, all that commerce which constitutes the body of our world, was gone. It was natural on that golden evening that I should jump at the idea of a social paradise. The difficulty of increasing population had been met, I guessed, and population had ceased to increase.

'But with this change in condition comes inevitably adaptations to the change. What, unless biological science is a mass of errors, is the cause of human intelligence and vigour? Hardship and freedom: conditions under which the active, strong, and subtle survive and the weaker go to the wall; conditions that put a premium upon the loyal alliance of capable men, upon self-restraint, patience, and decision. And the institution of the family, and the emotions that arise therein, the fierce jealousy, the tenderness for offspring, parental self-devotion, all found their justification and support in the imminent dangers of the young. *Now,* where are these imminent dangers? There is a sentiment arising, and it will grow, against connubial jealousy, against fierce maternity, against passion of all sorts; unnecessary things now, and things that make us uncomfortable, savage survivals, discords in a refined and pleasant life.

'I thought of the physical slightness of the people, their lack of intelligence, and those big abundant ruins, and it strengthened my belief in a perfect conquest of Nature. For after the battle comes Quiet. Humanity had been strong, energetic, and intelligent, and had used all its abundant vitality to alter the conditions under which it lived. And now came the reaction of the altered conditions.

'Under the new conditions of perfect comfort and security, that restless energy, that with us is strength, would become weakness. Even in our own time certain tendencies and desires, once necessary to survival, are a constant source of failure. Physical courage and the love of battle, for instance, are no great help—may even be hindrances—to a civilized man. And in a state of physical balance and security, power, intellectual as well as physical, would be out of place. For countless years I judged there had been no danger of war or solitary violence, no danger from wild beasts, no wasting disease to require strength of constitution, no need of toil. For such a life, what we should call the weak are as well equipped as the strong, are indeed no longer weak. Better equipped indeed they are, for the strong would be fretted by an energy for which there was no outlet. No doubt the exquisite beauty of the buildings I saw was the outcome of the last surgings of the now purposeless energy of mankind before it settled down into perfect harmony with the conditions under which it lived—the flourish of that triumph which began the last great peace. This has ever been the fate of energy in security; it takes to art and to eroticism,[13] and then come languor and decay.

'Even this artistic impetus would at last die away—had almost died in the Time I saw. To adorn themselves with flowers, to dance, to sing in the sunlight: so much was left of the artistic spirit, and no more. Even that would fade in the end into a contented inactivity. We are kept keen on the grindstone of pain and necessity, and, it seemed to me, that here was that hateful grindstone broken at last!

'As I stood there in the gathering dark I thought that in this simple explanation I had mastered the problem of the world—mastered the whole secret of these delicious people. Possibly the checks they had devised for the increase of population had succeeded too well, and their numbers had rather diminished than kept stationary. That would account for the abandoned ruins. Very simple was my explanation, and plausible enough—as most wrong theories are!

---

13. Again, a covert reference to the aestheticism of the *Yellow Book* artists and poets. While Beardsley, Wilde, et al., chose to regard their "decadence" as a revolt against the growth of technology, Wells insists that it is the history of technology that makes possible, and inevitable, the decadence of art.

V

'As I stood there musing over this too perfect triumph of man, the full moon, yellow and gibbous,[1] came up out of an overflow of silver light in the north-east. The bright little figures ceased to move about below, a noiseless owl flitted by, and I shivered with the chill of the night. I determined to descend and find where I could sleep.

'I looked for the building I knew. Then my eye travelled along to the figure of the White Sphinx upon the pedestal of bronze, growing distinct as the light of the rising moon grew brighter. I could see the silver birch against it. There was the tangle of rhododendron bushes, black in the pale light, and there was the little lawn. I looked at the lawn again. A queer doubt chilled my complacency. "No," said I stoutly to myself, "that was not the lawn."

'But it *was* the lawn. For the white leprous[2] face of the sphinx was towards it. Can you imagine what I felt as this conviction came home to me? But you cannot. The Time Machine was gone!

'At once, like a lash across the face, came the possibility of losing my own age, of being left helpless in this strange new world. The bare thought of it was an actual physical sensation. I could feel it grip me at the throat and stop my breathing. In another moment I was in a passion of fear and running with great leaping strides down the slope. Once I fell headlong and cut my face; I lost no time in stanching the blood, but jumped up and ran on, with a warm trickle down my cheek and chin. All the time I ran I was saying to myself: "They have moved it a little, pushed it under the bushes out of the way." Nevertheless, I ran with all my might. All the time, with the certainty that sometimes comes with excessive dread, I knew that such assurance was folly, knew instinctively that the machine was removed out of my reach. My breath came with pain. I suppose I covered the whole distance from the hill crest to the little lawn, two

1. The shape of the moon when it is more than half full (convex at both edges).
2. Covered with white splotches.

miles perhaps, in ten minutes. And I am not a young man. I cursed aloud, as I ran, at my confident folly in leaving the machine, wasting good breath thereby. I cried aloud, and none answered. Not a creature seemed to be stirring in that moonlit world.

'When I reached the lawn my worst fears were realized. Not a trace of the thing was to be seen. I felt faint and cold when I faced the empty space among the black tangle of bushes. I ran round it furiously, as if the thing might be hidden in a corner, and then stopped abruptly, with my hands clutching my hair. Above me towered the sphinx, upon the bronze pedestal, white, shining, leprous, in the light of the rising moon. It seemed to smile in mockery of my dismay.

'I might have consoled myself by imagining the little people had put the mechanism in some shelter for me, had I not felt assured of their physical and intellectual inadequacy. That is what dismayed me: the sense of some hitherto unsuspected power, through whose intervention my invention had vanished. Yet, of one thing I felt assured: unless some other age had produced its exact duplicate, the machine could not have moved in time. The attachment of the levers—I will show you the method later—prevented any one from tampering with it in that way when they were removed. It had moved, and was hid, only in space. But then, where could it be?

'I think I must have had a kind of frenzy. I remember running violently in and out among the moonlit bushes all round the sphinx, and startling some white animal that, in the dim light, I took for a small deer. I remember, too, late that night, beating the bushes with my clenched fists until my knuckles were gashed and bleeding from the broken twigs. Then, sobbing and raving in my anguish of mind, I went down to the great building of stone. The big hall was dark, silent, and deserted. I slipped on the uneven floor, and fell over one of the malachite[3] tables, almost breaking my shin. I lit a match and went on past the dusty curtains, of which I have told you.

'There I found a second great hall covered with cushions, upon which, perhaps, a score or so of the little people were sleeping. I

3. A greenish mineral (copper carbonate).

have no doubt they found my second appearance strange enough, coming suddenly out of the quiet darkness with inarticulate noises and the splutter and flare of a match. For they had forgotten about matches. "Where is my Time Machine?" I began, bawling like an angry child, laying hands upon them and shaking them up together. It must have been very queer to them. Some laughed, most of them looked sorely frightened. When I saw them standing round me, it came into my head that I was doing as foolish a thing as it was possible for me to do under the circumstances, in trying to revive the sensation of fear. For, reasoning from their daylight behaviour, I thought that fear must be forgotten.

'Abruptly, I dashed down the match, and, knocking one of the people over in my course, went blundering across the big dining-hall again, out under the moonlight. I heard cries of terror and their little feet running and stumbling this way and that. I do not remember all I did as the moon crept up the sky. I suppose it was the unexpected nature of my loss that maddened me. I felt hopelessly cut off from my own kind—a strange animal in an unknown world. I must have raved to and fro, screaming and crying upon God and Fate. I have a memory of horrible fatigue, as the long night of despair wore away; of looking in this impossible place and that; of groping among moonlit ruins and touching strange creatures in the black shadows; at last, of lying on the ground near the sphinx and weeping with absolute wretchedness. I had nothing left but misery. Then I slept, and when I woke again it was full day, and a couple of sparrows were hopping round me on the turf within reach of my arm.

'I sat up in the freshness of the morning, trying to remember how I had got there, and why I had such a profound sense of desertion and despair. Then things came clear in my mind. With the plain, reasonable daylight, I could look my circumstances fairly in the face. I saw the wild folly of my frenzy overnight, and I could reason with myself. "Suppose the worst?" I said. "Suppose the machine altogether lost—perhaps destroyed? It behoves me to be calm and patient, to learn the way of the people, to get a clear idea of the method of my loss, and the means of getting materials and tools; so that in the end, perhaps, I may make another." That would be my only hope, a poor hope perhaps, but better than despair. And, after all, it was a beautiful and curious world.

'But probably the machine had only been taken away. Still, I must be calm and patient, find its hiding-place, and recover it by force or cunning. And with that I scrambled to my feet and looked about me, wondering where I could bathe. I felt weary, stiff, and travel-soiled. The freshness of the morning made me desire an equal freshness. I had exhausted my emotion. Indeed, as I went about my business, I found myself wondering at my intense excitement overnight. I made a careful examination of the ground about the little lawn. I wasted some time in futile questionings, conveyed, as well as I was able, to such of the little people as came by. They all failed to understand my gestures; some were simply stolid, some thought it was a jest and laughed at me. I had the hardest task in the world to keep my hands off their pretty laughing faces. It was a foolish impulse, but the devil begotten of fear and blind anger was ill curbed and still eager to take advantage of my perplexity. The turf gave better counsel. I found a groove ripped in it, about midway between the pedestal of the sphinx and the marks of my feet where, on arrival, I had struggled with the overturned machine. There were other signs of removal about, with queer narrow footprints like those I could imagine made by a sloth. This directed my closer attention to the pedestal. It was, as I think I have said, of bronze. It was not a mere block, but highly decorated with deep framed panels on either side. I went and rapped at these. The pedestal was hollow. Examining the panels with care I found them discontinuous with the frames. There were no handles or keyholes, but possibly the panels, if they were doors, as I supposed, opened from within. One thing was clear enough to my mind. It took no very great mental effort to infer that my Time Machine was inside that pedestal. But how it got there was a different problem.

'I saw the heads of two orange-clad people coming through the bushes and under some blossom-covered apple-trees towards me.

I turned smiling to them and beckoned them to me. They came, and then, pointing to the bronze pedestal, I tried to intimate my wish to open it. But at my first gesture towards this they behaved very oddly. I don't know how to convey their expression to you. Suppose you were to use a grossly improper gesture to a delicate-minded woman—it is how she would look. They went off as if they had received the last possible insult. I tried a sweet-looking little chap in white next, with exactly the same result. Somehow, his manner made me feel ashamed of myself. But, as you know, I wanted the Time Machine, and I tried him once more. As he turned off, like the others, my temper got the better of me. In three strides I was after him, had him by the loose part of his robe round the neck, and began dragging him towards the sphinx. Then I saw the horror and repugnance of his face, and all of a sudden I let him go.

'But I was not beaten yet. I banged with my fist at the bronze panels. I thought I heard something stir inside—to be explicit, I thought I heard a sound like a chuckle—but I must have been mistaken. Then I got a big pebble from the river, and came and hammered till I had flattened a coil in the decorations, and the verdigris came off in powdery flakes. The delicate little people must have heard me hammering in gusty outbreaks a mile away on either hand, but nothing came of it. I saw a crowd of them upon the slopes, looking furtively at me. At last, hot and tired, I sat down to watch the place. But I was too restless to watch long; I am too Occidental[4] for a long vigil. I could work at a problem for years, but to wait inactive for twenty-four hours—that is another matter.

'I got up after a time, and began walking aimlessly through the bushes towards the hill again. "Patience," said I to myself. "If you want your machine again you must leave that sphinx alone. If they mean to take your machine away, it's little good your wrecking their bronze panels, and if they don't, you will get it back as soon as you can ask for it. To sit among all those unknown things before a puzzle like that is hopeless. That way lies monomania. Face this world. Learn its ways, watch it, be careful of too hasty guesses at

4. Western European.

its meaning. In the end you will find clues to it all." Then suddenly the humour of the situation came into my mind: the thought of the years I had spent in study and toil to get into the future age, and now my passion of anxiety to get out of it. I had made myself the most complicated and the most hopeless trap that ever a man devised. Although it was at my own expense, I could not help myself. I laughed aloud.

'Going through the big palace, it seemed to me that the little people avoided me. It may have been my fancy, or it may have had something to do with my hammering at the gates of bronze. Yet I felt tolerably sure of the avoidance. I was careful, however, to show no concern and to abstain from any pursuit of them, and in the course of a day or two things got back to the old footing. I made what progress I could in the language, and in addition I pushed my explorations here and there. Either I missed some subtle point, or their language was excessively simple—almost exclusively composed of concrete substantives and verbs. There seemed to be few, if any, abstract terms, or little use of figurative language. Their sentences were usually simple and of two words, and I failed to convey or understand any but the simplest propositions. I determined to put the thought of my Time Machine and the mystery of the bronze doors under the sphinx as much as possible in a corner of memory, until my growing knowledge would lead me back to them in a natural way. Yet a certain feeling, you may understand, tethered me in a circle of a few miles round the point of my arrival.

'So far as I could see, all the world displayed the same exuberant richness as the Thames valley. From every hill I climbed I saw the same abundance of splendid buildings, endlessly varied in material and style, the same clustering thickets of evergreens, the same blossom-laden trees and tree-ferns. Here and there water shone like silver, and beyond, the land rose into blue undulating hills, and so faded into the serenity of the sky. A peculiar feature, which presently attracted my attention, was the presence of certain circular wells, several, as it seemed to me, of a very great depth. One lay by the path up the hill, which I had followed during my first walk.

Like the others, it was rimmed with bronze, curiously wrought, and protected by a little cupola from the rain. Sitting by the side of these wells, and peering down into the shafted darkness, I could see no gleam of water, nor could I start any reflection with a lighted match. But in all of them I heard a certain sound: a thud—thud—thud, like the beating of some big engine; and I discovered, from the flaring of my matches, that a steady current of air set down the shafts. Further, I threw a scrap of paper into the throat of one, and, instead of fluttering slowly down, it was at once sucked swiftly out of sight.

'After a time, too, I came to connect these wells with tall towers standing here and there upon the slopes; for above them there was often just such a flicker in the air as one sees on a hot day above a sun-scorched beach. Putting things together, I reached a strong suggestion of an extensive system of subterranean ventilation, whose true import it was difficult to imagine. I was at first inclined to associate it with the sanitary apparatus of these people. It was an obvious conclusion, but it was absolutely wrong.

'And here I must admit that I learned very little of drains and bells and modes of conveyance, and the like conveniences, during my time in this real future. In some of these visions of Utopias[5] and coming times which I have read, there is a vast amount of detail about building, and social arrangements, and so forth. But while such details are easy enough to obtain when the whole world is contained in one's imagination, they are altogether inaccessible to a real traveller amid such realities as I found here. Conceive the tale of London which a negro, fresh from Central Africa, would take back to his tribe! What would he know of railway companies, of

5. The word "Utopia" itself, which in Greek means "nowhere," was invented by Sir Thomas More in his Renaissance description of a rationally managed, ideal state (1516). The late nineteenth century was rich in theories and presentations (often fictional) of Utopian societies, all of which Wells satirizes in his story of the Eloi; but he may be thinking explicitly here of *News from Nowhere* (1888) by William Morris (1834-1896), which presents an idealized future society of deindustrialized, antitechnological artisans of whom the feckless Eloi are nightmare parodies.

social movements, of telephone and telegraph wires, of the Parcels Delivery Company, and postal orders and the like? Yet we, at least, should be willing enough to explain these things to him! And even of what he knew, how much could he make his untravelled friend either apprehend or believe? Then, think how narrow the gap between a negro and a white man of our own times, and how wide the interval between myself and these of the Golden Age![6] I was sensible of much which was unseen, and which contributed to my comfort; but save for a general impression of automatic organization, I fear I can convey very little of the difference to your mind.

'In the matter of sepulture,[7] for instance, I could see no signs of crematoria nor anything suggestive of tombs. But it occurred to me that, possibly, there might be cemeteries (or crematoria) somewhere beyond the range of my explorings. This, again, was a question I deliberately put to myself, and my curiosity was at first entirely defeated upon the point. The thing puzzled me, and I was led to make a further remark, which puzzled me still more: that aged and infirm among this people there were none.

'I must confess that my satisfaction with my first theories of an automatic civilization and a decadent humanity did not long endure. Yet I could think of no other. Let me put my difficulties. The several big palaces I had explored were mere living places, great dining-halls and sleeping apartments. I could find no machinery, no appliances of any kind. Yet these people were clothed in pleasant fabrics that must at times need renewal, and their sandals, though undecorated, were fairly complex specimens of metalwork. Somehow such things must be made. And the little people displayed no vestige of a creative tendency. There were no shops, no workshops, no sign of importations among them. They spent all their time in playing gently, in bathing in the river, in making love in a half-

6. "The Golden Age," the era when men did not struggle under their burdens of labor, frustration, and mortality, is one of the most universal myths of human culture. Wells invokes the phrase here only to deny its reality—though, significantly, the phrase itself was one of the original chapter titles (see the appendix to *The Time Machine*).
7. Burial.

playful fashion, in eating fruit and sleeping. I could not see how things were kept going.

'Then, again, about the Time Machine: something, I knew not what, had taken it into the hollow pedestal of the White Sphinx. *Why?* For the life of me I could not imagine. Those waterless wells, too, those flickering pillars. I felt I lacked a clue. I felt—how shall I put it? Suppose you found an inscription, with sentences here and there in excellent plain English, and interpolated therewith, others made up of words, of letters even, absolutely unknown to you? Well, on the third day of my visit, that was how the world of Eight Hundred and Two Thousand Seven Hundred and One presented itself to me!

'That day, too, I made a friend—of a sort. It happened that, as I was watching some of the little people bathing in a shallow, one of them was seized with cramp and began drifting downstream. The main current ran rather swiftly, but not too strongly for even a moderate swimmer. It will give you an idea, therefore, of the strange deficiency in these creatures, when I tell you that none made the slightest attempt to rescue the weakly crying little thing which was drowning before their eyes. When I realized this, I hurriedly slipped off my clothes, and, wading in at a point lower down, I caught the poor mite and drew her safe to land. A little rubbing of the limbs soon brought her round, and I had the satisfaction of seeing she was all right before I left her. I had got to such a low estimate of her kind that I did not expect any gratitude from her. In that, however, I was wrong.

'This happened in the morning. In the afternoon I met my little woman, as I believe it was, as I was returning towards my centre from an exploration, and she received me with cries of delight and presented me with a big garland of flowers—evidently made for me and me alone. The thing took my imagination. Very possibly I had been feeling desolate. At any rate I did my best to display my appreciation of the gift. We were soon seated together in a little stone arbour, engaged in conversation, chiefly of smiles. The creature's friendliness affected me exactly as a child's might have done. We passed each other flowers, and she kissed my hands. I did the same to hers. Then I tried to talk, and found that her name was Weena, which, though I don't know what it meant, somehow seemed appropriate enough. That was the beginning of a queer friendship which lasted a week, and ended—as I will tell you!

'She was exactly like a child. She wanted to be with me always. She tried to follow me everywhere, and on my next journey out and about it went to my heart to tire her down, and leave her at last, exhausted and calling after me rather plaintively. But the problems of the world had to be mastered. I had not, I said to myself, come into the future to carry on a miniature flirtation. Yet her distress when I left her was very great, her expostulations at the parting were sometimes frantic, and I think, altogether, I had as much trouble as comfort from her devotion. Nevertheless she was, somehow, a very great comfort. I thought it was mere childish affection that made her cling to me. Until it was too late, I did not clearly know what I had inflicted upon her when I left her. Nor until it was too late did I clearly understand what she was to me. For, by merely seeming fond of me, and showing in her weak, futile way that she cared for me, the little doll of a creature presently gave my return to the neighbourhood of the White Sphinx almost the feeling of coming home; and I would watch for her tiny figure of white and gold so soon as I came over the hill.

'It was from her, too, that I learned that fear had not yet left the world. She was fearless enough in the daylight, and she had the oddest confidence in me; for once, in a foolish moment, I made threatening grimaces at her, and she simply laughed at them. But she dreaded the dark, dreaded shadows, dreaded black things. Darkness to her was the one thing dreadful. It was a singularly passionate emotion, and it set me thinking and observing. I discovered then, among other things, that these little people gathered into the great house after dark, and slept in droves. To enter upon them without a light was to put them into a tumult of apprehension. I never found one out of doors, or one sleeping alone within doors, after dark. Yet I was still such a blockhead that I missed the lesson of that fear, and in spite of Weena's distress I insisted upon sleeping away from these slumbering multitudes.

'It troubled her greatly, but in the end her odd affection for me triumphed, and for five of the nights of our acquaintance, including the last night of all, she slept with her head pillowed on my arm. But my story slips away from me as I speak of her. It must have been the night before her rescue that I was awakened about dawn. I had been restless, dreaming most disagreeably that I was drowned, and that sea-anemones were feeling over my face with their soft palps.[8] I woke with a start, and with an odd fancy that some greyish animal had just rushed out of the chamber. I tried to get to sleep again, but I felt restless and uncomfortable. It was that dim grey hour when things are just creeping out of darkness, when every-thing is colourless and clear cut, and yet unreal. I got up, and went down into the great hall, and so out upon the flagstones in front of the palace. I thought I would make a virtue of necessity, and see the sunrise.

'The moon was setting, and the dying moonlight and the first pallor of dawn were mingled in a ghastly half-light. The bushes were inky black, the ground a sombre grey, the sky colourless and cheerless. And up the hill I thought I could see ghosts. Three several times, as I scanned the slope, I saw white figures. Twice I fancied I saw a solitary white, ape-like creature running rather quickly up the hill, and once near the ruins I saw a leash[9] of them carrying some dark body. They moved hastily. I did not see what became of them. It seemed that they vanished among the bushes. The dawn was still indistinct, you must understand. I was feeling that chill, uncertain, early-morning feeling you may have known. I doubted my eyes.

'As the eastern sky grew brighter, and the light of the day came on and its vivid colouring returned upon the world once more, I scanned the view keenly. But I saw no vestige of my white figures.

8. The anemone, an aquatic fixed plant, grasps its food with the tiny, sensi-tive tendrils (called palps) that surround its mouth.
9. A group of three, usually three hounds.

They were mere creatures of the half-light. "They must have been ghosts," I said; "I wonder whence they dated." For a queer notion of Grant Allen's[10] came into my head, and amused me. If each generation die and leave ghosts, he argued, the world at last will get overcrowded with them. On that theory they would have grown innumerable some Eight Hundred Thousand Years hence, and it was no great wonder to see four at once. But the jest was unsatisfying, and I was thinking of these figures all the morning, until Weena's rescue drove them out of my head. I associated them in some indefinite way with the white animal I had startled in my first passionate search for the Time Machine. But Weena was a pleasant substitute. Yet all the same, they were soon destined to take far deadlier possession of my mind.

'I think I have said how much hotter than our own was the weather of this Golden Age. I cannot account for it. It may be that the sun was hotter, or the earth nearer the sun. It is usual to assume that the sun will go on cooling steadily in the future. But people, unfamiliar with such speculations as those of the younger Darwin,[11] forget that the planets must ultimately fall back one by one into the parent body. As these catastrophes occur, the sun will blaze with renewed energy; and it may be that some inner planet had suffered this fate. Whatever the reason, the fact remains that the sun was very much hotter than we know it.

'Well, one very hot morning—my fourth, I think—as I was seeking shelter from the heat and glare in a colossal ruin near the great house where I slept and fed, there happened this strange thing: Clambering among these heaps of masonry, I found a narrow gallery, whose end and side windows were blocked by fallen masses of stone. By contrast with the brilliancy outside, it seemed at first impenetrably dark to me. I entered it groping, for the change from

10. Allen (1848-1899) was a libertarian, advocate of female suffrage, novelist, historian, and scientist whose novel of 1895, *The Woman Who Did,* Wells reviewed and attacked bitterly.
11. Charles Darwin (1809-1882), called "the younger" to distinguish him from his grandfather Erasmus (1731-1802), once a widely known naturalist and versifier of biological science.

light to blackness made spots of colour swim before me. Suddenly I halted spellbound. A pair of eyes, luminous by reflection against the daylight without, was watching me out of the darkness.

'The old instinctive dread of wild beasts came upon me. I clenched my hands and steadfastly looked into the glaring eyeballs. I was afraid to turn. Then the thought of the absolute security in which humanity appeared to be living came to my mind. And then I remembered that strange terror of the dark. Overcoming my fear to some extent, I advanced a step and spoke. I will admit that my voice was harsh and ill-controlled. I put out my hand and touched something soft. At once the eyes darted sideways, and something white ran past me. I turned with my heart in my mouth, and saw a queer little ape-like figure, its head held down in a peculiar manner, running across the sunlit space behind me. It blundered against a block of granite, staggered aside, and in a moment was hidden in a black shadow beneath another pile of ruined masonry.

'My impression of it is, of course, imperfect; but I know it was a dull white, and had strange large greyish-red eyes; also that there was flaxen hair on its head and down its back. But, as I say, it went too fast for me to see distinctly. I cannot even say whether it ran on all-fours, or only with its forearms held very low. After an instant's pause I followed it into the second heap of ruins. I could not find it at first; but, after a time in the profound obscurity, I came upon one of those round well-like openings of which I have told you, half closed by a fallen pillar. A sudden thought came to me. Could this Thing have vanished down the shaft? I lit a match, and, looking down, I saw a small, white, moving creature, with large bright eyes which regarded me steadfastly as it retreated. It made me shudder. It was so like a human spider! It was clambering down the wall, and now I saw for the first time a number of metal foot and hand rests forming a kind of ladder down the shaft. Then the light burned my fingers and fell out of my hand, going out as it dropped, and when I had lit another the little monster had disappeared.

'I do not know how long I sat peering down that well. It was not for some time that I could succeed in persuading myself that the thing I had seen was human. But, gradually, the truth dawned on me: that Man had not remained one species, but had differentiated into two distinct animals: that my graceful children of the Upper-world were not the sole descendants of our generation, but that this bleached, obscene, nocturnal Thing, which had flashed before me, was also heir to all the ages.

'I thought of the flickering pillars and of my theory of an under-ground ventilation. I began to suspect their true import. And what, I wondered, was this Lemur[12] doing in my scheme of a perfectly balanced organization? How was it related to the indolent serenity of the beautiful Upper-worlders? And what was hidden down there, at the foot of that shaft? I sat upon the edge of the well telling my-self that, at any rate, there was nothing to fear, and that there I must descend for the solution of my difficulties. And withal I was absolutely afraid to go! As I hesitated, two of the beautiful Upper-world people came running in their amorous sport across the day-light into the shadow. The male pursued the female, flinging flowers at her as he ran.

'They seemed distressed to find me, my arm against the over-turned pillar, peering down the well. Apparently it was considered bad form to remark these apertures; for when I pointed to this one, and tried to frame a question about it in their tongue, they were still more visibly distressed and turned away. But they were inter-ested by my matches, and I struck some to amuse them. I tried them again about the well, and again I failed. So presently I left them, meaning to go back to Weena, and see what I could get from her. But my mind was already in revolution; my guesses and im-pressions were slipping and sliding to a new adjustment. I had now a clue to the import of these wells, to the ventilating towers, to the mystery of the ghosts; to say nothing of a hint at the meaning of the

12. A tree-dwelling, nocturnal mammal resembling a monkey with a fox-like, muzzled face.

bronze gates and the fate of the Time Machine! And very vaguely there came a suggestion towards the solution of the economic problem that had puzzled me.

'Here was the new view. Plainly, this second species of Man was subterranean. There were three circumstances in particular which made me think that its rare emergence above ground was the outcome of a long-continued underground habit. In the first place, there was the bleached look common in most animals that live largely in the dark—the white fish of the Kentucky caves,[13] for instance. Then, those large eyes, with that capacity for reflecting light, are common features of nocturnal things—witness the owl and the cat. And last of all, that evident confusion in the sunshine, that hasty yet fumbling and awkward flight towards dark shadow, and that peculiar carriage of the head while in the light—all reinforced the theory of an extreme sensitiveness of the retina.

'Beneath my feet, then, the earth must be tunnelled enormously, and these tunnellings were the habitat of the new race. The presence of ventilating shafts and wells along the hill slopes—everywhere, in fact, except along the river valley—showed how universal were its ramifications. What so natural, then, as to assume that it was in this artificial Under-world that such work as was necessary to the comfort of the daylight race was done? The notion was so plausible that I at once accepted it, and went on to assume the how of this splitting of the human species. I dare say you will anticipate the shape of my theory; though, for myself, I very soon felt that it fell far short of the truth.

'At first, proceeding from the problems of our own age, it seemed clear as daylight to me that the gradual widening of the present merely temporary and social difference between the Capitalist and the Labourer, was the key to the whole position. No doubt it will

13. *Amblyopsis spelaeus,* a variety of carp still to be found in Mammoth Cave, Kentucky. These fish, living for millennia in the absolutely light-less depths of the cave, have only small, vestigial, blind eyes. Their existence had been known since the early nineteenth century, but came to be adduced as unusually graphic evidence for Darwin's theory of the adaptation of organism to environment.

seem grotesque enough to you—and wildly incredible!—and yet even now there are existing circumstances to point that way. There is a tendency to utilize underground space for the less ornamental purposes of civilization; there is the Metropolitan Railway[14] in London, for instance, there are new electric railways, there are subways, there are underground workrooms and restaurants, and they increase and multiply. Evidently, I thought, this tendency had increased till Industry had gradually lost its birthright in the sky. I mean that it had gone deeper and deeper into larger and ever larger underground factories, spending a still-increasing amount of its time therein, till, in the end—! Even now, does an East-end worker[15] live in such artificial conditions as practically to be cut off from the natural surface of the earth?

'Again, the exclusive tendency of richer people—due, no doubt, to the increasing refinement of their education, and the widening gulf between them and the rude violence of the poor—is already leading to the closing, in their interest, of considerable portions of the surface of the land. About London, for instance, perhaps half the prettier country is shut in against intrusion. And this same widening gulf—which is due to the length and expense of the higher educational process and the increased facilities for and temptations towards refined habits on the part of the rich—will make that exchange between class and class, that promotion by intermarriage which at present retards the splitting of our species along lines of social stratification, less and less frequent. So, in the end, above ground you must have the Haves, pursuing pleasure and comfort and beauty, and below ground the Have-nots, the Workers getting continually adapted to the conditions of their labour. Once they were there, they would no doubt have to pay rent, and not a little

14. The Metropolitan Railway (origin of the present London Underground) opened in 1863. It was not until 1890 that the first electric underground railway line began operating between South London and the City.
15. Throughout the nineteenth century, the East End of London was the site of the most abject working-class slums. It was not until the period between the two World Wars that the area began to be cleared and renovated.

of it, for the ventilation of their caverns; and if they refused, they would starve or be suffocated for arrears. Such of them as were so constituted as to be miserable and rebellious would die; and, in the end, the balance being permanent, the survivors would become as well adapted to the conditions of underground life, and as happy in their way, as the Upper-world people were to theirs. As it seemed to me, the refined beauty and the etiolated[16] pallor followed naturally enough.

'The great triumph of Humanity I had dreamed of took a different shape in my mind. It had been no such triumph of moral education and general co-operation as I had imagined. Instead, I saw a real aristocracy, armed with a perfected science and working to a logical conclusion the industrial system of to-day. Its triumph had not been simply a triumph over Nature, but a triumph over Nature and the fellow-man. This, I must warn you, was my theory at the time. I had no convenient cicerone[17] in the pattern of the Utopian books. My explanation may be absolutely wrong. I still think it is the most plausible one. But even on this supposition the balanced civilization that was at last attained must have long since passed its zenith, and was now far fallen into decay. The too-perfect security of the Upper-worlders had led them to a slow movement of degeneration, to a general dwindling in size, strength, and intelligence. That I could see clearly enough already. What had happened to the Undergrounders I did not yet suspect; but from what I had seen of the Morlocks[18]—that, by the by, was the name by which these creatures were called—I could imagine that the modification of the human type was even far more profound than among the "Eloi," the beautiful race that I already knew.

16. Made pale or bleached through the protracted absence of light.
17. A professional guide for tourists. Wells refers contemptuously to the convention, in Utopian fictions, of having a character explain the workings of the ideal society in all its complexity to the wondering visitor from our own world.
18. It is interesting that, in the first version of *The Time Machine,* its 1894 serialization in the *National Observer,* the Morlocks were named as such, but the Eloi were not.

'Then came troublesome doubts. Why had the Morlocks taken my Time Machine? For I felt sure it was they who had taken it. Why, too, if the Eloi were masters, could they not restore the machine to me? And why were they so terribly afraid of the dark? I proceeded, as I have said, to question Weena about this Underworld, but here again I was disappointed. At first she would not understand my questions, and presently she refused to answer them. She shivered as though the topic was unendurable. And when I pressed her, perhaps a little harshly, she burst into tears. They were the only tears, except my own, I ever saw in that Golden Age. When I saw them I ceased abruptly to trouble about the Morlocks, and was only concerned in banishing these signs of the human inheritance from Weena's eyes. And very soon she was smiling and clapping her hands, while I solemnly burned a match.

VI

'It may seem odd to you, but it was two days before I could follow up the new-found clue in what was manifestly the proper way. I felt a peculiar shrinking from those pallid bodies. They were just the half-bleached colour of the worms and things one sees preserved in spirit in a zoological museum. And they were filthily cold to the touch. Probably my shrinking was largely due to the sympathetic influence of the Eloi, whose disgust of the Morlocks I now began to appreciate.

'The next night I did not sleep well. Probably my health was a little disordered. I was oppressed with perplexity and doubt. Once or twice I had a feeling of intense fear for which I could perceive no definite reason. I remember creeping noiselessly into the great hall where the little people were sleeping in the moonlight—that night Weena was among them—and feeling reassured by their presence. It occurred to me even then, that in the course of a few days the moon must pass through its last quarter, and the nights grow dark, when the appearances of these unpleasant creatures from below, these whitened Lemurs, this new vermin that had replaced the old, might be more abundant. And on both these days I had the restless feeling of one who shirks an inevitable duty. I felt assured that the Time Machine was only to be recovered by boldly penetrating these underground mysteries. Yet I could not face the mystery. If only I had had a companion it would have been different. But I was so horribly alone, and even to clamber down into the darkness of the well appalled me. I don't know if you will understand my feeling, but I never felt quite safe at my back.

'It was this restlessness, this insecurity, perhaps, that drove me further and further afield in my exploring expeditions. Going to the south-westward towards the rising country that is now called Combe Wood, I observed far off, in the direction of nineteenth-century Banstead,[1] a vast green structure, different in character from any I had hitherto seen. It was larger than the largest of the palaces or ruins I knew, and the façade had an Oriental look: the face of it having the lustre, as well as the pale-green tint, a kind of bluish-green, of a certain type of Chinese porcelain. This difference in aspect suggested a difference in use, and I was minded to push on and explore. But the day was growing late, and I had come upon the sight of the place after a long and tiring circuit; so I resolved to hold over the adventure for the following day, and I returned to the welcome and the caresses of little Weena. But next morning I perceived clearly enough that my curiosity regarding the Palace of Green Porcelain was a piece of self-deception, to enable me to shirk, by another day, an experience I dreaded. I resolved I would make the descent without further waste of time, and started out in the early morning towards a well near the ruins of granite and aluminium.

'Little Weena ran with me. She danced beside me to the well, but when she saw me lean over the mouth and look downward, she seemed strangely disconcerted. "Good-bye, little Weena," I said, kissing her; and then, putting her down, I began to feel over the parapet for the climbing hooks. Rather hastily, I may as well con-

1. See map.

fess, for I feared my courage might leak away! At first she watched me in amazement. Then she gave a most piteous cry, and, running to me, she began to pull at me with her little hands. I think her opposition nerved me rather to proceed. I shook her off, perhaps a little roughly, and in another moment I was in the throat of the well. I saw her agonized face over the parapet, and smiled to reassure her. Then I had to look down at the unstable hooks to which I clung.

'I had to clamber down a shaft of perhaps two hundred yards. The descent was effected by means of metallic bars projecting from the sides of the well, and these being adapted to the needs of a creature much smaller and lighter than myself, I was speedily cramped and fatigued by the descent. And not simply fatigued! One of the bars bent suddenly under my weight, and almost swung me off into the blackness beneath. For a moment I hung by one hand, and after that experience I did not dare to rest again. Though my arms and back were presently acutely painful, I went on clambering down the sheer descent with as quick a motion as possible. Glancing upward, I saw the aperture, a small blue disk, in which a star was visible, while little Weena's head showed as a round black projection. The thudding sound of a machine below grew louder and more oppressive. Everything save that little disk above was profoundly dark, and when I looked up again Weena had disappeared.

'I was in an agony of discomfort. I had some thought of trying to go up the shaft again, and leave the Under-world alone. But even while I turned this over in my mind I continued to descend. At last, with intense relief, I saw dimly coming up, a foot to the right of me, a slender loophole in the wall. Swinging myself in, I found it was the aperture of a narrow horizontal tunnel in which I could lie down and rest. It was not too soon. My arms ached, my back was cramped, and I was trembling with the prolonged terror of a fall. Besides this, the unbroken darkness had had a distressing effect upon my eyes. The air was full of the throb and hum of machinery pumping air down the shaft.

'I do not know how long I lay. I was roused by a soft hand touching my face. Starting up in the darkness I snatched at my matches and, hastily striking one, I saw three stooping white creatures similar to the one I had seen above ground in the ruin, hastily retreating before the light. Living, as they did, in what appeared to me impenetrable darkness, their eyes were abnormally large and sensitive, just as are the pupils of the abysmal fishes, and they reflected the light in the same way. I have no doubt they could see me in that rayless obscurity, and they did not seem to have any fear of me apart from the light. But, so soon as I struck a match in order to see them, they fled incontinently, vanishing into dark gutters and tunnels, from which their eyes glared at me in the strangest fashion.

'I tried to call to them, but the language they had was apparently different from that of the Over-world people; so that I was needs left to my own unaided efforts, and the thought of flight before exploration was even then in my mind. But I said to myself, "You are in for it now," and, feeling my way along the tunnel, I found the noise of machinery grow louder. Presently the walls fell away from me, and I came to a large open space, and, striking another match, saw that I had entered a vast arched cavern, which stretched into utter darkness beyond the range of my light. The view I had of it was as much as one could see in the burning of a match.

'Necessarily my memory is vague. Great shapes like big machines rose out of the dimness, and cast grotesque black shadows, in which dim spectral Morlocks sheltered from the glare. The place, by the by, was very stuffy and oppressive, and the faint halitus[2] of freshly shed blood was in the air. Some way down the central vista was a little table of white metal, laid with what seemed a meal. The Morlocks at any rate were carnivorous! Even at the time, I remember wondering what large animal could have survived to furnish the red joint I saw. It was all very indistinct: the heavy smell, the big unmeaning shapes, the obscene figures lurking in the shadows, and only waiting for the darkness to come at me again! Then the match

---

2. Breath or bad odor.

burned down, and stung my fingers, and fell, a wriggling red spot in the blackness.

'I have thought since how particularly ill-equipped I was for such an experience. When I had started with the Time Machine, I had started with the absurd assumption that the men of the Future would certainly be infinitely ahead of ourselves in all their appliances. I had come without arms, without medicine, without anything to smoke—at times I missed tobacco frightfully—even without enough matches. If only I had thought of a Kodak![3] I could have flashed that glimpse of the Under-world in a second, and examined it at leisure. But, as it was, I stood there with only the weapons and the powers that Nature had endowed me with—hands, feet, and teeth; these, and four safety-matches that still remained to me.

'I was afraid to push my way in among all this machinery in the dark, and it was only with my last glimpse of light I discovered that my store of matches had run low. It had never occurred to me until that moment that there was any need to economize them, and I had wasted almost half the box in astonishing the Upper-worlders, to whom fire was a novelty. Now, as I say, I had four left, and while I stood in the dark, a hand touched mine, lank fingers came feeling over my face, and I was sensible of a peculiar unpleasant odour. I fancied I heard the breathing of a crowd of those dreadful little beings about me. I felt the box of matches in my hand being gently disengaged, and other hands behind me plucking at my clothing. The sense of these unseen creatures examining me was indescribably unpleasant. The sudden realization of my ignorance of their ways of thinking and doing came home to me very vividly in the darkness. I shouted at them as loudly as I could. They started away, and then I could feel them approaching me again. They clutched at me more boldly, whispering odd sounds to each other. I shivered violently, and shouted again—rather discordantly. This time they were not so seriously alarmed, and they made a queer laughing noise as they came back at me. I will confess I was horribly fright-

3. George Eastman (1854-1932) introduced his first portable camera in 1888. Wells himself was an avid, and talented, amateur photographer.

ened. I determined to strike another match and escape under the protection of its glare. I did so, and eking out the flicker with a scrap of paper from my pocket, I made good my retreat to the narrow tunnel. But I had scarce entered this when my light was blown out, and in the blackness i could hear the Morlocks rustling like wind among leaves, and pattering like the rain, as they hurried after me.

'In a moment I was clutched by several hands, and there was no mistaking that they were trying to haul me back. I struck another light, and waved it in their dazzled faces. You can scarce imagine how nauseatingly inhuman they looked—those pale, chinless faces and great, lidless, pinkish-grey eyes!—as they stared in their blindness and bewilderment. But I did not stay to look, I promise you: I retreated again, and when my second match had ended, I struck my third. It had almost burned through when I reached the opening into the shaft. I lay down on the edge, for the throb of the great pump below made me giddy. Then I felt sideways for the projecting hooks, and, as I did so, my feet were grasped from behind, and I was violently tugged backward. I lit my last match . . . and it incontinently went out. But I had my hand on the climbing bars now, and, kicking violently, I disengaged myself from the clutches of the Morlocks and was speedily clambering up the shaft, while they stayed peering and blinking up at me: all but one little wretch who followed me for some way, and wellnigh secured my boot as a trophy.

'That climb seemed interminable to me. With the last twenty or thirty feet of it a deadly nausea came upon me. I had the greatest difficulty in keeping my hold. The last few yards was a frightful struggle against this faintness. Several times my head swam, and I felt all the sensations of falling. At last, however, I got over the well-mouth somehow, and staggered out of the ruin into the blinding sunlight. I fell upon my face. Even the soil smelt sweet and clean. Then I remember Weena kissing my hands and ears, and the voices of others among the Eloi. Then, for a time, I was insensible.

VII

'Now, indeed, I seemed in a worse case than before. Hitherto, except during my night's anguish at the loss of the Time Machine, I had felt a sustaining hope of ultimate escape, but that hope was staggered by these new discoveries. Hitherto I had merely thought myself impeded by the childish simplicity of the little people, and by some unknown forces which I had only to understand to overcome; but there was an altogether new element in the sickening quality of the Morlocks—a something inhuman and malign. Instinctively I loathed them. Before, I had felt as a man might feel who had fallen into a pit: my concern was with the pit and how to get out of it. Now I felt like a beast in a trap, whose enemy would come upon him soon.

'The enemy I dreaded may surprise you. It was the darkness of the new moon. Weena had put this into my head by some at first incomprehensible remarks about the Dark Nights. It was not now such a very difficult problem to guess what the coming Dark Nights might mean. The moon was on the wane: each night there was a longer interval of darkness. And I now understood to some slight degree at least the reason of the fear of the little Upper-world people for the dark. I wondered vaguely what foul villainy it might be that the Morlocks did under the new moon. I felt pretty sure now that my second hypothesis was all wrong. The Upper-world people might once have been the favoured aristocracy, and the Morlocks their mechanical servants; but that had long since passed away. The two species that had resulted from the evolution of man were sliding down towards, or had already arrived at, an altogether new relationship. The Eloi, like the Carlovingian kings,[1] had decayed to a mere beautiful futility. They still possessed the earth on sufferance: since the Morlocks, subterranean for innumerable genera-

1. The Carlovingian Dynasty of France, 751-987 A.D., was proverbial for its genetic degeneracy.

tions, had come at last to find the daylit surface intolerable. And the Morlocks made their garments, I inferred, and maintained them in their habitual needs, perhaps through the survival of an old habit of service. They did it as a standing horse paws with his foot, or as a man enjoys killing animals in sport: because ancient and departed necessities had impressed it on the organism. But, clearly, the old order was already in part reversed. The Nemesis[2] of the delicate ones was creeping on apace. Ages ago, thousands of generations ago, man had thrust his brother man out of the ease and the sunshine. And now that brother was coming back—changed! Already the Eloi had begun to learn one old lesson anew. They were becoming reacquainted with Fear. And suddenly there came into my head the memory of the meat I had seen in the Under-world. It seemed odd how it floated into my mind: not stirred up as it were by the current of my meditations, but coming in almost like a question from outside. I tried to recall the form of it. I had a vague sense of something familiar, but I could not tell what it was at the time.

'Still, however helpless the little people in the presence of their mysterious Fear, I was differently constituted. I came out of this age of ours, this ripe prime of the human race, when Fear does not paralyse and mystery has lost its terrors. I at least would defend myself. Without further delay I determined to make myself arms and a fastness[3] where I might sleep. With that refuge as a base, I could face this strange world with some of that confidence I had lost in realizing to what creatures night by night I lay exposed. I felt I could never sleep again until my bed was secure from them. I shuddered with horror to think how they must already have examined me.

'I wandered during the afternoon along the valley of the Thames, but found nothing that commended itself to my mind as inaccessible. All the buildings and trees seemed easily practicable to such dexterous climbers as the Morlocks, to judge by their wells, must

2. In Greek myth, an avenging deity.
3. Fortress.

be. Then the tall pinnacles of the Palace of Green Porcelain and the polished gleam of its walls came back to my memory; and in the evening, taking Weena like a child upon my shoulder, I went up the hills towards the south-west. The distance, I had reckoned, was seven or eight miles, but it must have been nearer eighteen. I had first seen the place on a moist afternoon when distances are decep-tively diminished. In addition, the heel of one of my shoes was loose, and a nail was working through the sole—they were comfort-able old shoes I wore about indoors—so that I was lame. And it was already long past sunset when I came in sight of the palace, sil-houetted black against the pale yellow of the sky.

'Weena had been hugely delighted when I began to carry her, but after a time she desired me to let her down, and ran along by the side of me, occasionally darting off on either hand to pick flowers to stick in my pockets. My pockets had always puzzled Weena, but at the last she had concluded that they were an eccentric kind of vase for floral decoration. At least she utilized them for that pur-pose. And that reminds me! In changing my jacket I found . . .'

The Time Traveller paused, put his hand into his pocket, and si-lently placed two withered flowers, not unlike very large white mallows, upon the little table. Then he resumed his narrative.[4]

'As the hush of evening crept over the world and we proceeded over the hill crest towards Wimbledon, Weena grew tired and wanted to return to the house of grey stone. But I pointed out the distant pinnacles of the Palace of Green Porcelain to her, and con-trived to make her understand that we were seeking a refuge there from her Fear. You know that great pause that comes upon things before the dusk? Even the breeze stops in the trees. To me there is always an air of expectation about that evening stillness. The sky was clear, remote, and empty save for a few horizontal bars far down in the sunset. Well, that night the expectation took the colour of my fears. In that darkling calm my senses seemed preternatu-

4. Mallows are small plants with purple, pink, or white flowers. This is the only point at which the narrative of the Time Traveller is interrupted: to produce the crucial evidence of his truthfulness.

rally[5] sharpened. I fancied I could even feel the hollowness of the ground beneath my feet: could, indeed, almost see through it the Morlocks on their ant-hill going hither and thither and waiting for the dark. In my excitement I fancied that they would receive my invasion of their burrows as a declaration of war. And why had they taken my Time Machine?

'So we went on in the quiet, and the twilight deepened into night. The clear blue of the distance faded, and one star after another came out. The ground grew dim and the trees black. Weena's fears and her fatigue grew upon her. I took her in my arms and talked to her and caressed her. Then, as the darkness grew deeper, she put her arms round my neck, and, closing her eyes, tightly pressed her face against my shoulder. So we went down a long slope into a valley, and there in the dimness I almost walked into a little river. This I waded, and went up the opposite side of the valley, past a number of sleeping houses, and by a statue—a Faun,[6] or some such figure, *minus* the head. Here too were acacias. So far I had seen nothing of the Morlocks, but it was yet early in the night, and the darker hours before the old moon rose were still to come.

'From the brow of the next hill I saw a thick wood spreading wide and black before me. I hesitated at this. I could see no end to it, either to the right or the left. Feeling tired—my feet, in particular, were very sore—I carefully lowered Weena from my shoulder as I halted, and sat down upon the turf. I could no longer see the Palace of Green Porcelain, and I was in doubt of my direction. I looked into the thickness of the wood and thought of what it might hide. Under that dense tangle of branches one would be out of sight of the stars. Even were there no other lurking danger—a danger I did not care to let my imagination loose upon—there would still be all the roots to stumble over and the tree-boles[7] to strike against.

5. Out of the ordinary course of nature.
6. In Greek myth, a woodland spirit with the ears and feet of a goat. The Faun is a perennial symbol of sensuality; the fact that here he has lost his head may well represent the author's judgment on the unintelligent eroticism of this future society.
7. Tree trunks.

'I was very tired, too, after the excitements of the day; so I decided that I would not face it, but would pass the night upon the open hill.

'Weena, I was glad to find, was fast asleep. I carefully wrapped her in my jacket, and sat down beside her to wait for the moonrise. The hill-side was quiet and deserted, but from the black of the wood there came now and then a stir of living things. Above me shone the stars, for the night was very clear. I felt a certain sense of friendly comfort in their twinkling. All the old constellations had gone from the sky, however: that slow movement which is imperceptible in a hundred human lifetimes, had long since rearranged them in unfamiliar groupings. But the Milky Way, it seemed to me, was still the same tattered streamer of star-dust as of yore. Southward (as I judged it) was a very bright red star that was new to me; it was even more splendid than our own green Sirius.[8] And amid all these scintillating points of light one bright planet[9] shone kindly and steadily like the face of an old friend.

'Looking at these stars suddenly dwarfed my own troubles and all the gravities of terrestrial life. I thought of their unfathomable distance, and the slow inevitable drift of their movements out of the unknown past into the unknown future. I thought of the great precessional cycle[10] that the pole of the earth describes. Only forty times had that silent revolution occurred during all the years that I had traversed. And during these few revolutions all the activity, all the traditions, the complex organizations, the nations, languages,

8. The Dog Star, in the constellation of Ursa Major, the brightest star in the heavens.
9. Venus, the morning and the evening star.
10. The phenomenon called the "precession of the equinoxes" was first explained by Sir Isaac Newton (1642-1727). The earth rotates on its axis; but because of the gravitational attractions of the moon and the sun, the earth's axis of rotation itself describes a much slower rotation, somewhat like a top spinning out of the vertical and slowly rotating as it spins. This is "precession," and the earth completes one full precession every 26,000 years. The Time Traveller, doubtless under the pressure of the moment, miscalculates: from the late nineteenth century to 802, 701 the precessional cycle would have been completed only thirty times.

literatures, aspirations, even the mere memory of Man as I knew him, had been swept out of existence. Instead were these frail creatures who had forgotten their high ancestry, and the white Things of which I went in terror. Then I thought of the Great Fear that was between the two species, and for the first time, with a sudden shiver, came the clear knowledge of what the meat I had seen might be. Yet it was too horrible! I looked at little Weena sleeping beside me, her face white and starlike under the stars, and forthwith dismissed the thought.

'Through that long night I held my mind off the Morlocks as well as I could, and whiled away the time by trying to fancy I could find signs of the old constellations in the new confusion. The sky kept very clear, except for a hazy cloud or so. No doubt I dozed at times. Then, as my vigil wore on, came a faintness in the eastward sky, like the reflection of some colourless fire, and the old moon rose, thin and peaked and white. And close behind, and overtaking it, and overflowing it, the dawn came, pale at first, and then growing pink and warm. No Morlocks had approached us. Indeed, I had seen none upon the hill that night. And in the confidence of renewed day it almost seemed to me that my fear had been unreasonable. I stood up and found my foot with the loose heel swollen at the ankle and painful under the heel; so I sat down again, took off my shoes, and flung them away.

'I awakened Weena, and we went down into the wood, now green and pleasant instead of black and forbidding. We found some fruit wherewith to break our fast. We soon met others of the dainty ones, laughing and dancing in the sunlight as though there was no such thing in nature as the night. And then I thought once more of the meat that I had seen. I felt assured now of what it was, and from the bottom of my heart I pitied this last feeble rill[11] from the great flood of humanity. Clearly, at some time in the Long-Ago of human decay the Morlocks' food had run short. Possibly they had lived on rats and suchlike vermin. Even now man is far less discriminating and exclusive in his food than he was—far less than any

11. A small rivulet or brook.

monkey. His prejudice against human flesh is no deep-seated instinct. And so these inhuman sons of men——! I tried to look at the thing in a scientific spirit. After all, they were less human and more remote than our cannibal ancestors of three or four thousand years ago. And the intelligence that would have made this state of things a torment had gone. Why should I trouble myself? These Eloi were mere fatted cattle, which the ant-like Morlocks preserved and preyed upon—probably saw to the breeding of. And there was Weena dancing at my side!

'Then I tried to preserve myself from the horror that was coming upon me, by regarding it as a rigorous punishment of human selfishness. Man had been content to live in ease and delight upon the labours of his fellow-man, had taken Necessity as his watchword and excuse, and in the fullness of time Necessity had come home to him. I even tried a Carlyle-like[12] scorn of this wretched aristocracy in decay. But this attitude of mind was impossible. However great their intellectual degradation, the Eloi had kept too much of the human form not to claim my sympathy, and to make me perforce a sharer in their degradation and their Fear.

'I had at that time very vague ideas as to the course I should pursue. My first was to secure some safe place of refuge, and to make myself such arms of metal or stone as I could contrive. That necessity was immediate. In the next place, I hoped to procure some means of fire, so that I should have the weapon of a torch at hand, for nothing, I knew, would be more efficient against these Morlocks. Then I wanted to arrange some contrivance to break open the doors of bronze under the White Sphinx. I had in mind a battering-ram. I had a persuasion that if I could enter those doors and carry a blaze of light before me I should discover the Time Machine and escape. I could not imagine the Morlocks were strong enough to move it far away. Weena I had resolved to bring with

12. Thomas Carlyle (1795-1881), the great Scottish historian and essayist, whose philosophy of history involved a romantic emphasis on the era-shaping influence of "great men" in their opposition to weak and outmoded traditions.

me to our own time. And turning such schemes over in my mind I pursued our way towards the building which my fancy had chosen as our dwelling.

VIII

'I found the Palace of Green Porcelain, when we approached it about noon, deserted and falling into ruin. Only ragged vestiges of glass remained in its windows, and great sheets of the green facing had fallen away from the corroded metallic framework. It lay very high upon a turfy down, and looking north-eastward before I entered it, I was surprised to see a large estuary,[1] or even creek, where I judged Wandsworth and Battersea must once have been. I thought then—though I never followed up the thought—of what might have happened, or might be happening, to the living things in the sea.

'The material of the Palace proved on examination to be indeed porcelain, and along the face of it I saw an inscription in some unknown character. I thought, rather foolishly, that Weena might help me to interpret this, but I only learned that the bare idea of writing had never entered her head. She always seemed to me, I fancy, more human than she was, perhaps because her affection was so human.

'Within the big valves[2] of the door—which were open and broken—we found, instead of the customary hall, a long gallery lit by many side windows. At the first glance I was reminded of a museum. The tiled floor was thick with dust, and a remarkable array of miscellaneous objects was shrouded in the same grey covering. Then I perceived, standing strange and gaunt in the centre of the hall, what was clearly the lower part of a huge skeleton. I recognized by the oblique feet that it was some extinct creature after the fashion of the Megatherium.[3] The skull and the upper bones lay be-

1. An arm or inlet of the sea; the point at which a river's current meets the sea's tide.
2. "Valve" is an archaic word for one of the leaves of a double door.
3. A giant ground sloth of the Pleistocene Era, approximately 1,000,000 B.C.

side it in the thick dust, and in one place, where rain-water had dropped through a leak in the roof, the thing itself had been worn away. Further in the gallery was the huge skeleton barrel of a Brontosaurus.[4] My museum hypothesis was confirmed. Going towards the side I found what appeared to be sloping shelves, and, clearing away the thick dust, I found the old familiar glass cases of our own time. But they must have been air-tight to judge from the fair preservation of some of their contents.

'Clearly we stood among the ruins of some latter-day South Kensington![5] Here, apparently, was the Palaeontological Section,[6] and a very splendid array of fossils it must have been, though the inevitable process of decay that had been staved off for a time, and had, through the extinction of bacteria and fungi, lost ninety-nine hundredths of its force, was, nevertheless, with extreme sureness if with extreme slowness at work again upon all its treasures. Here and there I found traces of the little people in the shape of rare fossils broken to pieces or threaded in strings upon reeds. And the cases had in some instances been bodily removed—by the Morlocks as I judged. The place was very silent. The thick dust deadened our footsteps. Weena, who had been rolling a sea-urchin down the sloping glass of a case, presently came, as I stared about me, and very quietly took my hand and stood beside me.

'And at first I was so much surprised by this ancient monument of an intellectual age, that I gave no thought to the possibilities it presented. Even my preoccupation about the Time Machine receded a little from my mind.

'To judge from the size of the place, this Palace of Green Porcelain had a great deal more in it than a Gallery of Palaeontology; possibly historical galleries; it might be, even a library! To me, at least in my present circumstances, these would be vastly more in-

---

4. The largest land animal ever evolved, a vegetarian dinosaur of the Jurassic Period, 180 to 135 million years ago.
5. This was the site of Wells's own science studies, at the Normal School of Science.
6. Paleontology is the study of prehistoric forms of life.

teresting than this spectacle of old-time geology in decay. Exploring, I found another short gallery running transversely to the first. This appeared to be devoted to minerals, and the sight of a block of sulphur set my mind running on gunpowder. But I could find no saltpetre; indeed, no nitrates[7] of any kind. Doubtless they had deliquesced[8] ages ago. Yet the sulphur hung in my mind, and set up a train of thinking. As for the rest of the contents of that gallery, though on the whole they were the best preserved of all I saw, I had little interest. I am no specialist in mineralogy, and I went on down a very ruinous aisle running parallel to the first hall I had entered. Apparently this section had been devoted to natural history, but everything had long since passed out of recognition. A few shrivelled and blackened vestiges of what had once been stuffed animals, desiccated[9] mummies in jars that had once held spirit, a brown dust of departed plants: that was all! I was sorry for that, because I should have been glad to trace the patent readjustments by which the conquest of animated nature had been attained. Then we came to a gallery of simply colossal proportions, but singularly ill-lit, the floor of it running downward at a slight angle from the end at which I entered. At intervals white globes hung from the ceiling—many of them cracked and smashed—which suggested that originally the place had been artifically lit. Here I was more in my element, for rising on either side of me were the huge bulks of big machines, all greatly corroded and many broken down, but some still fairly complete. You know I have a certain weakness for mechanism, and I was inclined to linger among these; the more so as for the most part they had the interest of puzzles, and I could make only the vaguest guesses at what they were for. I fancied that if I could solve their puzzles I should find myself in possession of powers that might be of use against the Morlocks.

'Suddenly Weena came very close to my side. So suddenly that

---

7. The basic ingredients of gunpowder. Saltpeter ("saltpetre," in British usage) is the natural form of potassium nitrate.
8. Melted away, become liquefied by absorbing moisture from the air.
9. Dried out.

she startled me. Had it not been for her I do not think I should have noticed that the floor of the gallery sloped at all.[10] The end I had come in at was quite above ground, and was lit by rare slit-like windows. As you went down the length, the ground came up against these windows, until at last there was a pit like the "area"[11] of a London house before each, and only a narrow line of daylight at the top. I went slowly along, puzzling about the machines, and had been too intent upon them to notice the gradual diminution of the light, until Weena's increasing apprehensions drew my attention. Then I saw that the gallery ran down at last into a thick darkness. I hesitated, and then, as I looked round me, I saw that the dust was less abundant and its surface less even. Further away towards the dimness, it appeared to be broken by a number of small narrow footprints. My sense of the immediate presence of the Morlocks revived at that. I felt that I was wasting my time in this academic examination of machinery. I called to mind that it was already far advanced in the afternoon, and that I had still no weapon, no refuge, and no means of making a fire. And then down in the remote blackness of the gallery I heard a peculiar pattering, and the same odd noises I had heard down the well.

'I took Weena's hand. Then, struck with a sudden idea, I left her and turned to a machine from which projected a lever not unlike those in a signal-box.[12] Clambering upon the stand, and grasping this lever in my hands, I put all my weight upon it sideways. Suddenly Weena, deserted in the central aisle, began to whimper. I had judged the strength of the lever pretty correctly, for it snapped after a minute's strain, and I rejoined her with a mace in my hand more than sufficient, I judged, for any Morlock skull I might encounter. And I longed very much to kill a Morlock or so. Very inhuman, you may think, to want to go killing one's own descendants! But it

10. "It may be, of course, that the floor did not slope, but that the museum was built into the side of a hill.—Ed." Wells's note.
11. The space, usually reserved for a garden, in front of a house.
12. In America, "signal tower": an enclosed metal box or platform from which railroad signals are displayed.

was impossible, somehow, to feel any humanity in the things. Only my disinclination to leave Weena, and a persuasion that if I began to slake my thirst for murder my Time Machine might suffer, re- strained me from going straight down the gallery and killing the brutes I heard.

'Well, mace in one hand and Weena in the other, I went out of that gallery and into another and still larger one, which at the first glance reminded me of a military chapel hung with tattered flags. The brown and charred rags that hung from the sides of it, I pres- ently recognized as the decaying vestiges of books. They had long since dropped to pieces, and every semblance of print had left them. But here and there were warped boards and cracked metallic clasps that told the tale well enough. Had I been a literary man I might, perhaps, have moralized upon the futility of all ambition. But as it was, the thing that struck me with keenest force was the enormous waste of labour to which this sombre wilderness of rotting paper testified. At the time I will confess that I thought chiefly of the *Philosophical Transactions*[13] and my own seventeen papers upon physical optics.

'Then, going up a broad staircase, we came to what may once have been a gallery of technical chemistry. And here I had not a little hope of useful discoveries. Except at one end where the roof had collapsed, this gallery was well preserved. I went eagerly to every unbroken case. And at last, in one of the really air-tight cases, I found a box of matches. Very eagerly I tried them. They were perfectly good. They were not even damp. I turned to Weena. "Dance," I cried to her in her own tongue. For now I had a weapon indeed against the horrible creatures we feared. And so, in that derelict museum, upon the thick soft carpeting of dust, to Weena's huge delight, I solemnly performed a kind of composite dance,

13. The *Philosophical Transactions,* begun in 1664, is the journal of the Royal Society, England's first and most famous scientific association; in 1887 it was divided into two journals, the "A" series devoted to mathe- matics and physics and the "B" series devoted to biological studies. The Time Traveller, obviously, is interested in perusing his own contributions to the journal.

whistling *The Land of the Leal*[14] as cheerfully as I could. In part it was a modest *cancan,* in part a step-dance, in part a skirt-dance (so far as my tail-coat permitted), and in part original. For I am naturally inventive, as you know.

'Now, I still think that for this box of matches to have escaped the wear of time for immemorial years was a most strange, as for me it was a most fortunate thing. Yet, oddly enough, I found a far unlikelier substance, and that was camphor.[15] I found it in a sealed jar, that by chance, I suppose, had been really hermetically sealed. I fancied at first that it was paraffin wax, and smashed the glass accordingly. But the odour of camphor was unmistakable. In the universal decay this volatile substance had chanced to survive, perhaps through many thousands of centuries. It reminded me of a sepia painting I had once seen done from the ink of a fossil Belemnite[16] that must have perished and become fossilized millions of years ago. I was about to throw it away, but I remembered that it was inflammable and burned with a good bright flame—was, in fact, an excellent candle—and I put it in my pocket. I found no explosives, however, nor any means of breaking down the bronze doors. As yet my iron crowbar was the most helpful thing I had chanced upon. Nevertheless I left that gallery greatly elated.

'I cannot tell you all the story of that long afternoon. It would require a great effort of memory to recall my explorations in at all the proper order. I remember a long gallery of rusting stands of arms, and how I hesitated between my crowbar and a hatchet or a sword. I could not carry both, however, and my bar of iron promised best against the bronze gates. There were numbers of guns, pistols, and rifles. The most were masses of rust, but many were of

14. A popular ballad by Carolina, Baroness Nairne (1766-1845), songwriter and contributor of lyrics to *The Scottish Minstrel* (1821-1824).
15. A whitish, highly flammable chemical used chiefly as a counterirritant and in the making of cellophane.
16. Sepia is a brown pigment made from the inklike secretions of the cuttlefish; a Belemnite is the cone-shaped, fossilized backbone of an extinct ancestor of the present-day cuttlefish.

some new metal, and still fairly sound. But any cartridges or powder there may once have been had rotted into dust. One corner I saw was charred and shattered; perhaps, I thought, by an explosion among the specimens. In another place was a vast array of idols—Polynesian, Mexican, Grecian, Phoenician, every country on earth I should think. And here, yielding to an irresistible impulse, I wrote my name upon the nose of a steatite[17] monster from South America that particularly took my fancy.

'As the evening drew on, my interest waned. I went through gallery after gallery, dusty, silent, often ruinous, the exhibits sometimes mere heaps of rust and lignite,[18] sometimes fresher. In one place I suddenly found myself near the model of a tin-mine, and then by the merest accident I discovered, in an air-tight case, two dynamite cartridges! I shouted "Eureka!" and smashed the case with joy. Then came a doubt. I hesitated. Then, selecting a little side gallery, I made my essay. I never felt such a disappointment as I did in waiting five, ten, fifteen minutes for an explosion that never came. Of course the things were dummies, as I might have guessed from their presence. I really believe that, had they not been so, I should have rushed off incontinently and blown Sphinx, bronze doors, and (as it proved) my chances of finding the Time Machine, all together into non-existence.

'It was after that, I think, that we came to a little open court within the palace. It was turfed, and had three fruit-trees. So we rested and refreshed ourselves. Towards sunset I began to consider our position. Night was creeping upon us, and my inaccessible hiding-place had still to be found. But that troubled me very little now. I had in my possession a thing that was, perhaps, the best of all defences against the Morlocks—I had matches! I had the camphor in my pocket, too, if a blaze were needed. It seemed to me that the best thing we could do would be to pass the night in the open, protected by a fire. In the morning there was the getting of the Time Machine. Towards that, as yet, I had only my iron mace. But now,

17. Soapstone, a soft, easily carved mineral.
18. Imperfectly formed, woody coal.

with my growing knowledge, I felt very differently towards those bronze doors. Up to this, I had refrained from forcing them, largely because of the mystery on the other side. They had never impressed me as being very strong, and I hoped to find my bar of iron not altogether inadequate for the work.

IX

'We emerged from the palace while the sun was still in part above the horizon. I was determined to reach the White Sphinx early the next morning, and ere the dusk I purposed pushing through the woods that had stopped me on the previous journey. My plan was to go as far as possible that night, and then, building a fire, to sleep in the protection of its glare. Accordingly, as we went along I gathered any sticks or dried grass I saw, and presently had my arms full of such litter. Thus loaded, our progress was slower than I had anticipated, and besides Weena was tired. And I began to suffer from sleepiness too; so that it was full night before we reached the wood. Upon the shrubby hill of its edge Weena would have stopped, fearing the darkness before us; but a singular sense of impending calamity, that should indeed have served me as a warning, drove me onward. I had been without sleep for a night and two days, and I was feverish and irritable. I felt sleep coming upon me, and the Morlocks with it.

'While we hesitated, among the black bushes behind us, and dim against their blackness, I saw three crouching figures. There was scrub and long grass all about us, and I did not feel safe from their insidious approach. The forest, I calculated, was rather less than a mile across. If we could get through it to the bare hill-side, there, as it seemed to me, was an altogether safer resting-place; I thought that with my matches and my camphor I could contrive to keep my path illuminated through the woods. Yet it was evident that if I was to flourish matches with my hands I should have to abandon my firewood; so, rather reluctantly, I put it down. And then it came into my head that I would amaze our friends behind by lighting it.

I was to discover the atrocious folly of this proceeding, but it came to my mind as an ingenious move for covering our retreat.

'I don't know if you have ever thought what a rare thing flame must be in the absence of man and in a temperate climate. The sun's heat is rarely strong enough to burn, even when it is focused by dewdrops, as is sometimes the case in more tropical districts. Lightning may blast and blacken, but it rarely gives rise to wide-spread fire. Decaying vegetation may occasionally smoulder with the heat of its fermentation, but this rarely results in flame. In this decadence, too, the art of fire-making had been forgotten on the earth. The red tongues that went licking up my heap of wood were an altogether new and strange thing to Weena.

'She wanted to run to it and play with it. I believe she would have cast herself into it had I not restrained her. But I caught her up, and, in spite of her struggles, plunged boldly before me into the wood. For a little way the glare of my fire lit the path. Looking back presently, I could see, through the crowded stems, that from my heap of sticks the blaze had spread to some bushes adjacent, and a curved line of fire was creeping up the grass of the hill. I laughed at that, and turned again to the dark trees before me. It was very black, and Weena clung to me convulsively, but there was still, as my eyes grew accustomed to the darkness, sufficient light for me to avoid the stems. Overhead it was simply black, except where a gap of remote blue sky shone down upon us here and there. I struck none of my matches because I had no hand free. Upon my left arm I carried my little one, in my right hand I had my iron bar.

'For some way I heard nothing but the crackling twigs under my feet, the faint rustle of the breeze above, and my own breathing and the throb of the blood-vessels in my ears. Then I seemed to know of a pattering about me. I pushed on grimly. The pattering grew more distinct, and then I caught the same queer sounds and voices I had heard in the Under-world. There were evidently several of the Morlocks, and they were closing in upon me. Indeed, in another minute I felt a tug at my coat, then something at my arm. And Weena shivered violently, and became quite still.

'It was time for a match. But to get one I must put her down. I did so, and, as I fumbled with my pocket, a struggle began in the darkness about my knees, perfectly silent on her part and with the same peculiar cooing sounds from the Morlocks. Soft little hands, too, were creeping over my coat and back, touching even my neck. Then the match scratched and fizzed. I held it flaring, and saw the white backs of the Morlocks in flight amid the trees. I hastily took a lump of camphor from my pocket, and prepared to light it as soon as the match should wane. Then I looked at Weena. She was lying clutching my feet and quite motionless, with her face to the ground. With a sudden fright I stooped to her. She seemed scarcely to breathe. I lit the block of camphor and flung it to the ground, and as it split and flared up and drove back the Morlocks and the shadows, I knelt down and lifted her. The wood behind seemed full of the stir and murmur of a great company!

'She seemed to have fainted. I put her carefully upon my shoulder and rose to push on, and then there came a horrible realization. In manœuvring with my matches and Weena, I had turned myself about several times, and now I had not the faintest idea in what direction lay my path. For all I knew, I might be facing back towards the Palace of Green Porcelain. I found myself in a cold sweat. I had to think rapidly what to do. I determined to build a fire and encamp where we were. I put Weena, still motionless, down upon a turfy bole, and very hastily, as my first lump of camphor waned, I began collecting sticks and leaves. Here and there out of the darkness round me Morlocks' eyes shone like carbuncles.[1]

'The camphor flickered and went out. I lit a match, and as I did so, two white forms that had been approaching Weena dashed hastily away. One was so blinded by the light that he came straight for me, and I felt his bones grind under the blow of my fist. He gave a whoop of dismay, staggered a little way, and fell down. I lit another piece of camphor, and went on gathering my bonfire. Presently I noticed how dry was some of the foliage above me, for since my arrival on the Time Machine, a matter of a week, no rain had

1. Semiprecious stones—garnets—cut in rounded, unfaceted form.

fallen. So, instead of casting about among the trees for fallen twigs, I began leaping up and dragging down branches. Very soon I had a choking smoky fire of green wood and dry sticks, and could economize my camphor. Then I turned to where Weena lay beside my iron mace. I tried what I could to revive her, but she lay like one dead. I could not even satsify myself whether or not she breathed.

'Now, the smoke of the fire beat over towards me, and it must have made me heavy of a sudden. Moreover, the vapour of camphor was in the air. My fire would not need replenishing for an hour or so. I felt very weary after my exertion, and sat down. The wood, too, was full of a slumbrous murmur that I did not understand. I seemed just to nod and open my eyes. But all was dark, and the Morlocks had their hands upon me. Flinging off their clinging fingers I hastily felt in my pocket for the match-box, and—it had gone! Then they gripped and closed with me again. In a moment I knew what had happened. I had slept, and my fire had gone out, and the bitterness of death came over my soul. The forest seemed full of the smell of burning wood. I was caught by the neck, by the hair, by the arms, and pulled down. It was indescribably horrible in the darkness to feel all these soft creatures heaped upon me. I felt as if I was in a monstrous spider's web. I was overpowered, and went down. I felt little teeth nipping at my neck. I rolled over, and as I did so my hand came against my iron lever. It gave me strength. I struggled up, shaking the human rats from me, and, holding the bar short, I thrust where I judged their faces might be. I could feel the succulent giving of flesh and bone under my blows, and for a moment I was free.

'The strange exultation that so often seems to accompany hard fighting came upon me. I knew that both I and Weena were lost, but I determined to make the Morlocks pay for their meat. I stood with my back to a tree, swinging the iron bar before me. The whole wood was full of the stir and cries of them. A minute passed. Their voices seemed to rise to a higher pitch of excitement, and their movements grew faster. Yet none came within reach. I stood glar-

ing at the blackness. Then suddenly came hope. What if the Morlocks were afraid? And close on the heels of that came a strange
thing. The darkness seemed to grow luminous. Very dimly I began
to see the Morlocks about me—three battered at my feet—and then
I recognized, with incredulous surprise, that the others were running, in an incessant stream, as it seemed, from behind me, and
away through the wood in front. And their backs seemed no longer
white, but reddish. As I stood agape, I saw a little red spark go
drifting across a gap of starlight between the branches, and vanish.
And at that I understood the smell of burning wood, the slumbrous
murmur that was growing now into a gusty roar, the red glow, and
the Morlocks' flight.

'Stepping out from behind my tree and looking back, I saw,
through the black pillars of the nearer trees, the flames of the burning forest. It was my first fire coming after me. With that I looked
for Weena, but she was gone. The hissing and crackling behind me,
the explosive thud as each fresh tree burst into flame, left little time
for reflection. My iron bar still gripped, I followed in the Morlocks'
path. It was a close race. Once the flames crept forward so swiftly
on my right as I ran that I was outflanked and had to strike off to
the left. But at last I emerged upon a small open space, and as I did
so, a Morlock came blundering towards me, and past me, and went
on straight into the fire!

'And now I was to see the most weird and horrible thing, I think,
of all that I beheld in that future age. This whole space was as
bright as day with the reflection of the fire. In the centre was a hillock or tumulus,[2] surmounted by a scorched hawthorn. Beyond this
was another arm of the burning forest, with yellow tongues already
writhing from it, completely encircling the space with a fence of
fire. Upon the hill-side were some thirty or forty Morlocks, dazzled
by the light and heat, and blundering hither and thither against each
other in their bewilderment. At first I did not realize their blindness,
and struck furiously at them with my bar, in a frenzy of fear, as
they approached me, killing one and crippling several more. But

2. An artificial mound, usually a grave mound.

when I had watched the gestures of one of them groping under the hawthorn against the red sky, and heard their moans, I was assured of their absolute helplessness and misery in the glare, and I struck no more of them.

'Yet every now and then one would come straight towards me, setting loose a quivering horror that made me quick to elude him. At one time the flames died down somewhat, and I feared the foul creatures would presently be able to see me. I was even thinking of beginning the fight by killing some of them before this should happen; but the fire burst out again brightly, and I stayed my hand. I walked about the hill among them and avoided them, looking for some trace of Weena. But Weena was gone.

'At last I sat down on the summit of the hillock, and watched this strange incredible company of blind things groping to and fro, and making uncanny noises to each other, as the glare of the fire beat on them. The coiling uprush of smoke streamed across the sky, and through the rare tatters of that red canopy, remote as though they belonged to another universe, shone the little stars. Two or three Morlocks came blundering into me, and I drove them off with blows of my fists, trembling as I did so.

'For the most part of that night I was persuaded it was a nightmare. I bit myself and screamed in a passionate desire to awake. I beat the ground with my hands, and got up and sat down again, and wandered here and there, and again sat down. Then I would fall to rubbing my eyes and calling upon God to let me awake. Thrice I saw Morlocks put their heads down in a kind of agony and rush into the flames. But, at last, above the subsiding red of the fire, above the streaming masses of black smoke and the whitening and blackening tree stumps, and the diminshing numbers of these dim creatures, came the white light of the day.

'I searched again for traces of Weena, but there were none. It was plain that they had left her poor little body in the forest. I cannot describe how it relieved me to think that it had escaped the awful fate to which it seemed destined. As I thought of that, I was almost moved to begin a massacre of the helpless abominations about me, but I contained myself. The hillock, as I have said, was a kind of island in the forest. From its summit I could now make out through a haze of smoke the Palace of Green Porcelain, and from that I could get my bearings for the White Sphinx. And so, leaving the remnant of these damned souls still going hither and thither and moaning, as the day grew clearer, I tied some grass about my feet and limped on across smoking ashes and among black stems, that still pulsated internally with fire, towards the hiding-place of the Time Machine. I walked slowly, for I was almost exhausted, as well as lame, and I felt the intensest wretchedness for the horrible death of little Weena. It seemed an overwhelming calamity. Now, in this old familiar room, it is more like the sorrow of a dream than an actual loss. But that morning it left me absolutely lonely again—terribly alone. I began to think of this house of mine, of this fireside, of some of you, and with such thoughts came a longing that was pain.

'But, as I walked over the smoking ashes under the bright morning sky, I made a discovery. In my trouser pocket were still some loose matches. The box must have leaked before it was lost.

X

'About eight or nine in the morning I came to the same seat of yellow metal from which I had viewed the world upon the evening of my arrival. I though of my hasty conclusions upon that evening and could not refrain from laughing bitterly at my confidence. Here was the same beautiful scene, the same abundant foliage, the same splendid palaces and magnificent ruins, the same silver river running between its fertile banks. The gay robes of the beautiful people moved hither and thither among the trees. Some were bathing in exactly the place where I had saved Weena, and that suddenly gave me a keen stab of pain. And like blots upon the landscape rose the cupolas above the ways to the Under-world. I understood now what all the beauty of the Over-world people covered. Very pleasant was their day, as pleasant as the day of the cattle in the field.

Like the cattle, they knew of no enemies and provided against no needs. And their end was the same.

'I grieved to think how brief the dream of the human intellect had been. It had committed suicide. It had set itself steadfastly towards comfort and ease, a balanced society with security and permanency as its watchword, it had attained its hopes—to come to this at last. Once, life and property must have reached almost absolute safety. The rich had been assured of his wealth and comfort, the toiler assured of his life and work. No doubt in that perfect world there had been no unemployed problem, no social question left unsolved. And a great quiet had followed.

'It is a law of nature we overlook, that intellectual versatility is the compensation for change, danger, and trouble. An animal perfectly in harmony with its environment is a perfect mechanism. Nature never appeals to intelligence until habit and instinct are useless. There is no intelligence where there is no change and no need of change. Only those animals partake of intelligence that have to meet a huge variety of needs and dangers.

'So, as I see it, the Upper-world man had drifted towards his feeble prettiness, and the Under-world to mere mechanical industry. But that perfect state had lacked one thing even for mechanical perfection—absolute permanency. Apparently as time went on, the feeding of the Under-world, however it was effected, had become disjointed. Mother Necessity, who had been staved off for a few thousand years, came back again, and she began below. The Under-world being in contact with machinery, which, however perfect, still needs some little thought outside habit, had probably retained perforce rather more initiative, if less of every other human character, than the Upper. And when other meat failed them, they turned to what old habit had hitherto forbidden. So I say I saw it in my last view of the world of Eight Hundred and Two Thousand Seven Hundred and One. It may be as wrong an explanation as mortal wit could invent. It is how the thing shaped itself to me, and as that I give it to you.

'After the fatigues, excitements, and terrors of the past days, and in spite of my grief, this seat and the tranquil view and the warm sunlight were very pleasant. I was very tired and sleepy, and soon my theorizing passed into dozing. Catching myself at that, I took my own hint, and spreading myself out upon the turf I had a long and refreshing sleep.

'I awoke a little before sunsetting. I now felt safe against being caught napping by the Morlocks, and, stretching myself, I came on down the hill towards the White Sphinx. I had my crowbar in one hand, and the other hand played with the matches in my pocket.

'And now came a most unexpected thing. As I approached the pedestal of the sphinx I found the bronze valves were open. They had slid down into grooves.

'At that I stopped short before them, hesitating to enter.

'Within was a small apartment, and on a raised place in the corner of this was the Time Machine. I had the small levers in my pocket. So here, after all my elaborate preparations for the siege of the White Sphinx, was a meek surrender. I threw my iron bar away, almost sorry not to use it.

'A sudden thought came into my head as I stooped towards the portal. For once, at least, I grasped the mental operations of the Morlocks. Suppressing a strong inclination to laugh, I stepped through the bronze frame and up to the Time Machine. I was surprised to find it had been carefully oiled and cleaned. I have suspected since that the Morlocks had even partially taken it to pieces while trying in their dim way to grasp its purpose.

'Now as I stood and examined it, finding a pleasure in the mere touch of the contrivance, the thing I had expected happened. The bronze panels suddenly slid up and struck the frame with a clang. I was in the dark—trapped. So the Morlocks thought. At that I chuckled gleefully.

'I could already hear their murmuring laughter as they came towards me. Very calmly I tried to strike the match. I had only to fix on the levers and depart then like a ghost. But I had overlooked one little thing. The matches were of that abominable kind that light only on the box.[1]

'You may imagine how all my calm vanished. The little brutes were close upon me. One touched me. I made a sweeping blow in the dark at them with the levers, and began to scramble into the saddle of the machine. Then came one hand upon me and then another. Then I had simply to fight against their persistent fingers for my levers, and at the same time feel for the studs over which these fitted. One, indeed, they almost got away from me. As it slipped from my hand, I had to butt in the dark with my head—I could hear the Morlock's skull ring—to recover it. It was a nearer thing than the fight in the forest, I think, this last scramble.

'But at last the lever was fixed and pulled over. The clinging hands slipped from me. The darkness presently fell from my eyes. I found myself in the same grey light and tumult I have already described.[2]

1. Safety matches, which can only be struck on their own box, had been invented in Sweden in 1855, but were still not as common in 1895 as they are now. (The most common form of match, the book match, was invented in America in 1895.)
2. This is the episode with which *The Time Machine* originally concluded, in its 1894 serialization in the *National Observer*. The next chapter with its vision of the end of all life on the planet was present in that version only as a final speculation on the part of the Time Traveller. It was at the suggestion of William Ernest Henley that Wells wrote the present chapter XI, for its 1895 serialization in Henley's *New Review*.

XI

'I have already told you of the sickness and confusion that comes with time travelling. And this time I was not seated properly in the saddle, but sideways and in an unstable fashion. For an indefinite time I clung to the machine as it swayed and vibrated, quite unheeding how I went, and when I brought myself to look at the dials again I was amazed to find where I had arrived. One dial records days, another thousands of days, another millions of days, and another thousands of millions.[1] Now, instead of reversing the levers, I had pulled them over so as to go forward with them, and when I came to look at these indicators I found that the thousands hand was sweeping round as fast as the seconds hand of a watch—into futurity.

'As I drove on, a peculiar change crept over the appearance of things. The palpitating greyness grew darker; then—though I was still travelling with prodigious velocity—the blinking succession of day and night, which was usually indicative of a slower pace, returned, and grew more and more marked. This puzzled me very much at first. The alternations of night and day grew slower and slower, and so did the passage of the sun across the sky, until they seemed to stretch through centuries. At last a steady twilight brooded over the earth, a twilight only broken now and then when a comet glared across the darkling sky. The band of light that had indicated the sun had long since disappeared; for the sun had ceased to set—it simply rose and fell in the west, and grew ever broader and more red. All trace of the moon had vanished. The circling of the stars, growing slower and slower, had given place to creeping points of light. At last, some time before I stopped, the sun, red and very large, halted motionless upon the horizon, a vast dome glowing with a dull heat, and now and then suffering a momentary extinction. At one time it had for a little while glowed more brilliantly again, but it speedily reverted to its sullen red heat. I perceived by this slowing down of its rising and setting that the work of the tidal drag[2] was done. The earth had come to rest with one face to the sun, even as in our own time the moon faces the earth. Very cautiously, for I remembered my former headlong fall, I be-

1. There is perhaps a slight inconsistency between this sentence and the Time Traveller's words in Chapter IV, where he says that "the year Eight Hundred and Two Thousand Seven Hundred and One A.D." was "the date the little dials of my machine recorded." The earlier passage seems to imply that the Time Machine's dials measured time in years, not days.
2. That is, the earth had ceased to revolve on its axis.

gan to reverse my motion. Slower and slower went the circling hands until the thousands one seemed motionless and the daily one was no longer a mere mist upon its scale. Still slower, until the dim outlines of a desolate beach grew visible.

'I stopped very gently and sat upon the Time Machine, looking round. The sky was no longer blue. North-eastward it was inky black, and out of the blackness shone brightly and steadily the pale white stars. Overhead it was a deep Indian red and starless, and south-eastward it grew brighter to a glowing scarlet where, cut by the horizon, lay the huge hull of the sun, red and motionless. The rocks about me were of a harsh reddish colour, and all the trace of life that I could see at first was the intensely green vegetation that covered every projecting point on their south-eastern face. It was the same rich green that one sees on forest moss or on the lichen[3] in caves: plants which like these grow in a perpetual twilight.

'The machine was standing on a sloping beach. The sea stretched away to the south-west, to rise into a sharp bright horizon against the wan sky. There were no breakers and no waves, for not a breath of wind was stirring. Only a slight oily swell rose and fell like a gentle breathing, and showed that the eternal sea was still moving and living. And along the margin where the water sometimes broke was a thick incrustation of salt—pink under the lurid sky. There was a sense of oppression in my head, and I noticed that I was breathing very fast. The sensation reminded me of my only experience of mountaineering, and from that I judged the air to be more rarefied than it is now.

'Far away up the desolate slope I heard a harsh scream, and saw a thing like a huge white butterfly go slanting and fluttering up into the sky and, circling, disappear over some low hillocks beyond. The sound of its voice was so dismal that I shivered and seated myself more firmly upon the machine. Looking round me again, I saw that, quite near, what I had taken to be a reddish mass of rock was moving slowly towards me. Then I saw the thing was really a mon-

3. A complex plant made up of an alga and a fungus living symbiotically.

strous crab-like creature. Can you imagine a crab as large as yonder table, with its many legs moving slowly and uncertainly, its big claws swaying, its long antennae, like carters' whips,[4] waving and feeling, and its stalked eyes gleaming at you on either side of its metallic front? Its back was corrugated and ornamented with ungainly bosses,[5] and a greenish incrustation blotched it here and there. I could see the many palps of its complicated mouth flickering and feeling as it moved.

'As I stared at this sinister apparition crawling towards me, I felt a tickling on my cheek as though a fly had lighted there. I tried to brush it away with my hand, but in a moment it returned, and almost immediately came another by my ear. I struck at this, and caught something threadlike. It was drawn swiftly out of my hand. With a frightful qualm, I turned, and saw that I had grasped the antenna of another monster crab that stood just behind me. Its evil eyes were wriggling on their stalks, its mouth was all alive with appetite, and its vast ungainly claws, smeared with an algal[6] slime, were descending upon me. In a moment my hand was on the lever, and I had placed a month between myself and these monsters. But I was still on the same beach, and I saw them distinctly now as soon as I stopped. Dozens of them seemed to be crawling here and there, in the sombre light, among the foliated[7] sheets of intense green.

'I cannot convey the sense of abominable desolation that hung over the world. The red eastern sky, the northward blackness, the salt Dead Sea, the stony beach crawling with these foul, slow-stirring monsters, the uniform poisonous-looking green of the lichenous plants, the thin air that hurts one's lungs: all contributed to an appalling effect. I moved on a hundred years, and there was the same red sun—a little larger, a little duller—the same dying sea, the same chill air, and the same crowd of earthly crustacea creeping

4. Horsewhips.
5. Ornamental reliefs.
6. Like alga (a primitive sea plant).
7. Divided into leaves.

in and out among the green weed and the red rocks. And in the westward sky I saw a curved pale line like a vast new moon.

'So I travelled, stopping ever and again, in great strides of a thousand years or more, drawn on by the mystery of the earth's fate, watching with a strange fascination the sun grow larger and duller in the westward sky, and the life of the old earth ebb away. At last, more than thirty million years hence, the huge red-hot dome of the sun had come to obscure nearly a tenth part of the darkling heavens.[8] Then I stopped once more, for the crawling multitude of crabs had disappeared, and the red beach, save for its livid green liverworts[9] and lichens, seemed lifeless. And now it was flecked with white. A bitter cold assailed me. Rare white flakes ever and again came eddying down. To the north-eastward, the glare of snow lay under the starlight of the sable sky, and I could see an undulating crest of hillocks pinkish white. There were fringes of ice along the sea margin, with drifting masses further out; but the main expanse of that salt ocean, all bloody under the eternal sunset, was still unfrozen.

'I looked about me to see if any traces of animal life remained. A certain indefinable apprehension still kept me in the saddle of the machine. But I saw nothing moving, in earth or sky or sea. The green slime on the rocks alone testified that life was not extinct. A shallow sand-bank had appeared in the sea and the water had receded from the beach. I fancied I saw some black object flopping about upon this bank, but it became motionless as I looked at it, and I judged that my eye had been deceived, and that the black object was merely a rock. The stars in the sky were intensely bright and seemed to me to twinkle very little.[10]

'Suddenly I noticed that the circular westward outline of the sun had changed; that a concavity, a bay, had appeared in the curve. I saw this grow larger. For a minute perhaps I stared aghast at this blackness that was creeping over the day, and then I realized that

8. The earth had fallen closer to the sun.
9. Mosslike plants growing on damp ground or on tree trunks.
10. Because the earth's atmosphere had all but disappeared.

an eclipse was beginning. Either the moon or the planet Mercury[11] was passing across the sun's disk. Naturally, at first I took it to be the moon, but there is much to incline me to believe that what I really saw was the transit of an inner planet passing very near to the earth.

'The darkness grew apace; a cold wind began to blow in freshening gusts from the east, and the showering white flakes in the air increased in number. From the edge of the sea came a ripple and whisper. Beyond these lifeless sounds the world was silent. Silent? It would be hard to convey the stillness of it. All the sounds of man, the bleating of sheep, the cries of birds, the hum of insects, the stir that makes the background of our lives—all that was over. As the darkness thickened, the eddying flakes grew more abundant, dancing before my eyes; and the cold of the air more intense. At last, one by one, swiftly, one after the other, the white peaks of the distant hills vanished into blackness. The breeze rose to a moaning wind. I saw the black central shadow of the eclipse sweeping towards me. In another moment the pale stars alone were visible. All else was rayless obscurity. The sky was absolutely black.

'A horror of this great darkness came on me. The cold, that smote to my marrow, and the pain I felt in breathing, overcame me. I shivered, and a deadly nausea seized me. Then like a red-hot bow in the sky appeared the edge of the sun. I got off the machine to recover myself. I felt giddy and incapable of facing the return journey. As I stood sick and confused I saw again the moving thing upon the shoal—there was no mistake now that it was a moving thing—against the red water of the sea. It was a round thing, the size of a football[12] perhaps, or, it may be, bigger, and tentacles trailed down from it; it seemed black against the weltering blood-red water, and it was hopping fitfully about. Then I felt I was fainting. But a terrible dread of lying helpless in that remote and awful twilight sustained me while I clambered upon the saddle.

11. As the earth falls toward the sun, the inner planets grow correspondingly larger as seen from the earth.
12. That is, a soccer ball, rounded in shape.

XII

'So I came back. For a long time I must have been insensible upon the machine. The blinking succession of the days and nights was resumed, the sun got golden again, the sky blue. I breathed with greater freedom. The fluctuating contours of the land ebbed and flowed. The hands spun backward upon the dials. At last I saw again the dim shadows of houses, the evidences of decadent humanity. These, too, changed and passed, and others came. Presently, when the million dial was at zero, I slackened speed. I began to recognize our own petty and familiar architecture, the thousands hand ran back to the starting-point, the night and day flapped slower and slower. Then the old walls of the laboratory came round me. Very gently, now, I slowed the mechanism down.

'I saw one little thing that seemed odd to me. I think I have told you that when I set out, before my velocity became very high, Mrs. Watchett had walked across the room, travelling, as it seemed to me, like a rocket. As I returned, I passed again across that minute when she traversed the laboratory. But now her every motion appeared to be the exact inversion of her previous ones.[1] The door at the lower end opened, and she glided quietly up the laboratory, back foremost, and disappeared behind the door by which she had previously entered. Just before that I seemed to see Hillyer[2] for a moment; but he passed like a flash.

'Then I stopped the machine, and saw about me again the old familiar laboratory, my tools, my appliances just as I had left them. I got off the thing very shakily, and sat down upon my bench. For

1. Another surprising anticipation of film technique.
2. Most readings of *The Time Machine* assume that this is the Time Traveller's manservant: but in fact it is the narrator of the story. At the end of this chapter, the narrator tells how he breaks into the Time Traveller's laboratory, on the day *after* the narrative, to see the Traveller disappearing on his last voyage into the future. Naturally, then, on his journey *back* to the day of his narrative, the Time Traveller might glimpse the narrator briefly—on the day, that is, after he tells his tale.

several minutes I trembled violently. Then I became calmer. Around me was my old workshop again, exactly as it had been. I might have slept there, and the whole thing have been a dream.

'And yet, not exactly! The thing had started from the south-east corner of the laboratory. It had come to rest again in the north-west, against the wall where you saw it. That gives you the exact distance from my little lawn to the pedestal of the White Sphinx, into which the Morlocks had carried my machine.

'For a time my brain went stagnant. Presently I got up and came through the passage here, limping, because my heel was still painful, and feeling sorely begrimed. I saw the *Pall Mall Gazette*[3] on the table by the door. I found the date was indeed to-day, and looking at the timepiece, saw the hour was almost eight o'clock. I heard your voices and the clatter of plates. I hesitated—I felt so sick and weak. Then I sniffed good wholesome meat, and opened the door on you. You know the rest. I washed, and dined, and now I am telling you the story.

'I know,' he said, after a pause, 'that all this will be absolutely incredible to you. To me the one incredible thing is that I am here to-night in this old familiar room looking into your friendly faces and telling you these strange adventures.'

He looked at the Medical Man. 'No. I cannot expect you to believe it. Take it as a lie—or a prophecy. Say I dreamed it in the workshop. Consider I have been speculating upon the destinies of our race until I have hatched this fiction. Treat my assertion of its truth as a mere stroke of art to enhance its interest. And taking it as a story, what do you think of it?'

He took up his pipe, and began, in his old accustomed manner, to tap with it nervously upon the bars of the grate. There was a momentary stillness. Then chairs began to creak and shoes to scrape upon the carpet. I took my eyes off the Time Traveller's face, and looked round at his audience. They were in the dark, and little spots of colour swam before them. The Medical Man seemed

3. Founded in 1865, this was a newspaper of Liberal sentiments and a rather sensationalist approach to journalism.

absorbed in the contemplation of our host. The Editor was looking hard at the end of his cigar—the sixth. The Journalist fumbled for his watch. The others, as far as I remember, were motionless.

The Editor stood up with a sigh. 'What a pity it is you're not a writer of stories!' he said, putting his hand on the Time Traveller's shoulder.

'You don't believe it?'

'Well——'

'I thought not.'

The Time Traveller turned to us. 'Where are the matches?' he said. He lit one and spoke over his pipe, puffing. 'To tell you the truth . . . I hardly believe it myself . . . And yet . . .'

His eye fell with a mute inquiry upon the withered white flowers upon the little table. Then he turned over the hand holding his pipe, and I saw he was looking at some half-healed scars on his knuckles.

The medical Man rose, came to the lamp, and examined the flowers. 'The gynaeceum's[4] odd,' he said. The Psychologist leant forward to see, holding out his hand for a specimen.

'I'm hanged if it isn't a quarter to one,' said the Journalist. 'How shall we get home?'

'Plenty of cabs at the station,' said the Psychologist.

'It's a curious thing,' said the Medical Man; 'but I certainly don't know the natural order of these flowers. May I have them?'

The Time Traveller hesitated. Then suddenly: 'Certainly not.'

'Where did you really get them?' said the Medical Man.

The Time Traveller put his hand to his head. He spoke like one who was trying to keep hold of an idea that eluded him. 'They were put into my pocket by Weena, when I travelled into Time.' He stared round the room. 'I'm damned if it isn't all going. This room and you and the atmosphere of every day is too much for my memory. Did I ever make a Time Machine, or a model of a Time Machine? Or is it all only a dream? They say life is a dream, a precious poor dream at times—but I can't stand another that won't fit.

4. The pistils of a flower.

It's madness. And where did the dream come from? . . . I must look at that machine. If there *is* one!'

He caught up the lamp swiftly, and carried it, flaring red, through the door into the corridor. We followed him. There in the flickering light of the lamp was the machine sure enough, squat, ugly, and askew; a thing of brass, ebony, ivory, and translucent glimmering quartz. Solid to the touch—for I put out my hand and felt the rail of it—and with brown spots and smears upon the ivory, and bits of grass and moss upon the lower parts, and one rail bent awry.

The Time Traveller put the lamp down on the bench, and ran his hand along the damaged rail. 'It's all right now,' he said. 'The story I told you was true. I'm sorry to have brought you out here in the cold.' He took up the lamp, and, in an absolute silence, we returned to the smoking-room.

He came into the hall with us and helped the Editor on with his coat. The Medical Man looked into his face and, with a certain hesitation, told him he was suffering from overwork, at which he laughed hugely. I remember him standing in the open doorway, bawling good night.

I shared a cab with the Editor. He thought the tale a 'gaudy lie.' For my own part I was unable to come to a conclusion. The story was so fantastic and incredible, the telling so credible and sober. I lay awake most of the night thinking about it. I determined to go next day and see the Time Traveller again. I was told he was in the laboratory, and being on easy terms in the house, I went up to him. The laboratory, however, was empty. I stared for a minute at the Time Machine and put out my hand and touched the lever. At that the squat substantial-looking mass swayed like a bough shaken by the wind. Its instability startled me extremely, and I had a queer reminiscence of the childish days when I used to be forbidden to meddle. I came back through the corridor. The Time Traveller met me in the smoking-room. He was coming from the house. He had a small camera under one arm and a knapsack under the other. He laughed when he saw me, and gave me an elbow to shake. 'I'm frightfully busy,' said he, 'with that thing in there.'

'But is it not some hoax?' I said. 'Do you really travel through time?'

'Really and truly I do.' And he looked frankly into my eyes. He hesitated. His eye wandered about the room. 'I only want half an hour,' he said. 'I know why you came, and it's awfully good of you. There's some magazines here. If you'll stop to lunch I'll prove you this time travelling up to the hilt, specimen and all. If you'll forgive my leaving you now?'

I consented, hardly comprehending then the full import of his words, and he nodded and went on down the corridor. I heard the door of the laboratory slam, seated myself in a chair, and took up a daily paper. What was he going to do before lunch-time? Then suddenly I was reminded by an advertisement that I had promised to meet Richardson, the publisher, at two. I looked at my watch, and saw that I could barely save that engagement. I got up and went down the passage to tell the Time Traveller.

As I took hold of the handle of the door I heard an exclamation, oddly truncated at the end, and a click and a thud. A gust of air whirled round me as I opened the door, and from within came the sound of broken glass falling on the floor. The Time Traveller was not there. I seemed to see a ghostly, indistinct figure sitting in a whirling mass of black and brass for a moment—a figure so transparent that the bench behind with its sheets of drawings was absolutely distinct; but this phantasm[5] vanished as I rubbed my eyes. The Time Machine had gone. Save for a subsiding stir of dust, the further end of the laboratory was empty. A pane of the skylight had, apparently, just been blown in.

I felt an unreasonable amazement. I knew that something strange had happened, and for the moment could not distinguish what the strange thing might be. As I stood staring, the door into the garden opened, and the man-servant appeared.

We looked at each other. Then ideas began to come. 'Has Mr. —— gone out that way?' said I.

5. Fantasy or ghost.

'No, sir. No one has come out this way. I was expecting to find him here.'

At that I understood. At the risk of disappointing Richardson I stayed on, waiting for the Time Traveller; waiting for the second, perhaps still stranger story, and the specimens and photographs he would bring with him. But I am beginning now to fear that I must wait a lifetime. The Time Traveller vanished three years ago. And, as everybody knows now, he has never returned.

EPILOGUE

One cannot choose but wonder. Will he ever return? It may be that he swept back into the past, and fell among the blood-drinking, hairy savages of the Age of Unpolished Stone;[1] into the abysses of the Cretaceous Sea;[2] or among the grotesque saurians, the huge reptilian brutes of the Jurassic[3] times. He may even now—if I may use the phrase—be wandering on some plesiosaurus-haunted Oolitic[4] coral reef, or beside the lonely saline lakes of the Triassic Age.[5] Or did he go forward, into one of the nearer ages, in which men are still men, but with the riddles of our own time answered and its wearisome problems solved? Into the manhood of the race: for I, for my own part, cannot think that these latter days of weak experiment, fragmentary theory, and mutual discord are indeed man's culminating time! I say, for my own part. He, I know—for the question had been discussed among us long before the Time Machine was made—thought but cheerlessly of the Advancement of Man-

1. The Paleolithic or Old Stone Age, 500,000 to 10,000 B.C.
2. The Cretaceous, from 135 to 70 million years ago, was the era of the extinction of the dinosaurs and the advent of insects and flowering plants.
3. 180 to 135 million years ago, the age of the dinosaurs and of the giant conifers.
4. Plesiosaurus was a seaborne dinosaur; Oolitic refers to large limestone deposits in the sea, made up of rounded bulges resembling the texture of fish roe.
5. The Triassic, from 220 to 180 million years ago, was the age of the earliest dinosaurs and marine reptiles.

kind, and saw in the growing pile of civilization only a foolish heaping that must inevitably fall back upon and destroy its makers in
the end. If that is so, it remains for us to live as though it were not
so. But to me the future is still black and blank—is a vast ignorance,
lit at a few casual places by the memory of his story. And I have by
me, for my comfort, two strange white flowers—shrivelled now, and
brown and flat and brittle—to witness that even when mind and
strength had gone, gratitude and a mutual tenderness still lived on
in the heart of man.

Appendix

The Chapters of The Time Machine

In the original English publication, *The Time Machine* was divided into sixteen chapters with descriptive titles, rather than the twelve untitled chapters and epilogue which Wells later standardized for the novel. Below are the original chapter headings correlated to the book as presented here.

   I.   *Introduction:* Chapter I to "Filby's anecdote collapsed."

   II.   *The Machine:* to the end of Chapter I.

   III.   *The Time Traveller Returns:* Chapter II.

   IV.   *Time Travelling:* Chapter III.

   V.   *In the Golden Age:* Chapter IV to "people more indolent or more easily fatigued."

   VI.   *The Sunset of Mankind:* to the end of Chapter IV.

   VII.   *A Sudden Shock:* Chapter V to "round the point of my arrival."

   VIII.   *Explanation:* to the end of Chapter V.

   IX.   *The Morlocks:* Chapter VI.

   X.   *When the Night Came:* Chapter VII.

   XI.   *The Palace of Green Porcelain:* Chapter VIII.

   XII.   *In the Darkness:* Chapter IX.

   XIII.   *The Trap of the White Sphinx:* Chapter X.

   XIV.   *The Further Vision:* Chapter XI.

   XV.   *The Time Traveller's Return:* Chapter XIII to "I am telling you the story."

   XVI.   *After the Story:* to the end of the epilogue.

ILLUSTRATIONS

Morlocks: George Pal's *The Time Machine,* 1960. Pal, one of the most influential science fiction directors, produced a remarkably faithful and convincing version of *The Time Machine* in this film. The Morlocks, especially, are realized almost exactly as Wells described them; but it is noteworthy that, in their position and in the machinery behind them, they owe at least as much to Fritz Lang's *Metropolis* as they do to Wells's original story. The contrast in this still between the hairy, primitive disorganization of the beast-men and the pure, crystalline order of the machines they tend is one that Wells himself would have appreciated.

The Evolution of the Morlocks: Fritz Lang's *Metropolis*, 1926. *Metropolis* was based upon a novel by Lang's wife, Thea von Harbou, but the Wellsian influence is obvious, though oddly altered. In the future city of Metropolis, the managerial classes live in self-indulgent splendor while the workers, bound to their machines, trudge along in somnolent submission. Lang's film, a parable of the soul-destroying powers of technology, was one that Wells disliked intensely, even though he was its most important source. And his own filmscript, *Things to Come*, was intended partly as a refutation of the vision of *Metropolis*.

The origin of a species: Aubrey Beardsley's "A Snare of Vintage," 1894. Wells's Eloi, with their consumptive, hectic beauty, their sensuality, and their odd suggestion of menace, are an obvious allusion to the aesthetic amorality of the *Yellow Book* Decadents of the 1890s. Aubrey Beardsley (1872-1898), the brilliant illustrator of the *Yellow Book* and one of the most famous of the "Decadents," may well have suggested the poisonous Eden of the Eloi in a drawing like this one (an illustration of Lucian's third-century A.D. *True History*—a book that Wells acknowledged as one of the influences on his own romances).

The imagination of disaster: *Things to Come*, 1936. Wells was fascinated with the possibilities of film as an educative as well as an artistic
medium; he had also been infuriated by the 1926 film, *Metropolis*, in
which some aspects of *The Time Machine* were utilized for the purposes of an anti-technological parable. The filmscript of *Things to
Come*, based upon his earlier stories *A Tale of Days to Come* and *The
War in the Air*, was intended as a refutation of *Metropolis*. But though
the film is a classic and influential myth of the glories of science, many
of its most memorable scenes are like the one here: a representation of
the effects of total war that owes more to the pessimistic visions of
The War of the Worlds and *The Time Machine* than it does to his later,
optimistic imagination of human possibility.

The discoverer of the future: Wells (with Raymond Massey and Ann Todd) on the set of *Things to Come,* 1936. By 1936 Wells was a world figure, a highly influential prophet of science, and—apparently—nothing like the young man who had written those grim parables *The Time Machine* and *The War of the Worlds.* The future imagined in *Things to Come,* supervised by benevolent engineer-dictators like the character played by Massey, seems to escape the twin dooms of Eloi and Morlocks: the engineers are masters of machinery (like the Morlocks) who nevertheless create a cleanly world of peaceful order (like the Eloi). But even in this radiant vision of possibility Wells's lifelong pessimism finds expression. The famous last lines of the film, intoned by Massey as the first rocket takes off for the moon, blend confidence with a profound doubt: "If we are no more than animals—we must snatch at our little scraps of happiness and live and suffer and pass, muttering no more—than all the other animals do—or have done." (He points out at the stars.) "Is it that—or this? All the universe—or nothing. . . . Which shall it be?"

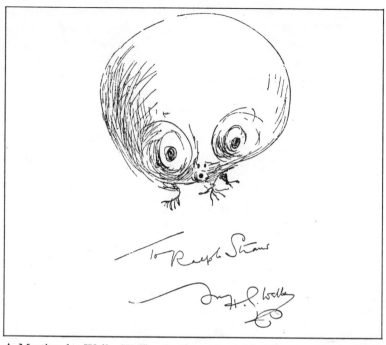

A Martian by Wells. Wells was throughout his life an enthusiastic if rough-edged amateur cartoonist. This drawing, inscribed in Ralph Straus's copy of *The War of the Worlds,* is a fairly accurate realization of his description of the Martians, even though it makes them look surprisingly *cuter* than does the professional illustrator, Alvim-Correa.

Man meets Martian. This is an early illustration (1906) of *The War of the Worlds* by the Belgian artist, Alvim-Correa. (Top right)

Martian war machines. Alvim-Correa, in 1906, could not resist the temptation (a temptation Wells himself refuses) to humanize the visitors from another planet. Note that the tripods in this illustration have *eyes*—eyes that are nowhere described in the novel the drawing is supposed to illustrate—and that their movements, though performed upon three rather than two feet, nevertheless appear oddly like the motions of human runners. The same tendency to imagine the unearthly Martians in terms of contemporary technology is obvious in the 1953 film of *The War of the Worlds,* where the war machines resemble the sportier automobiles of the period. (Bottom right)

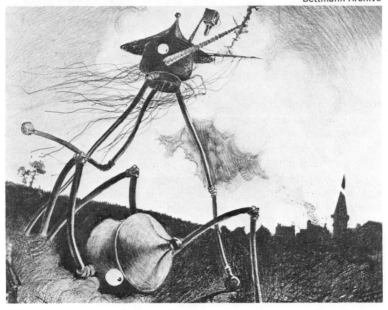

Martian war machines: Byron Haskin's 1953 *The War of the Worlds*. This film, in an attempt to make itself more relevant, was set not in southern England but in southern California; and the Martian invaders, instead of stalking about on tripodal legs, float upon a relatively undefined force field. But the influence of Wells's original concept, though muted, is nonetheless essential. The machines themselves may appear more and more dated—in fact, more and more dated than Wells's own description of the tripods—rather like automobile styles of two decades ago. But the terror they spread is not their phony-streamlined shape, rather it is their outrageous *presence* in the landscape of the familiar and the everyday. And that terror the film brilliantly realizes.

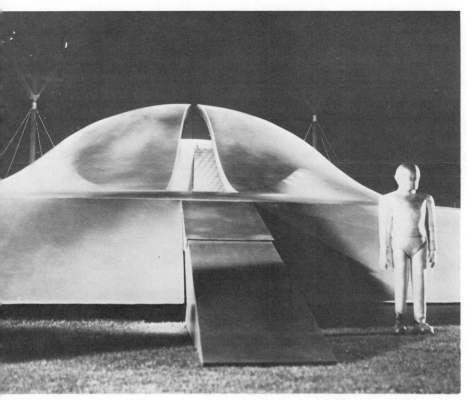

After Wells: *The Day the Earth Stood Still,* 1955. The concept of the
"flying saucer," though Wells himself did not articulate it, is nevertheless implicit in his romances of the 1890s: a machine based upon a
technology earthdwellers have not yet conceived of though they
might in the foreseeable future. *The Day the Earth Stood Still,* one of
the most literate and subtle science fiction films of the 1950s, can be
seen as a development and inversion of some Wellsian concepts. The
saucer is on a mission, not of war, but of peace: it has come to warn
earthmen of the dangers of their own warlike tendencies. And the
robot in the foreground (whose name, by the way, is "Gort") is not
the terrifyingly inhuman cyborg represented by Wells's own Martians,
but rather a docile and kindly servant of the human intelligences which
have created him. It is testimony to Wells's influence, though, that
much of the plot of *The Day the Earth Stood Still* turns upon the assumption by earthmen that any aliens from the other planets, any
intruders from the skies, *must* be hostile.

Man meets "Martian": *Earth Versus the Flying Saucers,* 1956. The origin of the invading aliens in this film is not specified; but, even for science fiction films of the fifties, it owes an unusually large debt to Wells's *War of the Worlds.* As the plot develops, it is revealed that the aliens are in fact shriveled, powerless parodies of human beings who depend upon the impressive armor shown in this still for even the simplest movement. Like Wells's Martians, they are a prophecy of the perils of technology if we allow our dependence upon machinery to isolate us from the life of our own bodies. The confrontation between man and a possible future recorded in this still, furthermore, is strikingly like that imagined in the early illustration of *The War of the Worlds.*

THE WAR OF THE WORLDS

To my brother,

Frank Wells,

This rendering of his idea.[1]

"But who shall dwell in these worlds if they be inhabited?
. . . Are we or they Lords of the World? . . . And how
are all things made for man?"

KEPLER (quoted in The Anatomy of Melancholy)[2]

1. Writing in the 1920 *Strand Magazine,* Wells explained the dedication:

The book was begotten by a remark of my brother Frank. We were walking together through some particularly peaceful Surrey scenery. "Suppose some beings from another planet were to drop out of the sky suddenly," said he, "and begin laying about them here!" Perhaps we had been talking of the discovery of Tasmania by the Europeans—a very frightful disaster for the native Tasmanians! But that was the point of departure.

For the relevance of the Tasmanians to the theme of the book, see Book I, Chapter One, note 9.

2. Johann Kepler (1571-1630), the great German astronomer and astrologer, accurately plotted the planetary orbits and suggested that the planets were peopled by genii or astral souls. Robert Burton (1576-1640) was an Oxford scholar whose *Anatomy of Melancholy,* first published in 1621, is one of the most desultory and most influential prose works in English. The quotation from Kepler occurs in Part Two, Section Two, Member Three of the *Anatomy.*

CONTENTS

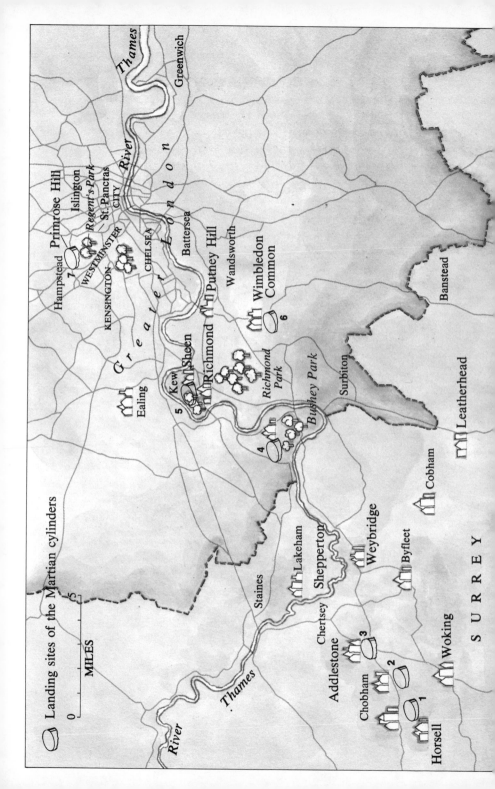

○ Landing sites of the Martian cylinders

MILES
0   5

Thames
Horsell
Woking
Chobham
Addlestone
Byfleet
Weybridge
Cobham
Leatherhead
Chertsey
Staines
Lakeham
Shepperton
Surbiton
Bushey Park
Richmond Park
Ealing
Kew
Sheen
Richmond
Putney Hill
Wandsworth
Wimbledon Common
Battersea
CHELSEA
KENSINGTON
WESTMINSTER
CITY
St. Pancras
Regent's Park
Islington
Primrose Hill
Hampstead
Greater London
Greenwich
Thames River
River Thames
SURREY
Banstead

BOOK I

THE COMING OF THE MARTIANS

CHAPTER ONE
THE EVE OF THE WAR

No one would have believed, in the last years of the nineteenth century, that human affairs were being watched keenly and closely by intelligences greater than man's and yet as mortal as his own; that as men busied themselves about their affairs they were scrutinized and studied, perhaps almost as narrowly as a man with a microscope might scrutinize the transient creatures[1] that swarm and multiply in a drop of water. With infinite complacency men went to and fro over this globe about their little affairs, serene in their assurance of their empire over matter. It is possible that the infusoria under the microscope do the same. No one gave a thought to the older worlds of space as sources of human danger, or thought of them only to dismiss the idea of life upon them as impossible and improbable. It is curious to recall some of the mental habits of those departed days. At most, terrestrial men fancied there might be other men upon Mars, perhaps inferior to themselves and ready to welcome a missionary enterprise. Yet, across the gulf of space, minds that are to our minds as ours are to those of the beasts that perish, intellects vast and cool and unsympathetic, regarded this earth with envious eyes, and slowly and surely drew their plans against us. And early in the twentieth century came the great disillusionment.

The planet Mars, I scarcely need remind the reader, revolves

---

1. Although the existence of microorganisms had been known since the seventeenth century, it was not until the 1860s, thanks to advances in microscopy, that the science of bacteriology really got under way. The first truly exhaustive classification of bacteria, by F. J. Cohn, was published in 1875.

about the sun at a mean distance of 140,000,000 miles, and the light and heat it receives from the sun is barely half of that received by this world. It must be, if the nebular hypothesis[2] has any truth, older than our world, and long before this earth ceased to be molten, life upon its surface must have begun its course. The fact that it is scarcely one-seventh of the volume of the earth must have accelerated its cooling to the temperature at which life could begin. It has air and water, and all that is necessary for the support of animated existence.

Yet so vain is man, and so blinded by his vanity, that no writer, up to the very end of the nineteenth century, expressed any idea that intelligent life might have developed there far, or indeed at all, beyond its earthly level. Nor was it generally understood that since Mars is older than our earth, with scarcely a quarter of the superficial area, and remoter from the sun, it necessarily follows that it is not only more distant from life's beginning but nearer its end.

The secular[3] cooling that must some day overtake our planet has already gone far indeed with our neighbour. Its physical condition is still largely a mystery, but we know now that even in its equatorial region the midday temperature barely approaches that of our coldest winter. Its air is much more attenuated than ours, its oceans[4] have shrunk until they cover but a third of its surface, and as its slow seasons change huge snowcaps gather and melt about either pole, and periodically inundate its temperate zones. That last stage of exhaustion, which to us is still incredibly remote, has become a present-day problem for the inhabitants of Mars. The immediate pressure of necessity had brightened their intellects, enlarged their powers, and hardened their hearts. And looking across space, with instruments and intelligences such as we have scarcely dreamt of,

2. The theory of Pierre Laplace (1749-1827) that the solar system originated as a single, densely compacted "cloud" or "nebula" of matter.
3. Ages-long.
4. The idea that there are oceans on Mars was a misapprehension caused by the inaccuracy of telescopic observation at the turn of the century. Of course, scientists did not have a fully accurate picture of the Martian surface until the unmanned Mariner space expeditions of the 1970s.

they see, at its nearest distance, only 35,000,000[5] of miles sunward of them, a morning star of hope, our own warmer planet, green with vegetation and grey with water, with a cloudy atmosphere eloquent of fertility, with glimpses through its drifting cloud-wisps of broad stretches of populous country and narrow navy-crowded seas.

And we men, the creatures who inhabit this earth, must be to them at least as alien and lowly as are the monkeys and lemurs[6] to us. The intellectual side of man already admits that life is an incessant struggle for existence,[7] and it would seem that this too is the belief of the minds upon Mars. Their world is far gone in its cooling, and this world is still crowded with life, but crowded only with what they regard as inferior animals. To carry warfare sunward is indeed their only escape from the destruction that generation after generation creeps upon them.

And before we judge of them too harshly, we must remember what ruthless and utter destruction our own species has wrought, not only upon animals, such as the vanished bison and dodo,[8] but upon its own inferior races. The Tasmanians,[9] in spite of their human likeness, were entirely swept out of existence in a war of extermination waged by European immigrants in the space of fifty

5. This is the distance in opposition at perihelion (the point at which the planets are closest to the sun). In opposition at aphelion (their farthest distance from the sun) they are 63,000,000 miles apart.
6. Small, nocturnal, tree-dwelling mammals akin to monkeys.
7. The phrase "struggle for existence" was made famous in Charles Darwin's *Origin of Species* (1859). In the work of Darwin and Darwin's defender (Wells's teacher) T. H. Huxley, it became a key phrase for the new, evolutionary view of man's embattled position in the universe.
8. The dodo, a large flightless bird of the island of Mauritius (in the Indian Ocean), was rendered completely extinct in the seventeenth century by English explorers. The bison of North America appeared, in 1898, to have suffered a like fate; fortunately, thanks to careful breeding and enlightened game laws, this has proved not to be the case.
9. The native inhabitants of Tasmania, an island south of Australia, were driven in great numbers from their land when, in the eighteenth century, England turned Tasmania into a prison colony. This reference is the first of many in *The War of the Worlds* to sound the theme of anticolonialism; just as the Martians heartlessly slaughter Earthlings, so have the European nations treated so-called "primitive" peoples.

years. Are we such apostles of mercy as to complain if the Martians warred in the same spirit?

The Martians seem to have calculated their descent with amazing subtlety—their mathematical learning is evidently far in excess of ours—and to have carried out their preparations with a well-nigh perfect unanimity. Had our instruments permitted it, we might have seen the gathering trouble far back in the nineteenth century. Men like Schiaparelli[10] watched the red planet—it is odd, by-the-by, that for countless centuries Mars has been the star of war—but failed to interpret the fluctuating appearances of the markings they mapped so well. All that time the Martians must have been getting ready.

During the opposition of 1894[11] a great light was seen on the illuminated part of the disc, first at the Lick Observatory,[12] then by Perrotin of Nice,[13] and then by other observers. English readers heard of it first in the issue of *Nature*[14] dated 2 August. I am inclined to think that the appearance may have been the casting of the huge gun, the vast pit sunk into their planet, from which their shots were fired at us. Peculiar markings, as yet unexplained, were seen near the site of that outbreak during the next two oppositions.

10. Giovanni Virginio Schiaparelli (1835-1910), the Italian astronomer who discovered the "canals" of Mars. Schiaparelli called them *canali,* which simply means "channels," with no implication of human (or non-human) excavation or conscious planning. But the mistranslation of his phrase as "canals" gave rise to widespread speculation about the inhabitants of Mars.

11. At opposition Mars is on the opposite side of the Earth from the Sun, and nearest the Earth. Schiaparelli's discovery of the "canals" (along with the discovery, by an American, of the moons of Mars) was made during the opposition of 1877. 1894 was a very favorable opposition, and gave rise to a flurry of observation and measurement of Mars throughout the civilized world.

12. Lick Observatory was built at Mount Hamilton, California, in 1888; it was named for James Lick, designer of its 36-inch refracting telescope, one of the largest telescopes at the time.

13. Henri Joseph Anastase Perrotin (1845-1904), French astronomer at Nice from 1880 till his death.

14. Founded in 1869, this was the greatest and most influential scientific journal in English. Its first editor, Sir Norman Lockyer, was one of Wells's teachers at the Normal School of Science in South Kensington.

The storm burst upon us six years ago now. As Mars approached opposition, Lavelle of Java[15] set the wires of the astronomical exchange palpitating with the amazing intelligence of a huge outbreak of incandescent gas upon the planet. It had occurred towards midnight of the 12th, and the spectroscope,[16] to which he had at once resorted, indicated a mass of flaming gas, chiefly hydrogen, moving with an enormous velocity towards this earth. This jet of fire had become invisible about a quarter-past twelve. He compared it to a colossal puff of flame, suddenly and violently squirted out of the planet, 'as flaming gas rushes out of a gun'.

A singularly appropriate phrase it proved. Yet the next day there was nothing of this in the papers, except a little note in the *Daily Telegraph*,[17] and the world went in ignorance of one of the gravest dangers that ever threatened the human race. I might not have heard of the eruption at all had I not met Ogilvy, the well-known astronomer, at Ottershaw. He was immensely excited at the news, and in the excess of his feelings invited me up to take a turn with him that night in a scrutiny of the red planet.

In spite of all that has happened since, I still remember that vigil very distinctly: the black and silent observatory, the shadowed lan-

15. Like all the scientists actually involved with the Martian invasion, a fictional character; but one whose name seems to have been invented by an interesting process. In 1894 a M. Javelle, an associate of Perrotin of Nice, actually had observed a "strange light" on Mars, giving rise to speculation about the possibility of intelligence on the planet; Wells had mentioned Javelle in an 1896 essay, "Intelligence on Mars." Transforming him into "Lavelle of Java" not only reminds the contemporary reader of the "strange light," though; it also would remind many of the cataclysmic eruption of Mt. Krakatoa in 1883, which killed 50,000 people in Java—the first in a series of historic disasters Wells invokes throughout the book.
16. With a spectroscope it is possible to describe the chemical composition of a substance by analyzing the wavelengths of the light generated by combustion of the substance. Its use was first demonstrated in 1860.
17. The late nineteenth century saw the birth (and the demise) of an immense number of newspapers in London, many of them aimed toward a specific political or social audience. The *Daily Telegraph,* founded in 1855, catered to the "great middle class" with flamboyant, often sensational journalism.

tern throwing a feeble glow upon the floor in the corner, the steady ticking of the clockwork of the telescope,[18] the little slit in the roof—an oblong profundity with the star dust streaked across it. Ogilvy moved about, invisible but audible. Looking through the telescope, one saw a circle of deep blue, and the little round planet swimming in the field. It seemed such a little thing, so bright and small and still, faintly marked with transverse stripes, and slightly flattened from the perfect round. But so little it was, so silvery warm, a pin's head of light! It was as if it quivered a little, but really this was the telescope vibrating with the activity of the clockwork that kept the planet in view.

As I watched, the little star seemed to grow larger and smaller, and to advance and recede, but that was simply that my eye was tired. Forty millions of miles it was from us—more than 40,000,000 miles of void. Few people realize the immensity of vacancy in which the dust of the material universe swims.

Near it in the field, I remember, were three little points of light, three telescopic stars infinitely remote, and all around it was the unfathomable darkness of empty space. You know how that blackness looks on a frosty starlight night. In a telescope it seems far profounder. And invisible to me, because it was so remote and small, flying swiftly and steadily towards me across that incredible distance, drawing nearer every minute by so many thousands of miles, came the Thing they were sending us, the Thing that was to bring so much struggle and calamity and death to the earth. I never dreamt of it then as I watched; no one on earth dreamt of that unerring missile.

That night, too, there was another jetting out of gas from the distant planet. I saw it. A reddish flash at the edge, the slightest projection of the outline, just as the chronometer[19] struck midnight, and at that I told Ogilvy, and he took my place. The night was warm and I was thirsty, and I went, stretching my legs clumsily, and

18. The clockwork would keep the telescope rotating in synchronization with the movement of its celestial object.
19. Timepiece.

feeling my way in the darkness, to the little table where the siphon stood, while Ogilvy exclaimed at the streamer of gas that came out towards us.

That night another invisible missile started on its way to the earth from Mars, just a second or so under twenty-four hours after the first one. I remember how I sat on the table there in the blackness, with patches of green and crimson swimming before my eyes. I wished I had a light to smoke by, little suspecting the meaning of the minute gleam I had seen, and all that it would presently bring me. Ogilvy watched till one, and then gave it up, and we lit the lantern and walked over to his house. Down below in the darkness were Ottershaw and Chertsey, and all their hundreds of people, sleeping in peace.

He was full of speculation that night about the condition of Mars, and scoffed at the vulgar idea of its having inhabitants who were signalling us. His idea was that meteorites might be falling in a heavy shower upon the planet, or that a huge volcanic explosion was in progress. He pointed out to me how unlikely it was that organic evolution had taken the same direction in the two adjacent planets.

'The chances against anything man-like on Mars are a million to one,' he said.

Hundreds of observers saw the flame that night and the night after, about midnight, and again the night after, and so for ten nights, a flame each night. Why the shots ceased after the tenth no one on earth has attempted to explain. It may be the gases of the firing caused the Martians inconvenience. Dense clouds of smoke or dust, visible through a powerful telescope on earth as little grey, fluctuating patches, spread through the clearness of the planet's atmosphere, and obscured its more familiar features.

Even the daily papers woke up to the disturbances at last, and popular notes appeared here, there, and everywhere concerning the volcanoes upon Mars. The serio-comic periodical *Punch*,[20] I re-

---

20. Founded in 1841, this was the influential and frequently brilliant satirical magazine of the middle classes.

member, made a happy use of it in the political cartoon. And, all unsuspected, those missiles the Martians had fired at us drew earthward, rushing now at a pace of many miles a second through the empty gulf of space, hour by hour and day by day, nearer and nearer. It seems to me now almost incredibly wonderful that, with that swift fate hanging over us, men could go about their petty concerns as they did. I remember how jubilant Markham was at securing a new photograph of the planet for the illustrated paper he edited in those days. People in these latter times scarcely realize the abundance and enterprise of our nineteenth-century papers. For my own part, I was much occupied in learning to ride the bicycle,[21] and busy upon a series of papers discussing the probable developments of moral ideas as civilization progressed.

One night (the first missile then could scarcely have been 10,000,000 miles away) I went for a walk with my wife. It was starlight, and I explained the signs of the zodiac to her, and pointed out Mars, a bright dot of light creeping zenithwards, towards which so many telescopes were pointed. It was a warm night. Coming home, a party of excursionists from Chertsey or Isleworth passed us singing and playing music. There were lights in the upper windows of the houses as the people went to bed. From the railway station in the distance came the sound of shunting trains, ringing and rumbling, softened almost into melody by the distance. My wife pointed out to me the brightness of the red, green and yellow signal lights, hanging in a framework against the sky. It seemed so safe and tranquil.

21. As, of course, was Wells himself.

CHAPTER TWO

THE FALLING STAR

Then came the night of the first falling star. It was seen early in the morning rushing over Winchester eastward, a line of flame, high in the atmosphere. Hundreds must have seen it, and taken it for an ordinary falling star. Albin described it as leaving a greenish streak behind it that glowed for some seconds. Denning, our greatest authority on meteorites, stated that the height of its first appearance was about ninety or one hundred miles. It seemed to him that it fell to earth about one hundred miles east of him.

I was at home at that hour and writing in my study, and although my French windows face towards Ottershaw and the blind was up (for I loved in those days to look up at the night sky), I saw nothing of it. Yet this strangest of all things that ever came to earth from outer space must have fallen while I was sitting there, visible to me had I only looked up as it passed. Some of those who saw its flight say it travelled with a hissing sound. I myself heard nothing of that. Many people in Berkshire, Surrey, and Middlesex must have seen the fall of it, and, at most, have thought that another meteorite had descended. No one seems to have troubled to look for the fallen mass that night.

But very early in the morning poor Ogilvy, who had seen the shooting star, and who was persuaded that a meteorite lay somewhere on the common between Horsell, Ottershaw and Woking, rose early with the idea of finding it. Find it he did, soon after dawn, and not far from the sand-pits. An enormous hole had been made by the impact of the projectile, and the sand and gravel had been flung violently in every direction over the heath and heather, forming heaps visible a mile and a half away. The heather was on fire eastward, and a thin blue smoke rose against the dawn.

The Thing itself lay almost entirely buried in sand, amidst the scattered splinters of a fir tree it had shivered to fragments in its descent. The uncovered part had the appearance of a huge cylinder, caked over, and its outline softened by a thick, scaly, dun-coloured incrustation. It had a diameter of about thirty yards. He approached the mass, surprised at the size and more so at the shape, since most meteorites are rounded more or less completely. It was, however, still so hot from its flight through the air as to forbid his near approach. A stirring noise within its cylinder he ascribed to the unequal cooling of its surface; for at that time it had not occurred to him that it might be hollow.

He remained standing at the edge of the pit that the Thing had made for itself, staring at its strange appearance, astonished chiefly at its unusual shape and colour, and dimly perceiving even then some evidence of design in its arrival. The early morning was wonderfully still, and the sun, just clearing the pine trees towards Weybridge, was already warm. He did not remember hearing any birds that morning, there was certainly no breeze stirring, and the only sounds were the faint movements from within the cindery cylinder. He was all alone on the common.

Then suddenly he noticed with a start that some of the grey clinker,[1] the ashy incrustation that covered the meteorite, was falling off the circular edge of the end. It was dropping off in flakes and raining down upon the sand. A large piece suddenly came off and fell with a sharp noise that brought his heart into his mouth.

For a minute he scarcely realized what this meant, and, although the heat was excessive, he clambered down into the pit close to the bulk to see the thing more clearly. He fancied even then that the cooling of the body might account for this, but what disturbed that idea was the fact that the ash was falling only from the end of the cylinder.

And then he perceived that, very slowly, the circular top of the cylinder was rotating on its body. It was such a gradual movement that he discovered it only through noticing that a black mark that had been near him five minutes ago was now at the other side of the circumference. Even then he scarcely understood what this indicated, until he heard a muffled grating sound and saw the black mark jerk forward an inch or so. Then the thing came upon him in a flash. The cylinder was artificial—hollow—with an end that screwed out! Something within the cylinder was unscrewing the top!

'Good heavens!' said Ogilvy. 'There's a man in it—men in it! Half roasted to death! Trying to escape!'

1. Solidified ash.

At once, with a quick mental leap, he linked the thing with the flash upon Mars.

The thought of the confined creature was so dreadful to him that he forgot the heat, and went forward to the cylinder to help turn. But luckily the dull radiation arrested him before he could burn his hands on the still glowing metal. At that he stood irresolute for a moment, then turned, scrambled out of the pit, and set off running wildly into Woking. The time then must have been somewhere about six o'clock. He met a waggoner and tried to make him understand, but the tale he told, and his appearance, were so wild—his hat had fallen off in the pit—that the man simply drove on. He was equally unsuccessful with the pot-man[2] who was just unlocking the doors of the public house by Horsell Bridge. The fellow thought he was a lunatic at large, and made an unsuccessful attempt to shut him into the tap-room.[3] That sobered him a little, and when he saw Henderson, the London journalist, in his garden, he called over the palings and made himself understood.

'Henderson,' he called, 'you saw that shooting star last night?'

'Well?' said Henderson.

'It's out on Horsell Common now.'

'Good Lord!' said Henderson. 'Fallen meteorite! That's good.'

'But it's something more than a meteorite. It's a cylinder—an artificial cylinder, man! And there's something inside.'

Henderson stood up with his spade in his hand.

'What's that?' he said. He is deaf in one ear.

Ogilvy told him all that he had seen. Henderson was a minute or so taking it in. Then he dropped his spade, snatched at his jacket, and came out into the road. The two men hurried back at once to the common, and found the cylinder still lying in the same position. But now the sounds inside had ceased, and a thin circle of bright metal showed between the top and the body of the cylinder. Air was either entering or escaping at the rim with a thin, sizzling sound.

They listened, rapped on the scale with a stick, and, meeting with

2. Bartender.
3. Barroom.

no response, they both concluded the man or men inside must be insensible or dead.

Of course the two were quite unable to do anything. They shouted consolation and promises, and went off back to the town again to get help. One can imagine them, covered with sand, excited and disordered, running up the little street in the bright sunlight, just as the shop folks were taking down their shutters and people were opening their bedroom windows. Henderson went into the railway station at once, in order to telegraph the news to London. The newspaper articles had prepared men's minds for the reception of the idea.

By eight o'clock a number of boys and unemployed men had already started for the common to see the 'dead men from Mars'. That was the form the story took. I heard of it first from my newspaper boy, about a quarter to nine, when I went out to get my *Daily Chronicle*.[4] I was naturally startled, and lost no time in going out and across the Ottershaw bridge to the sand-pits.

4. Founded 1877, this was one of the chief Liberal papers.

CHAPTER THREE

ON HORSELL COMMON

I found a little crowd of perhaps twenty people surrounding the huge hole in which the cylinder lay. I have already described the appearance of that colossal bulk, embedded in the ground. The turf and gravel about it seemed charred as if by a sudden explosion. No doubt its impact had caused a flash of fire. Henderson and Ogilvy were not there. I think they perceived that nothing was to be done for the present, and had gone away to breakfast at Henderson's house.

There were four or five boys sitting on the edge of the pit, with their feet dangling, and amusing themselves—until I stopped them—by throwing stones at the giant mass. After I had spoken to them about it, they began playing at 'touch'[1] in and out of the group of bystanders.

Among these were a couple of cyclists, a jobbing gardener[2] I employed sometimes, a girl carrying a baby, Gregg the butcher and his little boy, and two or three loafers and golf caddies who were accustomed to hang about the railway station. There was very little talking. Few of the common people in England had anything but the vaguest astronomical ideas in those days. Most of them were staring quietly at the big table-like end of the cylinder, which was still as Ogilvy and Henderson had left it. I fancy the popular expectation of a heap of charred corpses was disappointed at this inanimate bulk. Some went away while I was there, and other people came. I clambered into the pit and fancied I heard a faint movement under my feet. The top had certainly ceased to rotate.

It was only when I got thus close to it that the strangeness of this object was at all evident to me. At the first glance it was really no more exciting than an overturned carriage or a tree blown across the road. Not so much so, indeed. It looked like a rusty gas-float[3] half buried, more than anything else in the world. It required a certain amount of scientific education to perceive that the grey scale of the thing was no common oxide,[4] that the yellowish-white metal that gleamed in the crack between the lid and the cylinder had an unfamiliar hue. 'Extra-terrestrial' had no meaning for most of the onlookers.

At that time it was quite clear in my own mind that the Thing had come from the planet Mars, but I judged it improbable that it contained any living creature. I thought the unscrewing might be

1. Tag.
2. A free-lance gardener.
3. A hollow tube or ball used to regulate the flow of a liquid or gas. Throughout the novel, Wells imagines the unearthly Martian machines in terms of everyday shapes and objects.
4. Any chemical compound containing oxygen. The surface of the cylinder has been oxidized in the heat generated by its fall through the atmosphere.

automatic. In spite of Ogilvy, I still believed that there were men on Mars. My mind ran fancifully on the possibilities of its containing manuscript, on the difficulties in translation that might arise, whether we should find coins and models in it, and so forth. Yet it was a little too large for assurance on this idea. I felt an impatience to see it opened. About eleven, as nothing seemed happening, I walked back, full of such thoughts, to my home in Maybury. But I found it difficult to get to work[5] upon my abstract investigations.

In the afternoon the appearance of the common had altered very much. The early editions of the evening papers had startled London with enormous headlines:

A MESSAGE RECEIVED FROM MARS

REMARKABLE STORY FROM WOKING

and so forth. In addition, Ogilvy's wire to the Astronomical Exchange[6] had roused every observatory in the three kingdoms.[7]

There were half a dozen flys or more from the Woking station standing in the road by the sand-pits, a basket chaise[8] from Chobham, and a rather lordly carriage. Besides that, there was quite a heap of bicycles. In addition, a large number of people must have walked, in spite of the heat of the day, from Woking and Chertsey, so that there was altogether quite a considerable crowd—one or two gaily dressed ladies among the others.

It was glaringly hot, not a cloud in the sky, nor a breath of wind, and the only shadow was that of the few scattered pine trees. The burning heather had been extinguished, but the level ground towards Ottershaw was blackened as far as one could see, and still giving off vertical streamers of smoke. An enterprising sweet-stuff dealer in the Chobham Road had sent up his son with a barrow-load of green apples and ginger-beer.

Going to the edge of the pit, I found it occupied by a group of

5. For the subject of this "work," see Book II, Chapter Nine, note 5.
6. A prophecy. The International Astronomical Union was organized at Brussels only in 1919.
7. England, Scotland, and Ireland.
8. Both flies and basket chaises are light, two-wheeled one-horse vehicles.

about half a dozen men—Henderson, Ogilvy, and a tall fair-haired
man that I afterwards learnt was Stent, the Astronomer Royal, with
several workmen wielding spades and pickaxes. Stent was giving
directions in a clear, high-pitched voice. He was standing on the
cylinder, which was now evidently much cooler; his face was crimson and streaming with perspiration, and something seemed to have
irritated him.

A large portion of the cylinder had been uncovered, though its
lower end was still embedded. As soon as Ogilvy saw me among
the staring crowd on the edge of the pit, he called to me to come
down, and asked me if I would mind going over to see Lord Hilton,
the lord of the manor.

The growing crowd, he said, was becoming a serious impediment
to their excavations, especially the boys. They wanted a light railing
put up, and help to keep the people back. He told me that a faint
stirring was occasionally still audible within the case, but that the
workmen had failed to unscrew the top, as it afforded no grip to
them. The case appeared to be enormously thick, and it was possible that the faint sounds we heard represented a noisy tumult in the
interior.

I was very glad to do as he asked, and so become one of the priv-
ileged spectators within the contemplated enclosure. I failed to find
Lord Hilton at his house, but I was told he was expected from London by the six o'clock train from Waterloo; and as it was then
about a quarter past five, I went home, had some tea, and walked
up to the station to waylay him.

CHAPTER FOUR

THE CYLINDER UNSCREWS

When I returned to the common the sun was setting. Scattered
groups were hurrying from the direction of Woking, and one or
two persons were returning. The crowd about the pit had increased,
and stood out black against the lemon-yellow of the sky—a couple

of hundred people, perhaps. There were a number of voices raised, and some sort of struggle appeared to be going on about the pit. Strange imaginings passed through my mind. As I drew nearer I heard Stent's voice:

'Keep back! Keep back!'

A boy came running towards me.

'It's a movin',' he said to me as he passed—'a-screwin' and a-screwin' out. I don't like it. I'm a-goin' 'ome, I am.'

I went on to the crowd. There were really, I should think, two or three hundred people elbowing and jostling one another, the one or two ladies there being by no means the least active.

'He's fallen in the pit!' cried someone.

'Keep back!' said several.

The crowd swayed a little, and I elbowed my way through. Everyone seemed greatly excited. I heard a peculiar humming sound from the pit.

'I say!' said Ogilvy, 'help keep these idiots back. We don't know what's in the confounded thing you know!'

I saw a young man, a shop assistant in Woking I believe he was, standing on the cylinder and trying to scramble out of the hole again. The crowd had pushed him in.

The end of the cylinder was being screwed out from within. Nearly two feet of shining screw projected. Somebody blundered against me, and I narrowly missed being pitched on to the top of the screw. I turned, and as I did so the screw must have come out, and the lid of the cylinder fell upon the gravel with a ringing concussion. I stuck my elbow into the person behind me and turned my head towards the Thing again. For a moment that circular cavity seemed perfectly black. I had the sunset in my eyes.

I think everyone expected to see a man emerge—possibly something a little unlike us terrestrial men, but in all essentials a man. I know I did. But, looking, I presently saw something stirring within the shadow—greyish billowy movements, one above another, and then two luminous discs like eyes. Then something resembling a little grey snake, about the thickness of a walking-stick, coiled up out of the writhing middle, and wriggled in the air towards me—and then another.

A sudden chill came over me. There was a loud shriek from a woman behind. I half turned, keeping my eyes fixed upon the cylinder still, from which other tentacles were now projecting, and began pushing my way back from the edge of the pit. I saw astonishment giving place to horror on the faces of the people about me. I heard inarticulate exclamations on all sides. There was a general movement backward. I saw the shopman struggling still on the edge of the pit. I found myself alone, and saw the people on the other side of the pit running off, Stent among them. I looked again at the cylinder, and ungovernable terror gripped me. I stood petrified and staring.

A big greyish, rounded bulk, the size perhaps, of a bear, was rising slowly and painfully out of the cylinder. As it bulged up and caught the light, it glistened like wet leather. Two large darkcoloured eyes were regarding me steadfastly. It was rounded, and had, one might say, a face. There was a mouth under the eyes, the lipless brim of which quivered and panted, and dropped saliva. The body heaved and pulsated convulsively. A lank tentacular appendage gripped the edge of the cylinder, another swayed in the air.

Those who have never seen a living Martian can scarcely imagine the strange horror of their appearance. The peculiar V-shaped mouth with its pointed upper lip, the absence of brow ridges, the absence of a chin beneath the wedge-like lower lip, the incessant quivering of this mouth, the Gorgon[1] groups of tentacles, the tumultuous breathing of the lungs in a strange atmosphere, the evident heaviness and painfulness of movement, due to the greater gravitational energy of the earth—above all, the extraordinary intensity of the immense eyes—culminated in an effect akin to nausea. There was something fungoid[2] in the oily brown skin, something in the

1. In Greek myth, the Gorgons were monsters whose gaze turned men to stone, and who had, instead of hair, bundles of writhing snakes on their heads.
2. Fungus-like.

clumsy deliberation of their tedious movements unspeakably terrible. Even at this first encounter, this first glimpse, I was overcome
with disgust and dread.

Suddenly the monster vanished. It had toppled over the brim of
the cylinder and fallen into the pit, with a thud like the fall of a
great mass of leather. I heard it give a peculiar thick cry, and forthwith another of these creatures appeared in the deep shadow of the
aperture.

At that my rigour of terror passed away. I turned and, running
madly, made for the first group of trees, perhaps a hundred yards
away; but I ran slantingly and stumbling, for I could not avert my
face from these things.

There, among some young pine trees and furze bushes, I stopped,
panting, and waited further developments. The common round the
sand-pits was dotted with people, standing, like myself, in a half-
fascinated terror, staring at these creatures, or, rather, at the heaped
gravel at the edge of the pit in which they lay. And then, with a
renewed horror, I saw a round, black object bobbing up and down
on the edge of the pit. It was the head of the shopman who had
fallen in, but showing as a little black object against the hot western
sky. Now he got his shoulder and knee up, and again he seemed to
slip back until only his head was visible. Suddenly he vanished, and
I could have fancied a faint shriek had reached me. I had a
momentary impulse to go back and help him that my fears over-
ruled.

Everything was then quite invisible, hidden by the deep pit and
the heap of sand that the fall of the cylinder had made. Anyone
coming along the road from Chobham or Woking would have been
amazed at the sight—a dwindling multitude of perhaps a hundred
people or more standing in a great irregular circle, in ditches, behind bushes, behind gates and hedges, saying little to one another,
and that in short, excited shouts, and staring, staring hard at a few
heaps of sand. The barrow of ginger-beer stood a queer derelict,
black against the burning sky, and in the sand-pits was a row of de-

serted vehicles with their horses feeding out of nose-bags or pawing the ground.

CHAPTER FIVE

THE HEAT-RAY

After the glimpse I had had of the Martians emerging from the cylinder in which they had come to the earth from their planet, a kind of fascination paralysed my actions. I remained standing knee-deep in the heather, staring at the mound that hid them. I was a battleground of fear and curiosity.

I did not dare to go back towards the pit, but I felt a passionate longing to peer into it. I began walking, therefore, in a big curve, seeking some point of vantage, and continually looking at the sand-heaps that hid these newcomers to our earth. Once a leash of thin black whips, like the arms of an octopus, flashed across the sunset and was immediately withdrawn, and afterwards a thin rod rose up, joint by joint, bearing at its apex a circular disc that spun with a wobbling motion. What could be going on there?

Most of the spectators had gathered in one or two groups—one a little crowd towards Woking, the other a knot of people in the direction of Chobham. Evidently they shared my mental conflict. There were few near me. One man I approached—he was, I perceived, a neighbour of mine, though I did not know his name—and accosted. But it was scarcely a time for articulate conversation.

'What ugly *brutes*!' he said. 'Good God! what ugly brutes!' He repeated this over and over again.

'Did you see a man in the pit?' I said; but he made me no answer to that. We became silent, and stood watching for a time side by side, deriving, I fancy, a certain comfort in one another's company. Then I shifted my position to a little knoll that gave me the advantage of a yard or more of elevation, and when I looked for him presently he was walking towards Woking.

The sunset faded to twilight before anything further happened. The crowd far away on the left, towards Woking, seemed to grow, and I heard now a faint murmur from it. The little knot of people towards Chobham dispersed. There was scarcely an intimation of movement from the pit.

It was this, as much as anything, that gave people courage, and I suppose the new arrivals from Woking also helped to restore confidence. At any rate, as the dusk came on, a slow, intermittent movement upon the sand-pits began, a movement that seemed to gather force as the stillness of the evening about the cylinder remained unbroken. Vertical black figures in twos and threes would advance, stop, watch, and advance again, spreading out as they did so in a thin irregular crescent that promised to enclose the pit in its attenuated horns. I, too, on my side began to move towards the pit.

Then I saw some cabmen and others had walked boldly into the sand-pits, and heard the clatter of hoofs and the grind of wheels. I saw a lad trundling off the barrow of apples. And then, within thirty yards of the pit, advancing from the direction of Horsell, I noted a little black knot of men, the foremost of whom was waving a white flag.

This was the Deputation. There had been a hasty consultation, and, since the Martians were evidently, in spite of their repulsive forms, intelligent creatures, it had been resolved to show them, by approaching them with signals, that we, too, were intelligent.

Flutter, flutter, went the flag, first to the right, then to the left. It was too far for me to recognize anyone there, but afterwards I learnt that Ogilvy, Stent and Henderson were with others in this attempt at communication. This little group had in its advance dragged inward, so to speak, the circumference of the now almost complete circle of people, and a number of dim black figures followed it at discreet distances.

Suddenly there was a flash of light, and a quantity of luminous greenish smoke came out of the pit in three distinct puffs, which drove up, one after the other, straight into the still air.

This smoke (or flame, perhaps, would be the better word for it) was so bright that the deep blue sky overhead, and the hazy stretches of brown common towards Chertsey, set with black pine trees, seemed to darken abruptly as these puffs arose, and to remain the darker after their dispersal. At the same time a faint hissing sound became audible.

Beyond the pit stood the little wedge of people, with the white flag at its apex, arrested by these phenomena, a little knot of small vertical black shapes upon the black ground. As the green smoke rose, their faces flashed out pallid green, and faded again as it vanished.

Then slowly the hissing passed into a humming, into a long, loud, droning noise. Slowly a humped shape rose out of the pit, and the ghost of a beam of light seemed to flicker out from it.

Forthwith flashes of actual flame, a bright glare leaping from one to another, sprang from the scattered group of men. It was as if some invisible jet impinged upon them and flashed into white flame. It was as if each man suddenly and momentarily turned to fire.

Then, by the light of their own destruction, I saw them staggering and falling, and their supporters turning to run.

I stood staring, not as yet realizing that this was death leaping from man to man in that little distant crowd. All I felt was that it was something strange. An almost noiseless and blinding flash of light, and a man fell headlong and lay still, and as the unseen shaft of heat passed over them, pine trees burst into fire, and every dry furze bush[1] became with one dull thud a mass of flames. And far away towards Knaphill I saw the flashes of trees and hedges and wooden buildings suddenly set alight.

It was sweeping round swiftly and steadily, this invisible, inevitable sword of heat. I perceived it coming towards me by the flashing bushes it touched, and was too astounded and stupefied to stir. I heard the crackle of fire in the sand-pits and the sudden squeal of a horse that was as suddenly stilled. Then it was as if an invisible yet intensely-heated finger was drawn through the heather between me

1. A spiny shrub with yellow flowers, very common throughout England and Europe.

and the Martians, and all along a curving line beyond the sand-pits the dark ground smoked and cracked. Something fell with a crash, far away to the left, where the road from Woking Station opens out on the common. Forthwith the hissing and humming ceased and the black, dome-like object sank slowly out of sight into the pit.

All this had happened with such swiftness that I had stood motionless, dumbfounded and dazzled by the flashes of light. Had that death swept through a full circle, it must inevitably have slain me in my surprise. But it passed and spared me, and left the night about me suddenly dark and unfamiliar.

The undulating common seemed now dark almost to blackness, except where its roadways lay grey and pale under the deep-blue sky of the early night. It was dark, and suddenly void of men. Overhead the stars were mustering, and in the west the sky was still a pale, bright, almost greenish blue. The tops of the pine trees and the roofs of Horsell came out sharp and black against the western afterglow. The Martians and their appliances were altogether invisible, save for that thin mast upon which their restless mirror wobbled. Patches of bush and isolated trees here and there smoked and glowed still, and the houses towards Woking Station were sending up spires of flame into the stillness of the evening air.

Nothing was changed save for that and a terrible astonishment. The little group of black specks with the flag of white had been swept out of existence, and the stillness of the evening, so it seemed to me, had scarcely been broken.

It came to me that I was upon this dark common, helpless, unprotected and alone. Suddenly like a thing falling upon me from without came—Fear.

With an effort I turned and began a stumbling run through the heather.

The fear I felt was no rational fear, but a panic terror, not only of the Martians, but of the dusk and stillness all about me. Such an extraordinary effect in unmanning me it had that I ran weeping silently as a child might do. Once I had turned, I did not dare to look back.

I remember I felt an extraordinary persuasion that I was being played with, that presently, when I was upon the very verge of safety, this mysterious death—as swift as the passage of light— would leap after me from the pit about the cylinder, and strike me down.

CHAPTER SIX

THE HEAT-RAY IN THE CHOBHAM ROAD

It is still a matter of wonder how the Martians are able to slay men so swiftly and so silently. Many think that in some way they are able to generate an intense heat in a chamber of practically absolute non-conductivity. This intense heat they project in a parallel beam against any object they choose by means of a polished parabolic mirror[1] of unknown composition—much as the parabolic mirror of a lighthouse projects a beam of light. But no one has absolutely proved these details. However it is done, it is certain that a beam of heat is the essence of the matter. Heat, and invisible, instead of visible light. Whatever is combustible flashes into flame at its touch, lead runs like water, it softens iron, cracks and melts glass, and when it falls upon water incontinently that explodes into steam.

That night nearly forty people lay under the starlight about the pit, charred and distorted beyond recognition, and all night long the common from Horsell to Maybury was deserted, and brightly ablaze.

The news of the massacre probably reached Chobham, Woking, and Ottershaw about the same time. In Woking the shops had closed when the tragedy happened, and a number of people, shop-people and so forth, attracted by the stories they had heard, were walking over Horsell Bridge and along the road between the hedges that run out at last upon the common. You may imagine the young people brushed up after the labours of the day, and making this

1. Though the details of the heat-ray are vague, they do anticipate in some remarkable ways the development of the laser beam in the 1950s.

novelty, as they would make any novelty, the excuse for walking together and enjoying a trivial flirtation. You may figure to yourself
the hum of voices along the road in the gloaming.[2] . . .

As yet, of course, few people in Woking even knew that the
cylinder had opened, though poor Henderson had sent a messenger
on a bicycle to the post office with a special wire to an evening
paper.

As these folks came out by twos and threes upon the open they
found little knots of people talking excitedly, and peering at the
spinning mirror over the sand-pits, and the newcomers were, no
doubt, soon infected by the excitement of the occasion.

By half-past eight, when the Deputation was destroyed, there
may have been a crowd of 300 people or more at this place, besides
those who had left the road to approach the Martians nearer. There
were three policemen, too, one of whom was mounted, doing their
best under instructions from Stent, to keep the people back and
deter them from approaching the cylinder. There was some booing
from those more thoughtless and excitable souls to whom a crowd
is always an occasion for noise and horse-play.

Stent and Ogilvy, anticipating some possibilities of a collision,
had telegraphed from Horsell to the barracks as soon as the Martians emerged, for the help of a company of soldiers to protect these
strange creatures from violence. After that they returned to lead
that ill-fated advance. The description of their death, as it was seen
by the crowd, tallies very closely with my own impressions: the
three puffs of green smoke, the deep humming note, and the flashes
of flame.

But that crowd of people had a far narrower escape than mine.
Only the fact that a hummock[3] of heathery sand intercepted the
lower part of the Heat-Ray saved them. Had the elevation of the
parabolic mirror been a few yards higher, none could have lived
to tell the tale. They saw the flashes and the men falling, and an
invisible hand, as it were, lit the bushes as it hurried towards them

2. Twilight.
3. A small knoll or hill.

through the twilight. Then, with a whistling note that rose above the droning of the pit, the beam swung close over their heads, lighting the tops of the beech trees that line the road, and splitting the bricks, smashing the windows, firing the window-frames, and bringing down in crumbling ruin a portion of the gable of the house nearest the corner.

In the sudden thud, hiss and glare of the igniting trees the panic-stricken crowd seems to have swayed hesitatingly for some moments.

Sparks and burning twigs began to fall into the road, and single leaves like puffs of flame. Hats and dresses caught fire. Then came a crying from the common.

There were shrieks and shouts, and suddenly a mounted policeman came galloping through the confusion with his hands clasped over his head, screaming.

'They're coming!' a woman shrieked, and incontinently everyone was turning and pushing at those behind, in order to clear their way to Woking again. They must have bolted as blindly as a flock of sheep. Where the road grows narrow and black between the high banks the crowd jammed and a desperate struggle occurred. All that crowd did not escape; three persons at least, two women and a little boy, were crushed and trampled there and left to die amidst the terror and the darkness.

CHAPTER SEVEN

HOW I REACHED HOME

For my own part, I remember nothing of my flight except the stress of blundering against trees and stumbling through the heather. All about me gathered the invisible terrors of the Martians; that pitiless sword of heat seemed whirling to and fro, flourishing overhead before it descended and smote me out of life. I came into the road between the cross-roads and Horsell, and ran along this to the cross-roads.

At last I could go no farther; I was exhausted with the violence of my emotion and of my flight and I staggered and fell by the wayside. That was near the bridge that crosses the canal by the gasworks. I fell and lay still.

I must have remained there some time.

I sat up, strangely perplexed. For a moment, perhaps, I could not clearly understand how I came there. My terror had fallen from me like a garment. My hat had gone, and my collar had burst away from its stud.[1] A few minutes before there had only been three real things before me—the immensity of the night and space and nature, my own feebleness and anguish, and the near approach of death. Now it was as if something turned over, and the point of view altered abruptly. There was no sensible transition from one state of mind to the other. I was immediately the self of every day again, a decent ordinary citizen. The silent common, the impulse of my flight, the starting flames, were as if it were a dream. I asked myself had these latter things indeed happened. I could not credit it.

I rose and walked unsteadily up the steep incline of the bridge. My mind was blank wonder. My muscles and nerves seemed drained of their strength. I dare say I staggered drunkenly. A head rose over the arch, and the figure of a workman carrying a basket appeared. Beside him ran a little boy. He passed me, wishing me good-night. I was minded to speak to him, and did not. I answered his greeting with a meaningless mumble and went on over the bridge.

Over the Maybury arch a train, a billowing tumult of white, firelit smoke, and a long caterpillar of lighted windows, went flying south: clatter, clatter, clap, rap, and it had gone. A dim group of people talked in the gate of one of the houses in the pretty little row of gables that was called Oriental Terrace. It was all so real and so familiar. And that behind me! It was frantic, fantastic! Such things, I told myself, could not be.

Perhaps I am a man of exceptional moods. I do not know how

---

1. Collars at the time were detached from the shirt, generally made of celluloid, and fastened around the neck with a stud.

far my experience is common. At times I suffer from the strangest sense of detachment from myself and the world about me; I seem to watch it all from the outside, from somewhere inconceivably remote, out of time, out of space, out of the stress and tragedy of it all. This feeling was very strong upon me that night. Here was another side to my dream.

But the trouble was the blank incongruity of this serenity and the swift death flying yonder, not two miles away. There was a noise of business from the gas-works, and the electric lamps were all alight. I stopped at the group of people.

'What news from the common?' said I.

There were two men and a woman at the gate.

'Eh?' said one of the men, turning.

'What news from the common?' I said.

'Ain't yer just *been* there?' asked the men.

'People seem fair silly about the common,' said the woman over the gate. 'What's it all abart?'

'Haven't you heard of the men from Mars?' said I. 'The creatures from Mars?'

'Quite enough,' said the woman over the gate. 'Thenks,' and all three of them laughed.

I felt foolish and angry. I tried and found I could not tell them what I had seen. They laughed again at my broken sentences.

'You'll hear more yet,' I said, and went on to my home.

I startled my wife at the doorway, so haggard was I. I went into the dining-room, sat down, drank some wine, and so soon as I could collect myself sufficiently told her the things I had seen. The dinner, which was a cold one, had already been served, and remained neglected on the table while I told my story.

'There is one thing,' I said to allay the fears I had aroused. 'They are the most sluggish things I ever saw crawl. They may keep the pit and kill people who come near them, but they cannot get out of it. . . . But the horror of them!'

'Don't, dear!' said my wife, knitting her brows and putting her hand on mine.

'Poor Ogilvy!' I said. 'To think he may be lying dead there!'

My wife at least did not find my experience incredible. When I saw how deadly white her face was, I ceased abruptly.

'They may come here,' she said again and again.

I pressed her to take wine, and tried to reassure her.

'They can scarcely move,' I said.

I began to comfort her and myself by repeating all that Ogilvy had told me of the impossibility of the Martians establishing themselves on the earth. In particular I laid stress on the gravitational difficulty. On the surface of the earth the force of gravity is three times what it is on the surface of Mars. A Martian, therefore, would weigh three times more than on Mars, albeit his muscular strength would be the same. His own body would be a cope of lead to him, therefore. That indeed was the general opinion. Both *The Times* and the *Daily Telegraph,* for instance, insisted on it the next morning, and both overlooked, just as I did, two obvious modifying influences.

The atmosphere of the earth, we now know, contains far more oxygen or far less argon[2] (whichever way one likes to put it) than does Mars. The invigorating influences of this excess of oxygen upon the Martians indisputably did much to counterbalance the increased weight of their bodies. And, in the second place, we all overlooked the fact that such mechanical intelligence as the Martian possessed was quite able to dispense with muscular exertion at a pinch.

But I did not consider these points at the time, and so my reasoning was dead against the chances of the invaders. With wine and food, the confidence of my own table, and the necessity of reassuring my wife, I grew, by insensible degrees, courageous and secure.

'They have done a foolish thing,' said I, fingering my wineglass. 'They are dangerous, because no doubt they are mad with terror. Perhaps they expected to find no living things—certainly no intelli-

2. An inactive, gaseous element.

gent living things. A shell in the pit,' said I, 'if the worst comes to the worst, will kill them all.'

The intense excitement of the events had no doubt left my perceptive powers in a state of erethism.[3] I remember that dinner-table with extraordinary vividness even now. My dear wife's sweet, anxious face peering at me from under the pink lamp-shade, the white cloth with its silver and glass table furniture—for in those days even philosophical writers had many little luxuries—the crimson-purple wine in my glass, are photographically distinct. At the end of it I sat, tempering[4] nuts with a cigarette, regretting Ogilvy's rashness, and denouncing the short-sighted timidity of the Martians.

So some respectable dodo in the Mauritius[5] might have lorded it in his nest, and discussed the arrival of that shipful of pitiless sailors in want of animal food. 'We will peck them to death tomorrow, my dear.'

I did not know it, but that was the last civilized dinner I was to eat for very many strange and terrible days.

3. Term describing an unusual state of irritability or stimulation in an organism.
4. Burning, roasting.
5. This is the second reference to man's fate at the hands of the Martians in terms of the extinction of the dodo species; see Chapter One, note 8.

CHAPTER EIGHT
FRIDAY NIGHT

The most extraordinary thing to my mind, of all the strange and wonderful things that happened upon that Friday, was the dovetailing of the commonplace habits of our social order[1] with the first beginnings of the series of events that was to topple that social order headlong. If on Friday night you had taken a pair of com-

1. This introduces another "Darwinian" theme of the story: the transformation of an established, normal-seeming social order by extreme stress from outside.

passes and drawn a circle with a radius of five miles round the Woking sand-pits, I doubt if you would have had one human being outside it, unless it was some relation of Stent or of the three or four cyclists[2] or London people who lay dead on the common, whose emotions or habits were at all affected by the newcomers. Many people had heard of the cylinder, of course, and talked about it in their leisure, but it certainly did not make the sensation an ultimatum to Germany would have done.

In London that night poor Henderson's telegram describing the gradual unscrewing of the shot was judged to be a canard,[3] and his evening paper, after wiring for authentication from him and receiving no reply—the man was killed—decided not to print a special edition.

Within the five-mile circle even the great majority of people were inert. I have already described the behaviour of the men and women to whom I spoke. All over the district people were dining and supping; working-men were gardening after the labours of the day, children were being put to bed, young people were wandering through the lanes love-making, students sat over their books.

Maybe there was a murmur in the village streets, a novel and dominant topic in the public houses, and here and there a messenger, or even an eye-witness of the later occurrences, caused a whirl of excitement, a shouting and a running to and fro; but for the most part the daily routine of working, eating, drinking, sleeping, went on as it had done for countless years—as though no planet Mars existed in the sky. Even at Woking Station and Horsell and Chobham that was the case.

In Woking Junction, until a late hour, trains were stopping and going on, others were shunting on the sidings, passengers were

2. Cycling was a widespread enthusiasm in the 1890s, and the young Wells was an ardent cyclist. The first practical safety bicycle had been patented in 1884, but it was not until 1888, when Dunlop patented the first pneumatic tire, that the sport became a comfortable and inexpensive form of entertainment.
3. Hoax.

alighting and waiting, and everything was proceeding in the most ordinary way. A boy from town, trenching on Smith's monopoly,[4] was selling papers with the afternoon's news. The ringing and impact of trucks, the sharp whistle of the engines from the junction, mingled with his shouts of: 'Men from Mars!' Excited men came into the station with incredible tidings about nine o'clock, and caused no more disturbance than drunkards might have done. People rattling Londonwards peered into the darkness outside the carriage windows and saw only a rare, flickering, vanishing spark dance up from the direction of Horsell, a red glow and a thin veil of smoke driving across the stars, and thought that nothing more serious than a heath fire was happening. It was only round the edge of the common that any disturbance was perceptible. There were half a dozen villas burning on the Woking border. There were lights in all the houses on the common side of the three villages, and the people there kept awake till dawn.

A curious crowd lingered restlessly, people coming and going but the crowd remaining, both on the Chobham and Horsell bridges. One or two adventurous souls, it was afterwards found, went into the darkness and crawled quite near the Martians; but they never returned, for now and again a light-ray, like the beam of a warship's searchlight, swept the common, and the Heat-Ray was ready to follow. Save for such, that big area of common was silent and desolate, and the charred bodies lay about on it all night under the stars, and all the next day. A noise of hammering from the pit was heard by many people.

So you have the state of things on Friday night. In the centre, sticking into the skin of our old planet Earth like a poisoned dart, was this cylinder. But the poison was scarcely working yet. Around it was a patch of silent common, smouldering in places, and with a few dark, dimly-seen objects lying in contorted attitudes here and there. Here and there was a burning bush or tree. Beyond was a

4. "Trenching" means encroaching. The newsboy is selling his papers at a
   station where Mr. Smith has a permanent newsstand.

fringe of excitement, and farther than that fringe the inflammation had not crept as yet. In the rest of the world the stream of life still flowed as it had flowed for immemorial years. The fever of war that would presently clog in vein and artery, deaden nerve and destroy brain, had still to develop.

All night long the Martians were hammering and stirring, sleepless, indefatigable, at work upon the machines they were making ready, and ever and again a puff of greenish-white smoke whirled up to the starlit sky.

About eleven a company of soldiers came through Horsell, and deployed along the edge of the common to form a cordon. Later a second company marched through Chobham to deploy on the north side of the common. Several officers from the Inkerman barracks[5] had been on the common earlier in the day, and one, Major Eden, was reported to be missing. The Colonel of the regiment came to the Chobham bridge, and was busy questioning the crowd at midnight. The military authorities were certainly alive to the seriousness of the business. About eleven, the next morning's papers were able to say, a squadron of hussars, two Maxims,[6] and about 400 men of the Cardigan[7] regiment, started from Aldershot.

A few seconds after midnight the crowd in the Chertsey road, Woking, saw a star fall from heaven into the pine-woods to the north-west. It fell with a greenish light, causing a flash of light like summer lightning. This was the second cylinder.

5. The Inkerman Barracks were named for the Battle of Inkerman where, in 1854, English and French troops defeated an attacking Prussian Army. Throughout the late nineteenth century, the armies of Europe were in the process of massive and ominous expansion and reorganization. But the British had a long-standing aversion to the idea of a standing army. Their reorganization, beginning in 1870, emphasized the localization of garrisons and short enlistment terms for civilian volunteers. In 1881 the infantry of the line was remodeled into two-battalion regiments with territorial names.
6. Hussars are light cavalry. The Maxim is the Maxim-Vickers, the first truly automatic machine gun, manufactured in the 1880s.
7. A regiment from Cardiganshire, a county of West Wales.

CHAPTER NINE

THE FIGHTING BEGINS

Saturday lives in my memory as a day of suspense. It was a day of lassitude too, hot and close, with, I am told, a rapidly fluctuating barometer. I had slept but little, though my wife had succeeded in sleeping, and I rose early. I went into my garden before breakfast, and stood listening, but towards the common there was nothing stirring but a lark.

The milkman came as usual. I heard the rattle of his chariot, and I went round to the side gate to ask the latest news. He told me that during the night the Martians had been surrounded by troops, and that guns were expected. Then, a familiar reassuring note, I heard a train running towards Woking.

'They aren't to be killed,' said the milkman, 'if that can possibly be avoided.'

I saw my neighbour gardening, chatted with him for a time, and then strolled in to breakfast. It was a most unexceptional morning. My neighbour was of opinion that the troops would be able to capture or to destroy the Martians during the day.

'It's a pity they make themselves so unapproachable,' he said. 'It would be curious to learn how they live on another planet; we might learn a thing or two.'

He came up to the fence and extended a handful of strawberries, for his gardening was as generous as it was enthusiastic. At the same time he told me of the burning of the pine-woods about the Byfleet Golf Links.

'They say,' said he, 'that there's another of those blessed things fallen there—number two. But one's enough, surely. This lot'll cost the insurance people a pretty penny before everything's settled.' He laughed with an air of the greatest good-humour as he said this. The woods, he said, were still burning, and pointed out a haze of smoke to me. 'They will be hot under foot for days on account of the thick soil of pine-needles and turf,' he said, and then grew serious over 'poor Ogilvy'.

After breakfast, instead of working, I decided to walk down towards the common. Under the railway bridge I found a group of soldiers—sappers,[1] I think, men in small round caps, dirty red jackets unbuttoned, and showing their blue shirts, dark trousers, and boots coming to the calf. They told me no one was allowed over the canal, and, looking along the road towards the bridge, I saw one of the Cardigan men standing sentinel there. I talked with these soldiers for a time; I told them of my sight of the Martians on the previous evening. None of them had seen the Martians, and they had but the vaguest ideas of them, so that they plied me with questions. They said that they did not know who had authorized the movements of the troops; their idea was that a dispute had arisen at the Horse Guards.[2] The ordinary sapper is a great deal better educated than the common soldier, and they discussed the peculiar conditions of the possible fight with some acuteness. I described the Heat-Ray to them, and they began to argue among themselves.

'Crawl up under cover and rush 'em, say I,' said one.

'Get aht!' said another. 'What's cover against this 'ere 'eat? Sticks to cook yer! What we got to do is to go as near as the ground'll let us, and then drive a trench.'

'Blow yer trenches! You always want trenches; you ought to ha' been born a rabbit, Snippy.'

'Ain't they got any necks, then?' said a third abruptly—a little, contemplative, dark man, smoking a pipe.

I repeated my description.

'Octopuses,' said he, 'that's what I calls 'em. Talk about fishers of men[3]—fighters of fish it is this time!'

---

1. Military engineers, builders of trenches, fortifications, etc.
2. The famous "Blues," or Royal Horse Guards, consolidated in 1819.
3. In Matthew 4:19 Christ tells Peter and Andrew that He will make them "fishers of men."

'It ain't no murder killing beasts like that,' said the first speaker.

'Why not shell the darned things strite off and finish 'em?' said the little dark man. 'You carn tell what they might do.'

'Where's your shells?' said the first speaker. 'There ain't no time. Do it in a rush, that's my tip, and do it at once.'

So they discussed it. After a while I left them, and went on to the railway-station to get as many morning papers as I could.

But I will not weary the reader with a description of that long morning and of the longer afternoon. I did not succeed in getting a glimpse of the common, for even Horsell and Chobham church towers were in the hands of the military authorities. The soldiers I addressed didn't know anything; the officers were mysterious as well as busy. I found people in the town quite secure again in the presence of the military, and I heard for the first time from Marshall, the tobacconist, that his son was among the dead on the common. The soldiers had made the people on the outskirts of Horsell lock up and leave their houses.

I got back to lunch about two, very tired, for, as I have said, the day was extremely hot and dull, and in order to refresh myself I took a cold bath in the afternoon. About half-past four I went up to the railway-station to get an evening paper, for the morning papers had contained only a very inaccurate description of the killing of Stent, Henderson, Ogilvy, and the others. But there was little I didn't know. The Martians did not show an inch of themselves. They seemed busy in their pit, and there was a sound of hammering and an almost continuous streamer of smoke. Apparently, they were busy getting ready for a struggle. 'Fresh attempts have been made to signal, but without success,' was the stereotyped formula of the papers. A sapper told me it was done by a man in a ditch with a flag on a long pole. The Martians took as much notice of such advances as we should of the lowing of a cow.

I must confess the sight of all this armament, all this preparation, greatly excited me. My imagination became belligerent, and defeated the invaders in a dozen striking ways; something of my schoolboy dreams of battle and heroism came back. It hardly seemed a fair fight to me at that time. They seemed very helpless in this pit of theirs.

About three o'clock there began the thud of a gun at measured intervals from Chertsey or Addlestone. I learnt that the smouldering pine-wood into which the second cylinder had fallen was being shelled, in the hope of destroying that object before it opened. It was only about five, however, that a field-gun reached Chobham for use against the first body of Martians.

About six in the evening, as I sat at tea with my wife in the summer-house talking vigorously about the battle that was lowering upon us, I heard a muffled detonation from the common, and immediately after a gust of firing. Close on the heels of that came a violent, rattling crash, quite close to us, that shook the ground; and, starting out upon the lawn, I saw the tops of the trees about the Oriental College burst into smoky red flame, and the tower of the little church beside it slide down into ruin. The pinnacle of the mosque had vanished, and the roof-line of the college itself looked as if a hundred-ton gun had been at work upon it. One of our chimneys cracked as if a shot had hit it, flew, and the piece of it came clattering down the tiles and made a heap of broken red fragments upon the flower-bed by my study window.

I and my wife stood amazed. Then I realized that the crest of Maybury Hill must be within range of the Martians' Heat-Ray now that the college was cleared out of the way.

At that I gripped my wife's arm, and without ceremony ran her out into the road. Then I fetched out the servant, telling her I would go upstairs myself for the box she was clamouring for.

'We can't possibly stay here,' I said; and as I spoke the firing re-opened for a moment upon the common.

'But where are we to go?' said my wife in terror.

I thought, perplexed. Then I remembered her cousins[4] at Leatherhead.

---

4. An apparent slip. Everywhere else these cousins are the narrator's cousins, not his wife's (see Book I, Chapter Ten, first paragraph, for instance).

'Leatherhead!' I shouted above the sudden noise.

She looked away from me downhill. The people were coming out of their houses astonished.

'How are we to get to Leatherhead?' she said.

Down the hill I saw a bevy of hussars ride under the railway bridge; three galloped through the open gates of the Oriental College; two others dismounted, and began running from house to house. The sun, shining through the smoke that drove up from the tops of the trees, seemed blood-red, and threw an unfamiliar lurid light upon everything.

'Stop here,' said I; 'you are safe here;' and I started off at once for the Spotted Dog, for I knew the landlord had a horse and dog-cart.[5] I ran, for I perceived that in a moment everyone upon this side of the hill would be moving. I found him in his bar, quite unaware of what was going on behind his house. A man stood with his back to me, talking to him.

'I must have a pound,' said the landlord, 'and I've no one to drive it.'

'I'll give you two,' said I, over the stranger's shoulder.

'What for?'

'And I'll bring it back by midnight,' I said.

'Lord!' said the landlord, 'what's the hurry? I'm selling my bit of a pig.[6] Two pounds, and you bring it back? What's going on now?'

I explained hastily that I had to leave my home, and so secured the dog-cart. At the time it did not seem to me nearly so urgent that the landlord should leave his. I took care to have the cart there and then, drove it off down the road, and, leaving it in charge of my wife and servant, rushed into my house and packed a few valuables, such plate as we had, and so forth. The beech trees below the house were burning while I did this, and the palings[7] up the road glowed red. While I was occupied in this way, one of the dis-

5. A light, two-wheeled vehicle with two seats, back to back: *horse*-drawn.
6. The landlord fears he may be selling (not buying) a "pig in a poke."
7. Fence pickets.

mounted hussars came running up. He was going from house to house, warning people to leave. He was going on as I came out of my front door, lugging my treasures, done up in a table-cloth. I shouted after him:

'What news?'

He turned, stared, bawled something about 'crawling out in a thing like a dish-cover',[8] and ran on to the gate of the house at the crest. A sudden whirl of black smoke driving across the road hid him for a moment. I ran to my neighbour's door, and rapped to satisfy myself, what I already knew, that his wife had gone to London with him, and had locked up their house. I went in again according to my promise to get my servant's box, lugged it out, clapped it beside her on the tail of the dog-cart, and then caught the reins and jumped up into the driver's seat beside my wife. In another moment we were clear of the smoke and noise, and spanking down the opposite slope of Maybury Hill towards Old Woking.

In front was a quiet sunny landscape, a wheat-field ahead on either side of the road, and the Maybury Inn with its swinging sign. I saw the doctor's cart ahead of me. At the bottom of the hill I turned my head to look at the hillside I was leaving. Thick streamers of black smoke shot with threads of red fire were driving up into the still air, and throwing dark shadows upon the green tree-tops eastward. The smoke already extended far away to the east and west—to the Byfleet pine-woods eastward, and to Woking on the west. The road was dotted with people running towards us. And very faint now, but very distinct through the hot, quiet air, one heard the whirr of a machine-gun[9] that was presently stilled, and

8. A dome-shaped cover to keep the food on a plate warm. Again, Wells describes the unearthly in terms of the everyday and the domestic.
9. The period from 1890 to the First World War has been called the "golden age" of the machine gun, and was an era of intensive development of new weapons of all sorts. The first, semi-automatic machine gun, the Gatling gun, saw wide use in the American Civil War, and was superseded by the fully automatic Maxim gun in 1884. But by 1898 technology had produced an amazingly wide range of designs.

an intermittent cracking of rifles. Apparently, the Martians were setting fire to everything within range of their Heat-Ray.

I am not an expert driver, and I had immediately to turn my attention to the horse. When I looked back again the second hill had hidden the black smoke. I slashed the horse with the whip, and gave him a loose rein until Woking and Send lay between us and that quivering tumult. I overtook and passed the doctor between Woking and Send.

CHAPTER TEN

IN THE STORM

Leatherhead is about twelve miles from Maybury Hill. The scent of hay was in the air through the lush meadows beyond Pyrford, and the hedges on either side were sweet and gay with multitudes of dog-roses.[1] The heavy firing that had broken out while we were driving down Maybury Hill ceased as abruptly as it began, leaving the evening very peaceful and still. We got to Leatherhead without misadventure about nine o'clock, and the horse had an hour's rest while I took supper with my cousins and commended my wife to their care.

My wife was curiously silent throughout the drive, and seemed oppressed with forebodings of evil. I talked to her reassuringly, pointing out that the Martians were tied to the pit by sheer heaviness, and, at the utmost, could but crawl a little out of it, but she answered only in monosyllables. Had it not been for my promise to the innkeeper, she would, I think, have urged me to stay in Leatherhead that night. Would that I had! Her face, I remember, was very white as we parted.

For my own part, I had been feverishly excited all day. Something very like the war fever, that occasionally runs through a civilized community, had got into my blood, and in my heart I was not so very sorry that I had to return to Maybury that night. I was even

1. European variety of rose, with very pale red flowers.

afraid that the last fusillade[2] I had heard might mean the extermination of our invaders from Mars. I can best express my state of
mind by saying that I wanted to be in at the death.

It was nearly eleven when I started to return. The night was unexpectedly dark; to me, walking out of the lighted passage of my
cousin's house, it seemed indeed black, and it was as hot and close
as the day. Overhead the clouds were driving fast, albeit not a
breath stirred the shrubs about us. My cousins' man lit both lamps.
Happily, I knew the road intimately. My wife stood in the light of
the doorway, and watched me until I jumped up into the dogcart.
Then abruptly she turned and went in, leaving my cousins side by
side wishing me good hap.

I was a little depressed at first with the contagion of my wife's
fears, but very soon my thoughts reverted to the Martians. At that
time I was absolutely in the dark as to the course of the evening's
fighting. I did not know even the circumstances that had precipitated the conflict. As I came through Ockham (for that was the way
I returned, and not through Send and Old Woking) I saw along the
western horizon a blood-red glow, which, as I drew nearer, crept
slowly up the sky. The driving clouds of the gathering thunderstorm
mingled there with masses of black and red smoke.

Ripley Street was deserted, and except for a lighted window or
so the village showed not a sign of life; but I narrowly escaped an
accident at the corner of the road to Pyrford, where a knot of people stood with their backs to me. They said nothing to me as I
passed. I do not know what they knew of the things happening beyond the hill, nor do I know if the silent houses I passed on my
way were sleeping securely, or deserted and empty, or harassed and
watching against the terror of the night.

From Ripley until I came through Pyrford I was in the valley
of the Wey, and the red glare was hidden from me. As I ascended
the little hill beyond Pyrford Church the glare came into view
again, and the trees about me shivered with the first intimation of
the storm that was upon me. Then I heard midnight pealing out

2. A volley of shots.

from Pyrford Church behind me, and then came the silhouette of Maybury Hill, with its tree-tops and roofs black and sharp against the red.

Even as I beheld this a lurid green glare lit the road about me, and showed the distant woods towards Addlestone. I felt a tug at the reins. I saw that the driving clouds had been pierced as it were by a thread of green fire, suddenly lighting their confusion and falling into the fields to my left. It was the Third Falling Star!

Close on its apparition, and blindingly violet by contrast, danced out the first lightning of the gathering storm, and the thunder burst like a rocket overhead. The horse took the bit between his teeth and bolted.

A moderate incline runs down towards the foot of Maybury Hill, and down this we clattered. Once the lightning had begun, it went on in as rapid a succession of flashes as I have ever seen. The thunder-claps, treading one on the heels of another and with a strange crackling accompaniment, sounded more like the working of a gigantic electric machine than the usual detonating reverberations. The flickering light was blinding and confusing, and a thin hail smote gustily at my face as I drove down the slope.

At first I regarded little but the road before me, and then abruptly my attention was arrested by something that was moving rapidly down the opposite slope of Maybury Hill. At first I took it for the wet roof of a house, but one flash following another showed it to be in swift rolling movement. It was an elusive vision—a moment of bewildering darkness, and then a flash like daylight, the red masses of the Orphanage near the crest of the hill, the green tops of the pine trees, and this problematical object came out clear and sharp and bright.

And this thing I saw! How can I describe it? A monstrous tripod,[3] higher than many houses, striding over the young pine trees,

3. Any three-legged support, although the most common instance of the "tripod" for Wells's readers would probably have been the tripod on which older cameras were mounted. Note that, in Chapter Twelve, the box the Martian tripods hold to generate the heat-ray is described as a "camera."

and smashing them aside in its career; a walking engine of glittering metal, striding now across the heather; articulate[4] ropes of steel dangling from it, and the clattering tumult of its passage mingling with the riot of the thunder. A flash, and it came out vividly, heeling over one way with two feet in the air, to vanish and reappear almost instantly as it seemed, with the next flash, a hundred yards nearer.[5] Can you imagine a milking-stool tilted and bowled violently along the ground? That was the impression those instant flashes gave. But instead of a milking-stool imagine it a great body of machinery on a tripod stand.

Then suddenly the trees in the pine-wood ahead of me were parted, as brittle reeds are parted by a man thrusting through them; they were snapped off and driven headlong, and a second huge tripod appeared, rushing, as it seemed, headlong towards me. And I was galloping hard to meet it! At the sight of the second monster my nerve went altogether. Not stopping to look again, I wrenched the horse's head hard round to the right, and in another moment the dog-cart had heeled over upon the horse; the shafts smashed noisily, and I was flung sideways and fell heavily into a shallow pool of water.

I crawled out almost immediately, and crouched, my feet still in the water, under a clump of furze. The horse lay motionless (his neck was broken, poor brute!), and by the lightning flashes I saw the black bulk of the overturned dog-cart, and the silhouette of the wheel still spinning slowly. In another moment the colossal mechanism went striding by me, and passed up-hill towards Pyrford.

Seen nearer, the thing was incredibly strange, for it was no mere insensate machine driving on its way. Machine it was, with a ringing metallic pace, and long flexible glittering tentacles (one of which gripped a young pine tree) swinging and rattling about its strange body. It picked its road as it went striding along, and the

4. Jointed.
5. This is a remarkable anticipation of the "strobe effect" of rapid flashes of light, which we have come to associate (through films as much as through real experience of warfare) with modern battle scenes.

brazen hood that surmounted it moved to and fro with the inevitable suggestion of a head looking about it. Behind the main body was a huge thing of white metal like a gigantic fisherman's basket, and puffs of green smoke squirted out from the joints of the limbs as the monster swept by me. And in an instant it was gone.

So much I saw then, all vaguely for the flickering of the lightning, in blinding high lights and dense black shadows.

As it passed it set up an exultant deafening howl that drowned the thunder: 'Aloo! aloo!' and in another minute it was with its companion, and half a mile away, stooping over something in the field. I have no doubt this thing in the field was the third of the ten cylinders they had fired at us from Mars.

For some minutes I lay there in the rain and darkness watching, by the intermittent light, these monstrous beings of metal moving about in the distance over the hedge-tops. A thin hail was now beginning, and as it came and went, their figures grew misty and then flashed into clearness again. Now and then came a gap in the lightning, and the night swallowed them up.

I was soaked with hail above and puddle-water below. It was some time before my blank astonishment would let me struggle up the bank to a drier position, or think at all of my imminent peril.

Not far from me was a little one-roomed squatter's hut of wood, surrounded by a patch of potato-garden. I struggled to my feet at last, and, crouching and making use of every chance of cover, I made a run for this. I hammered at the door, but I could not make the people hear (if there were any people inside), and after a time I desisted, and, availing myself of a ditch for the greater part of the way, succeeded in crawling, unobserved by these monstrous machines, into the pine-wood towards Maybury.

Under cover of this I pushed on, wet and shivering now, towards my own house. I walked among the trees trying to find the footpath. It was very dark indeed in the wood, for the lightning was now becoming infrequent, and the hail, which was pouring down in a torrent, fell in columns through the gaps in the heavy foliage.

If I had fully realized the meaning of all the things I had seen I should have immediately worked my way round through Byfleet to Street Cobham, and so gone back to rejoin my wife at Leatherhead. But that night the strangeness of things about me, and my physical wretchedness, prevented me, for I was bruised, weary, wet to the skin, deafened and blinded by the storm.

I had a vague idea of going on to my own house, and that was as much motive as I had. I staggered through the trees, fell into a ditch and bruised my knees against a plank, and finally splashed out into the lane that ran down from the College Arms. I say splashed, for the storm water was sweeping the sand down the hill in a muddy torrent. There in the darkness a man blundered into me and sent me reeling back.

He gave a cry of terror, sprung sideways, and rushed on before I could gather my wits sufficiently to speak to him. So heavy was the stress of the storm just at this place that I had the hardest task to win my way up the hill. I went close up to the fence on the left and worked my way along its palings.

Near the top I stumbled upon something soft, and, by a flash of lightning, saw between my feet a heap of black broadcloth and a pair of boots. Before I could distinguish clearly how the man lay, the flicker of light had passed. I stood over him waiting for the next flash. When it came, I saw that he was a sturdy man, cheaply but not shabbily dressed; his head was best under his body, and he lay crumpled up close to the fence, as though he had been flung violently against it.

Overcoming the repugnance natural to one who had never before touched a dead body, I stooped and turned him over to feel for his heart. He was quite dead. Apparently his neck had been broken. The lightning flashed for a third time, and his face leapt upon me. I sprang to my feet. It was the landlord of the Spotted Dog, whose conveyance I had taken.

I stepped over him gingerly and pushed on up the hill. I made my way by the police station and the College Arms towards my own house. Nothing was burning on the hillside, though from the common there still came a red glare and a rolling tumult of ruddy smoke beating up against the drenching hail. So far as I could see by the flashes, the houses about me were mostly uninjured. By the College Arms a dark heap lay in the road.

Down the road towards Maybury Bridge there were voices and the sound of feet, but I had not the courage to shout or to go to them. I let myself in with my latch-key, closed, locked and bolted the door, staggered to the foot of the staircase and sat down. My imagination was full of those striding metallic monsters, and of the dead body smashed against the fence.

I crouched at the foot of the staircase with my back to the wall, shivering violently.

CHAPTER ELEVEN

AT THE WINDOW

I have said already that my storms of emotion have a trick of exhausting themselves. After a time I discovered that I was cold and wet, and with little pools of water about me on the stair-carpet. I got up almost mechanically, went into the dining-room and drank some whisky, and then I was moved to change my clothes.

After I had done that I went upstairs to my study, but why I did so I do not know. The window of my study looks over the trees and the railway towards Horsell Common. In the hurry of our departure this window had been left open. The passage was dark, and, by contrast with the picture the window-frame enclosed, that side of the room seemed impenetrably dark. I stopped short in the doorway.

The thunderstorm had passed. The towers of the Oriental College and the pine trees about it had gone, and very far away, lit by a vivid red glare, the common about the sand-pits was visible. Across the light, huge black shapes, grotesque and strange, moved busily to and fro.

It seemed, indeed, as if the whole country in that direction was on fire—a broad hillside set with minute tongues of flame, swaying and writhing with the gusts of the dying storm, and throwing a red reflection upon the cloud scud above. Every now and then a haze of smoke from some nearer conflagration drove across the window and hid the Martian shapes. I could not see what they were doing, nor the clear form of them, nor recognize the black objects they were busied upon. Neither could I see the nearer fire, though the reflections of it danced on the wall and ceiling of the study. A sharp, resinous twang of burning was in the air.

I closed the door noiselessly and crept towards the window. As I did so, the view opened out until, on the one hand, it reached to the houses about Woking Station, and on the other to the charred and blackened pine-woods of Byfleet. There was a light down below the hill, on the railway, near the arch, and several of the houses along the Maybury road and the streets near the station were glowing ruins. The light upon the railway puzzled me at first; there was a black heap and a vivid glare, and to the right of that a row of yellow oblongs. Then I perceived this was a wrecked train, the fore part smashed and on fire, the hinder carriages still upon the rails.

Between these three main centres of light, the houses, the train, and the burning country towards Chobham, stretched irregular patches of dark country, broken here and there by intervals of dimly-glowing and smoking ground. It was the strangest spectacle, that black expanse set with fire. It reminded me, more than anything else, of the Potteries[1] seen at night. People at first I could distinguish none, though I peered intently for them. Later I saw against the light of Woking Station a number of black figures hurrying one after the other across the line.

And this was the little world in which I had been living securely for years, this fiery chaos! What had happened in the last seven hours I still did not know, nor did I know, though I was beginning

---

1. A district in central England, also called the "Five Towns," famous for its pottery and china factories. The area was a favorite subject of Wells's friend, the novelist Arnold Bennett (1867-1931).

to guess, the relation between these mechanical colossi[2] and the sluggish lumps I had seen disgorged from the cylinder. With a queer feeling of impersonal interest I turned my desk-chair to the window, sat down, and stared at the blackened country, and particularly at the three gigantic black things that were going to and fro in the glare about the sand-pits.

They seemed amazingly busy. I began to ask myself what they could be. Were they intelligent mechanisms? Such a thing I felt was impossible. Or did a Martian sit within each, ruling, directing, using, much as a man's brain sits and rules in his body?[3] I began to compare the things to human machines, to ask myself for the first time in my life how an ironclad[4] or a steam-engine would seem to an intelligent lower animal.

The storm had left the sky clear, and over the smoke of the burning land the little fading pin-point of Mars was dropping into the west, when the soldier came into my garden. I heard a slight scraping at the fence, and rousing myself from the lethargy that had fallen upon me, I looked down and saw him dimly clambering over the palings. At the sight of another human being my torpor passed, and I leant out of the window eagerly.

'Hist!' said I in a whisper.

He stopped astride of the fence in doubt. Then he came over and across the lawn to the corner of the house. He bent down and stepped softly.

'Who's there?' he said, also whispering, standing under the window and peering up.

2. Giant figures.
3. One of Wells's most resonant prophecies. The Martians, hyper-evolved brains dependent upon mechanical bodies, are an early version of that mind-machine symbiosis which recent thinkers (and science-fiction writers) call the *cyborg,* or "cybernetic organism."
4. A warship with iron or steel armor. The first battle between ironclad ships was that of the Union *Monitor* and the Confederate *Merrimac* in the American Civil War in 1862; and the growth of ironclad fleets in the later nineteenth century revolutionized the balance and tactics of European seapower, as did the steam engine, liberating warships from dependence upon the wind and tides.

'Where are you going?' I asked.

'God knows.'

'Are you trying to hide?'

'That's it.'

'Come into the house,' I said.

I went down, unfastened the door and let him in, and locked the door again. I could not see his face. He was hatless, and his coat was unbuttoned.

'My God!' he said as I drew him in.

'What has happened?' I asked.

'What hasn't?' In the obscurity I could see he made a gesture of despair. 'They wiped us out—simply wiped us out,' he repeated again and again.

He followed me, almost mechanically, into the dining-room.

'Take some whisky,' I said, pouring out a stiff dose.

He drank it. Then abruptly he sat down before the table, put his head on his arms, and began to sob and weep like a little boy, in a perfect passion of emotion, while I, with a curious forgetfulness of my own despair, stood beside him wondering.

It was a long time before he could steady his nerves to answer my questions, and then he answered perplexingly and brokenly. He was a driver[5] in the artillery, and had only come into action about seven. At that time firing was going on across the common, and it was said the first party of Martians were crawling towards their second cylinder under cover of a metal shield.

Later this shield staggered up on tripod legs, and became the first of the fighting machines I had seen. The gun he drove had been unlimbered[6] near Horsell, in order to command the sand-pits, and its arrival had precipitated the action. As the limber gunners went to the rear, his horse trod in a rabbit-hole and came down, throwing him into a depression of the ground. At the same moment the gun exploded behind him, the ammunition blew up, there was fire

---

5. That is, he drove the horse-drawn carriage of the heavy field guns.
6. To "unlimber" a gun is to detach it from its limber, a two-wheeled carriage drawn by four to six horses, and prepare it for firing.

all about him, and he found himself lying under a heap of charred dead men and dead horses.

'I lay still,' he said, 'scared out of my wits, with the fore-quarter of a horse atop of me. We'd been wiped out. And the smell—good God! Like burnt meat! I was hurt across the back by the fall of the horse, and there I had to lie until I felt better. Just like parade it had been a minute before—then stumble, bang, swish!'

'Wiped out!' he said.

He had hid under the dead horse for a long time, peeping out furtively across the common. The Cardigan men had tried a rush, in skirmishing order,[7] at the pit, simply to be swept out of existence. Then the monster had risen to its feet, and had begun to walk leisurely to and fro across the common, among the few fugtives, with its head-like hood turning about exactly like the head of a cowled human being. A kind of arm carried a complicated metallic case, about which green flashes scintillated, and out of the funnel of this there smote the Heat-Ray.

In a few minutes there was, so far as the soldier could see, not a living thing left upon the common, and every bush and tree upon it that was not already a blackened skeleton was burning. The hussars had been on the road beyond the curvature of the ground, and he saw nothing of them. He heard the Maxims rattle for a time, and then become still. The giant saved Woking Station and its cluster of houses until last; then in a moment the Heat-Ray was brought to bear, and the town became a heap of fiery ruins. Then the thing shut off the Heat-Ray, and, turning its back upon the artilleryman, began to waddle away towards the smouldering pine-woods that sheltered the second cylinder. As it did so, a second glittering Titan[8] built itself up out of the pit.

The second monster followed the first, and at that the artilleryman began to crawl very cautiously across the hot heather ash towards Horsell. He managed to get alive into the ditch along by the

7. Formation for a conventional attack.
8. In Greek myth the Titans were the gigantic and violent pre-Olympian gods whom Zeus vanquished in establishing the rule of reason and order.

side of the road, and so escaped to Woking. There his story became ejaculatory.[9] The place was impassable. It seems there were a few people alive there, frantic for the most part, and many burnt and scalded. He was turned aside by the fire, and hid among some almost scorching heaps of broken wall as one of the Martian giants returned. He saw this one pursue a man, catch him up in one of its steely tentacles, and knock his head against the trunk of a pine tree. At last, after nightfall, the artilleryman made a rush for it and got over the railway embankment.

Since then he had been skulking along towards Maybury, in the hope of getting out of danger Londonwards. People were hiding in trenches and cellars, and many of the survivors had made off towards Woking Village and Send. He had been consumed with thirst until he found one of the water mains near the railway arch smashed, and the water bubbling out like a spring upon the road.

That was the story I got from him bit by bit. He grew calmer telling me and trying to make me see the things he had seen. He had eaten no food since mid-day, he told me early in his narrative, and I found some mutton and bread in the pantry and brought it into the room. We lit no lamp, for fear of attracting the Martians, and ever and again our hands would touch upon bread or meat. As he talked, things about us came darkly out of the darkness, and the trampled bushes and broken rose trees outside the window grew distinct. It would seem that a number of men or animals had rushed across the lawn. I began to see his face, blackened and haggard, as no doubt mine was also.

When we had finished eating we went softly upstairs to my study, and I looked again out of the open window. In one night the valley had become a valley of ashes. The fires had dwindled now. Where flames had been there were now streamers of smoke; but the countless ruins of shattered and gutted houses and blasted and blackened trees that the night had hidden stood out now gaunt and terrible in the pitiless light of dawn. Yet here and there some object had had the luck to escape—a white railway signal here, the end of a green-

9. Disjointed, told in oaths and exclamations.

house there, white and fresh amidst the wreckage. Never before in the history of warfare[10] had destruction been so indiscriminate and so universal. And, shining with the growing light of the east, three of the metallic giants stood about the pit, their cowls rotating as though they were surveying the desolation they had made.

It seemed to me that the pit had been enlarged, and ever and again puffs of vivid green vapour streamed up out of it towards the brightening dawn—streamed up, whirled, broke and vanished.

Beyond were the pillars of fire[11] about Chobham. They became pillars of bloodshot smoke at the first touch of day.

10. In many ways, *The War of the Worlds* is a startling anticipation of the grim and unprecedented realities of World Wars I and II. But the novel itself arises from a long tradition of speculations on the future "history of warfare," without which it probably would not or could not have been written. During the massive weapons development and military conscription of the late nineteenth century, numerous fictions were written to warn of the dangers of sudden invasion and military unpreparedness. The first and most famous of these was *The Battle of Dorking* (1871) by Sir George Tomkyns Chesney, which described the invasion of England by Germany; the form became a popular but—except for Wells—now forgotten subgenre throughout Europe.
11. In Exodus 15:21-22, God sends a pillar of fire to guide the Israelites through the Sinai Desert by night, and a pillar of cloud to guide them by day.

CHAPTER TWELVE

WHAT I SAW OF THE DESTRUCTION OF WEYBRIDGE AND SHEPPERTON

As the dawn grew brighter we withdrew ourselves from the window from which we had watched the Martians, and went very quietly downstairs.

The artilleryman agreed with me that the house was no place to stay in. He proposed, he said, to make his way Londonwards, and thence rejoin his battery[1]—No. 12, of the Horse Artillery. My plan

1. Four to eight guns in the Horse Artillery of the time.

was to return at once to Leatherhead, and so greatly had the strength of the Martians impressed me that I had determined to take my wife to Newhaven, and go with her out of the country forthwith. For I already perceived clearly that the country about London must inevitably be the scene of a disastrous struggle before such creatures as these could be destroyed.

Between us and Leatherhead, however, lay the third cylinder, with its guarding giants. Had I been alone, I think I should have taken my chance and struck across country. But the artilleryman dissuaded me: 'It's no kindness to the right sort of wife,' he said, 'to make her a widow'; and in the end I agreed to go with him, under cover of the woods, northward as far as Street Chobham before I parted with him. Thence I would make a big detour by Epsom to reach Leatherhead.

I should have started at once, but my companion had been in active service, and he knew better than that. He made me ransack the house for a flask, which he filled with whisky; and we lined every available pocket with packets of biscuits and slices of meat. Then we crept out of the house, and ran as quickly as we could down the ill-made road by which I had come overnight. The houses seemed deserted. In the road lay a group of three charred bodies close together, struck dead by the Heat-Ray; and here and there were things that the people had dropped—a clock, a slipper, a silver spoon, and the like poor valuables. At the corner turning up towards the post office a little cart, filled with boxes and furniture, and horseless, heeled over on a broken wheel. A cash-box had been hastily smashed open, and thrown under the debris.

Except the lodge at the Orphanage, which was still on fire, none of the houses had suffered very greatly here. The Heat-Ray had shaved the chimney-tops and passed. Yet, save ourselves, there did not seem to be a living soul on Maybury Hill. The majority of the inhabitants had escaped, I suppose, by way of the Old Woking road—the road I had taken when I drove to Leatherhead—or they had hidden.

We went down the lane, by the body of the man in black, sodden now from the overnight hail, and broke into the woods at the foot of the hill. We pushed through these towards the railway, without meeting a soul. The woods across the line were but the scarred and blackened ruins of woods; for the most part the trees had fallen, but a certain proportion still stood, dismay grey stems, with dark-brown foliage instead of green.

On our side the fire had done no more than scorch the nearer trees; it had failed to secure its footing. In one place the woodmen had been at work on Saturday, trees, felled and freshly trimmed, lay in a clearing, with heaps of sawdust, by the sawing machine and its engine. Hard by was a temporary hut, deserted. There was not a breath of wind this morning, and everything was strangely still. Even the birds were hushed, and as we hurried along, I and the artilleryman talked in whispers, and looked now and again over our shoulders. Once or twice we stopped to listen.

After a time we drew near the road, and as we did so we heard the clatter of hoofs, and saw through the tree-stems three cavalry soldiers riding slowly towards Woking. We hailed them, and they halted while we hurried towards them. It was a lieutenant and a couple of privates of the 8th Hussars, with a stand like a theodolite, which the artilleryman told me was a heliograph.[2]

'You are the first men I've seen coming this way this morning,' said the lieutenant. 'What's brewing?'

His voice and face were eager. The men behind him stared curiously. The artilleryman jumped down the bank into the road and saluted.

'Gun destroyed last night, sir. Have been hiding. Trying to rejoin battery, sir. You'll come in sight of the Martians, I expect, about half a mile along this road.'

'What the dickens are they like?' asked the lieutenant.

2. A theodolite is a surveying instrument with a telescopic sight, for establishing horizontal and vertical angles. A heliograph was a moveable mirror, usually mounted on a tripod, used to transmit signals by sun flashes.

'Giants in armour, sir. Hundred feet high. Three legs and a body like 'luminium,[3] with a mighty great head in a hood, sir.'

'Get out!' said the lieutenant. 'What confounded nonsense!'

'You'll see, sir. They carry a kind of box, sir, that shoots fire and strikes you dead.'

'What d'ye mean—a gun?'

'No, sir,' and the artilleryman began a vivid account of the Heat-Ray. Half-way through the lieutenant interrupted him and looked up at me. I was still standing on the bank by the side of the road.

'Did you see it?' said the lieutenant.

'It's perfectly true,' I said.

'Well,' said the lieutenant, 'I suppose it's my business to see it too. Look here'—to the artilleryman—'we're detailed here clearing people out of their houses. You'd better go along and report yourself to Brigadier-General Marvin, and tell him all you know. He's at Weybridge. Know the way?'

'I do,' I said; and he turned his horse southward again.

'Half a mile, you say?' said he.

'At most,' I answered, and pointed over the tree-tops southward. He thanked me and rode on, and we saw them no more.

Further along we came upon a group of three women and two children in the road, busy clearing out a labourer's cottage. They had got hold of a little hand-truck, and were piling it up with unclean-looking bundles and shabby furniture. They were all too assiduously engaged to talk to us as we passed.

By Byfleet Station we emerged from the pine trees, and found the country calm and peaceful under the morning sunlight. We were far beyond the range of the Heat-Ray there, and had it not been for the silent desertion of some of the houses, the stirring movement of packing in others, and the knot of soldiers standing on the bridge

3. First isolated in 1825, aluminum ("aluminium," in British usage) began to be produced in massive quantities only after the discovery, in 1866, of a cheap method of production by electrolysis.

over the railway and staring down the line towards Woking, the day would have seemed very like any other Sunday.

Several farm wagons and carts were moving creakily along the road to Addlestone, and suddenly through the gate of a field we saw, across a stretch of flat meadow, six twelve-pounders,[4] standing neatly at equal distances and pointing towards Woking. The gunners stood by the guns waiting, and the ammunition wagons were at a business-like distance. The men stood almost as if under inspection.

'That's good!' said I. 'They will get one fair shot, at any rate.'

The artilleryman hesitated at the gate.

'I shall go on,' he said.

Further on towards Weybridge, just over the bridge, there were a number of men in white fatigue jackets throwing up a long rampart, and more guns behind.

'It's bows and arrows against the lightning, anyhow,' said the artilleryman. 'They 'aven't seen that fire-beam yet.'

The officers who were not actively engaged stood and stared over the tree-tops south-westward, and the men digging would stop every now and again to stare in the same direction.

Byfleet was in a tumult, people packing, and a score of hussars, some of them dismounted, some on horseback, were hunting them about. Three or four black Government wagons, with crosses in white circles,[5] and an old omnibus, among other vehicles, were being loaded in the village street. There were scores of people, most of them sufficiently Sabbatical[6] to have assumed their best clothes. The soldiers were having the greatest difficulty in making them re-

---

4. Guns capable of firing a twelve-pound ball. Heavy artillery, like every other aspect of warfare, underwent a gigantic growth in the late nineteenth century—especially after the German munitions maker, Alfred Krupp, developed the first all-steel gun in 1851.

5. The insignia, then as now, of the Red Cross, founded in 1864 as a result of the Geneva Convention on international warfare.

6. That is, dressed for the Sabbath, or Sunday—ironically, the day of rest and peace.

alize the gravity of their position. We saw one shrivelled old fellow with a huge box and a score or more of flower-pots containing orchids, angrily expostulating with the corporal who would leave them behind. I stopped and gripped his arm.

'Do you know what's over there?' I said, pointing at the pine-tops that hid the Martians.

'Eh?' said he, turning. 'I was explainin' these is vallyble.'

'Death!' I shouted. 'Death is coming! Death!' and, leaving him to digest that if he could, I hurried on after the artilleryman. At the corner I looked back. The soldier had left him, and he was still standing by his box with the pots of orchids on the lid of it, and staring vaguely over the trees.

No one in Weybridge could tell us where the headquarters were established; the whole place was in such confusion as I had never seen in any town before. Carts, carriages everywhere, the most astonishing miscellany of conveyances and horseflesh. The respectable inhabitants of the place, men in golf and boating costumes, wives prettily dressed, were packing, riverside loafers, energetically helping, children excited, and, for the most part, highly delighted at this astonishing variation of their Sunday experiences. In the midst of it all the worthy vicar[7] was very pluckily holding an early celebration, and his bell was jangling out above the excitement.

I and the artilleryman, seated on the step of the drinking-fountain, made a very passable meal upon what we had brought with us. Patrols of soldiers—here no longer hussars, but grenadiers in white[8]—were warning people to move now or to take refuge in their cellars as soon as the firing began. We saw as we crossed the railway bridge that a growing crowd of people had assembled in and about the railway station, and the swarming platform was piled with boxes

7. The priest of a parish.
8. Originally, grenadiers were especially tall soldiers in a regiment employed to throw grenades. This practice was discontinued by the end of the eighteenth century, though the tallest and finest soldiers of their regiments continued to be called "grenadiers." After 1858, the only regiment officially referred to by the name was the Grenadier Guards, the First Regiment of the Household Cavalry.

and packages. The ordinary traffic had been stopped, I believe, in order to allow of the passage of troops and guns to Chertsey, and I had heard since that a savage struggle occurred for places in the special trains that were put on at a later hour.

We remained at Weybridge until midday, and at that hour we found ourselves at the place near Shepperton Lock where the Wey and Thames join. Part of the time we spent helping two old women to pack a little cart. The Wey has a treble mouth, and at this point boats are to be hired, and there was a ferry across the river. On the Shepperton side was an inn, with a lawn, and beyond that the tower of Shepperton Church—it has been replaced by a spire—rose above the trees.

Here we found an excited and noisy crowd of fugitives. As yet the flight had not grown to a panic, but there were already far more people than all the boats going to and fro could enable to cross. People came panting along under heavy burdens; one husband and wife were even carrying a small out-house door between them, with some of their household goods piled thereon. One man told us he meant to try to get away from Shepperton Station.

There was a lot of shouting, and one man was even jesting. The idea people seemed to have here was that the Martians were simply formidable human beings, who might attack and sack the town, to be certainly destroyed in the end. Every now and then people would glance nervously across the Wey, at the meadows towards Chertsey, but everything over there was still.

Across the Thames, except just where the boats landed, everything was quiet, in vivid contrast with the Surrey side. The people who landed there from the boats went tramping off down the lane. The big ferry-boat had just made a journey. Three or four soldiers stood on the lawn of the inn, staring and jesting at the fugitives, without offering to help. The inn was closed, as it was now within prohibited hours.[9]

'What's that!' cried a boatman, and 'Shut up, you fool!' said a man near me to a yelping dog. Then the sound came again, this

9. The hours of the day during which British pubs are required to close.

time from the direction of Chertsey, a muffled thud—the sound of a gun.

The fighting was beginning. Almost immediately unseen batteries across the river to our right, unseen because of the trees, took up the chorus, firing heavily one after the other. A woman screamed. Everyone stood arrested by the sudden stir of battle, near us and yet invisible to us. Nothing was to be seen save flat meadows, cows feeding unconcernedly for the most part, and silvery pollard willows[10] motionless in the warm sunlight.

'The sojers 'll stop 'em,' said a woman beside me doubtfully. A haziness rose over the tree-tops.

Then suddenly we saw a rush of smoke far away up the river, a puff of smoke that jerked up into the air, and hung, and forthwith the ground heaved underfoot and a heavy explosion shook the air, smashing two or three windows in the houses near, and leaving us astonished.

'Here they are!' shouted a man in a blue jersey. 'Yonder! D'yer see them? Yonder!'

Quickly, one after the other, one, two, three, four of the armoured Martians appeared, far away over the little trees, across the flat meadows that stretch towards Chertsey, and striding hurriedly towards the river. Little cowled figures they seemed at first, going with a rolling motion and as fast as flying birds.

Then, advancing obliquely towards us, came a fifth. Their armoured bodies glittered in the sun, as they swept swiftly forward upon the guns, growing rapidly larger as they drew nearer. One on the extreme left, the remotest, that is, flourished a huge case high in the air, and the ghostly terrible Heat-Ray I had already seen on Friday night smote towards Chertsey, and struck the town.

At sight of these strange, swift, and terrible creatures, the crowd along by the water's edge seemed to me to be for a moment horror-struck. There was no screaming or shouting, but a silence. Then a hoarse murmur and a movement of feet—a splashing from the wa-

---

10. Willows cut back nearly to the trunk, so as to produce dense masses of branches.

ter. A man, too frightened to drop the portmanteau[11] he carried on his shoulder, swung round and sent me staggering with a blow from the corner of his burden. A woman thrust at me with her hand and rushed past me. I turned, too, with the rush of the people, but I was not too terrified for thought. The terrible Heat-Ray was in my mind. To get under water! That was it!

'Get under water!' I shouted unheeded.

I faced about again, and rushed towards the approaching Martian—rushed right down the gravelly beach and headlong into the water. Others did the same. A boatload of people putting back came leaping out as I rushed past. The stones under my feet were muddy and slippery, and the river was so low that I ran perhaps twenty feet scarcely waist-deep. Then, as the Martian towered overhead scarcely a couple of hundred yards away, I flung myself forward under the surface. The splashes of the people in the boats leaping into the river sounded like thunder-claps in my ears. People were landing hastily on both sides of the river.

But the Martian machine took no more notice for the moment of the people running this way and that than a man would of the confusion of ants in a nest against which his foot has kicked. When, half suffocated, I raised my head above water the Martian's hood pointed at the batteries that were still firing across the river, and as it advanced it swung loose what must have been the generator of the Heat-Ray.

In another moment it was on the bank, and in a stride wading half-way across. The knees of its foremost legs bent at the farther bank, and in another moment it had raised itself to its full height again, close to the village of Shepperton. Forthwith the six guns, which, unknown to anyone on the right bank, had been hidden behind the outskirts of that village, fired simultaneously. The sudden near concussions, the last close upon the first, made my heart jump. The monster was already raising the case generating the Heat-Ray, as the first shell burst six yards above the hood.

I gave a cry of astonishment. I saw and thought nothing of the

11. A large leather trunk or suitcase.

other four Martian monsters: my attention was riveted upon the nearer incident. Simultaneously two other shells burst in the air near the body as the hood twisted round in time to receive, but not in time to dodge, the fourth shell.

The shell burst clean in the face of the thing. The hood bulged, flashed, was whirled off in a dozen tattered fragments of glittering metal.

'Hit!' shouted I, with something between a scream and a cheer.

I heard answering shouts from the people in the water about me. I could have leapt out of the water with that momentary exultation.

The decapitated colossus reeled like a drunken giant; but it did not fall over. It recovered its balance by a miracle, and, no longer heeding its steps, and with the camera[12] that fired the Heat-Ray now rigidly upheld, it reeled swiftly upon Shepperton. The living intelligence, the Martian within the hood, was slain and splashed to the four winds of heaven, and the thing was now but a mere intricate device of metal whirling to destruction. It drove along in a straight line, incapable of guidance. It struck the tower of Shepperton Church, smashing it down as the impact of a battering-ram might have done, swerved aside, blundered on, and collapsed with a tremendous impact into the river out of my sight.

A violent explosion shook the air, and a spout of water, steam, mud, and shattered metal, shot far up into the sky. As the camera of the Heat-Ray hit the water, the latter had incontinently flashed into steam. In another moment a huge wave, like a muddy tidal bore,[13] but almost scaldingly hot, came sweeping round the bend up-stream. I saw people struggling shorewards, and heard their screaming and shouting faintly above the seething and roar of the Martian's collapse.

For the moment I heeded nothing of the heat, forgot the patent

12. The first portable camera, the Kodak, had been patented by George Eastman in 1888. Wells himself was an ardent amateur photographer.
13. An abrupt rise of the tidal water flowing inland from the mouth of an estuary.

need of self-preservation. I splashed through the tumultuous water, pushing aside a man in black to do so, until I could see round the bend. Half a dozen deserted boats pitched aimlessly upon the confusion of the waves. The fallen Martian came into sight downstream, lying across the river, and for the most part submerged.

Thick clouds of steam were pouring off the wreckage, and through the tumultuously whirling wisps I could see, intermittently and vaguely, the gigantic limbs churning the water and flinging a splash and spray of mud and froth into the air. The tentacles swayed and struck like living arms, and, save for the helpless purposelessness of these movements, it was as if some wounded thing struggled for life amidst the waves. Enormous quantities of a ruddy brown fluid were spurting up in noisy jets out of the machine.

My attention was diverted from this sight by a furious yelling, like that of the thing called a siren[14] in our manufacturing towns. A man, knee-deep near the towing-path,[15] shouted inaudibly to me and pointed. Looking back, I saw the other Martians advancing with gigantic strides down the river-bank from the direction of Chertsey. The Shepperton guns spoke this time unavailingly.

At that I ducked at once under water, and, holding my breath until movement was an agony, blundered painfully along under the surface as long as I could. The water was in a tumult about me, and rapidly growing hotter.

When for a moment I raised my head to take breath, and throw the hair and water from my eyes, the steam was rising in a whirling white fog that at first hid the Martians altogether. The noise was deafening. Then I saw them dimly, colossal figures of grey, magnified by the mist. They had passed by me, and two were stooping over the frothing tumultuous ruins of their comrade.

The third and fourth stood beside him in the water, one perhaps

14. The word was still new at the time, and referred primarily to factory whistles.
15. A path along the bank of a river for the horses or men who tow boats on the river.

200 yards from me, the other towards Laleham. The generators of the Heat-Rays waved high, and the hissing beams smote down this way and that.

The air was full of sound, a deafening and confusing conflict of noises, the clangorous din of the Martians, the crash of falling houses, the thud of trees, fences, sheds, flashing into flame, and the crackling and roaring of fire. Dense black smoke was leaping up to mingle with the steam from the river, and as the Heat-Ray went to and fro over Weybridge, its impact was marked by flashes of incandescent white, that gave place at once to a smoky dance of lurid flames. The nearer houses still stood intact, awaiting their fate, shadowy, faint and pallid in the steam, with the fire behind them going to and fro.

For a moment, perhaps, I stood there, breast-high in the almost boiling water, dumbfounded at my position, hopeless of escape. Through the reek I could see the people who had been with me in the river scrambling out of the water through the reeds, like little frogs hurrying through grass from the advance of a man, or running to and fro in utter dismay on the towing-path.

Then suddenly the white flashes of the Heat-Ray came leaping towards me. The houses caved in as they dissolved at its touch, and darted out flames; the trees changed to fire with a roar. It flickered up and down the towing-path, licking off the people who ran this way and that, and came down to the water's edge not fifty yards from where I stood. It swept across the river to Shepperton, and the water in its track rose in a boiling wheal[16] crested with steam. I turned shoreward.

In another moment the huge wave, well-night at the boiling-point, had rushed upon me. I screamed aloud, and scalded, half blinded, agonized, I staggered through the leaping, hissing water towards the shore. Had my foot stumbled, it would have been the end. I fell helplessly, in full sight of the Martians, upon the broad, bare gravelly spit that runs down to mark the angle of the Wey and Thames. I expected nothing but death.

16. Welt or ridge.

I have a dim memory of the foot of a Martian coming down within a score of yards of my head, driving straight into the loose gravel, whirling it this way and that, and lifting again; of a long suspense, and then of the four carrying the débris of their comrade between them, now clear, and then presently faint, through a veil of smoke, receding interminably, as it seemed to me, across a vast space of river and meadow. And then, very slowly, I realized that by a miracle I had escaped.

CHAPTER THIRTEEN
HOW I FELL IN WITH THE CURATE[1]

After giving this sudden lesson in the power of terrestrial weapons, the Martians retreated to their original position upon Horsell Common, and in their haste, and encumbered with the debris of their smashed companion, they no doubt overlooked many such a stray and unnecessary victim as myself. Had they left their comrade, and pushed on forthwith, there was nothing at that time between them and London but batteries of twelve-pounder guns, and they would certainly have reached the capital in advance of the tidings of their approach; as sudden, dreadful and destructive their advent would have been as the earthquake that destroyed Lisbon a century ago.[2]

But they were in no hurry. Cylinder followed cylinder in its interplanetary flight; every twenty-four hours brought them reinforcement. And meanwhile the military and naval authorities, now fully alive to the tremendous power of their antagonists, worked with furious energy. Every minute a fresh gun came into position, until, before twilight, every copse, every row of suburban villas on the hilly slopes about Kingston and Richmond, masked an expectant

1. A clergyman employed to assist the rector or vicar of a parish.
2. The Lisbon earthquake, on November 1, 1755, produced tremors felt throughout Europe, destroyed almost the entire city, and killed thirty thousand people.

black muzzle. And through the charred and desolated area—perhaps twenty square miles altogether—that encircled the Martian encampment on Horsell Common, through charred and ruined villages among the green trees, through the blackened and smoking arcades that had been but a day ago pine spinneys,[3] crawled the devoted scouts with the heliographs that were presently to warn the gunners of the Martian approach. But the Martians now understood our command of artillery and the danger of human proximity, and not a man ventured within a mile of either cylinder, save at the price of his life.

It would seem these giants spent the earlier part of the afternoon in going to and fro, transferring everything from the second and third cylinders—the second in Addlestone Golf Links, and the third at Pyrford—to their original pit on Horsell Common. Over that, above the blackened heather and ruined buildings that stretched far and wide, stood one as sentinel, while the rest abandoned their vast fighting machines and descended into the pit. They were hard at work there far into the night, and the towering pillar of dense green smoke that rose therefrom could be seen from the hills about Merrow, and even, it is said, from Banstead and Epsom Downs.

And while the Martians behind me were thus preparing for their next sally, and in front of me Humanity gathered for the battle, I made my way, with infinite pains and labour, from the fire and smoke of burning Weybridge towards London.

I saw an abandoned boat, very small and remote, drifting downstream, and, throwing off the most of my sodden clothes, I went after it, gained it, and so escaped out of that destruction. There were no oars in the boat, but I contrived to paddle, as much as my parboiled hands would allow, down the river towards Halliford and Walton, going very tediously, and continually looking behind me, as you may well understand. I followed the river because I considered the water gave me my best chance of escape, should these giants return.

The hot water from the Martian's overthrow drifted down-stream

3. Small woods or thickets.

with me, so that for the best part of a mile I could see little of either bank. Once, however, I made out a string of black figures hurrying across the meadows from the direction of Weybridge. Halliford, it seemed, was quite deserted, and several of the houses facing the river were on fire. It was strange to see the place quite tranquil, quite desolate under the hot blue sky, with the smoke and little threads of flame going straight up into the heat of the afternoon. Never before had I seen houses burning without the accompaniment of an inconvenient crowd.[4] A little farther on the dry reeds up the bank were smoking and glowing, and a line of fire inland was marching steadily across a late field of hay.

For a long time I drifted, so painful and weary was I after the violence I had been through, and so intense the heat upon the water. Then my fears got the better of me again, and I resumed my paddling. The sun scorched my bare back. At last, the bridge at Walton was coming into sight round the bend, my fever and faintness overcame my fears, and I landed on the Middlesex bank, and lay down, deadly sick, amidst the long grass. I suppose the time was then about four or five o'clock. I got up presently, walked perhaps half a mile without meeting a soul, and then lay down again in the shadow of a hedge. I seem to remember talking wanderingly to myself during that last spurt. I was also very thirsty, and bitterly regretful I had drunk no more water. It is a curious thing that I felt angry with my wife; I cannot account for it, but my impotent desire to reach Leatherhead worried me excessively.

I do not clearly remember the arrival of the curate, so that I probably dozed. I became aware of him as a seated figure in soot-smudged shirt-sleeves, and with his upturned clean-shaven face staring at a faint flickering that danced over the sky. The sky was what is called a mackerel sky, rows and rows of faint down-plumes of cloud, just tinted with the midsummer sunset.

I sat up, and at the rustle of my motion he looked at me quickly.

'Have you any water?' I asked abruptly.

He shook his head.

4. Another grim prophecy of the First World War.

'You have been asking for water for the last hour,' he said.

For a moment we were silent, taking stock of one another. I dare say he found me a strange enough figure, naked save for my water-soaked trousers and socks, scalded, and my face and shoulders blackened from the smoke. His face was a fair weakness, his chin retreated, and his hair lay in crisp, almost flaxen curls on his low forehead; his eyes were rather large, pale blue, and blankly staring. He spoke abruptly, looking vacantly away from me.

'What does it mean?' he said. 'What do these things mean?'

I stared at him and made no answer.

He extended a thin white hand and spoke in almost a complaining tone.

'Why are these things permitted? What sins have we done? The morning service was over, I was walking through the roads to clear my brain for the afternoon, and then—fire, earthquake, death! As if it were Sodom and Gomorrah![5] All our work undone, all the work . . . What are these Martians?'

'What are we?' I answered, clearing my throat.

He gripped his knees and turned to look at me again. For half a minute, perhaps, he stared silently.

'I was walking through the roads to clear my brains,' he said. 'And suddenly fire, earthquake, death!'

He relapsed into silence, with his chin now sunken almost to his knees.

Presently he began waving his hand:

'All the work—all the Sunday schools. What have we done—what has Weybridge done? Everything gone—everything destroyed. The church! We rebuilt it only three years ago. Gone!—swept out of existence! Why?'

Another pause, and he broke out again like one demented.

'The smoke of her burning goeth up for ever and ever!'[6] he shouted.

5. In Genesis 18:20-28, the Lord sends fire from heaven to destroy the sinful people of Sodom and Gomorrah.
6. A slightly inaccurate quotation from Genesis 18:28.

His eyes flamed, and he pointed a lean finger in the direction of Weybridge.

By this time I was beginning to take his measure. The tremendous tragedy in which he had been involved—it was evident that he was a fugitive from Weybridge—had driven him to the very verge of his reason.

'Are we far from Sunbury?' I said in a matter-of-fact tone.

'What are we to do?' he asked. 'Are these creatures everywhere? Has the earth been given over to them?'

'Are we far from Sunbury?'

'Only this morning I officiated at early celebration . . .'

'Things have changed,' I said quietly. 'You must keep your head. There is still hope.'

'Hope!'

'Yes; plentiful hope—for all this destruction!'

I began to explain my view of our position. He listened at first, but as I went on the interest in his eyes changed to their former stare, and his regard wandered from me.

'This must be the beginning of the end,' he said, interrupting me. 'The end! The great and terrible day of the Lord! When men shall call upon the mountains and the rocks to fall upon them and hide them—hide them from the face of Him that sitteth upon the throne!'[7]

I began to understand the position. I ceased my laboured reasoning, struggled to my feet, and, standing over him, laid my hand on his shoulder.

'Be a man,' said I. 'You are scared out of your wits. What good is religion if it collapses at calamity? Think of what earthquakes and floods, wars and volcanoes, have done before to men. Did you think God had exempted Weybridge? . . . He is not an insurance agent, man.'

For a time he sat in blank silence.

'But how can we escape?' he asked suddenly. 'They are invulnerable, they are pitiless. . . .'

7. Another slightly inaccurate quotation, this one from Revelation 6:16-17, describing the end of the world.

'Neither the one nor, perhaps, the other,' I answered. 'And the mightier they are, the more sane and wary should we be. One of them was killed yonder not three hours ago.'

'Killed!' he said, staring about him. 'How can God's ministers be killed?'

'I saw it happen,' I proceeded to tell him. 'We have chanced to come in for the thick of it,' said I, 'and that is all.'

'What is that flicker in the sky?' he asked abruptly.

I told him it was the heliograph signalling—that it was the sign of human help and effort in the sky.

'We are in the midst of it,' I said, 'quiet as it is. That flicker in the sky tells of the gathering storm. Yonder, I take it, are the Martians, and Londonward, where those hills rise about Richmond and Kingston, and the trees give cover, earthworks are being thrown up and guns are being laid. Presently the Martians will be coming this way again. . . .'

And even as I spoke, he sprang to his feet and stopped me by a gesture.

'Listen!' he said. . . .

From beyond the low hills across the water came the dull resonance of distant guns and a remote, weird crying. Then everything was still. A cockchafer[8] came droning over the hedge and past us. High in the west the crescent moon hung faint and pale, above the smoke of Weybridge and Shepperton and the hot still splendour of the sunset.

'We had better follow this path,' I said, 'northward.'[9]

8. The European scarab beetle.
9. "Northward" is the movement of the whole book: of the Martian invasion, of the successive landings of the cylinders, and of the narrator's own wanderings. Uttered here, the word is a cue—almost a stage direction—for the radical shift in point of view in the following chapter.

CHAPTER FOURTEEN

IN LONDON

My younger brother[1] was in London when the Martians fell at Woking. He was a medical student, working for an imminent examination, and he heard nothing of the arrival until Saturday morning. The morning papers on Saturday contained, in addition to lengthy special articles on the planet Mars, on life in the planets, and so forth, a brief and vaguely-worded telegram, all the more striking for its brevity.

The Martians, alarmed by the approach of a crowd, had killed a number of people with a quick-firing gun, so the story ran. The telegram concluded with the words: 'Formidable as they seem to be, the Martians have not moved from the pit into which they have fallen, and, indeed, seem incapable of doing so. Probably this is due to the relative strength of the earth's gravitational energy.' On that last text the leader-writers expanded very comfortingly.

Of course, all the students in the crammer's[2] biology class, to which my brother went that day, were intensely interested, but there were no signs of any unusual excitement in the streets. The afternoon papers puffed scraps of news under big headlines. They had nothing to tell beyond the movements of troops about the common, and the burning of the pine-woods between Woking and Weybridge, until eight. Then the St James's Gazette,[3] in an extra special edition, announced the bare fact of the interruption of telegraphic

1. For the next four chapters, Wells shifts the main point of view from the narrator to the narrator's brother in London: a technical feat of some brilliance. For by doing this Wells enhances the verisimilitude of his most violent scenes, the panic in London and the mass exodus to the north—being presented at second hand, they gain rather than lose conviction. And also, by suspending most of the narrator's own story till the beginning of Book II, he increases the suspense of the whole novel.
2. An advanced student or younger teacher who, for a fee, tutors other students in preparation for their examinations.
3. An evening paper published from 1880 to 1905.

communication. This was thought to be due to the falling of burning pine trees across the line. Nothing more of the fighting was known that night, the night of my drive to Leatherhead and back.

My brother felt no anxiety about us, as he knew from the description in the papers that the cylinder was a good two miles from my house. He made up his mind to run down that night to me, in order, as he says, to see the things before they were killed. He despatched a telegram, which never reached me, about four o'clock, and spent the evening at a music-hall.

In London, also, on Saturday night there was a thunderstorm, and my brother reached Waterloo in a cab. On the platform from which the midnight train usually starts he learnt, after some waiting, that an accident prevented trains from reaching Woking that night. The nature of the accident he could not ascertain; indeed, the railway authorities did not clearly know at that time. There was very little excitement in the station, as the officials, failing to realize that anything further than a breakdown between Byfleet and Woking Junction had occurred, were running the theatre trains, which usually passed through Woking, round by Virginia Water or Guildford. They were busy making the necessary arrangements to alter the route of the Southampton and Portsmouth Sunday League[4] excursions. A nocturnal newspaper reporter, mistaking my brother for the traffic manager, whom he does to a slight extent resemble, waylaid and tried to interview him. Few people, excepting the railway officials, connected the breakdown with the Martians.

I have read, in another account of these events, that on Sunday morning 'all London was electrified by the news from Woking.' As a matter of fact, there was nothing to justify that very extravagant phrase. Plenty of people in London did not hear of the Martians until the panic of Monday morning. Those who did took some time to realize all that the hastily-worded telegrams in the Sunday papers conveyed. The majority of people in London do not read Sunday papers.

4. One of a number of religious groups which gathered to protest the opening of pubs on the Sabbath.

The habit of personal security, moreover, is so deeply fixed in the Londoner's mind, and startling intelligence so much a matter of course in the papers, that they could read without any personal tremors: 'About seven o'clock last night the Martians came out of the cylinder, and, moving about under an armour of metallic shields, have completely wrecked Woking Station, with the adjacent houses, and massacred an entire battalion of the Cardigan Regiment. No details are known. Maxims have been absolutely useless against their armour; the field-guns have been disabled by them. Flying hussars[5] have been galloping into Chertsey. The Martians appear to be moving slowly towards Chertsey or Windsor. Great anxiety prevails in West Surrey, and earthworks are being thrown up to check the advance Londonwards.' That was how the *Sunday Sun* put it, and a clever and remarkable prompt 'hand-book' article in the *Referee*[6] compared the affair to a menagerie suddenly let loose in a village.

No one in London knew positively of the nature of the armoured Martians, and there was still a fixed idea that these monsters must be sluggish: 'crawling,' 'creeping painfully'—such expressions occurred in almost all the earlier reports. None of the telegrams could have been written by an eye-witness of their advance. The Sunday papers printed separate editions as further news came to hand, some even in default of it. But there was practically nothing more to tell people until late in the afternoon, when the authorities gave the press agencies the news in their possession. It was stated that the people of Walton and Weybridge, and all that district, were pouring along the roads Londonward, and that was all.

My brother went to church at the Foundling Hospital[7] in the morning, still in ignorance of what had happened on the previous night. There he heard allusions made to the invasion, and a special

5. Light cavalry specializing in swift attack.
6. Two evening papers. The *Sun* was published 1893-1906, the *Referee* 1877-1928.
7. One of the first hospitals and nurseries for abandoned or illegitimate children, the Foundling Hospital was founded in 1739 in the London district of Bloomsbury.

prayer for peace. Coming out, he bought a *Referee*. He became alarmed at the news in this, and went again to Waterloo Station to find out if communication were restored. The omnibuses, carriages, cyclists, and innumerable people walking in their best clothes, seemed scarcely affected by the strange intelligence that the news-vendors were disseminating. People were interested, or, if alarmed, alarmed only on account of the local residents. At the station he heard for the first time that the Windsor and Chertsey lines were now interrupted. The porters hold him that several remarkable tele-grams had been received in the morning from Byfleet and Chertsey Stations, but that these had abruptly ceased. My brother could get very little precise detail out of them. 'There's fighting going on about Weybridge,' was the extent of their information.

The train service was now very much disorganized. Quite a num-ber of people, who had been expecting friends from places on the South-Western network,[8] were standing about the station. One grey-headed old gentleman came and abused the South-Western Company bitterly to my brother. 'It wants showing up,' he said.

One or two trains came in from Richmond, Putney, and Kings-ton, containing people who had gone out for a day's boating, and found the locks closed and a feeling of panic in the air. A man in a blue and white blazer addressed my brother, full of strange tidings.

'There's hosts of people driving into Kingston in traps[9] and carts and things, with boxes of valuables and all that,' he said. 'They come from Molesey and Weybridge and Walton, and they say there's been guns heard at Chertsey, heavy firing, and that mounted soldiers have told them to get off at once because the Martians are coming. *We* heard guns firing at Hampton Court Station, but we thought it was thunder. What the dickens does it all mean? The Martians can't get out of their pit, can they?'

8. The London transit system grew rapidly after the passage, in 1870, of the Tramways Act, establishing horsedrawn trams from the burgeoning suburbs to the central city. But it was not until 1890 that the first "tube" or underground railway was opened from south London into the City.
9. Light, two-wheeled carriages.

My brother could not tell him.

Afterwards he found that the vague feeling of alarm had spread to the clients of the underground railway, and that the Sunday excursionists began to return from all the South-Western 'lungs'—Barnes, Wimbledon, Richmond Park, Kew, and so forth—at unnaturally early hours;[10] but not a soul had anything but vague hearsay to tell of. Everyone connected with the terminus seemed ill-tempered.

About five o'clock the gathering crowd in the station was immensely excited by the opening of the line of communication, which is almost invariably closed, between the South-Eastern and the South-Western stations, and the passage of carriage-trucks bearing huge guns, and carriages crammed with soldiers. These were the guns that were brought up from Woolwich and Chatham to cover Kingston. There was an exchange of pleasantries: 'You'll get eaten!' 'We're the beast-tamers!' and so forth. A little while after that a squad of police came into the station, and began to clear the public off the platforms, and my brother went out into the street again.

The church bells were ringing for evensong, and a squad of Salvation Army lasses[11] came singing down Waterloo Road. On the bridge a number of loafers were watching a curious brown scum that came drifting down the stream in patches. The sun was just setting, and the Clock Tower and the Houses of Parliament rose against one of the most peaceful skies it is possible to imagine, a sky of gold, barred with long transverse stripes of reddish-purple gold. There was talk of a floating body. One of the men there, a reservist[12] he said he was, told my brother he had seen the heliograph flickering in the west.

10. That is, the authorities are blocking off the area from which the Martian invasion comes.
11. The Salvation Army was founded in 1878 by the Methodist minister and social worker William Booth, for the purpose of aiding the inhabitants of the terrible slums in the East End of London.
12. The reorganization of the British Army included an emphasis upon the reserve forces; but there was considerable doubt throughout the years before World War I whether a "reserve" soldier would really be able to function in a battlefield situation.

In Wellington Street my brother met a couple of sturdy roughs, who had just rushed out of Fleet Street with still wet newspapers and staring placards. 'Dreadful catastrophe!' they bawled one to the other down Wellington Street. 'Fighting at Weybridge! Full description! Repulse of the Martians! London said to be in danger!' He had to give threepence for a copy of that paper.

Then it was, and then only, that he realized something of the full power and terror of these monsters. He learnt that they were not merely a handful of small sluggish creatures, but that they were minds swaying vast mechanical bodies, and that they could move swiftly and smite with such power that even the mightiest guns could not stand against them.

They were described as 'vast spider-like machines, nearly a hundred feet high, capable of the speed of an express train, and able to shoot out a beam of intense heat.' Masked batteries, chiefly of field-guns,[13] had been planted in the country about Horsell Common, and especially between the Woking district and London. Five of the machines had been seen moving towards the Thames, and one, by a freak of chance, had been destroyed. In the other cases the shells had missed, and the batteries had been at once annihilated by the Heat-Rays. Heavy losses of soldiers were mentioned, but the tone of the despatch was optimistic.

The Martians had been repulsed; they were not invulnerable. They had retreated to their triangle of cylinders again, in the circle about Woking. Signallers with heliographs were pushing forward upon them from all sides. Guns were in rapid transit from Windsor, Portsmouth, Aldershot, Woolwich—even from the north; among others, long wire guns of ninety-five tons[14] from Woolwich. Altogether one hundred and sixteen were in position or being hastily

---

13. Heavy cannon mounted on carriages.
14. Field pieces with finely-wound wire, coiled under tension, inside their barrels. An early form of rifling (introduced in 1855), the wire coil made it possible to construct a much thinner and lighter barrel than previously, and also increased greatly the effective range of the projectile. Wire guns were used extensively during the period, and in the First World War.

laid, chiefly covering London. Never before in England had there been such a vast or rapid concentration of military material.

Any further cylinders that fell, it was hoped, could be destroyed at once by high explosives, which were being rapidly manufactured and distributed. No doubt, ran the report, the situation was of the strangest and gravest description, but the public was exhorted to avoid and discourage panic. No doubt the Martians were strange and terrible in the extreme, but at the outside there could not be more than twenty of them against our millions.

The authorities had reason to suppose, from the size of the cylinders, that at the outside there could not be more than five in each cylinder—fifteen altogether. And one at least was disposed of—perhaps more. The public would be fairly warned of the approach of danger, and elaborate measures were being taken for the protection of the people in the threatened south-western suburbs. And so, with reiterated assurances of the safety of London, and the confidence of the authorities to cope with the difficulty, this *quasi* proclamation[15] closed.

This was printed in enormous type, so fresh that the paper was still wet, and there had been no time to add a word of comment. It was curious, my brother said, to see how ruthlessly the other contents of the paper had been hacked and taken out to give this place.

All down Wellington Street, people could be seen fluttering out the pink sheets and reading, and the Strand was suddenly noisy with the voices of an army of hawkers following these pioneers. Men came scrambling off buses to secure copies. Certainly this news excited people intensely, whatever their previous apathy. The shutters of a map-shop in the Strand were being taken down, my brother said, and a man in his Sunday raiment, lemon-yellow gloves[16] even, was visible inside the window, hastily fastening maps of Surrey to the glass.

Going on along the Strand to Trafalgar Square, the paper in his

15. That is, an official statement which does not quite claim to *be* an official statement.
16. Highly fashionable, even somewhat dandified, at the time.

hand, my brother saw some of the fugitives from West Surrey. There was a man driving a cart such as greengrocers use, and his wife and two boys and some articles of furniture. He was driving from the direction of Westminster Bridge, and close behind him came a hay-wagon with five or six respectable-looking people in it, and some boxes and bundles. The faces of these people were haggard, and their entire appearance contrasted conspicuously with the Sabbath-best appearance of the people on the omnibuses. People in fashionable clothing peeped at them out of cabs. They stopped at the Square as if undecided which way to take, and finally turned eastward along the Strand. Some way after these came a man in work-day clothes, riding one of those old-fashioned tricycles[17] with a small front wheel. He was dirty and white in the face.

My brother turned down towards Victoria, and met a number of such people. He had a vague idea that he might see something of me. He noticed an unusual number of police regulating the traffic. Some of the refugees were exchanging news with the people on the omnibuses. One was professing to have seen the Martians. 'Boilers on stilts, I tell you, striding along like men.' Most of them were excited and animated by their strange experience.

Beyond Victoria the public-houses were doing a lively trade with these arrivals. At all the street corners groups of people were reading papers, talking excitedly, or staring at these unusual Sunday visitors. They seemed to increase as night drew on, until at last the roads, my brother said, were like the Epsom High Street on a Derby Day.[18] My brother addressed several of these fugitives and got unsatisfactory answers from most.

None of them could tell him any news of Woking except one man, who assured him that Woking had been entirely destroyed on the previous night.

'I come from Byfleet,' he said; 'a man on a bicycle came through the place in the early morning, and ran from door to door warning

17. The "Coventry" tricycle, two wheels with a much larger supporting wheel to one side, current around 1876.
18. The town of Epsom, south of London, is the annual site of the Derby.

us to come away. Then came soldiers. We went out to look, and there were clouds of smoke to the south—nothing but smoke, and not a soul coming that way. Then we heard the guns at Chertsey, and folks coming from Weybridge. So I've locked up my house and come on.'

At that time there was a strong feeling in the streets that the authorities were to blame for their incapacity to dispose of the invaders without all this inconvenience.

About eight o'clock, a noise of heavy firing was distinctly audible all over the south of London. My brother could not hear it for the traffic in the main streets, but by striking through the quiet back streets to the river he was able to distinguish it quite plainly.

He walked back from Westminster to his apartments near Regent's Park about two. He was now very anxious on my account, and disturbed at the evident magnitude of the trouble. His mind was inclined to run, even as mine had run on Saturday, on military details. He thought of all those silent expectant guns, of the suddenly nomadic countryside; he tried to imagine 'boilers on stilts' a hundred feet high.

There were one or two cart-loads of refugees passing along Oxford Street, and several in the Marylebone Road, but so slowly was the news spreading that Regent Street and Portland Road were full of their usual Sunday night promenaders, albeit they talked in groups, and along the edge of Regent's Park there were as many silent couples 'walking out'[19] together under the scattered gas-lamps[20] as ever there had been. The night was warm and still, and a little oppressive, the sound of guns continued intermittently, and after midnight there seemed to be sheet lightning in the south.

He read and re-read the paper, fearing the worst had happened to me. He was restless, and after supper prowled out again aimlessly. He returned and tried to divert his attention by his examina-

19. Courting.
20. The first practical electric light had been developed by Thomas Edison in 1879, but the cities of Europe and America were still lit by gas at the time of the story.

tion notes in vain. He went to bed a little after midnight, and he was awakened out of some lurid dreams in the small hours of Monday by the sound of door-knockers, feet running in the street, distant drumming, and a clamour of bells. Red reflections danced on the ceiling. For a moment he lay astonished, wondering whether day had come or the world had gone mad. Then he jumped out of bed and ran to the window.

His room was an attic, and as he thrust his head out, up and down the street there were a dozen echoes to the noise of his window-sash, and heads in every kind of night disarray appeared. Inquiries were being shouted. 'They are coming!' bawled a policeman, hammering at the door; 'the Martians are coming!' and hurried to the next door.

The noise of drumming and trumpeting came from the Albany Street Barracks, and every church within earshot was hard at work killing sleep with a vehement disorderly tocsin.[21] There was a noise of doors opening, and window after window in the houses opposite flashed from darkness into yellow illumination.

Up the street came galloping a closed carriage, bursting abruptly into noise at the corner, rising to a clattering climax under the window, and dying away slowly in the distance. Close on the rear of this came a couple of cabs, the forerunners of a long procession of flying vehicles, going for the most part to Chalk Farm Station, where the North-Western special trains were loading up, instead of coming down the gradient into Euston.

For a long time my brother stared out of the window in blank astonishment, watching the policemen hammering at door after door, and delivering their incomprehensible message. Then the door behind him opened, and the man who lodged across the landing came in, dressed only in shirt, trousers, and slippers, his braces loose about his waist, his hair disordered from his pillow.

'What the devil is it?' he asked. 'A fire? What a devil of a row!'

They both craned their heads out of the window, straining to

21. Alarm bell.

hear what the policemen were shouting. People were coming out of the side streets, and standing in groups at the corners talking.

'What the devil is it all about?' said my brother's fellow-lodger.

My brother answered him vaguely and began to dress, running with each garment to the window in order to miss nothing of the growing excitement of the streets. And presently men selling unnaturally early newspapers came bawling into the street:

'London in danger of suffocation! The Kingston and Richmond defences forced! Fearful massacres in the Thames Valley!'

And all about him—in the rooms below, in the houses on either side and across the road, and behind in the Park Terraces and in the hundred other streets of that part of Marylebone, and the Westbourne Park district and St Pancras, and westward and northward in Kilburn and St John's Wood and Hampstead, and eastward in Shoreditch and Highbury and Haggerston and Hoxton, and, indeed, through all the vastness of London from Ealing to East Ham—people were rubbing their eyes, and opening windows to stare out and ask aimless questions, and dressing hastily as the first breath of the coming storm of Fear blew through the streets. It was the dawn of the great panic. London, which had gone to bed on Sunday night stupid and inert, was awakened in the small hours of Monday morning to a vivid sense of danger.

Unable from his window to learn what was happening, my brother went down and out into the street, just as the sky between the parapets of the houses grew pink with the early dawn. The flying people on foot and in vehicles grew more numerous every moment. 'Black Smoke!' he heard people crying, and again 'Black Smoke!' The contagion of such a unanimous fear was inevitable. As my brother hesitated on the doorstep, he saw another newsvendor approaching him, and got a copy forthwith. The man was running away with the rest, and selling his papers as he ran for a shilling each[22]—a grotesque mingling of profit and panic.

22. A shilling was worth approximately twenty-five cents American in 1898. This was nearly fifty times the normal price of a newspaper.

And from this paper my brother read that catastrophic despatch of the Commander-in-Chief:

'The Martians are able to discharge enormous clouds of a black and poisonous vapour by means of rockets. They have smothered our batteries, destroyed Richmond, Kingston, and Wimbledon, and are advancing slowly towards London, destroying everything on the way. It is impossible to stop them. There is no safety from the Black Smoke but in instant flight.'

That was all, but it was enough. The whole population of the great six-million city was stirring, slipping, running; presently it would be pouring *en masse*[23] northward.

'Black Smoke!' the voices cried. 'Fire!'

The bells of the neighbouring church made a jangling tumult, a cart carelessly driven smashed amidst shrieks and curses against the water-trough up the street. Sickly yellow light went to and fro in the houses, and some of the passing cabs flaunted unextinguished lamps. And overhead the dawn was growing brighter, clear and steady and calm.

He heard footsteps running to and fro in the rooms, and up and down stairs behind him. His landlady came to the door, loosely wrapped in dressing-gown and shawl; her husband followed, ejaculating.

As my brother began to realize the import of all these things, he turned hastily to his own room, put all his available money—some ten pounds[24] altogether—into his pockets, and went out again into the streets.

23. In a body, in a crowd.
24. The equivalent of fifty dollars at the time.

CHAPTER FIFTEEN

WHAT HAD HAPPENED IN SURREY

It was while the curate had sat and talked so wildly to me under the hedge in the flat meadows near Halliford, and while my brother was watching the fugitives stream over Westminster Bridge, that the Martians had resumed the offensive. So far as one can ascertain from the conflicting accounts that have been put forth, the majority of them remained busied with preparations in the Horsell pit until nine that night, hurrying on some operation that disengaged huge volumes of green smoke.

But three certainly came out about eight o'clock, and, advancing slowly and cautiously, made their way through Byfleet and Pyrford towards Ripley and Weybridge, and so came in sight of the expectant batteries against the setting sun. These Martians did not advance in a body, but in a line, each perhaps a mile and a half from his nearest fellow. They communicated with each other by means of siren-like howls, running up and down the scale from one note to another.

It was this howling and the firing of the guns at Ripley and St George's Hill that we had heard at Upper Halliford. The Ripley gunners, unseasoned artillery volunteers who ought never to have been placed in such a position, fired one wild, premature, ineffectual volley, and bolted on horse and foot through the deserted village, and the Martian walked over their guns serenely without using his Heat-Ray, stepped gingerly among them, passed in front of them, and so came unexpectedly upon the guns in Painshill Park, which he destroyed.

The St George's Hill men, however, were better led or of a better mettle. Hidden by a pine wood as they were, they seem to have been quite unexpected by the Martian nearest to them. They laid their guns[1] as deliberately as if they had been on parade, and fired at about a thousand yards' range.

The shells flashed all round the Martian, and they saw him advance a few paces, stagger, and go down. Everybody yelled together, and the guns were re-loaded in frantic haste. The overthrown Martian set up a prolonged ululation,[2] and immediately a second glittering giant, answering him, appeared over the trees to

1. Prepared to fire.
2. Crying or moaning.

the south. It would seem that a leg of the tripod had been smashed by one of the shells. The whole of the second volley flew wide of the Martian on the ground, and simultaneously both his companions brought their Heat-Rays to bear on the battery. The ammunition blew up, the pine trees all about the guns flashed into fire, and only one or two of the men who were already running over the crest of the hill escaped.

After this it would seem that the three took counsel together and halted, and the scouts who were watching them report that they remained absolutely stationary for the next half-hour. The Martian who had been overthrown crawled tediously out of his hood, a small brown figure, oddly suggestive from that distance of a speck of blight, and apparently engaged in the repair of his support. About nine he had finished, for his cowl was then seen above the trees again.

It was a few minutes past nine that night when these three sentinels were joined by four other Martians, each carrying a thick black tube. A similar tube was handed to each of the three, and the seven proceeded to distribute themselves at equal distances along a curved line between St George's Hill, Weybridge, and the village of Send, south-west of Ripley.

A dozen rockets sprang out of the hills before them as soon as they began to move, and warned the waiting batteries about Ditton and Esher. At the same time four of their Fighting Machines, similarly armed with tubes, crossed the river, and two of them, black against the western sky, came into sight of myself and the curate as we hurried wearily and painfully along the road that runs northward out of Halliford. They moved, as it seemed to us, upon a cloud, for a milky mist covered the fields and rose to a third of their height.

At this sight the curate cried faintly in his throat, and began running; but I knew it was no good running from a Martian, and I turned aside and crawled through dewy nettles and brambles into the broad ditch by the side of the road. He looked back, saw what I was doing, and turned to join me.

The two Martians halted, the nearer to us standing and facing Sunbury, the remoter being a grey indistinctness towards the evening star, away towards Staines.

The occasional howling of the Martians had ceased; they took up their positions in the huge crescent about their cylinders in absolute silence. It was a crescent with twelve miles between its horns. Never since the devising of gunpowder was the beginning of a battle so still. To us and to an observer about Ripley it would have had precisely the same effect—the Martians seemed in solitary possession of the darkling night, lit only as it was by the slender moon, the stars, the after-glow of the daylight, and the ruddy glare from St George's Hill and the woods of Painshill.

But facing that crescent everywhere, at Staines, Hounslow, Ditton, Esher, Ockham, behind hills and woods south of the river, and across the flat grass meadows to the north of it, wherever a cluster of trees or village houses gave sufficient cover, the guns were waiting. The signal rockets burst and rained their sparks through the night and vanished, and the spirit of all those watching batteries rose to a tense expectation. The Martians had but to advance into the line of fire, and instantly those motionless black forms of men, those guns glittering so darkly in the early night, would explode into a thunderous fury of battle.

No doubt the thought that was uppermost in a thousand of those vigilant minds, even as it was uppermost in mine, was the riddle how much they understood of us. Did they grasp that we in our millions were organized, disciplined, working together? Or did they interpret our spurts of fire, the sudden stinging of our shells, our steady investment of their encampment, as we should the furious unanimity of onslaught in a disturbed hive of bees? Did they dream they might exterminate us? (At that time no one knew what food they needed.) A hundred such questions struggled together in my mind as I watched that vast sentinel shape. And in the back of my mind was the sense of all the huge unknown and hidden forces Londonward. Had they prepared pitfalls? Were the powder-mills at Hounslow ready as a snare? Would the Londoners have the heart and courage to make a greater Moscow[3] of their mighty province of houses?

Then, after an interminable time as it seemed to us, crouching and peering through the hedge, came a sound like the distant concussion of a gun. Another nearer, and then another. And then the Martian beside us raised his tube on high and discharged it gunwise, with a heavy report that made the ground heave. The Martian towards Staines answered him. There was no flash, no smoke, simply that loaded detonation.

I was so excited by these heavy minute-guns[4] following one another that I so far forgot my personal safety and my scalded hands as to clamber up into the hedge and stare towards Sunbury. As I did so a second report followed, and a big projectile hurtled overhead towards Hounslow. I expected at least to see smoke or fire or some other evidence of its work. But all I saw was the deep-blue sky above, with one solitary star, and the white mist spreading wide and low beneath. And there had been no crash, no answering explosion. The silence was restored; the minute lengthened to three.

'What has happened?' said the curate, standing up beside me.

'Heaven knows!' said I.

A bat flickered by and vanished. A distant tumult of shouting began and ceased. I looked again at the Martian, and saw he was now moving eastward along the river-bank, with a swift rolling motion.

Every moment I expected the fire of some hidden battery to spring upon him; but the evening calm was unbroken. The figure of the Martian grew smaller as he receded, and presently the mist and the gathering night had swallowed him up. By a common impulse we clambered higher. Towards Sunbury was a dark appearance, as though a conical hill had suddenly come into being there,

3. From September 2 to October 7, 1812, the French Army of Napoleon occupied Moscow, burning and destroying more than three-fourths of the city. They were finally compelled to retreat, however, due to Russian guerilla resistance and the impossibility of acquiring adequate provisions.
4. Guns designed to be fired at intervals of one minute.

hiding our view of the further country; and then, remoter across the river, over Walton, we saw another such summit. These hill-like forms grew lower and broader even as we stared.

Moved by a sudden thought, I looked northward, and there I perceived a third of these cloudy black kopjes[5] had arisen.

Everything had suddenly become very still. Far away to the south-east, marking the quiet, we heard the Martians hooting to one another, and then the air quivered again with the distant thud of their guns. But the earthly artillery made no reply.

Now, at the time we could not understand these things; but later I was to learn the meaning of these ominous kopjes that gathered in the twilight. Each of the Martians, standing in the great crescent I have described, had discharged at some unknown signal, by means of a gun-like tube he carried, a huge canister over whatever hill, copse, cluster of houses, or other possible cover for guns, chanced to be in front of him. Some fired only one of these, some two, as in the case of the one we had seen; the one at Ripley is said to have discharged no fewer than five at that time. These canisters smashed on striking the ground—they did not explode—and incontinently disengaged an enormous volume of a heavy inky vapour, coiling and pouring upwards in a huge and ebony cumulous cloud,[6] a gaseous hill that sank and spread itself slowly over the surrounding country. And the touch of that vapour, the inhaling of its pungent wisps, was death to all that breathes.

It was heavy, this vapour, heavier than the densest smoke, so that, after the first tumultuous uprush and outflow of its impact, it sank down through the air and poured over the ground in a manner rather liquid than gaseous, abandoning the hills, and streaming into the valleys and ditches and water-courses, even as I have heard the carbonic acid gas[7] that pours from volcanic clefts is wont to do. And where it came upon water some chemical action occurred,

5. Small hills or mounds.
6. A tall, dense, puffy cloud. Many readers during the First World War viewed this as a forecast of the use of poison gas.
7. Carbon dioxide.

and the surface would be instantly covered with a powdery scum that sank slowly and made way for more. The scum was absolutely insoluble, and it is a strange thing, seeing the instant effect of the gas, that one could drink the water from which it had been strained without hurt. The vapour did not diffuse as a true gas would do. It hung together in banks, flowing sluggishly down the slope of the land and driving reluctantly before the wind, and very slowly it combined with the mist and moisture of the air, and sank to the earth in the form of dust. Save that an unknown element giving a group of four lines in the blue of the spectrum[8] is concerned, we are still entirely ignorant of the nature of this substance.

Once the tumultuous upheaval of its dispersion was over, the black smoke clung so closely to the ground, even before its precipitation, that, fifty feet up in the air, on the roofs and upper stories of high houses and on great trees, there was a chance of escaping its poison altogether, as was proved even that night at Street Cobham and Ditton.

The man who escaped at the former place tells a wonderful story of the strangeness of its coiling flow, and how he looked down from the church spire and saw the houses of the village rising like ghosts out of its inky nothingness. For a day and a half he remained there, weary, starving, and sun-scorched, the earth under the blue sky and against the prospect of the distant hills a velvet black expanse, with red roofs, green trees, and, later, black-veiled shrubs and gates, barns, outhouses, and walls, rising here and there into the sunlight.

But that was at Street Cobham, where the black vapour was allowed to remain until it sank of its own accord into the ground. As a rule, the Martians, when it had served its purpose, cleared the air of it again by wading into it and directing a jet of steam upon it.

That they did with the vapour-banks near us, as we saw in the starlight from the window of a deserted house at Upper Halliford, whither we had returned. From there we could see the searchlights on Richmond Hill and Kingston Hill going to and fro, and about

8. A contradiction in the novel; see Book II, Chapter Ten, note 1.

eleven the window rattled, and we heard the sound of the huge siege guns[9] that had been put in position there. These continued intermittently for the space of a quarter of an hour, sending chance shots at the invisible Martians at Hampton and Ditton, and then the pale beams of the electric light vanished, and were replaced by a bright red glow.

Then the fourth cylinder fell—a brilliant green meteor—as I learnt afterwards, in Bushey Park. Before the guns on the Richmond and Kingston line of hills began, there was a fitful cannonade far away in the south-west, due, I believe, to guns being fired haphazard before the black vapour could overwhelm the gunners.

So, setting about it as methodically as men might smoke out a wasps' nest, the Martians spread this strange stifling vapour over the Londonward country. The horns of the crescent slowly spread apart, until at last they formed a line from Hanwell to Coombe and Malden. All night through their destructive tubes advanced. Never once, after the Martian at St George's Hill was brought down, did they give the artillery the ghost of a chance against them. Wherever there was a possibility of guns being laid for them unseen, a fresh canister of the black vapour was discharged, and where the guns were openly displayed the Heat-Ray was brought to bear.

By midnight the blazing trees along the slopes of Richmond Park, and the glare of Kingston Hill, threw their light upon a network of black smoke, blotting out the whole Valley of the Thames, and extending as far as the eye could reach. And through this two Martians slowly waded, and turned their hissing steam-jets this way and that.

The Martians were sparing of the Heat-Ray that night, either because they had but a limited supply of material for its production, or because they did not wish to destroy the country, but only to crush and overawe the opposition they had aroused. In the latter aim they certainly succeeded. Sunday night was the end of the organized opposition to their movements. After that no body of men

9. Heavy artillery.

could stand against them, so hopeless was the enterprise. Even the crews of the torpedo-boats and destroyers[10] that had brought their quick-firers up the Thames refused to stop, mutinied, and went down again. The only offensive operation men ventured upon after that night was the preparation of mines and pitfalls, and even in that men's energies were frantic and spasmodic.

One has to imagine the fate of those batteries towards Esher, waiting so tensely in the twilight, as well as one may. Survivors there were none. One may picture the orderly expectation, the officers alert and watchful, the gunners ready, the ammunition piled to hand, the limber gunners with their horses and wagons, the groups of civilian spectators standing as near as they were permitted, the evening stillness; the ambulances and hospital tents, with the burnt and wounded from Weybridge; then the dull resonance of the shots the Martians fired, and the clumsy projectile whirling over the trees and houses, and smashing amidst the neighbouring fields.

One may picture, too, the sudden shifting of the attention, the swiftly spreading coils and bellyings of that blackness advancing headlong, towering heavenward, turning the twilight to a palpable darkness, a strange and horrible antagonist of vapour striding upon its victims, men and horses near it seen dimly, running, shrieking, falling headlong, shouts of dismay, the guns suddenly abandoned, men choking and writhing on the ground, and the swift broadening out of the opaque cone of smoke. And then, night and extinction— nothing but a silent mass of impenetrable vapour hiding its dead.

Before dawn the black vapour was pouring through the streets of Richmond, and the disintegrating organism of government was,

10. The first British destroyer, the *Havoc,* was commissioned in 1893. The development of steam power in the second half of the century had revolutionized the concept of naval warfare, and put in jeopardy Britain's traditional bulwark of defense, the Royal Navy. In the growing war-fever of the end of the century, much concern was generated around what seemed to be the increased power of European navies, especially the French, and the Naval Defense Act of 1889 laid down rules for the refurbishing of the Navy similar to those which had earlier attempted to reinvigorate the Army.

with a last expiring effort, rousing the population of London to the necessity of flight.

CHAPTER SIXTEEN

THE EXODUS FROM LONDON

So you understand the roaring wave of fear that swept through the greatest city in the world just as Monday[1] was dawning—the stream of flight rising swiftly to a torrent, lashing in a foaming tumult round the railway stations, banked up into a horrible struggle about the shipping in the Thames, and hurrying by every available channel northward and eastward. By ten o'clock the police organization, and by midday even the railway organizations, were losing coherency, losing shape and efficiency, guttering, softening, running at last in that swift liquefaction of the social body.

All the railway lines north of the Thames and the South-Eastern people at Cannon Street had been warned by midnight on Sunday, and trains were being filled, people were fighting savagely for standing room in the carriages, even at two o'clock. By three people were being trampled and crushed even in Bishopsgate Street; a couple of hundred yards or more from Liverpool Street Station revolvers were fired, people stabbed, and the policemen who had been sent to direct the traffic, exhausted and infuriated, were breaking the heads of the people they were called out to protect.

And as the day advanced and the engine-drivers and stokers refused to return to London, the pressure of the flight drove the people in an ever-thickening multitude away from the stations and along the northward-running roads. By midday a Martian had been seen at Barnes, and a cloud of slowly-sinking black vapour drove along the Thames and across the flats of Lambeth, cutting off all

1. The reference helps clarify the time scheme of the book. The first cylinder had landed on Thursday night; the fighting began on Friday; and Chapter Fourteen, with the beginning of the panic in London, began on Saturday morning.

escape over the bridges in its sluggish advance. Another bank drove over Ealing, and surrounded a little island of survivors on Castle Hill, alive, but unable to escape.

After a fruitless struggle to get aboard a North-Western train at Chalk Farm—the engines of the trains that had loaded in the goods yard there *ploughed* through shrieking people, and a dozen stalwart men fought to keep the crowd from crushing the driver against his furnace—my brother emerged upon the Chalk Farm Road, dodged across through a hurrying swarm of vehicles, and had the luck to be foremost in the sack of a cycle shop. The front tyre of the machine he got was punctured in dragging it through the window, but he got up and off, notwithstanding, with no further injury than a cut wrist. The steep foot of Haverstock Hill was impassable owing to several overturned horses, and my brother struck into Belsize Road.

So he got out of the fury of the panic, and, skirting the Edgware Road, reached Edgware about seven, fasting and wearied, but well ahead of the crowd. Along the road people were standing in the roadway curious, wondering. He was passed by a number of cyclists, some horsemen, and two motor-cars. A mile from Edgware the rim of the wheel broke, and the machine became unrideable. He left it by the roadside and trudged through the village. There were shops half opened in the main street of the place, and people crowded on the pavement and in the doorways and windows, staring astonished at this extraordinary procession of fugitives that was beginning. He succeeded in getting some food at an inn.

For a time he remained in Edgware, not knowing what next to do. The flying people increased in number. Many of them, like my brother, seemed inclined to stop in the place. There was no fresh news of the invaders from Mars.

At that time the road was crowded, but as yet far from congested. Most of the fugitives at that hour were mounted on cycles, but there were soon motor-cars, hansom-cabs,[2] and carriages hurry-

2. One-horse, two-wheeled cabs for two passengers, with the driver seated above and behind the cab itself.

ing along, and the dust hung in heavy clouds along the road to St Albans.

It was perhaps a vague idea of making his way to Chelmsford, where some friends of his lived, that at last induced my brother to strike into a quiet lane running eastward. Presently he came upon a stile,[3] and, crossing it, followed a footpath north-eastward. He passed near several farm-houses and some little places whose names he did not learn. He saw few fugitives until, in a grass lane towards High Barnet, he happened upon the two ladies who became his fellow-travellers. He came upon them just in time to save them.

He heard their screams, and, hurrying round the corner, saw a couple of men struggling to drag them out of the little pony-chaise in which they had been driving, while a third with difficulty held the frightened pony's head. One of the ladies, a short woman dressed in white, was simply screaming; the other, a dark, slender figure, slashed at the man who gripped her arm with a whip she held in her disengaged hand.

My brother immediately grasped the situation, shouted, and hurried towards the struggle. One of the men desisted and turned towards him, and my brother, realizing from his antagonist's face that a fight was unavoidable, and being an expert boxer, went into him forthwith, and sent him down against the wheel of the chaise.

It was no time for pugilistic chivalry, and my brother laid him quiet with a kick, and gripped the collar of the man who pulled at the slender lady's arm. He heard the clatter of hoofs, the whip stung across his face, a third antagonist struck him between the eyes, and the man he held wrenched himself free and made off down the lane in the direction from which he had come.

Partly stunned, he found himself facing the man who had held the horse's head, and became aware of the chaise receding from him down the lane, swaying from side to side and with the woman in it looking back. The man before him, a burly rough, tried to close, and he stopped him with a blow in the face. Then, realizing that he

3. Steps or rungs for going over a wall.

was deserted, he dodged round and made off down the lane after the chaise, with the sturdy man close behind him, and the fugitive, who had turned now, following remotely.

Suddenly he stumbled and fell: his immediate pursuer went headlong, and he rose to his feet to find himself with a couple of antagonists again. He would have had little chance against them had not the slender lady very pluckily pulled up and returned to his help. It seems that she had had a revolver all this time, but it had been under the seat when she and her companion were attacked. She fired at six yards' distance, narrowly missing my brother. The less courageous of the robbers made off, and his companion followed him, cursing his cowardice. They both stopped in sight down the lane, where the third man lay insensible.

'Take this!' said the slender lady, and gave my brother her revolver.

'Go back to the chaise,' said my brother, wiping the blood from his split lip.

She turned without a word—they were both panting—and they went back to where the lady in white struggled to hold back the frightened pony.

The robbers had evidently had enough of it. When my brother looked again they were retreating.

'I'll sit here,' said my brother, 'if I may,' and he got up on the empty front seat. The lady looked over her shoulder.

'Give me the reins,' she said, and laid the whip along the pony's side. In another moment a bend in the road hid the three men from my brother's eyes.

So, quite unexpectedly, my brother found himself, panting, with a cut mouth, a bruised jaw and blood-stained knuckles, driving along an unknown lane with these two women.

He learnt they were the wife and the younger sister of a surgeon living at Stanmore, who had come in the small hours from a dangerous case at Pinner, and heard at some railway station on his way of the Martian advance. He had hurried home, roused the women— their servant had left them two days before—packed some provisions, put his revolver under the seat—luckily for my brother—and told them to drive on to Edgware, with the idea of getting a train there. He stopped behind to tell the neighbours. He would overtake them, he said, at about half-past four in the morning, and now it was nearly nine and they had seen nothing of him since. They could not stop in Edgware because of the growing traffic through the place, and so they had come into this side lane.

That was the story they told my brother in fragments when presently they stopped again, nearer to New Barnet. He promised to stay with them at least until they could determine what to do, or until the missing man arrived, and professed to be an expert shot with the revolver—a weapon strange to him—in order to give them confidence.

They made a sort of encampment by the wayside, and the pony became happy in the hedge. He told them of his own escape out of London, and all that he knew of these Martians and their ways. The sun crept higher in the sky, and after a time their talk died out and gave place to an uneasy state of anticipation. Several wayfarers came along the lane, and of these my brother gathered such news as he could. Every broken answer he had deepened his impression of the great disaster that had come on humanity, deepened his persuasion of the immediate necessity for prosecuting[4] this flight. He urged the matter upon them.

'We have money,' said the elder woman, and hesitated.

Her eyes met my brother's and her hesitation ended.

'So have I,' said my brother.

She explained that they had as much as thirty pounds in gold, besides a five-pound note,[5] and suggested that with that they might get upon a train at St Albans or New Barnet. My brother thought that was hopeless, seeing the fury of the Londoners to crowd upon the trains, and broached his own idea of striking across Essex towards Harwich and thence escaping from the country altogether.

4. Pressing on.
5. A pound was the equivalent of five dollars.

Mrs Elphinstone—that was the name of the woman in white—would listen to no reasoning, and kept calling upon 'George'; but her sister-in-law was astonishingly quiet and deliberate, and at last agreed to my brother's suggestion. So they went on towards Barnet, designing to cross the Great North Road, my brother leading the pony to save it as much as possible.

As the sun crept up the sky the day became excessively hot, and under foot a thick whitish sand grew burning and blinding, so that they travelled only very slowly. The hedges were grey with dust. And as they advanced towards Barnet, a tumultuous murmuring grew stronger.

They began to meet more people. For the most part these were staring before them, murmuring indistinct questions, jaded, haggard, unclean. One man in evening-dress passed them on foot, his eyes on the ground. They heard his voice, and, looking back at him, saw one hand clutched in his hair and the other beating invisible things. His paroxysm of rage over, he went on his way without once looking back.

As my brother's party went on towards the crossroads to the south of Barnet, they saw a woman approaching the road across some fields on their left, carrying a child and with two other children, and then a man in dirty black, with a thick stick in one hand and a small portmanteau in the other, passed. Then round the corner of the lane, from between the villas that guarded it at its confluence with the highroad, came a little cart drawn by a sweating black pony and driven by a sallow youth in a bowler hat, grey with dust. There were three girls like East End factory girls,[6] and a couple of little children, crowded in the cart.

'This'll tike us rahnd Edgware?' asked the driver, wild-eyed, white-faced; and when my brother told him it would if he turned to the left, he whipped up at once without the formality of thanks.

My brother noticed a pale grey smoke or haze rising among the houses in front of them, and veiling the white façade of a terrace

6. The East End of London, until well into the 1930s, was a notorious working-class slum.

beyond the road that appeared between the backs of the villas. Mrs Elphinstone suddenly cried out at a number of tongues of smoky red flame leaping up above the houses in front of them against the hot blue sky. The tumultuous noise resolved itself now into the disorderly mingling of many voices, the grind of many wheels, the creaking of wagons, and the staccato of hoofs. The lane came round sharply not fifty yards from the cross-roads.

'Good heavens!' cried Mrs Elphinstone. 'What is this you are driving us into?'

My brother stopped.

For the main road was a boiling stream of people, a torrent of human beings rushing northward, one pressing on another. A great bank of dust, white and luminous in the blaze of the sun, made everything within twenty feet of the ground grey and indistinct, and was perpetually renewed by the hurrying feet of a dense crowd of horses and men and women on foot, and by the wheels of vehicles of every description.

'Way!' my brother heard voices crying. 'Make way!'

It was like riding into the smoke of a fire to approach the meeting-point of the lane and road; the crowd roared like a fire, and the dust was hot and pungent. And, indeed, a little way up the road a villa was burning and sending rolling masses of black smoke across the road to add to the confusion.

Two men came past them. Then a dirty woman carrying a heavy bundle and weeping. A lost retriever dog with hanging tongue circled dubiously round them, scared and wretched, and fled at my brother's threat.

So much as they could see of the road Londonward between the houses to the right, was a tumultuous stream of dirty, hurrying people pent in between the villas on either side; the black heads, the crowded forms, grew into distinctness as they rushed towards the corner, hurried past, and merged their individuality again in a receding multitude that was swallowed up at last in a cloud of dust.

'Go on! Go on!' cried the voices. 'Way! Way!'

One man's hands pressed on the back of another. My brother

stood at the pony's head. Irresistibly attracted, he advanced slowly, pace by pace, down the lane.

Edgware had been a scene of confusion, Chalk Farm a riotous tumult, but this was a whole population in movement. It is hard to imagine that host. It had no character of its own. The figures poured out past the corner, and receded with their backs to the group in the lane. Along the margin came those who were on foot threatened by the wheels, stumbling in the ditches, blundering into one another.

The carts and carriages crowded close upon one another, making little way for those swifter and more impatient vehicles that darted forward every now and then when an opportunity showed itself of doing so, sending the people scattering against the fences and gates of the villas.

'Push on!' was the cry. 'Push on! they are coming!'

In one cart stood a blind man in the uniform of the Salvation Army, gesticulating with his crooked fingers and bawling: 'Eternity! eternity!' His voice was hoarse and very loud, so that my brother could hear him long after he was lost to sight in the southward dust. Some of the people who crowded in the carts whipped stupidly at their horses and quarrelled with other drivers; some sat motionless, staring at nothing with miserable eyes; some gnawed their hands with thirst or lay prostrate in the bottoms of their conveyances. The horses' bits were covered with foam, their eyes bloodshot.

There were cabs, carriages, shop-carts, wagons, beyond counting; a mail-cart, a road-cleaner's cart marked 'Vestry of St Pancras',[7] a huge timber-wagon crowded with roughs. A brewer's dray rumbled by with its two near wheels splashed with recent blood.

'Clear the way!' cried the voices. 'Clear the way!'

'Eter—nity! eter—nity!' came echoing up the road.

There were sad, haggard women tramping by, well dressed, with children that cried and stumbled, their dainty clothes smothered in

7. A vestry, in the Church of England, is not only the room in a church where vestments are stored, but also the committee of parishioners empowered to arrange such local matters as streetcleaning.

dust, their weary faces smeared with tears. With many of these came men, sometimes helpful, sometimes lowering and savage. Fighting side by side with them pushed some weary street outcast in faded black rags, wide-eyed, loud-voiced, and foul-mouthed. There were sturdy workmen thrusting their way along, wretched unkempt men clothed like clerks or shopmen, struggling spasmodically, a wounded soldier my brother noticed, men dressed in the clothes of railway porters, one wretched creature in a night-shirt with a coat thrown over it.

But, varied as its composition was, certain things all that host had in common. There was fear and pain on their faces, and fear behind them. A tumult up the road, a quarrel for a place in a wagon, sent the whole host of them quickening their pace; even a man so scared and broken that his knees bent under him was galvanized for a moment into renewed activity. The heat and dust had already been at work upon this multitude. Their skins were dry, their lips black and cracked. They were all thirsty, weary and footsore. And amid the various cries one heard disputes, reproaches, groans of weariness and fatigue; the voices of most of them were hoarse and weak. Through it all ran a refrain:

'Way! way! The Martians are coming!'

Few stopped and came aside from that flood. The lane opened slantingly into the main road with a narrow opening, and had a delusive appearance of coming from the direction of London. Yet a kind of eddy of people drove into its mouth; weaklings elbowed out of the stream, who for the most part rested but a moment before plunging into it again. A little way down the lane, with two friends bending over him, lay a man with a bare leg, wrapped about with bloody rags. He was a lucky man to have friends.

A little old man, with a grey military moustache and a filthy black frock-coat, limped out and sat down beside the trap, removed his boot—his sock was blood-stained—shook out a pebble, and hobbled on again; and then a little girl of eight or nine, all alone, threw herself under the hedge close by my brother, weeping.

'I can't go on! I can't go on!'

My brother woke from his torpor of astonishment, and lifted her up, speaking gently to her, and carried her to Miss Elphinstone. So soon as my brother touched her she became quite still, as if frightened.

'Ellen!' shrieked a woman in the crowd, with tears in her voice. 'Ellen!' And the child suddenly darted away from my brother, crying: 'Mother!'

'They are coming,' said a man on horseback, riding past along the lane.

'Out of the way, there!' bawled a coachman, towering high; and my brother saw a closed carriage turning into the lane.

The people crushed back on one another to avoid the horse. My brother pushed the pony and chaise back into the hedge, and the man drove by and stopped at the turn of the way. It was a carriage, with a pole for a pair of horses, but only one was in the traces.

My brother saw dimly through the dust that two men lifted out something on a white stretcher, and put this gently on the grass beneath the privet hedge.[8]

One of the men came running to my brother.

'Where is there any water?' he said. 'He is dying fast, and very thirsty. It is Lord Garrick.'

'Lord Garrick!' said my brother, 'the Chief Justice.'[9]

'The water?' he said.

'There may be a tap,' said my brother, 'in some of the houses. We have no water. I dare not leave my people.'

The man pushed against the crowd towards the gate of the corner house.

'Go on!' said the people, thrusting at him. 'They are coming! Go on!'

Then my brother's attention was distracted by a bearded, eagle-faced man lugging a small hand-bag, which split even as my brother's eyes rested on it, and disgorged a mass of sovereigns[10] that

8. A European evergreen with white flowers.
9. In England, the presiding judge of any court with several members.
10. Gold coins worth two pounds eighteen shillings each.

seemed to break up into separate coins as it struck the ground. They rolled hither and thither among the struggling feet of men and horses. The man stopped, and looked stupidly at the heap, and the shaft of a cab struck his shoulder and sent him reeling. He gave a shriek and dodged back, and a cart-wheel shaved him narrowly.

'Way!' cried the men all about him. 'Make way!'

So soon as the cab had passed, he flung himself, with both hands open, upon the heap of coins, and began clutching handfuls in his pockets. A horse rose close upon him, and in another moment he had half risen, and had been borne down under the horse's hoofs.

'Stop!' screamed my brother, and, pushing a woman out of the way, tried to clutch the bit of the horse.

Before he could get to it, he heard a scream under the wheels, and saw through the dust the rim passing over the poor wretch's back. The driver of the cart slashed his whip at my brother, who ran round behind the cart. The multitudinous shouting confused his ears. The man was lying in the dust among his scattered money, unable to rise, for the wheel had broken his back, and his lower limbs lay limp and dead. My brother stood up and yelled at the next driver, and a man on a black horse came to his assistance.

'Get him out of the road,' said he; and, clutching the man's collar with his free hand, my brother lugged him sideways. But he still clutched after his money, and regarded my brother fiercely, hammering at his arm with a handful of gold. 'Go on! Go on!' shouted angry voices behind. 'Way! Way!'

There was a smash as the pole of a carriage crashed into the cart that the man on horseback stopped. My brother looked up, and the man with the gold twisted his head round and bit the wrist that held his collar. There was a concussion, and the black horse came staggering sideways, and the cart-horse pushed beside it. A hoof missed my brother's foot by a hair's breadth. He released his grip on the fallen man and jumped back. He saw anger change to terror on the face of the poor wretch on the ground, and in a moment he was hidden and my brother was borne backward and carried past

the entrance of the lane, and had to fight hard in the torrent to recover it.

He saw Miss Elphinstone covering her eyes, and a little child,
with all a child's want of sympathetic imagination, staring with di-
lated eyes at a dusty something that lay black and still, ground and
crushed under the rolling wheels. 'Let us go back!' he shouted, and
began turning the pony round. 'We cannot cross this—hell,' he said;
and they went back a hundred yards the way they had come, until
the fighting crowd was hidden. As they passed the bend in the lane,
my brother saw the face of the dying man in the ditch under the
privet, deadly white and drawn, and shining with perspiration. The
two women sat silent, crouching in their seats and shivering.

Then beyond the bend my brother stopped again. Miss Elphinstone was white and pale, and her sister-in-law sat weeping, too
wretched even to call upon 'George'. My brother was horrified and
perplexed. So soon as they had retreated, he realized how urgent
and unavoidable it was to attempt this crossing. He turned to Miss
Elphinstone suddenly, resolute.

'We must go that way,' he said, and led the pony round again.

For the second time that day this girl proved her quality. To
force their way into the torrent of people, my brother plunged into
the traffic and held back a cab-horse, while she drove the pony
across its head. A wagon locked wheels for a moment, and ripped a
long splinter from the chaise. In another moment they were caught
and swept forward by the stream. My brother, with the cabman's
whip-marks red across his face and hands, scrambled into the
chaise, and took the reins from her.

'Point the revolver at the man behind,' he said, giving it to her,
'if he presses us too hard. No!—point it at his horse.'

Then he began to look out for a chance of edging to the right
across the road. But once in the stream, he seemed to lose volition,
to become a part of that dusty rout. They swept through Chipping
Barnet with the torrent; they were nearly a mile beyond the centre
of the town before they had fought across to the opposite side of the
way. It was din and confusion indescribable; but in and beyond the

town the road forks repeatedly, and this to some extent relieved the stress.

They struck eastward through Hadley, and there on either side of the road, and at another place farther on, they came upon a great multitude of people drinking at the stream, some fighting to come at the water. And farther on, from a hill near East Barnet, they saw two trains running slowly one after the other without signal or or-der—trains swarming with people, with men even among the coals behind the engines—going northward along the Great Northern Railway. My brother supposes they must have filled outside Lon-don, for at that time the furious terror of the people had rendered the central termini impossible.

Near this place they halted for the rest of the afternoon, for the violence of the day had already utterly exhausted all three of them. They began to suffer the beginnings of hunger, the night was cold, and none of them dared to sleep. And in the evening many people came hurrying along the road near by their stopping-place, fleeing from unknown dangers before them and going in the direction from which my brother had come.

CHAPTER SEVENTEEN

THE 'THUNDER CHILD'

Had the Martians aimed only at destruction, they might on Monday have annihilated the entire population of London, as it spread itself slowly through the home counties.[1] Not only along the road through Barnet, but also through Edgware and Waltham Abbey, and along the roads eastward to Southend and Shoeburyness, and south of the Thames to Deal and Broadstairs, poured the same frantic rout. If one could have hung that June morning in a balloon[2] in the blazing

1. The counties, rural and highly conservative, southeast of London.
2. Ballooning began in the late eighteenth century. It was employed for military purposes in the American Civil War, and many prophecies of the late nineteenth century envisaged the wartime use of balloons for both reconnaissance and bombardment.

blue above London, every northward and eastward road running out of the infinite tangle of streets would have seemed stippled black with the streaming fugitives, each dot a human agony of terror and physical distress. I have set forth at length in the last chapter my brother's account of the road through Chipping Barnet, in order that my readers may realize how that swarming of black dots appeared to one of those concerned. Never before in the history of the world had such a mass of human beings moved and suffered together. The legendary hosts of Goths and Huns,[3] the hugest armies Asia has ever seen, would have been but a drop in that current. And this was no disciplined march; it was a stampede—a stampede gigantic and terrible—without order and without a goal, six million people, unarmed and unprovisioned, driving headlong. It was the beginning of the rout of civilization, of the massacre of mankind.

Directly below him the balloonist would have seen the network of streets far and wide, houses, churches, squares, crescents, gardens—already derelict—spread out like a huge map, and in the southward *blotted*. Over Ealing, Richmond, Wimbledon, it would have seemed as if some monstrous pen had flung ink upon the chart. Steadily, incessantly, each black splash grew and spread, shooting out ramifications[4] this way and that, now banking itself against rising ground, now pouring swiftly over a crest into a new-found valley, exactly as a gout of ink would spread itself upon blotting-paper.

And beyond, over the blue hills that rise southward of the river, the glittering Martians went to and fro, calmly and methodically spreading their poison-cloud over this patch of country, and then over that, laying it again with their steam-jets when it had served its purpose, and taking possession of the conquered country. They do not seem to have aimed at extermination so much as at com-

---

3. The Goths were a Teutonic people who invaded and settled in the Roman Empire between the third and fifth centuries A.D. The Huns, an Asiatic people, invaded and pillaged the Empire during the fifth century A.D.
4. Extensions.

plete demoralization and the destruction of the opposition. They exploded any stores of powder they came upon, cut every telegraph, and wrecked the railways here and there. They were hamstringing[5] mankind. They seemed in no hurry to extend the field of their operations, and did not come beyond the central part of London all that day. It is possible that a very considerable number of people in London stuck to their houses through Monday morning. Certain it is that many died at home, suffocated by the Black Smoke.

Until about midday, the Pool of London[6] was an astonishing scene. Steamboats and shipping of all sorts lay there, tempted by the enormous sums of money offered by fugitives, and it is said that many who swam out to these vessels were thrust off with boat-hooks and drowned. About one o'clock in the afternoon the thinning remnant of a cloud of the black vapour appeared between the arches of Blackfriars Bridge. At that the Pool became a scene of mad confusion, fighting and collision, and for some time a multitude of boats and barges jammed in the northern arch of the Tower Bridge, and the sailors and lightermen[7] had to fight savagely against the people who swarmed upon them from the river front. People were actually clambering down the piers of the bridge from above. . . .

When, an hour later, a Martian appeared beyond the Clock Tower and waded down the river, nothing but wreckage floated above Limehouse.

Of the falling of the fifth cylinder I have presently to tell. The sixth star fell at Wimbledon. My brother, keeping watch beside the women sleeping in the chaise in a meadow, saw the green flash of it far beyond the hills. On Tuesday the little party, still set upon getting across the sea, made its way through the swarming country towards Colchester. The news that the Martians were now in possession of the whole of London was confirmed. They had been seen at

5. Crippling.
6. The artificially enlarged shipping area of the Thames.
7. Crewmembers of a lighter, or unpowered barge used to unload cargo ships in harbor.

Highgate, and even, it was said, at Neasden. But they did not come into my brother's view until the morrow.

That day the scattered multitudes began to realize the urgent need of provisions. As they grew hungry the rights of property ceased to be regarded. Farmers were out to defend their cattle-sheds, granaries, and ripening root crops with arms in their hands. A number of people now, like my brother, had their faces eastward, and there were some desperate souls even going back towards London to get food. These were chiefly people from the northern suburbs, whose knowledge of the Black Smoke came by hearsay. He heard that about half the members of the Government had gathered at Birmingham, and that enormous quantities of high explosives were being prepared to be used in automatic mines across the Midland counties.[8]

He was also told that the Midland Railway Company had replaced the desertions of the first day's panic, had resumed traffic, and were running northward trains from St Albans to relieve the congestion of the home counties. There was also a placard in Chipping Ongar announcing that large stores of flour were available in the northern towns, and that within twenty-four hours bread would be distributed among the starving people in the neighbourhood. But this intelligence did not deter him from the plan of escape he had formed, and the three pressed eastward all day, and saw no more of the bread distribution than this promise. Nor, as a matter of fact, did anyone else see more of it. That night fell the seventh star, falling upon Primrose Hill. It fell while Miss Elphinstone was watching, for she took that duty alternately with my brother. She saw it.

On Wednesday the three fugitives—they had passed the night in

8. "Automatic mines" are mines set to detonate on contact with any moving object; they are so called to distinguish them from mines exploded by electric current from the shore—a variety still experimented with in the nineties, but soon abandoned as impractical. The mines are set to block the expected advance of the Martians into the counties (Leicester, Warwick, Nottinghamshire, etc.) in the middle of England.

a field of unripe wheat—reached Chelmsford, and there a body of the inhabitants, calling itself the Committee of Public Supply, seized the pony as provisions, and would give nothing in exchange for it but the promise of a share in it the next day. Here there were rumours of Martians at Epping, and news of the destruction of Waltham Abbey Powder Mills in a vain attempt to blow up one of the invaders.

People were watching for Martians here from the church towers. My brother, very luckily for him as it chanced, preferred to push on at once to the coast, rather than wait for food, although all three of them were very hungry. By midday they passed through Tillingham, which strangely enough seemed to be quite silent and deserted, save for a few furtive plunderers, hunting for food. Near Tillingham they suddenly came in sight of the sea, and the most amazing crowd of shipping of all sorts that it is possible to imagine.

For after the sailors could no longer come up the Thames, they came on to the Essex coast, to Harwich, and Walton, and Clacton, and afterwards to Foulness and Shoebury, to bring off the people. They lay in a huge sickle-shaped curve that vanished into mist at last towards the Naze.[9] Close inshore was a multitude of fishing-smacks, English, Scotch, French, Dutch and Swedish; steam-launches from the Thames, yachts, electric boats; and beyond were ships of larger burthen, a multitude of filthy colliers,[10] trim merchantmen, cattle-ships, passenger-boats, petroleum-tanks, ocean tramps, an old white transport even, neat white and grey liners from Southampton and Hamburg; and along the blue coast across the Blackwater my brother could make out dimly a dense swarm of boats chaffering[11] with the people on the beach, a swarm which also extended up the Blackwater almost to Maldon.

About a couple of miles out lay an ironclad very low in the

9. A promontory, north of London (in the county of Essex), extending into the North Sea.
10. Ships carrying coal.
11. Haggling.

water, almost, to my brother's perception, like a waterlogged ship. This was the ram[12] *Thunder Child*. It was the only warship in sight, but far away to the right over the smooth surface of the sea—for that day there was a dead calm—lay a serpent of black smoke to mark the next ironclads of the Channel Fleet, which hovered in an extended line, steam up and ready for action, across the Thames Estuary[13] during the course of the Martian conquest, vigilant and yet powerless to prevent it.

At the sight of the sea, Mrs Elphinstone, in spite of the assurances of her sister-in-law, gave way to panic. She had never been out of England before, she would rather die than trust herself friendless in a foreign country, and so forth. She seemed, poor woman! to imagine that the French and the Martians might prove very similar. She had been growing increasingly hysterical, fearful and depressed, during the two days' journeyings. Her great idea was to return to Stanmore. Things had been always well and safe at Stanmore. They would find George at Stanmore. . . .

It was with the greatest difficulty they could get her down to the beach, where presently my brother succeeded in attracting the attention of some men on a paddle-steamer out of the Thames. They sent a boat and drove a bargain for thirty-six pounds[14] for the three. The steamer was going, these men said, to Ostend.[15]

It was about two o'clock when my brother, having paid their fares on the gangway, found himself safely aboard the steamboat with his charges. There was food aboard, albeit at exorbitant prices, and the three of them contrived to eat a meal on one of the seats forward.

There were already a couple of score of passengers aboard, some of whom had expended their last money in securing a passage, but the captain lay off the Blackwater until five in the afternoon, pick-

12. A warship with a heavy iron beak or prow for penetrating the hull of an enemy.
13. The point at which the river meets the sea's tide.
14. One hundred eighty dollars at the time.
15. A seaport in northwest Belgium.

ing up passengers until the seated decks were even dangerously crowded. He would probably have remained longer had it not been for the sound of guns that began about that hour in the south. As if in answer, the ironclad seaward fired a small gun and hoisted a string of flags. A jet of smoke sprang out of her funnels.

Some of the passengers were of opinion that this firing came from Shoeburyness, until it was noticed that it was growing louder. At the same time, far away in the south-east, the masts and upper-works of three ironclads rose one after the other out of the sea, beneath clouds of black smoke. But my brother's attention speedily reverted to the distant firing in the south. He fancied he saw a column of smoke rising out of the distant grey haze.

The little steamer was already flapping her way eastward of the big crescent of shipping, and the low Essex coast was growing blue and hazy, when a Martian appeared, small and faint in the remote distance, advancing along the muddy coast from the direction of Foulness. At that the captain on the bridge swore at the top of his voice with fear and anger at his own delay, and the paddles seemed infected with his terror. Every soul aboard stood at the bulwarks[16] or on the seats of the steamer, and stared at that distant shape, higher than the trees or church towers inland, and advancing with a leisurely parody of a human stride.

It was the first Martian my brother had seen, and he stood, more amazed than terrified, watching this Titan advancing deliberately towards the shipping, wading farther and farther into the water as the coast fell away. Then, far away beyond the Crouch,[17] came another striding over some stunted trees, and then yet another still farther off, wading deeply through a shiny mudflat that seemed to hang half-way up between sea and sky. They were all stalking seaward, as if to intercept the escape of the multitudinous vessels that were crowded between Foulness and the Naze. In spite of the

16. Walls above the main deck to protect the passengers from wind and driving rain.
17. The River Crouch, south of the Naze, meets the North Sea at Foulness Point.

throbbing exertions of the engines of the little paddle-boat, and the pouring foam that her wheels flung behind her, she receded with terrifying slowness from this ominous advance.

Glancing north-eastward, my brother saw the large crescent of shipping already writhing with the approaching terror; one ship passing behind another, another coming round from broadside to end on, steamships whistling and giving off volumes of steam, sails being let out, launches rushing hither and thither. He was so fascinated by this and by the creeping danger away to the left that he had no eyes for anything seaward. And then a swift movement of the steamboat (she had suddenly come round to avoid being run down) flung him headlong from the seat upon which he was standing. There was a shouting all about him, a trampling of feet, and a cheer that seemed to be answered faintly. The steamboat lurched, and rolled him over upon his hands.

He sprang to his feet and saw to starboard, and not a hundred yards from their heeling, pitching boat, a vast iron bulk like the blade of a plough tearing through the water, tossing it on either side in huge waves of foam that leapt towards the steamer, flinging her paddles helplessly in the air, and then sucking her deck down almost to the water-line.

A douche[18] of spray blinded my brother for a moment. When his eyes were clear again, he saw the monster had passed and was rushing landward. Big iron upper-works rose out of this headlong structure, and from that twin funnels projected, and spat a smoking blast shot with fire into the air. It was the torpedo-ram, *Thunder Child,* steaming headlong, coming to the rescue of the threatened shipping.

Keeping his footing on the heaving deck by clutching the bulwarks, my brother looked past this charging leviathan[19] at the Martians again, and he saw the three of them now close together, and standing so far out to sea that their tripod supports were almost entirely submerged. Thus sunken, and seen in remote perspective,

18. Spray of water.
19. Gigantic sea beast of Biblical legend.

they appeared far less formidable than the huge iron bulk in whose wake the steamer was pitching so helplessly. It would seem they were regarding this new antagonist with astonishment. To their intelligence, it may be, the giant was even such another as themselves. The *Thunder Child* fired no gun, but simply drove full speed towards them. It was probably her not firing that enabled her to get so near the enemy as she did. They did not know what to make of her. One shell, and they would have sent her to the bottom forthwith with the Heat-Ray.

She was steaming at such a pace that in a minute she seemed halfway between the steamboat and the Martians—a diminishing black bulk against the receding horizontal expanse of the Essex coast.

Suddenly the foremost Martian lowered his tube, and discharged a canister of the black gas at the ironclad. It hit her larboard[20] side, and glanced off in an inky jet, that rolled away to seaward, an unfolding torrent of black smoke, from which the ironclad drove clear. To the watchers from the steamer, low in the water and with the sun in their eyes, it seemed as though she was already among the Martians.

They saw the gaunt figures separating and rising out of the water as they retreated shoreward, and one of them raised the cameralike generator of the Heat-Ray. He held it pointing obliquely downward, and a bank of steam sprang from the water at its touch. It must have driven through the iron of the ship's side like a white-hot iron rod through paper.

A flicker of flame went up through the rising steam, and then the Martian reeled and staggered. In another moment he was cut down, and a great body of water and steam shot high in the air. The guns of the *Thunder Child* sounded through the reek, going off one after the other, and one shot splashed the water high close by the steamer, ricocheted towards the other flying ships to the north, and smashed a smack to matchwood.

But no one heeded that very much. At the sight of the Martian's collapse, the captain on the bridge yelled inarticulately, and all the

20. Port, left.

crowding passengers on the steamer's stern shouted together. And then they yelled again. For, surging out beyond the white tumult drove something long and black, the flames streaming from its middle parts, its ventilators and funnels spouting fire.

She was alive still; the steering gear, it seems, was intact and her engines working. She headed straight for a second Martian, and was within a hundred yards of him when the Heat-Ray came to her. Then with a violent thud, a blinding flash, her decks, her funnels, leapt upward. The Martian staggered with the violence of her explosion, and in another moment the flaming wreckage, still driving forward with the impetus of its pace, had struck him and crumpled him up like a thing of cardboard. My brother shouted involuntarily. A boiling tumult of steam hid everything again.

'Two!' yelled the captain.

Everyone was shouting; the whole steamer from end to end rang with frantic cheering that was taken up first by one and then by all in the crowding multitude of ships and boats that was driving out to sea.

The steam hung upon the water for many minutes, hiding the third Martian and the coast altogether. And all this time the boat was paddling steadily out to sea and away from the fight; and when at last the confusion cleared, the drifting bank of black vapour intervened, and nothing of the *Thunder Child* could be made out, nor could the third Martian be seen. But the ironclads to seaward were now quite close, and standing in towards shore past the steamboat.

The little vessel continued to beat its way seaward, and the ironclads receded slowly towards the coast, which was hidden still by a marbled bank of vapour, part steam, part black gas, eddying and combining in the strangest ways. The fleet of refugees was scattering to the north-east; several smacks[21] were sailing between the ironclads and the steamboat. After a time, and before they reached the sinking cloud-bank, the warships turned northwards, and then abruptly went about and passed into the thickening haze of evening southward. The coast grew faint, and at last indistinguishable

21. Single-masted, light sailing vessels used as tenders for warships.

amidst the low banks of clouds that were gathering about the sinking sun.

Then suddenly out of the golden haze of the sunset came the vibration of guns, and a form of black shadows moving. Everyone struggled to the rail of the steamer and peered into the blinding furnace of the west, but nothing was to be distinguished clearly. A mass of smoke rose slantingly and barred the face of the sun. The steamboat throbbed on its way through an interminable suspense.

The sun sank into grey cloud, the sky flushed and darkened, the evening star trembled into sight. It was deep twilight when the captain cried out and pointed. My brother strained his eyes. Something[22] rushed up into the sky out of the greyness, rushed slantingly upward and very swiftly into the luminous clearness above the clouds in the western sky, something flat and broad and very large, that swept round in a vast curve, grew smaller, sank slowly, and vanished again into the grey mystery of the night. And as it flew it rained down darkness upon the land.

22. This prophecy of flying machines once again anticipates an important military advance of the First World War.

BOOK II

THE EARTH UNDER THE MARTIANS

CHAPTER I

UNDER FOOT

In the first book I have wandered so much from my own adventures to tell of the experiences of my brother, that all through the last two chapters I and the curate have been lurking in the empty house at Halliford, whither we fled to escape the Black Smoke. There I will resume. We stopped there all Sunday night and all the next day—the day of the panic—in a little island of daylight, cut off by the Black Smoke from the rest of the world. We could do nothing but wait, in an aching inactivity, during those two weary days.

My mind was occupied by anxiety for my wife. I figured her at Leatherhead, terrified, in danger, mourning me already as a dead man. I paced the rooms and cried aloud when I thought of how I was cut off from her, of all that might happen to her in my absence. My cousin I knew was brave enough for any emergency, but he was not the sort of man to realize danger quickly, to rise promptly. What was needed now was not bravery, but circumspection. My only consolation was to believe that the Martians were moving Londonward and away from her. Such vague anxieties keep the mind sensitive and painful. I grew very weary and irritable with the curate's perpetual ejaculations, I tired of the sight of his selfish despair. After some ineffectual remonstrance I kept away from him, staying in a room containing globes, forms, and copy-books,[1] that was evidently a children's schoolroom. When at last he followed

---

1. Workbooks with models of penmanship for elementary students to imitate.

me thither, I went to a box-room[2] at the top of the house and locked myself in, in order to be alone with my aching miseries.

We were hopelessly hemmed in by the Black Smoke all that day, and the morning of the next. There were signs of people in the next house on Sunday evening—a face at a window and moving lights, and later the slamming of a door. But I do not know who these people were, nor what became of them. We saw nothing of them next day. The Black Smoke drifted slowly riverward all through Monday morning, creeping nearer and nearer to us, driving at last along the roadway outside the house that hid us.

A Martian came across the fields about midday, laying the stuff with a jet of superheated steam that hissed against the walls, smashed all the windows it touched, and scalded the curate's hand as he fled out of the front room. When at last we crept across the sodden rooms and looked out again, the country northward was as though a black snowstorm had passed over it. Looking towards the river, we were astonished to see an unaccountable redness mingling with the black of the scorched meadows.

For a time we did not see how this change affected our position, save that we were relieved of our fear of the Black Smoke. But later I perceived that we were no longer hemmed in, that now we might get away. So soon as I realized the way of escape was open, my dream of action returned. But the curate was lethargic, unreasonable.

'We are safe here,' he repeated—'safe here.'

I resolved to leave him—would that I had! Wiser now for the artilleryman's teaching, I sought out food and drink. I had found oil and rags for my burns, and I also took a hat and a flannel shirt that I found in one of the bedrooms. When it was clear to him that I meant to go alone, had reconciled myself to going alone, he suddenly roused himself to come. And, all being quiet throughout the afternoon, we started, as I should judge, about five along the blackened road to Sunbury.

2. Storage room.

In Sunbury, and at intervals along the road, were dead bodies lying in contorted attitudes—horses as well as men—overturned carts and luggage, all covered thickly with black dust. That pall of cindery powder made me think of what I had read of the destruction of Pompeii.[3] We got to Hampton Court without misadventure, our minds full of strange and unfamiliar appearances, and at Hampton Court our eyes were relieved to find a patch of green that had escaped the suffocating drift. We went through Bushey Park, with its deer going to and fro under the chestnuts, and some men and women hurrying in the distance towards Hampton, and so came to Twickenham. These were the first people we saw.

Away across the road the woods beyond Ham and Petersham were still afire. Twickenham was uninjured by either Heat-Ray or Black Smoke, and there were more people about here, though none could give us news. For the most part, they were like ourselves, taking advantage of a lull to shift their quarters. I have an impression that many of the houses here were still occupied by scared inhabitants, too frightened even for flight. Here, too, the evidence of a hasty rout was abundant along the road. I remember most vividly three smashed bicycles in a heap, pounded into the road by the wheels of subsequent carts. We crossed Richmond Bridge about half-past eight. We hurried across the exposed bridge, of course, but I noticed floating down the stream a number of red masses, some many feet across. I did not know what these were—there was no time for scrutiny—and I put a more horrible interpretation on them than they deserved. Here, again, on the Surrey side, was black dust that had once been smoke, and dead bodies—a heap near the approach to the station—and never a sight of the Martians until we were some way towards Barnes.

We saw in the blackened distance a group of three people running down a side-street towards the river, but otherwise it seemed deserted. Up the hill Richmond town was burning briskly; outside the town of Richmond there was no trace of the Black Smoke.

3. The Roman city on the Bay of Naples, completely buried by the eruption of Mt. Vesuvius in 79 A.D.

Then suddenly, as we approached Kew, came a number of people running, and the upper-works of a Martian Fighting Machine loomed in sight over the house-tops, not a hundred yards away from us. We stood aghast at our danger, and had he looked down we must immediately have perished. We were so terrified that we dared not go on, but turned aside and hid in a shed in a garden. There the curate crouched, weeping silently, and refusing to stir again.

But my fixed idea of reaching Leatherhead would not let me rest, and in the twilight I ventured out again. I went through a shrubbery, and along a passage beside a big house standing in its own grounds, and so emerged upon the road towards Kew. The curate I left in the shed, but he came hurrying after me.

That second start was the most foolhardy thing I ever did. For it was manifest the Martians were about us. Scarcely had he overtaken me than we saw either the Fighting Machine we had seen before or another, far away across the meadows in the direction of Kew Lodge. Four or five little black figures hurried before it across the green-grey of the field, and in a moment it was evident this Martian pursued them. In three strides he was among them, and they ran radiating from his feet in all directions. He used no Heat-Ray to destroy them, but picked them up one by one. Apparently he tossed them into the great metallic carrier which projected behind him, much as a workman's basket hangs over his shoulder.

It was the first time I realized the Martians might have any other purpose than destruction with defeated humanity. We stood for a moment petrified, then turned and fled through a gate behind us into a walled garden, fell into rather than found a fortunate ditch, and lay there, scarce daring to whisper to one another until the stars were out.

I suppose it was nearly eleven at night before we gathered courage to start again, no longer venturing into the road, but sneaking along hedgerows and through plantations, and watching keenly through the darkness, he on the right and I on the left, for the Martians, who seemed to be all about us. In one place we blundered upon a scorched and blackened area, now cooling and ashen, and a number of scattered dead bodies of men; who had obviously been killed by the Heat-Ray; and of dead horses, fifty feet, perhaps, behind a line of four ripped guns and smashed gun-carriages.

Sheen, it seemed, had escaped destruction but the place was silent and deserted. Here we happened on no dead, though the night was too dark for us to see into the side roads of the place. In Sheen my companion suddenly complained of faintness and thirst, and we decided to try one of the houses.

The first house we entered, after a little difficulty with the window, was a small semi-detached villa,[4] and I found nothing eatable left in the place but some mouldy cheese. There was, however, water to drink, and I took a hatchet, which promised to be useful in our next house-breaking.

We crossed the road to a place where the road turns towards Mortlake. Here there stood a white house within a walled garden, and in the pantry of this we found a store of food—two loaves of bread in a pan, an uncooked steak, and the half of a ham. I give this catalogue so precisely because, as it happened, we were destined to subsist upon this store for the next fortnight. Bottled beer stood under a shelf, and there were two bags of haricot beans and some limp lettuces. This pantry opened into a kind of wash-up kitchen, and in this was firewood, and a cupboard in which we found nearly a dozen of burgundy, tinned soups and salmons, and two tins of biscuits.

We sat in the adjacent kitchen in the dark—for we dared not strike a light—and ate bread and ham and drank beer out of one bottle. The curate, who was still timorous and restless, was now oddly enough for pushing on, and I was urging him to keep up his strength by eating, when the thing that was to imprison us happened.

'It can't be midnight yet,' I said, and then came a blinding glare of vivid green light. Everything in the kitchen leapt out, clearly

4. A still-common English term for a suburban dwelling house.

visible in green and black, and then vanished again. And then followed such a concussion as I have never heard before or since. So close on the heels of this as to seem instantaneous, came a thud behind me, a clash of glass, a crash and rattle of falling masonry all about us, and incontinently the plaster of the ceiling came down upon us, smashing into a multitude of fragments upon our heads. I was knocked headlong across the floor against the oven handle and stunned. I was insensible for a long time, the curate told me, and when I came to we were in darkness again, and he, with a face wet as I found afterwards with blood from a cut forehead, was dabbing water over me.

For some time I could not recollect what had happened. Then things came to me slowly. A bruise on my temple asserted itself.

'Are you better?' asked the curate, in a whisper.

At last I answered him. I sat up.

'Don't move,' he said. 'The floor is covered with smashed crockery from the dresser. You can't possibly move without making a noise, and I fancy *they* are outside.'

We both sat quite silent, so that we could scarcely hear one another breathing. Everything seemed deadly still, though once something near us, some plaster or broken brickwork, slid down with a rumbling sound. Outside and very near was an intermittent, metallic rattle.

'That!' said the curate, when presently it happened again.

'Yes,' I said. 'But what is it?'

'A Martian!' said the curate.

I listened again.

'It was not like the Heat-Ray,' I said, and for a time I was inclined to think one of the great Fighting Machines had stumbled against the house, as I had seen one stumble against the tower of Shepperton Church.

Our situation was so strange and incomprehensible that for three or four hours, until the dawn came, we scarcely moved. And then the light filtered in, not through the window, which remained black, but through a triangular aperture between a beam and a heap of broken bricks in the wall behind us. The interior of the kitchen we now saw greyly for the first time.

The window had been burst in by a mass of garden mould, which flowed over the table upon which we had been sitting and lay about our feet. Outside the soil was banked high against the house. At the top of the window-frame we could see an uprooted drain-pipe. The floor was littered with smashed hardware; the end of the kitchen towards the house was broken into, and since the daylight shone in there it was evident the greater part of the house had collapsed. Contrasting vividly with this ruin was the neat dresser, stained in the fashion, pale green, and with a number of copper and tin vessels below it, the wallpaper imitating blue and white tiles, and a couple of coloured supplements[5] fluttering from the walls above the kitchen range.

As the dawn grew clearer, we saw through the gap in the wall the body of a Martian standing sentinel, I suppose, over the still glowing cylinder. At the sight of that we crawled as circumspectly as possible out of the twilight of the kitchen into the darkness of the scullery.

Abruptly the right interpretation of the things dawned upon my mind.

'The fifth cylinder,'[6] I whispered, 'the fifth shot from Mars, has struck this house and buried us under the ruins!'

For a space the curate was silent, and then he whispered:

'God have mercy upon us!'

I heard him presently whimpering to himself.

---

5. Popular newspapers frequently issued these supplements, cheap and crude reproductions, "suitable for framing," of famous works of art or stirring historical scenes; they decorated the homes of many lower middle class families.

6. A contradiction. The fourth star had fallen late Sunday night, north of where the narrator and the curate are hiding (Book I, Chapter Sixteen), and the narrator only hears of it later, from his brother. So it is impossible for him to know, at the time, that this is the *fifth* star; he should think it the fourth.

Save for that sound we lay quite still in the scullery.[7] I for my part scarce dared breathe, and sat with my eyes fixed on the faint light of the kitchen door. I could just see the curate's face, a dim oval shape, and his collar and cuffs. Outside there began a metallic hammering, and then a violent hooting, and then, after a quiet interval, a hissing, like the hissing of an engine. These noises, for the most part problematical, continued intermittently, and seemed, if anything, to increase in number as the time wore on. Presently a measured thudding, and a vibration that made everything about us quiver and the vessels in the pantry ring and shift, began and continued. Once the light was eclipsed, and the ghostly kitchen doorway became absolutely dark. For many hours we must have crouched there, silent and shivering, until our tired attention failed. . . .

At last I found myself awake and very hungry. I am inclined to believe we must have been the greater portion of a day before that awakening. My hunger was at a stride so insistent that it moved me to action. I told him I was going to seek food, and felt my way towards the pantry. He made me no answer, but so soon as I began eating, the faint noise I made stirred him to action, and I heard him crawling after me.

7. Room in which food is cleaned or cut before being taken to the kitchen for cooking; hence, the most malodorous and usually the dirtiest room of the house.

CHAPTER II
WHAT WE SAW FROM THE RUINED HOUSE

After eating we crept back to the scullery, and there I must have dozed again, for when presently I stirred I was alone. The thudding vibration continued with wearisome persistence. I whispered for the curate several times, and at last felt my way to the door of the kitchen. It was still daylight, and I perceived him across the room, lying against the triangular hole that looked out upon the Martians.

His shoulders were hunched, so that his head was hidden from me.

I could hear a number of noises, almost like those of an engine-shed, and the place rocked with that beating thud. Through the aperture in the wall I could see the top of a tree touched with gold, and the warm blue of a tranquil evening sky. For a minute or so I remained watching the curate, and then I advanced, crouching and stepping with extreme care amidst the broken crockery that littered the floor.

I touched the curate's leg, and he started so violently that a mass of plaster went sliding down outside and fell with a loud impact. I gripped his arm, fearing he might cry out, and for a long time we crouched motionless. Then I turned to see how much of our rampart remained. The detachment of the plaster had left a vertical slit open in the débris, and by raising myself cautiously across a beam I was able to see out of this gap into what had been overnight a quiet suburban roadway. Vast indeed was the change that we beheld.

The fifth cylinder must have fallen right into the midst of the house we had first visited. The building had vanished, completely smashed, pulverized and dispersed by the blow. The cylinder lay now far beneath the original foundations, deep in a hole, already vastly larger than the pit I had looked into at Woking. The earth all around it had splashed under that tremendous impact—'splashed' is the only word—and lay in heaped piles that hid the masses of the adjacent houses. It had behaved exactly like mud under the violent blow of a hammer. Our house had collapsed backwards; the front portion, even on the ground-floor, had been destroyed completely; by a chance, the kitchen and scullery had escaped, and stood buried now under soil and ruins, closed in by tons of earth on every side, save towards the cylinder. Over that aspect we hung now on the very verge of the great circular pit the Martians were engaged in making. The heavy beating sound was evidently just behind us, and ever and again a bright green vapour drove up like a veil across our peephole.

The cylinder was already opened in the centre of the pit, and on the further edge of the pit, amidst the smashed and gravel-heaped shrubbery, one of the great Fighting Machines stood, deserted by its occupant, stiff and tall against the evening sky. At first I scarcely noticed the pit or the cylinder, although it has been convenient to describe them first, on account of the extraordinary glittering mechanism I saw, busy in the excavation, and on account of the strange creatures that were crawling slowly and painfully across the heaped mould near it.

The mechanism it was that held my attention first. It was one of those complicated fabrics that have since been called Handling Machines, and the study of which has already given such an enormous impetus to terrestrial invention. As it dawned upon me first it presented a sort of metallic spider with five jointed agile legs, and with an extraordinary number of jointed levers, bars, and reaching and clutching tentacles about its body. Most of its arms were retracted, but with three long tentacles it was fishing out a number of rods, plates and bars which lined the covering of, and apparently strengthened the walls of, the cylinder. These, as it extracted them, were lifted out and deposited upon a level surface of earth behind it.

Its motion was so swift, complex and perfect that at first I did not see it as a machine, in spite of its metallic glitter. The Fighting Machines were co-ordinated and animated to an extraordinary pitch, but nothing to compare with this. People who have never seen these structures, and have only the ill-imagined efforts of artists or the imperfect descriptions of such eye-witnesses as myself to go upon, scarcely realize that living quality.

I recall particularly the illustration of one of the first pamphlets to give a consecutive account of the war. The artist had evidently made a hasty study of one of the Fighting Machines, and there his knowledge ended. He presented them as tilted, stiff tripods, without either flexibility or subtlety, and with an altogether misleading monotony of effect. The pamphlet containing these renderings had a considerable vogue, and I mention them here simply to warn the reader against the impression they may have created. They were no more like the Martians I saw in action than a Dutch doll is like a human being. To my mind, the pamphlet would have been much better without them.

At first, I say, the Handling Machine did not impress me as a machine, but as a crab-like creature with a glittering integument,[1] the controlling Martian, whose delicate tentacles actuated its movements, seeming to be simply the equivalent of the crab's cerebral portion. But then I perceived the resemblance of its grey-brown, shiny, leathery integument to that of the other sprawling bodies beyond, and the true nature of this dexterous workman dawned upon me. With this realization, my interest shifted to those other creatures, the real Martians. Already I had had a transient impression of these, and the first nausea no longer obscured my observation. Moreover, I was concealed and motionless, and under no urgency of action.

They were, I now saw, the most unearthly creatures it is possible to conceive. They were huge round bodies—or, rather, heads—about four feet in diameter, each body having in front of it a face. This face had no nostrils—indeed, the Martians do not seem to have had any sense of smell—but it had a pair of very large, dark-coloured eyes, and just beneath this a kind of fleshy beak. In the back of this head or body—I scarcely know how to speak of it—was the single tight tympanic[2] surface, since known to be anatomically an ear, though it must have been almost useless in our denser air. In a group round the mouth were sixteen slender, almost whip-like tentacles, arranged in two bunches of eight each. These bunches have since been named rather aptly, by that distinguished anatomist Professor Howes, the *hands*. Even as I saw these Martians for the first time they seemed to be endeavouring to raise themselves on these hands, but of course, with the increased weight of terrestrial conditions, this was impossible. There is reason to suppose that on Mars they may have progressed upon them with some facility.

The internal anatomy, I may remark here, dissection has since shown, was almost equally simple. The greater part of the structure

1. Rind or outer shell.
2. Like the tympanum, the vibrating membrane of the middle ear.

was the brain, sending enormous nerves to the eyes, ear and tactile tentacles. Besides this were the complex lungs, into which the mouth opened, and the heart and its vessels. The pulmonary[3] distress caused by the denser atmosphere and greater gravitational attraction was only too evident in the convulsive movements of the outer skin.

And this was the sum of the Martian organs. Strange as it may seem to a human being, all the complex apparatus of digestion, which makes up the bulk of our bodies, did not exist in the Martians. They were heads, merely heads. Entrails they had none. They did not eat, much less digest. Instead, they took the fresh living blood of other creatures, and *injected* it into their own veins. I have myself seen this being done, as I shall mention in its place. But, squeamish as I may seem, I cannot bring myself to describe what I could not endure even to continue watching. Let it suffice to say, blood obtained from a still living animal, in most cases from a human being, was run directly by means of a little pipette[4] into the recipient canal. . . .

The physiological advantages of the practice of injection are undeniable, if one thinks of the tremendous waste of human time and energy occasioned by eating and the digestive process. Our bodies are half made up of glands and tubes and organs occupied in turning heterogenous food into blood. The digestive processes and their reaction upon the nervous system sap our strength, colour our minds. Men go happy or miserable as they have healthy or unhealthy livers, or sound gastric glands. But the Martians were lifted above all these organic fluctuations of mood and emotion.

Their source of nourishment is partly explained by the nature of the remains of the victims they had brought with them as provisions from Mars. These creatures, to judge from the shrivelled remains that had fallen into human hands, were bipeds, with flimsy siliceous skeletons (almost like those of the siliceous sponges)[5] and feeble

3. Relating to the lungs.
4. A slender tube for measuring or transferring liquids in laboratory work.
5. Growing in silica-rich soil, crystalline.

musculature, standing about six feet high, and having round erect heads, and large eyes in flinty sockets.

And while I am engaged in this description, I may add in this place certain further details, which, although they were not all evident to us at the time, will enable the reader who is unacquainted with them to form a clearer picture of these offensive creatures.

In three other points their physiology differed strangely from ours. Their organisms did not sleep, any more than the heart of man sleeps. Since they had no extensive muscular mechanism to recuperate, that periodical extinction was unknown to them. They had little or no sense of fatigue, it would seem. On earth they can never have moved without effort, yet even to the last they kept in action. In twenty-four hours they did twenty-four hours of work, as even on earth is perhaps the case with the ants.

In the next place, wonderful as it seems in a sexual world, the Martians were absolutely without sex, and therefore without any of the tumultuous emotions that arise from that difference among men. A young Martian, there can now be no dispute, was really born upon earth during the war, and it was found attached to its parent, partially *budded* off, just as young lily bulbs bud off, or the young animals in the fresh-water polyp.[6]

In man, in all the higher terrestrial animals, such a method of increase has disappeared; but even on this earth it was certainly the primitive method. Among the lower animals, up even to those first cousins of the vertebrated animals, the Tunicates,[7] the two processes occur side by side. On Mars, however, just the reverse has apparently been the case.

It is worthy of remark that a certain speculative writer[8] of quasi-

6. A sedentary marine animal with a fixed base like a plant, and sensitive tendrils (palps) around its mouth with which it snares its prey.
7. Marine animals with saclike bodies and two protruding openings for the ingestion and expulsion of water (their means of locomotion).
8. The "certain speculative writer" is Wells himself. In 1893 he published a sketch, "The Man of the Year Million," in the *Pall Mall Budget,* in which he speculated that the men of the distant future might evolve into gigantic

scientific repute, writing long before the Martian invasion, did forecast for man a final structure not unlike the actual Martian condition. His prophecy, I remember, appeared in November or
December, 1893, in a long defunct publication, the *Pall Mall
Budget,* and I recall a caricature of it in a pre-Martian periodical
called *Punch.* He pointed out—writing in a foolish facetious tone—
that the perfection of mechanical appliances must ultimately supersede limbs, the perfection of chemical devices, digestion—that such
organs as hair, external nose, teeth, ears, chin, were no longer essential parts of the human being, and that the tendency of natural
selection[9] would lie in the direction of their steady diminution
through the coming ages. The brain alone remained a cardinal
necessity. Only one other part of the body had a strong case for
survival, and that was the hand, 'teacher and agent of the brain'.
While the rest of the body dwindled, the hands would grow larger.

There is many a true word spoken in jest, and here in the Martians we have beyond dispute the actual accomplishment of such a
suppression of the animal side of the organism by the intelligence.
To me it is quite credible that the Martians may be descended from
beings not unlike ourselves, by a gradual development of brain and
hands (the latter giving rise to the two bunches of delicate tentacles
at last) at the expense of the rest of the body. Without the body
the brain would of course become a mere selfish intelligence, without any of the emotional substratum[10] of the human being.

The last salient point in which the systems of these creatures
differed from ours was in what one might have thought a very trivial
particular. Micro-organisms, which cause so much disease and pain

---

heads supported by tiny, vestigial limbs. The sketch was very widely
read, and was satirized in *Punch* in the same year.

9. In Darwinian theory, this is the central principle and motive force of
   evolution: the process whereby successive generations of a species retain
   and elaborate those characteristics which aid their survival in the environment, and eliminate or diminish those characteristics which inhibit
   survival.

10. Underlying quality or essence.

on earth, have either never appeared upon Mars, or Martian sanitary science eliminated them ages ago. A hundred diseases, all the fevers and contagions of human life, consumption, cancers, tumours, and such morbidities, never enter the scheme of their life. And speaking of the differences between the life on Mars and terrestrial life, I may allude here to the curious suggestions of the Red Weed.

Apparently the vegetable kingdom in Mars, instead of having green for a dominant colour, is of a vivid blood-red tint. At any rate, the seeds which the Martians (intentionally or accidentally) brought with them gave rise in all cases to red-coloured growths. Only that known popularly as the Red Weed, however, gained any footing in competition with terrestrial forms. The Red Creeper was quite a transitory growth, and few people have seen it growing. For a time, however, the Red Weed grew with astonishing vigour and luxuriance. It spread up the sides of the pit by the third or fourth day of our imprisonment, and its cactus-like branches formed a carmine fringe to the edges of our triangular window. And afterwards I found it broadcast throughout the country, and especially wherever there was a stream of water.

The Martians had what appears to have been an auditory organ, a single round drum at the back of the head-body, and eyes with a visual range not very different from ours, except that, according to Philips, blue and violet were as black to them. It is commonly supposed that they communicated by sounds and tentacular gesticulations; this is asserted, for instance, in the able but hastily compiled pamphlet (written evidently by someone not an eye-witness of Martian actions) to which I have already alluded, and which, so far, has been the chief source of information concerning them. Now, no surviving human being saw so much of the Martians in action as I did. I take no credit to myself for an accident, but the fact is so. And I assert that I watched them closely time after time, and that I have seen four, five, and (once) six of them sluggishly performing the most elaborately complicated operations together, without either sound or gesture. Their peculiar hooting invariably preceded feeding; it had no modulations, and was, I believe, in no sense a signal, but merely the expiration of air preparatory to the suctional operation. I have a certain claim to at least an elementary knowledge of psychology, and in this matter I am convinced—as firmly as I am convinced of anything—that the Martians interchanged thoughts without any physical intermediation. And I have been convinced of this in spite of strong preconceptions. Before the Martian invasion, as an occasional reader here or there may remember, I had written, with some little vehemence, against the telepathic theory.

The Martians wore no clothing. Their conceptions of ornament and decorum were necessarily different from ours; and not only were they evidently much less sensible of changes of temperature than we are, but changes of pressure do not seem to have affected their health at all seriously. But if they wore no clothing, yet it was in the other artificial additions to their bodily resources, certainly, that their great superiority over man lay. We men, with our bicycles and road skates, our Lilienthal[11] soaring-machines, our guns and sticks, and so forth, are just in the beginning of the evolution that the Martians have worked out. They have become practically mere brains, wearing different bodies according to their needs, just as men wear suits of clothes, and take a bicycle in a hurry or an umbrella in the wet. And of their appliances, perhaps nothing is more wonderful to a man than the curious fact that what is the dominant feature of almost all human devices in mechanism is absent—the *wheel* is absent; amongst all the things they brought to earth there is no trace or suggestion of their use of wheels. One would have at least expected it in locomotion. And in this connection it is curious to remark that even on this earth Nature has never hit upon the wheel, or has preferred other expedients to its development. And not only did the Martians either not know of (which is incredible) or abstain from the wheel, but in their apparatus singularly little use is made of the fixed pivot, or relatively fixed pivot, with circular

11. Otto Lilienthal (1848-1896), German engineer, was the chief developer of glider flight.

motions thereabout confined to one plane. Almost all the joints of the machinery present a complicated system of sliding parts moving over small, but beautifully curved friction bearings.[12] And while upon this matter of detail, it is remarkable that the long leverages of their machines are in most cases actuated by a sort of sham musculature of discs in an elastic sheath; these discs become polarized and drawn closely and powerfully together when traversed by a current of electricity. In this way the curious parallelism to animal motions, which was so striking and disturbing to the human beholder, was attained. Such quasi-muscles abounded in the crab-like Handling Machine which I watched unpacking the cylinder, on my first peeping out of the slit. It seemed infinitely more alive than the actual Martians lying beyond it in the sunset light, panting, stirring ineffectual tentacles, and moving feebly, after their vast journey across space.

While I was still watching their feeble motions in the sunlight, and noting each strange detail of their form, the curate reminded me of his presence by pulling violently at my arm. I turned to a scowling face, and silent, eloquent lips. He wanted the slit, which permitted only one of us to peep through at a time; and so I had to forego watching them for a time while he enjoyed that privilege.

When I looked again, the busy Handling Machine had already put together several of the pieces of apparatus it had taken out of the cylinder into a shape having an unmistakable likeness to its own; and down on the left a busy little digging mechanism had

12. A friction bearing is any device interposed between two moving surfaces to reduce the friction they generate. Wells's description of Martian technology is a subtle reinforcement of his previous allusion to "natural selection." Since the Martians do not use the principle of the wheel—the great originating principle of all human machinery—they have been forced to develop a technology that imitates the muscular activity of the body. But in doing this, they have rendered the activity of the *real* body superfluous; they have been trapped, by their own engineering genius, into becoming the physically pathetic monsters, dependent upon a kind of absolute prosthetics, which the narrator sees. This passage is a more elaborate version of the earlier vision of the Martians as cyborgs (see Book I, Chapter Eleven, note 3).

come into view, emitting jets of green vapour and working its way round the pit, excavating and embanking in a methodical and dis-criminating manner. This it was had caused the regular beating noise, and the rhythmic shocks that had kept our ruinous refuge quivering. It piped and whistled as it worked. So far as I could see, the thing was without a directing Martian at all.[13]

13. Another important anticipation by Wells. The fully automatic Digging Machine is, in fact, a robot—though the word itself was not invented until 1921 by the Czech writer, Karel Čapek.

CHAPTER III
THE DAYS OF IMPRISONMENT

The arrival of a second Fighting Machine drove us from our peep-hole into the scullery, for we feared that from his elevation the Martian might see down upon us behind our barrier. At a later date we began to feel less in danger of their eyes, for to an eye in the dazzle of the sunlight outside our refuge must have seemed a blind of blackness, but at first the slightest suggestion of approach drove us into the scullery in heart-throbbing retreat. Yet, terrible as was the danger we incurred, the attraction of peeping was for both of us irresistible. And I recall now with a sort of wonder that, spite of the infinite danger in which we were between starvation and a still more terrible death, we could yet struggle bitterly for that horrible privilege of sight. We would race across the kitchen in a grotesque pace between eagerness and the dread of making a noise and strike one another, and thrust and kick, within a few inches of exposure.

The fact is that we had absolutely incompatible dispositions and habits of thought and action, and our danger and isolation only accentuated the incompatibility. At Halliford I had already come to hate his trick of helpless exclamation, his stupid rigidity of mind. His endless muttering monologue vitiated every effort I made to think out a line of action, and drove me at times, thus pent up and intensified, almost to the verge of craziness. He was as lacking in restraint as a silly woman. He would weep for hours together, and I verily believe that to the very end this spoilt child of life thought his weak tears in some way efficacious. And I would sit in the darkness unable to keep my mind off him by reason of his importunities. He ate more than I did, and it was in vain I pointed out that our only chance of life was to stop in the house until the Martians had done with their pit, that in that long patience a time might presently come when we should need food. He ate and drank impulsively in heavy meals at long intervals. He slept little.

As the days wore on, his utter carelessness of any consideration so intensified our distress and danger that I had, much as I loathed doing it, to resort to threats, and at last to blows. That brought him to reason for a time. But he was one of those weak creatures full of a shifty cunning—who face neither God nor man, who face not even themselves, void of pride, timorous, anæmic, hateful souls.

It is disagreeable for me to recall and write these things, but I set them down that my story may lack nothing. Those who have escaped the dark and terrible aspects of life will find my brutality, my flash of rage in our final tragedy, easy enough to blame; for they know what is wrong as well as any, but not what is possible to tortured men. But those who have been under the shadow, who have gone down at last to elemental things, will have a wider charity.

And while within we fought out our dark dim contest of whispers, snatched food and drink and gripping hands and blows, without in the pitiless sunlight of that terrible June was the strange wonder, the unfamiliar routine of the Martians in the pit. Let me return to those first new experiences of mine. After a long time I ventured back to the peep-hole, to find that the newcomers had been reinforced by the occupants of no less than three of the Fighting Machines. These last had brought with them certain fresh appliances that stood in an orderly manner about the cylinder. The second Handling Machine was now completed, and was busied in serving one of the novel contrivances the big machine had brought. This was a body resembling a milk-can in its general form above which oscillated a pear-shaped receptable, and from which a stream of white powder flowed into a circular basin below.

The oscillatory motion was imparted to this by one tentacle of the Handling Machine. With two spatulate[1] hands the Handling Machine was digging out and flinging masses of clay into the pear-shaped receptacle above, while with another arm it periodically opened a door and removed rusty and blackened clinkers from the middle part of the machine. Another steely tentacle directed the powder from the basin along a ribbed channel towards some receiver that was hidden from me by the mound of bluish dust. From this unseen receiver a little thread of green smoke rose vertically into the quiet air. As I looked, the Handling Machine, with a faint and musical clinking, extended, telescopic fashion, a tentacle that had been a moment before a mere blunt projection, until its end was hidden behind the mound of clay. In another second it had lifted a bar of white aluminium into sight, untarnished as yet and shining dazzlingly and deposited it in a growing stack of bars that stood at the side of the pit. Between sunset and starlight this dexterous machine must have made more than a hundred such bars out of the crude clay, and the mound of bluish dust rose steadily until it topped the side of the pit.

The contrast between the swift and complex movements of these contrivances and the inert, panting clumsiness of their masters was acute, and for days I had to tell myself repeatedly that these latter were indeed the living of the two things.

The curate had possession of the slit when the first men were brought to the pit. I was sitting below, crouched together, listening with all my ears. He made a sudden movement backward, and I, fearful that we were observed, crouched in a spasm of terror. He came sliding down the rubbish, and crouched beside me in the darkness, inarticulate, gesticulating, and for a moment I shared his terror. His gesture suggested a resignation of the slit, and after a little while my curiosity gave me courage, and I rose up, stepped across him, and clambered up to it. At first I could see no reason for his

1. Spoonlike: broad, flat, and rounded.

terror. The twilight had now come, the stars were little and faint, but the pit was illuminated by the flickering green fire that came from the aluminium making. The whole picture was a flickering scheme of green gleams and shifting rusty black shadows, strangely trying to the eyes. Over and through it all went the bats, heeding it not at all. The sprawling Martians were no longer to be seen, the mound of blue-green powder had risen to cover them from sight, and a Fighting Machine, with its legs contracted, crumpled and abbreviated, stood across the corner of the pit. And then, amidst the clangour of the machinery, came a drifting suspicion of human voices, that I entertained at first only to dismiss.

I crouched, watching this Fighting Machine closely, satisfying myself now for the first time that the hood did indeed contain a Martian. As the green flames lifted I could see the oily gleam of his integument and the brightness of his eyes. And suddenly I heard a yell, and saw a long tentacle reaching over the shoulder of the machine, to the little cage that hunched upon its back. Then something—something struggling violently—was lifted high against the sky, a black vague enigma[2] against the starlight, and as this black object came down again, I saw by the green brightness that it was a man. For an instant he was clearly visible. He was a stout, ruddy, middle-aged man, well dressed; three days before he must have been walking the world, a man of considerable consequence. I could see his staring eyes and gleams of light on his studs and watch-chain. He vanished behind the mound, and for a moment there was silence. And then began a shrieking and a sustained and cheerful hooting from the Martians. . . .

I slid down the rubbish, struggled to my feet, clapped my hands over my ears, and bolted into the scullery. The curate, who had been crouching silently with his arms over his head, looked up as I passed, cried out quite loudly at my desertion of him, and came running after me. . . .

That night, as we lurked in the scullery, balanced between our horror and the horrible fascination this peeping had, although I felt

2. Riddle.

an urgent need for action, I tried in vain to conceive any plan of escape; but afterwards, during the second day, I was able to consider our position with great clearness. The curate, I found, was quite incapable of discussion; strange terrors had already made him a creature of violent impulses, had robbed him of reason or forethought. Practically he had already sunk to the level of an animal. But, as the saying goes, I gripped myself with both hands. It grew upon my mind, once I could face the facts, that, terrible as our position was, there was as yet no justification for absolute despair. Our chief chance lay in the possibility of the Martians making the pit nothing more than a temporary encampment. Or even if they kept it permanently, they might not consider it necessary to guard it, and a chance of escape might be afforded us. I also weighed very carefully the possibility of our digging a way out in a direction away from the pit, but the chances of our emerging within sight of some sentinel Fighting Machine seemed at first too enormous. And I should have had to have done all the digging myself. The curate would certainly have failed me.

It was on the third day, if my memory serves me right, that I saw the lad killed. It was the only occasion on which I actually saw the Martians feed. After that experience, I avoided the hole in the wall for the better part of a day. I went into the scullery, removed the door, and spent some hours digging with my hatchet as silently as possible; but when I had made a hole about a couple of feet deep the loose earth collapsed noisily, and I did not dare continue. I lost heart, and lay down on the scullery floor for a long time, having no spirit even to move. And after that I abandoned altogether the idea of escaping by excavation.

It says much for the impression the Martians had made upon me, that at first I entertained little or no hope of our escape being brought about by their overthrow through any human effort. But on the fourth or fifth night I heard a sound like heavy guns.

It was very late in the night, and the moon was shining brightly. The Martians had taken away the Excavating Machine, and, save for a Fighting Machine that stood on the remoter bank of the pit, and a Handling Machine that was busied out of my sight in a corner of the pit immediately beneath my peep-hole, the place was deserted by them. Except for the pale glow from the Handling Machine, and the bars and patches of white moonlight, the pit was in darkness, and except for the clinking of the Handling Machine, quite still. That night was a beautiful serenity; save for one planet, the moon seemed to have the sky to herself. I heard a dog howling, and that familiar sound it was made me listen. Then I heard quite distinctly a booming exactly like the sound of great guns. Six distinct reports I counted, and after a long interval six again. And that was all.

CHAPTER IV

THE DEATH OF THE CURATE

It was on the sixth day of our imprisonment that I peeped for the last time, and presently found myself alone. Instead of keeping close to me and trying to oust me from the slit, the curate had gone back into the scullery. I was struck by a sudden thought. I went back quickly and quietly into the scullery. In the darkness I heard the curate drinking. I snatched in the darkness, and my fingers caught a bottle of burgundy.

For a few minutes there was a tussle. The bottle struck the floor and broke, and I desisted and rose. We stood panting, threatening one another. In the end I planted myself between him and the food, and told him of my determination to begin a discipline. I divided the food in the pantry into rations to last us ten days. I would not let him eat any more that day. In the afternoon he made a feeble effort to get at the food. I had been dozing, but in an instant I was awake. All day and all night we sat face to face, I weary but resolute, and he weeping and complaining of his immediate hunger. It was, I know, a night and a day, but to me it seemed—it seems now—an interminable length of time.

And so our widened incompatibility ended at last in open conflict. For two vast days we struggled in undertones and wrestling contests. There were times when I beat and kicked him madly, times when I cajoled and persuaded him, and once I tried to bribe him with the last bottle of burgundy, for there was a rain-water pump from which I could get water. But neither force nor kindness availed: he was indeed beyond reason. He would neither desist from his attacks on the food nor from his noisy babbling to himself. The rudimentary precautions to keep our imprisonment endurable he would not observe. Slowly I began to realize the complete overthrow of his intelligence, to perceive that my sole companion in this close and sickly darkness was a man insane.

From certain vague memories I am inclined to think my own mind wandered at times. I had strange and hideous dreams whenever I slept. It sounds strange, but I am inclined to think that the weakness and insanity of the curate warned me, braced me and kept me a sane man.

On the eighth day he began to talk aloud instead of whisper, and nothing I could do would moderate his speech.

'It is just, O God!' he would say over and over again. 'It is just. On me and mine be the punishment laid. We have sinned, we have fallen short. There was poverty, sorrow; the poor were trodden in the dust, and I held my peace. I preached acceptable folly—my God, what folly!—when I should have stood up, though I died for it, and called upon them to repent—repent! . . . Oppressors of the poor and needy. . . . The wine-press of God!'[1]

Then he would suddenly revert to the matter of the food I withheld from him, praying, begging, weeping, at last threatening. He began to raise his voice—I prayed him not to; he perceived a hold on me—he threatened he would shout and bring the Martians upon us. For a time that scared me; but any concession would have shortened our chance of escape beyond estimating. I defied him, although I felt no assurance that he might not do this thing. But that day, at any rate, he did not. He talked with his voice rising slowly,

---

1. A jumble of Biblical allusions, probably the most important of which is to Isaiah 63:3, an image of apocalypse or the vengeance of God.

through the greater part of the eighth and ninth days—threats, entreaties, mingled with a torrent of half-sane and always frothy repentance for his vacant sham of God's service, such as made me pity him. Then he slept awhile, and began again with renewed strength, so loudly that I must needs make him desist.

'Be still!' I implored.

He rose to his knees, for he had been sitting in the darkness near the copper.[2]

'I have been still too long,' he said in a tone that must have reached the pit, 'and now I must bear my witness. Woe unto this unfaithful city! Woe! woe! Woe! woe! woe! to the inhabitants of the earth by reason of the other voices of the trumpet—'[3]

'Shut up!' I said rising to my feet, and in a terror lest the Martians should hear us. 'For God's sake—'

'Nay,' shouted the curate at the top of his voice, standing likewise and extending his arms. 'Speak! The word of the Lord is upon me.'

In three strides he was at the door into the kitchen.

'I must bear my witness. I go. It has already been too long delayed.'

I put out my hand and felt the meat-chopper hanging to the wall. In a flash I was after him. I was fierce with fear. Before he was halfway across the kitchen I had overtaken him. With one last touch of humanity I turned the blade back and struck him with the butt. He went headlong forward, and lay stretched on the ground. I stumbled over him, and stood panting. He lay still.

Abruptly I heard a noise without, the run and smash of slipping plaster, and the triangular aperture in the wall was darkened. I looked up and saw the lower surface of a Handling Machine coming slowly across the hole. One of its gripping limbs curled amidst the

2. A very large kettle, usually made of iron; a common feature of kitchens at the turn of the century.
3. Another jumble of Biblical allusions, mainly to the Book of Amos in the Old Testament and to Revelation in the New.

debris; another limb appeared, feeling its way over the fallen beams. I stood petrified, staring. Then I saw through a sort of glass plate near the edge of the body the face, as we may call it, and the large dark eyes of a Martian peering, and then a long metallic snake of tentacle came feeling slowly through the hole.

I turned by an effort, stumbled over the curate, and stopped at the scullery door. The tentacle was now some way, two yards or more, in the room, and twisting and turning with queer sudden movements, this way and that. For a while I stood fascinated by that slow, fitful advance. Then, with a faint, hoarse cry, I forced myself across the scullery. I trembled violently; I could scarcely stand upright. I opened the door of the coal-cellar, and stood there in the darkness, staring at the faintly lit doorway into the kitchen, and listening. Had the Martian seen me? What was it doing now?

Something was moving to and fro there, very quietly; every now and then it tapped against the wall, or started on its movements with a faint metallic ringing, like the movement of keys on a split-ring.[4] Then a heavy body—I knew too well what—was dragged across the floor of the kitchen towards the opening. Irresistibly attracted, I crept to the door and peeped into the kitchen. In the triangle of bright outer sunlight I saw the Martian in its Briareus[5] of a Handling Machine, scrutinizing the curate's head. I thought at once that it would infer my presence from the mark of the blow I had given him.

I crept back to the coal-cellar, shut the door, and began to cover myself up as much as I could, and as noiselessly as possible, in the darkness, among the firewood and coal therein. Every now and then I paused rigid, to hear if the Martian had thrust its tentacle through the opening again.

Then the faint metallic jingle returned. I traced it slowly feeling

4. A large key-ring, for keeping all the keys of a household.
5. In Greek myth, a pre-Olympian giant with fifty heads and a hundred hands.

over the kitchen. Presently I heard it nearer—in the scullery, as I judged. I thought that its length might be insufficient to reach me. I prayed copiously. It passed, scraping faintly across the cellar door. An age of almost intolerable suspense intervened; then I heard it fumbling at the latch. It had found the door! The Martians understood doors!

It worried at the catch for a minute, perhaps, and then the door opened.

In the darkness I could just see the thing—like an elephant trunk more than anything else—waving towards me and touching and examining the wall, coals, wood, and ceiling. It was like a black worm swaying its blind head to and fro.

Once, even, it touched the heel of my boot. I was on the verge of screaming; I bit my hand. For a time it was silent. I could have fancied it had been withdrawn. Presently, with an abrupt click, it gripped something—I thought it had me!—and seemed to go out of the cellar again. For a minute I was not sure. Apparently, it had taken a lump of coal to examine.

I seized the opportunity of slightly shifting my position, which had become cramped, and listened. I whispered passionate prayers for safety.

Then I heard the slow, deliberate sound creeping towards me again. Slowly, slowly it drew near, scratching against the walls and tapping furniture.

While I was still doubtful, it rapped smartly against the cellar door and closed it. I heard it go into the pantry, and the biscuit-tins rattled and a bottle smashed, and then came a heavy bump against the cellar door. Then silence, that passed into an infinity of suspense.

Had it gone?

At last I decided that it had.

It came into the scullery no more; but I lay all the tenth day, in the close darkness, buried among coals and firewood, not daring even to crawl out for the drink for which I craved. It was the eleventh day before I ventured so far from my security.

CHAPTER V

THE STILLNESS

My first act, before I went into the pantry, was to fasten the door between kitchen and scullery. But the pantry was empty; every scrap of food had gone. Apparently, the Martian had taken it all on the previous day. At that discovery I despaired for the first time. I took no food and no drink either on the eleventh or the twelfth day.

At first my mouth and throat were parched, and my strength ebbed sensibly. I sat about in the darkness of the scullery, in a state of despondent wretchedness. My mind ran on eating. I thought I had become deaf, for the noises of movement I had been accustomed to hear from the pit ceased absolutely. I did not feel strong enough to crawl noiselessly to the peep-hole, or I would have gone there.

On the twelfth day my throat was so painful that, taking the chance of alarming the Martians, I attacked the creaking rain-water pump that stood by the sink, and got a couple of glassfuls of blackened and tainted rain-water. I was greatly refreshed by this, and emboldened by the fact that no inquiring tentacle followed the noise of my pumping.

During these days I thought much of the curate, and of the manner of his death, in a rambling, inconclusive manner.

On the thirteenth day I drank some more water, and dozed and thought disjointedly of eating and of vague impossible plans of escape. Whenever I dozed I dreamt of horrible phantasms,[1] of the death of the curate, or of sumptuous dinners; but, sleeping or awake, I felt a keen pain that urged me to drink again and again. The light that came into the scullery was no longer grey but red. To my disordered imagination it seemed the colour of blood.

On the fourteenth day I went into the kitchen, and I was sur-

1. Fantasies.

prised to find that the fronds of the Red Weed had grown right across the hole in the wall, turning the half-light of the place into a crimson-coloured obscurity.

It was early on the fifteenth day that I heard a curious familiar sequence of sounds in the kitchen, and, listening, identified it as the snuffing and scratching of a dog. Going into the kitchen, I saw a dog's nose peering in through a break among the ruddy fronds. This greatly surprised me. At the scent of me he barked shortly.

I thought if I could induce him to come into the place quietly I should be able, perhaps, to kill and eat him, and in any case it would be advisable to kill him, lest his actions attracted the attention of the Martians.

I crept forward, saying 'Good dog!' very softly; but he suddenly withdrew his head and disappeared.

I listened—I was not deaf—but certainly the pit was still. I heard a sound like the flutter of a bird's wings, and a hoarse croaking, but that was all.

For a long while I lay close to the peep-hole, but not daring to move aside the red plants that obscured it. Once or twice I heard a faint pitter-patter like the feet of the dog going hither and thither on the sand far below me, and there were more bird-like sounds, but that was all. At length, encouraged by the silence, I looked out.

Except in the corner, where a multitude of crows hopped and fought over the skeletons of the dead the Martians had consumed, there was not a living thing in the pit.

I stared about me, scarcely believing my eyes. All the machinery had gone. Save for the big mound of greyish-blue powder in one corner, certain bars of aluminium in another, the black birds and the skeletons of the killed, the place was merely an empty circular pit in the sand.

Slowly I thrust myself out through the red weed, and stood up on the mound of rubble. I could see in any direction save behind me, to the north, and neither Martian nor sign of Martian was to be seen. The pit dropped sheerly from my feet, but a little way along, the rubbish afforded a practicable slope to the summit of the ruins. My chance of escape had come. I began to tremble.

I hesitated for some time, and then, in a gust of desperate resolution and with a heart that throbbed violently, I scrambled to the top of the mound in which I had been buried so long.

I looked about again. To the northward, too, no Martian was visible.

When I had last seen this part of Sheen in the daylight, it had been a straggling street of comfortable white and red houses, interspersed with abundant shady trees. Now I stood on a mound of smashed brickwork, clay and gravel, over which spread a multitude of red cactus-shaped plants, knee-high, without a solitary terrestrial growth to dispute their footing. The trees near me were dead and brown, but farther, a network of red threads scaled the still living stems.

The neighbouring houses had all been wrecked, but none had been burned; their walls stood sometimes to the second storey, with smashed windows and shattered doors. The Red Weed grew tumultuously in their roofless rooms. Below me was the great pit, with the crows struggling for its refuse. A number of other birds hopped about among the ruins. Far away I saw a gaunt cat slink crouchingly along a wall, but traces of men there were none.

The day seemed, by contrast with my recent confinement, dazzlingly bright, the sky a glowing blue. A gentle breeze kept the Red Weed, that covered every scrap of unoccupied ground, gently swaying. And oh! the sweetness of the air!

CHAPTER VI

THE WORK OF FIFTEEN DAYS

For some time I stood tottering on the mound, regardless of my safety. Within that noisome den from which I had emerged, I had thought with a narrow intensity only of our immediate security. I had not realized what had been happening to the world, had not anticipated this startling vision of unfamiliar things. I had expected to see Sheen in ruins—I found about me the landscape, weird and lurid, of another planet.

For that moment I touched an emotion beyond the common range of men, yet one that the poor brutes we dominate know only too well. I felt as a rabbit might feel returning to his burrow, and suddenly confronted by the work of a dozen busy navvies[1] digging the foundations of a house. I felt the first inkling of a thing that presently grew quite clear in my mind, that oppressed me for many days, a sense of dethronement, a persuasion that I was no longer a master, but an animal among the animals, under the Martian heel. With us it would be as with them, to lurk and watch, to run and hide; the fear and empire of man had passed away.

But so soon as this strangeness had been realized, it passed, and my dominant motive became the hunger of my long and dismal fast. In the direction away from the pit, I saw, beyond a red-covered wall, a patch of garden ground unburied. This gave me a hint, and I went knee-deep, and sometimes neck-deep, in the Red Weed. The density of the weed gave me a reassuring sense of hiding. The wall was some six feet high and when I attempted to clamber it I found I could not lift my feet to the crest. So I went along by the side of it, and came to a corner and a rockwork that enabled me to get to the top and tumble into the garden I coveted. Here I found some young onions, a couple of gladiolus bulbs, and a quantity of imma- ture carrots, all of which I secured, and, scrambling over a ruined wall, went on my way through scarlet and crimson trees towards Kew—it was like walking through an avenue of gigantic blood- drops—possessed with two ideas: to get more food, and to limp as soon and as far as my strength permitted, out of this accursed unearthly region of the pit.

Some way farther, in a grassy place, was a group of mushrooms, which I also devoured, and then I came upon a brown sheet of flow- ing shallow water, where meadows used to be. These fragments of

1. Manual laborers employed to excavate roads, canals, railroad lines, etc.

nourishment served only to whet my hunger. At first I was surprised at this flood in a hot, dry summer, but afterwards I discovered that this was caused by the tropical exuberance of the Red
Weed. Directly this extraordinary growth encountered water, it
straightway became gigantic and of unparalleled fecundity. Its seeds
were simply poured down into the water of the Wey and Thames,
and its swiftly-growing and Titanic water-fronds speedily choked
both these rivers.

At Putney, as I afterwards saw, the bridge was almost lost in a
tangle of this weed, and at Richmond, too, the Thames water
poured in a broad and shallow stream across the meadows of
Hampton and Twickenham. As the waters spread the weed followed them, until the ruined villas of the Thames Valley were for a
time lost in this red swamp, whose margin I explored, and much of
the desolation the Martians had caused was concealed.

In the end the Red Weed succumbed almost as quickly as it
spread. A cankering[2] disease, due, it is believed, to the action of
certain bacteria, presently seized upon it. Now, by the action of natural selection, all terrestrial plants have acquired a resisting power
against bacterial diseases—they never succumb without a severe
struggle; but the Red Weed rotted like a thing already dead. The
fronds became bleached, and then shrivelled and brittle. They
broke off at the least touch, and the waters that had stimulated
their early growth carried their last vestiges out to sea. . . .

My first act on coming to this water was, of course, to slake my
thirst. I drank a great bulk of water, and, moved by an impulse,
gnawed some fronds of Red Weed; but they were watery, and had a
sickly metallic taste. I found the water was sufficiently shallow for
me to wade securely, although the Red Weed impeded my feet a
little; but the flood evidently got deeper towards the river, and I
turned back towards Mortlake. I managed to make out the road by

2. Rotting from within. This is an instance of "foreshadowing" in the classic
tradition of the Victorian novel. The death of the red Martian weed is our
first hint that the invasion of the Martians themselves may be doomed to
failure through the same "natural" processes.

means of occasional ruins of its villas and fences and lamps, and so presently I got out of this spate, and made my way to the hill going up towards Roehampton, and came out on Putney Common.

Here the scenery changed from the strange and unfamiliar to the wreckage of the familiar; patches of ground exhibited the devastation of a cyclone, and in a few score yards I would come upon perfectly undisturbed spaces, houses with their blinds trimly drawn and doors closed, as if they had been left for a day by the owners, or as if the inhabitants slept within. The Red Weed was less abundant; the tall trees along the lane were free from the red creeper. I hunted for food among the trees, finding nothing, and I also raided a couple of silent houses, but they had already been broken into and ransacked. I rested for the remainder of the daylight in a shrubbery, being, in my enfeebled condition, too fatigued to push on.

All this time I saw no human beings, and no signs of the Martians. I encountered a couple of hungry-looking dogs, but both hurried circuitously away from the advances I made them. Near Roehampton I had seen two human skeletons—not bodies, but skeletons, picked clean—and in the wood by me I found the crushed and scattered bones of several cats and rabbits, and the skull of a sheep. But though I gnawed parts of these in my mouth, there was nothing to be got from them.

After sunset, I struggled on along the road towards Putney, where I think the Heat-Ray must have been used for some reason. And in a garden beyond Roehampton I got a quantity of immature potatoes sufficient to stay my hunger. From this garden one saw down upon Putney and the river. The aspect of the place in the dusk was singularly desolate: blackened trees, blackened, desolate ruins, and down the hill the sheets of the flooded river, red-tinged with the weed. And over all—silence. It filled me with indescribable terror to think how swiftly that desolating change had come.

For a time I believed that mankind had been swept out of existence, and that I stood there alone, the last man left alive. Hard by the top of Putney Hill I came upon another skeleton, with the arms dislocated and removed several yards from the rest of the body. As

I proceeded I became more and more convinced that the extermination of mankind was, save for such stragglers as myself, already accomplished in this part of the world. The Martians, I thought, had gone on, and left the country desolated, seeking food elsewhere. Perhaps even now they were destroying Berlin or Paris, or it might be they had gone northward. . . .

CHAPTER VII

THE MAN ON PUTNEY HILL

I spent that night in the inn that stands at the top of Putney Hill, sleeping in a made bed for the first time since my flight to Leatherhead. I will not tell the needless trouble I had breaking into that house—afterwards I found the front door was on the latch—nor how I ransacked every room for food, until, just on the verge of despair, in what seemed to me to be a servant's bedroom, I found a ratgnawed crust and two tinned pineapples. The place had been already searched and emptied. In the bar I afterwards found some biscuits and sandwiches that had been overlooked. The latter I could not eat, but the former not only stayed my hunger, but filled my pockets. I lit no lamps, fearing some Martian might come beating that part of London for food in the night. Before I went to bed I had an interval of restlessness, and prowled from window to window, peering out for some sign of these monsters. I slept little. As I lay in bed I found myself thinking consecutively—a thing I do not remember to have done since my last argument with the curate. During all the intervening time my mental condition had been a hurrying succession of vague emotional states, or a sort of stupid receptivity. But in the night my brain, reinforced, I suppose, by the food I had eaten, grew clear again, and I thought.

Three things struggled for possession of my mind: the killing of the curate, the whereabouts of the Martians, and the possible fate of my wife. The former gave me no sensation of horror or remorse to recall; I saw it simply as a thing done, a memory infinitely disagreeable, but quite without the quality of remorse. I saw myself then as I see myself now, driven step by step towards that hasty blow, the creature of a sequence of accidents leading inevitably to that. I felt no condemnation; yet the memory, static, unprogressive, haunted me. In the silence of the night, with that sense of the near-ness of God that sometimes comes into the stillness and the dark-ness, I stood my trial, my only trial, for that moment of wrath and fear. I retraced every step of our conversation from the moment when I had found him crouching beside me, heedless of my thirst, and pointing to the fire and smoke that streamed up from the ruins of Weybridge. We had been incapable of co-operation—grim chance had taken no heed of that. Had I foreseen, I should have left him at Halliford. But I did not foresee; and crime is to foresee and do. And I set this down as I have set all this story down, as it was. There were no witnesses—all these things I might have concealed. But I set it down, and the reader must form his judgment as he will.

And when, by an effort, I had set aside that picture of a prostrate body, I faced the problem of the Martians and the fate of my wife. For the former I had no data; I could imagine a hundred things, and so, unhappily, I could for the latter. And suddenly that night became terrible. I found myself sitting up in bed, staring at the dark. I found myself praying that the Heat-Ray may have suddenly and painlessly struck her out of being. Since the night of my return from Leatherhead I had not prayed. I had uttered prayers, fetich[1] prayers, had prayed as heathens mutter charms when I was in ex-tremity; but now I prayed indeed, pleading steadfastly and sanely, face to face with the darkness of God. Strange night! strangest in this, that so soon as dawn had come, I, who had talked with God, crept out of the house like a rat leaving its hiding-place—a creature scarcely larger, an inferior animal, a thing that for any passing whim of our masters might be hunted and killed. Perhaps they also prayed confidently to God. Surely, if we have learnt nothing else, this war has taught us pity—pity for those witless souls that suffer our dominion.

---

1. I.e., superstitious prayers, believed to have magical powers in themselves, apart from the speaker's own state of mind or spirit.

The morning was bright and fine, and the eastern sky glowed pink, and was fretted with little golden clouds. In the road that runs from the top of Putney Hill to Wimbledon was a number of pitiful vestiges of the panic torrent that must have poured Londonward on the Sunday night after the fighting began. There was a little two-wheeled cart inscribed with the name of Thomas Lobb, Greengrocer, New Malden, with a smashed wheel and an abandoned tin trunk; there was a straw hat trampled into the now hardened mud, and at the top of West Hill a lot of blood-stained glass about the over-turned water-trough. My movements were languid, my plans of the vaguest. I had an idea of going to Leatherhead, though I knew that there I had the poorest chance of finding my wife. Certainly, unless death had overtaken them suddenly, my cousins and she would have fled thence; but it seemed to me I might find or learn there whither the Surrey people had fled. I knew I wanted to find my wife, that my heart ached for her and the world of men, but I had no clear idea how the finding might be done. I was also clearly aware now of my intense loneliness. From the corner I went, under cover of a thicket of trees and bushes, to the edge of Wimbledon Common, stretching wide and far.

That dark expanse was lit in patches by yellow gorse and broom;[2] there was no Red Weed to be seen, and as I prowled, hesitating, on the verge of the open, the sun rose, flooding it all with light and vitality. I came upon a busy swarm of little frogs in a swampy place among the trees. I stopped to look at them, drawing a lesson from their stout resolve to live.[3] And presently, turning suddenly, with an

2. "Gorse" is a British term for furze, a spiny shrub with yellow flowers; broom is another yellow-flowered, scrubby plant.
3. A version of a crucial moment in Wells's own life. During 1888 he was seriously ill, with what was diagnosed as tuberculosis, and staying at Up Park in Sussex where his mother was in service. One day in midsummer he walked into the surrounding woods and lay in the sun for some hours, after which, he later reported, he said to himself, "I have been dying for nearly two-thirds of a year, and I have died enough." It was after this resolution to live that he returned to London and began his career as a writer.

odd feeling of being watched, I beheld something crouching amidst a clump of bushes. I stood regarding this. I made a step towards it, and it rose up, and became a man armed with a cutlass. I approached him slowly. He stood silent and motionless, regarding me.

As I drew nearer, I perceived he was dressed in clothes as dusty and filthy as my own; he looked, indeed, as though he had been dragged through a culvert.[4] Nearer, I distinguished the green slime of ditches mixing with the pale drab of dried clay and shiny coaly patches. His black hair fell over his eyes, and his face was dark and dirty and sunken, so that at first I did not recognize him. There was a red cut across the lower part of his face.

'Stop!' he cried, when I was within ten yards of him, and I stopped. His voice was hoarse. 'Where do you come from?' he said.

I thought, surveying him.

'I come from Mortlake,' I said. 'I was buried near the pit the Martians made about their cylinder. I have worked my way out and escaped.'

'There is no food about here,' he said. 'This is my country. All this hill down to the river, and back to Clapham, and up to the edge of the Common. There is only food for one. Which way are you going?'

I answered slowly.

'I don't know,' I said. 'I have been buried in the ruins of a house thirteen or fourteen days. I don't know what has happened.'

He looked at me doubtfully, then started, and looked with a changed expression.

'I've no wish to stop about here,' said I. 'I think I shall go to Leatherhead, for my wife was there.'

He shot out a pointing finger.

'It is you,' said he. 'The man from Woking. And you weren't killed at Weybridge?'

I recognized him at the same moment.

'You are the artilleryman who came into my garden.'

'Good luck!' he said. 'We are the lucky ones! Fancy *you!*' He put

4. A sewer or drain under a sidewalk.

out a hand, and I took it. 'I crawled up a drain,' he said. 'But they didn't kill everyone. And after they went away I got off towards Walton across the fields. But— It's not sixteen days altogether—and your hair is grey.' He looked over his shoulder suddenly. 'Only a rook,' he said. 'One gets to know that birds have shadows these days. This *is* a bit open. Let us crawl under those bushes and talk.'

'Have you seen any Martians?' I said. 'Since I crawled out—'

'They've gone away across London,' he said. 'I guess they've got a bigger camp there. Of a night, all over there, Hampstead way, the sky is alive with their lights. It's like a great city, and in the glare you can just see them moving. By daylight you can't. But nearer— I haven't seen them—' He counted on his fingers. 'Five days. Then I saw a couple across Hammersmith way carrying something big. And the night before last'—he stopped, and spoke impressively—'it was just a matter of lights, but it was something up in the air. I believe they've built a flying-machine, and are learning to fly.'

I stopped, on hands and knees, for we had come to the bushes.

'Fly!'

'Yes,' he said, 'fly.'

I went on into a little bower, and sat down.

'It is all over with humanity,' I said. 'If they can do that they will simply go round the world. . . .'

He nodded.

'They will. But— It will relieve things over here a bit. And besides—' He looked at me. 'Aren't you satisfied it *is* up with humanity? I am. We're down; we're beat.'

I stared. Strange as it may seem, I had not arrived at this fact—a fact perfectly obvious so soon as he spoke. I had still held a vague hope; rather, I had kept a lifelong habit of mind. He repeated his words: 'We're beat.' They carried absolute conviction.

'It's all over,' he said. 'They've lost *one*—just one.[5] And they've made their footing good, and crippled the greatest power in the

5. The Martians have lost more than one machine by this time, though the narrator and the Artilleryman do not know it: the loss has been described in the narrator's brother's portion of Book I, Chapter Seventeen.

world. They've walked over us. The death of that one at Weybridge was an accident. And these are only pioneers. They keep on coming. These green stars—I've seen none these five or six days, but I've no doubt they're falling somewhere every night. Nothing's to be done. We're under! We're beat!'

I made him no answer. I sat staring before me, trying in vain to devise some countervailing thought.

'This isn't a war,' said the artilleryman. 'It never was a war, any more than there's war between men and ants.'

Suddenly I recalled the night in the observatory.

'After the tenth shot they fired no more—at least, until the first cylinder came.'

'How do you know?' said the artilleryman. I explained. He thought. 'Something wrong with the gun,' he said. 'But what if there is? They'll get it right again. And even if there's a delay, how can it alter the end? It's just men and ants. There's the ants builds their cities, live their lives, have wars, revolutions, until the men want them out of the way, and then they go out of the way. That's what we are now—just ants. Only—'

'Yes,' I said.

'We're eatable ants.'

We sat looking at each other.

'And what will they do with us,' I said.

'That's what I've been thinking,' he said—'that's what I've been thinking. After Weybridge I went south—thinking. I saw what was up. Most of the people were hard at it squealing and exciting themselves. But I'm not so fond of squealing. I've been in sight of death once or twice; I'm not an ornamental soldier, and at the best and worst, death—it's just death. And it's the man that keeps on thinking comes through. I saw everyone tracking away south. Says I: "Food won't last this way," and I turned right back. I went for the Martians like a sparrow goes for man.[6] All round'—he waved a hand to the horizon—'they're starving in heaps, bolting, treading on each other. . . .'

6. I.e., to pick up the crumbs men drop.

He saw my face, and halted awkwardly.

'No doubt lots who had money have gone away to France,' he said. He seemed to hesitate whether to apologize, met my eyes, and went on: 'There's food all about here. Canned things in shops; wines, spirits, mineral waters; and the water mains and drains are empty. Well, I was telling you what I was thinking. "Here's intelligent things," I said, "and it seems they want us for food. First, they'll smash us up—ships, machines, guns, cities, all the order and organization. All that will go. If we were the size of ants we might pull through. But we're not. It's all too bulky to stop. That's the first certainty." Eh?'

I assented.

'It is; I've thought it out. Very well, then, next: at present we're caught as we're wanted. A Martian has only to go a few miles to get a crowd on the run. And I saw one, one day out by Wandsworth, picking houses to pieces and routing among the wreckage. But they won't keep on doing that. So soon as they've settled all our guns and ships, and smashed our railways, and done all the things they are doing over there, they will begin catching us systematic, picking the best and storing us in cages and things. That's what they will start doing in a bit. Lord! they haven't begun on us yet. Don't you see that?'

'Not begun!' I exclaimed.

'Not begun. All that's happened so far is through our not having the sense to keep quiet—worrying them with guns and such foolery. And losing our heads, and rushing off in crowds to where there wasn't any more safety than where we were. They don't want to bother us yet. They're making their things—making all the things they couldn't bring with them, getting things ready for the rest of their people. Very likely that's why the cylinders have stopped for a bit, for fear of hitting those who are here. And instead of our rushing about blind, on the howl, or getting dynamite on the chance of busting them up, we've got to fix ourselves up according to the new state of affairs. That's how I figure it out. It isn't quite according to what a man wants for his species, but it's about what the facts point to. And that's the principle I acted upon. Cities, nations, civilization, progress—it's all over. That game's up. We're beat.'

'But if that is so, what is there to live for?'

The artilleryman looked at me for a moment.

'There won't be any more blessed concerts for a million years or so; there won't be any Royal Academy of Arts, and no nice little feeds at restaurants. If it's amusement you're after, I reckon the game is up. If you've got any drawing-room manners, or a dislike to eating peas with a knife or dropping aitches,[7] you'd better chuck 'em away. They ain't no further use.'

'You mean—'

'I mean, that men like me are going on living—for the sake of the breed. I tell you, I'm grim set on living. And, if I'm not mistaken, you'll show what insides *you've* got, too, before long. We aren't going to be exterminated. And I don't mean to be caught, either, and tamed and fattened and bred like a thundering ox. Ugh! Fancy those brown creepers!'

'You don't mean to say—'

'I do. I'm going on. Under their feet. I've got it planned; I've thought it out. We men are beat. We don't know enough. We've got to learn before we've got a chance. And we've got to live, and keep independent while we learn. See? That's what has to be done.'

I stared, astonished, and stirred profoundly by the man's resolution.

'Great God!' cried I. 'But you are a man indeed!' And suddenly I gripped his hand.

'Eh?' he said, with his eyes shining. 'I've thought it out, eh?'

'Go on,' I said.

'Well, those who mean to escape their catching must get ready.

7. Failure to pronounce initial *h*—e.g., "In 'Artford, 'Ereford, and 'Ampshire, 'urricanes 'ardly 'appen"—is still one of the most distinctive speech habits of the working-class, especially London-born, English. It is important not only linguistically, but also as a social and political class distinction. Wells's friend George Bernard Shaw satirized the class prejudices arising from such speech peculiarities in his 1913 comedy *Pygmalion*.

I'm getting ready. Mind you, it isn't all of us are made for wild beasts; and that's what it's got to be. That's why I watched you. I had my doubts. You're thin and slender. I didn't know it was you, you see, or just how you'd been buried. All these—the sort of people that lived in these houses, and all those damn little clerks that used to live down *that* way—they'd be no good. They haven't any spirit in them—no proud dreams and no proud lusts; and a man who hasn't one or the other—Lord! what is he but funk[8] and precautions? They just used to skedaddle off to work—I've seen hundreds of 'em, bit of breakfast in hand, running wild and shining to catch their little season-ticket train,[9] for fear they'd get dismissed if they didn't; working at businesses they were afraid to take the trouble to understand; skedaddling back for fear they wouldn't be in time for dinner; keeping indoors after dinner for fear of the back-streets; and sleeping with the wives they married, not because they wanted them, but because they had a bit of money that would make for safety in their one little miserable skedaddle through the world. Lives insured and a bit invested for fear of accidents. And on Sundays—fear of the hereafter. As if hell was built for rabbits. Well, the Martians will just be a godsend to these. Nice roomy cages, fattening food, careful breeding, no worry. After a week or so chasing about the fields and lands on empty stomachs, they'll come and be caught cheerful. They'll be quite glad after a bit. They'll wonder what people did before there were Martians to take care of them. And the bar-loafers, and mashers,[10] and singers—I can imagine them. I can imagine them,' he said, with a sort of sombre gratification. 'There'll be any amount of sentiment and religion loose among them. There's hundreds of things I saw with my eyes, that I've only begun to see clearly these last few days. There's lots will take things as they are, fat and stupid; and lots will be worried by a sort of feeling that it's all wrong, and that they ought to be doing something. Now, whenever things are so that a lot of people feel they ought to

8. Cowardice, fear.
9. I.e., their commuter train to the City.
10. Dandies, cads, flirtatious men.

be doing something, the weak, and those who go weak with a lot of complicated thinking, always make for a sort of do-nothing religion, very pious and superior, and submit to persecution and the will of the Lord. Very likely you've seen the same thing. It's energy in a gale of funk, and turned clean inside out. These cages will be full of psalms and hymns and piety. And those of a less simple sort will work in a bit of—what is it?—eroticism.'

He paused.

'Very likely these Martians will make pets of some of them; train them to do tricks—who knows?—get sentimental over the pet boy who grew up and had to be killed. And some, maybe, they will train to hunt us.'

'No,' I cried, 'that's impossible! No human being—'

'What's the good of going on with such lies?' said the artillery-man. 'There's men who'd do it cheerful. What nonsense to pretend there isn't!'

And I succumbed to his conviction.

'If they come after me,' he said—'Lord! if they come after me!' and subsided into a grim meditation.

I sat contemplating these things. I could find nothing to bring against this man's reasoning. In the days before the invasion no one would have questioned my intellectual superiority to his—I, a pro-fessed and recognized writer on philosophical themes, and he, a common soldier—and yet he had already formulated a situation that I had scarcely realized.

'What are you doing?' I said presently. 'What plans have you made?'

He hesitated.

'Well, it's like this,' he said. 'What have we to do? We have to invent a sort of life where men can live and breed, and be suffi-ciently secure to bring the children up. Yes—wait a bit, and I'll make it clearer what I think ought to be done. The tame ones will go like all tame beasts; in a few generations they'll be big, beautiful, rich-blooded, stupid—rubbish! The risk is that we who keep wild will go savage—degenerate into a sort of big savage rat. . . . You see, how I mean to live is underground. I've been thinking about the drains. Of course, those who don't know drains think horrible things; but under this London are miles and miles—hundreds of miles—and a few days' rain and London empty will leave them sweet and clean. The main drains are big enough and airy enough for anyone. Then there's cellars, vaults, stores, from which bolting passages may be made to the drains. And the railway tunnels and subways. Eh? You begin to see? And we form a band—able-bodied, clean-minded men. We're not going to pick up any rubbish that drifts in. Weaklings go out again.'

'As you meant me to go?'

'Well—I parleyed, didn't I?'

'We won't quarrel about that. Go on.'

'Those who stop, obey orders. Able-bodied, clean-minded women we want also—mothers and teachers. No lackadaisical ladies —no blasted rolling eyes. We can't have any weak or silly. Life is real again, and the useless and cumbersome and mischievous have to die. They ought to die. They ought to be willing to die. It's a sort of disloyalty, after all, to live and taint the race. And they can't be happy. Moreover, dying's none so dreadful;—it's the funking makes it bad. And in all those places we shall gather. Our district will be London. And we may even be able to keep a watch, and run about in the open when the Martians keep away. Play cricket, perhaps. That's how we shall save the race. Eh? It's a possible thing? But saving the race is nothing in itself. As I say, that's only being rats. It's saving our knowledge and adding to it is the thing. There men like you come in. There's books, there's models. We must make great safe places down deep, and get all the books we can; not novels and poetry swipes,[11] but ideas, science books. That's where men like you come in. We must go to the British Museum and pick all those books through. Especially we must keep up our science—learn more. We must watch these Martians. Some of us must go as spies. When it's all working, perhaps I will. Get caught, I mean. And the

---

11. "Swipes" is a working-class word for watery, spoiled beer: the Artillery-
    man's opinion, obviously, of all poetry.

great thing is, we must leave the Martians alone. We mustn't even steal. If we get in their way, we clear out. We must show them we mean no harm. Yes, I know. But they're intelligent things, and they won't hunt us down if they have all they want, and think we're just harmless vermin.'

The artilleryman paused, and laid a brown hand upon my arm.

'After all, it may not be so much we may have to learn before— Just imagine this: Four or five of their Fighting Machines suddenly starting off—Heat-Rays right and left, and not a Martian in 'em. Not a Martian in 'em, but men—men who have learnt the way how. It may be in my time, even—those men. Fancy having one of them lovely things, with its Heat-Ray wide and free! Fancy having it in control! What would it matter if you smashed to smithereens at the end of the run, after a bust like that? I reckon the Martians'll open their beautiful eyes! Can't you see them, man? Can't you see them hurrying, hurrying—puffing and blowing and hooting to their other mechanical affairs? Something out of gear in every case. And swish, bang, rattle, swish! just as they are fumbling over it, *swish* comes the Heat-Ray, and, behold! man has come back to his own.'

For a while the imaginative daring of the artilleryman, and the tone of assurance and courage he assumed, completely dominated my mind. I believed unhesitatingly both in his forecast of human destiny and in the practicability of his astonishing scheme, and the reader who thinks me susceptible and foolish must contrast his position, reading steadily, with all his thoughts about his subject, and mine, crouching fearfully in the bushes and listening, distracted by apprehension. We talked in this manner through the early morning time, and later crept out of the bushes, and, after scanning the sky for Martians, hurried precipitately to the house on Putney Hill where he had made his lair. It was the coal-cellar of the place, and when I saw the work he had spent a week upon—it was a burrow scarcely ten yards long, which he designed to reach to the main drain on Putney Hill—I had my first inkling of the gulf between his dreams and his powers. Such a hole I could have dug in a day. But

I believed in his sufficiently to work with him all that morning until past midday at his digging. We had a garden barrow, and shot[12] the earth we removed against the kitchen range. We refreshed ourselves with a tin of mock-turtle soup and wine from the neighbouring pantry. I found a curious relief from the aching strangeness of the world in this steady labour. As we worked, I turned his project over in my mind, and presently objections and doubts began to arise; but I worked there all the morning, so glad was I to find myself with a purpose again. After working an hour, I began to speculate on the distance one had to go before the cloaca[13] was reached—the chances we had of missing it altogether. My immediate trouble was why we should dig this long tunnel, when it was possible to get into the drain at once down one of the manholes, and work back to the house. It seemed to me, too, that the house was inconveniently chosen, and required a needless length of tunnel. And just as I was beginning to face these things, the artilleryman stopped digging, and looked at me.

'We're working well,' he said. He put down his spade. 'Let us knock off a bit,' he said. 'I think it's time we reconnoitred from the roof of the house.'

I was for going on, and after a little hesitation he resumed his spade; and then suddenly I was struck by a thought. I stopped, and so did he at once.

'Why were you walking about the Common,' I said, 'instead of being here?'

'Taking the air,' he said. 'I was coming back. It's safer by night.'

'But the work?'

'Oh, one can't always work,' he said, and in a flash I saw the man plain. He hesitated, holding his spade. 'We ought to reconnoitre now,' he said, 'because if any come near they may hear the spades and drop upon us unaware.'

I was no longer disposed to object. We went together to the roof

12. Dumped out of the wheelbarrow.
13. Sewer.

and stood on a ladder peeping out of the roof door. No Martians were to be seen, and we ventured out on the tiles, and slipped down under shelter of the parapet.

From this position a shrubbery hid the greater portion of Putney, but we could see the river below, a bubbly mass of Red Weed, and the low parts of Lambeth flooded and red. The red creeper swarmed up the trees about the old palace, and their branches stretched gaunt and dead, and set with shrivelled leaves, from amidst its clusters. It was strange how entirely dependent both these things were upon flowing water for their propagation. About us neither had gained a footing; laburnums, pink mays, snowballs, and trees of arbor vitae,[14] rose out of laurels and hydrangeas, green and brilliant, into the sunlight. Beyond Kensington dense smoke was rising, and that and a blue haze hid the northward hills.

The artilleryman began to tell me of the sort of people who still remained in London.

'One night last week,' he said, 'some fools got the electric light in order, and there was all Regent's Street and the Circus ablaze, crowded with painted and ragged drunkards, men and women, dancing and shouting till dawn. A man who was there told me. And as the day came they beheld a Fighting Machine standing nearby the Langham, and looking down at them. Heaven knows how long he had been there. He came down the road towards them, and picked up nearly a hundred too drunk or frightened to run away.'

Grotesque gleam of a time no history will ever fully describe!

From that, in answer to my questions, he came round to his grandiose plans again. He grew enthusiastic. He talked so eloquently of the possibility of capturing a Fighting Machine, that I more than half believed in him again. But now that I was beginning to understand something of his quality, I could divine the stress he laid on doing nothing precipitately. And I noted that now there was no question that he personally was to capture and fight the great machine.

14. All spring shrubs—suggestive of a rebirth of natural life, in contrast to the canker of the Martian red weed.

After a time we went to the cellar. Neither of us seemed disposed to resume digging, and when he suggested a meal, I was nothing loath. He became suddenly very generous, and when he had eaten he went away, and returned with some excellent cigars. We lit these, and his optimism glowed. He was inclined to regard my coming as a great occasion.

'There's some champagne in the cellar,' he said.

'We can dig better on this Thames-side burgundy,'[15] said I.

'No,' said he; 'I am host today. Champagne! Great God! we've a heavy enough task before us! Let us take a rest, and gather strength while we may. Look at these blistered hands!'

And pursuant to this idea of a holiday, he insisted upon playing cards after we had eaten. He taught me euchre,[16] and after dividing London between us, I taking the northern side, and he the southern, we played for parish points.[17] Grotesque and foolish as this will seem to the sober reader, it is absolutely true, and what is more remarkable, I found the card game and several others we played extremely interesting.

Strange mind of man! that, with our species upon the edge of extermination or appalling degradation, with no clear prospect before us but the chance of a horrible death, we could sit following the chance of this painted pasteboard and playing the 'joker'[18] with vivid delight. Afterwards he taught me poker, and I beat him at three tough chess games. When dark came we were so interested that we decided to take the risk and light a lamp.

After an interminable string of games, we supped, and the artilleryman finished the champagne. We continued smoking the cigars. He was no longer the energetic regenerator of his species I had

15. Inexpensive, mediocre wine.
16. A game much like pinochle, played with the thirty-two highest cards in the pack.
17. That is, the narrator and the artilleryman are playing for the "parishes" or areas of London that they will command in the new world of their daydreaming.
18. In some card games—very seldom played anymore—the joker is the trump that takes any trick.

encountered in the morning. He was still optimistic, but it was a less kinetic, a more thoughtful optimism. I remember he wound up with my health, proposed in a speech of small variety and considerable intermittence.[19] I took a cigar, and went upstairs to look at the lights he had spoken of, that blazed so greenly along the Highgate hills.

At first I stared across the London valley, unintelligently. The northern hills were shrouded in darkness; the fires near Kensington glowed redly, and now and then an orange-red tongue of flame flashed up and vanished in the deep blue night. All the rest of London was black. Then, nearer, I perceived a strange light, a pale violet-purple fluorescent glow, quivering under the night breeze. For a space I could not understand it, and then I knew that it must be the Red Weed from which this faint irradiation proceeded. With that realization, my dormant sense of wonder, my sense of the proportion of things, awoke again. I glanced from that to Mars, red and clear, glowing high in the west, and then gazed long and earnestly at the darkness of Hampstead and Highgate.

I remained a very long time upon the roof, wondering at the grotesque changes of the day. I recalled my mental states from the midnight prayer to the foolish card-playing. I had a violent revulsion of feeling. I remember I flung away the cigar with a certain wasteful symbolism. My folly came to me with glaring exaggeration. I seemed a traitor to my wife and to my kind; I was filled with remorse. I resolved to leave this strange undisciplined dreamer of great things to his drink and gluttony, and to go on into London. There, it seemed to me, I had the best chance of learning what the Martians and my fellow-men were doing. I was still upon the roof when the late moon rose.[20]

19. With frequent pauses or hesitations (since he is drunk).
20. In the original serialization of *The War of the Worlds* in *Pearson's Weekly,* this chapter was not included.

CHAPTER VIII

DEAD LONDON

After I had parted from the artilleryman, I went down the hill, and by the High Street across the bridge to Lambeth. The Red Weed was tumultuous at that time, and nearly choked the bridge roadway, but its fronds were already whitened in patches by the spreading disease that presently removed it so swiftly.

At the corner of the lane that runs to Putney Bridge Station I found a man lying. He was as black as a sweep with the black dust, alive, but helplessly and speechlessly drunk. I could get nothing from him but curses and furious lunges at my head. I think I should have stayed by him but for the brutal type of his face.

There was black dust along the roadway from the bridge onwards, and it grew thicker in Fulham. The streets were horribly quiet. I got food—sour, hard, and mouldy, but quite eatable—in a baker's shop here. Some way towards Walham Green the streets became clear of powder, and I passed a white terrace of houses on fire; the noise of the burning was an absolute relief. Going on towards Brompton, the streets were quiet again.

Here I came once more upon the black powder in the streets and upon dead bodies. I saw altogether about a dozen in the length of the Fulham Road. They had been dead many days, so that I hurried quickly past them. The black powder covered them over, and softened their outlines. One or two had been disturbed by dogs.

Where there was no black powder, it was curiously like a Sunday in the City,[1] with the closed shops, the houses locked up and the blinds drawn, the desertion, and the stillness. In some places plunderers had been at work, but rarely at other than the provision and wine-shops. A jeweller's window had been broken open in one

1. The area north of the Thames, from the Tower of London on the East to St. Paul's Cathedral on the West, enclosed within the original walls of London.

place, but apparently the thief had been disturbed, and a number of gold chains and a watch were scattered on the pavement. I did not trouble to touch them. Further on was a tattered woman in a heap on a doorstep; the hand that hung over her knee was gashed and bled down her rusty brown dress, and a smashed magnum of champagne formed a pool across the pavement. She seemed asleep, but she was dead.

The further I penetrated into London, the profounder grew the stillness. But it was not so much the stillness of death—it was the stillness of suspense, of expectation. At any time the destruction that had already singed the north-western borders of the Metropolis, and had annihilated Ealing and Kilburn, might strike among these houses and leave them smoking ruins. It was a city condemned and derelict. . . .

In South Kensington the streets were clear of dead and of black powder. It was near South Kensington that I first heard the howling. It crept almost imperceptibly upon my senses. It was a sobbing alternation of two notes, 'Ulla, ulla, ulla, ulla,' keeping on perpetually. When I passed streets that ran northward it grew in volume, and houses and buildings seemed to deaden and cut it off again. It came to a full tide down Exhibition Road. I stopped, staring towards Kensington Gardens, wondering at this strange remote wailing. It was as if that mighty desert of houses had found a voice for its fear and solitude.

'Ulla, ulla, ulla, ulla,' wailed that superhuman note—great waves of sound sweeping down the broad, sunlit roadway, between the tall buildings on either side. I turned northward, marvelling, towards the iron gates of Hyde Park. I had half a mind to break into the Natural History Museum and find my way up to the summits of the towers, in order to see across the park. But I decided to keep to the ground, where quick hiding was possible, and so went on up the Exhibition Road. All the large mansions on either side of the road were empty and still, and my footsteps echoed against the sides of the houses. At the top, near the park gate, I came upon a strange sight—a bus overturned, and the skeleton of a horse picked clean.

I puzzled over this for a time, and then went on to the bridge over the Serpentine. The Voice grew stronger and stronger, though I could see nothing above the housetops on the north side of the park, save a haze of smoke to the north-west.

'Ulla, ulla, ulla, ulla,' cried the Voice, coming, as it seemed to me, from the district about Regent's Park. The desolating cry worked upon my mind. The mood that had sustained me passed. The wailing took possession of me. I found I was intensely weary, footsore, and again hungry and thirsty.

It was already past noon. Why was I wandering alone in this city of the dead? Why was I alone when all London was lying in state, and in its black shroud? I felt intolerably lonely. My mind ran on old friends that I had forgotten for years. I thought of the poisons in the chemists' shops, of the liquors the wine-merchants stored; I recalled the two sodden creatures of despair who, so far as I knew, shared the city with myself. . . .

I came into Oxford Street by the Marble Arch, and here again was black powder and several bodies, and an evil, ominous smell from the gratings of the cellars of some of the houses. I grew very thirsty after the heat of my long walk. With infinite trouble I managed to break into a public-house and get food and drink. I was weary after eating, and went into the parlour behind the bar, and slept on a black horsehair sofa I found there.

I awoke to find that dismal howling still in my ears, 'Ulla, ulla, ulla, ulla.' It was now dusk, and after I had routed out some biscuits and a cheese in the bar—there was a meat-safe, but it contained nothing but maggots—I wandered on through the silent residential squares to Baker Street—Portman Square is the only one I can name—and so came out at last upon Regent's Park. And as I emerged from the top of Baker Street, I saw far away over the trees in the clearness of the sunset the hood of the Martian giant from which this howling proceeded. I was not terrified. I came upon him as if it were a matter of course. I watched him for some time, but he did not move. He appeared to be standing and yelling, for no reason that I could discover.

I tried to formulate a plan of action. That perpetual sound of 'Ulla, ulla, ulla, ulla', confused my mind. Perhaps I was too tired to be very fearful. Certainly I was rather curious to know the reason of this monotonous crying than afraid. I turned back away from the park and struck into Park Road, intending to skirt the park, went along under shelter of the terraces, and got a view of this stationary howling Martian from the direction of St John's Wood. A couple of hundred yards out of Baker Street I heard a yelping chorus, and saw, first a dog with a piece of putrescent[2] red meat in his jaws coming headlong towards me, and then a pack of starving mongrels in pursuit of him. He made a wide curve to avoid me, as though he feared I might prove a fresh competitor. As the yelping died away down the silent road, the wailing sound of 'Ulla, ulla, ulla, ulla' re-asserted itself.

I came upon the wrecked Handling Machine half-way to St John's Wood Station. At first I thought a house had fallen across the road. It was only as I clambered among the ruins that I saw, with a start, this mechanical Samson[3] lying, with its tentacles bent and smashed and twisted, among the ruins it had made. The fore-part was shattered. It seemed as if it had driven blindly at the house, and had been overwhelmed in its overthrow. It seemed to me then that this might have happened by a Handling Machine escaping from the guidance of its Martian. I could not clamber among the ruins to see it, and the twilight was now so far advanced that the interior was invisible to me.

Wondering still more at all that I had seen, I pushed on towards Primrose Hill. Far away, through a gap in the trees, I saw a second Martian, motionless as the first, standing in the park towards the Zoological Gardens, and silent. A little beyond the ruins about the smashed Handling Machine I came upon the Red Weed again, and found Regent's Canal a spongy mass of dark red vegetation.

2. Growing rotten or decayed.
3. The incredibly strong, unruly hero of Jewish folklore whose exploits are celebrated in Judges 13:1–16:31. Taken prisoner by the Philistines, he destroyed himself and them by pulling down the walls of their palace.

Abruptly, as I crossed the bridge, the sound of 'Ulla, ulla, ulla' ceased. It was, as it were, cut off. The silence came like a thunder-clap.

The dusky houses about me stood faint, and tall and dim; the trees towards the park were growing black. All about me the Red Weed clambered among the ruins, writhing to get above me in the dim. Night, the Mother of Fear and Mystery, was coming upon me. But while that voice sounded, the solitude, the desolation, had been endurable; by virtue of it London had still seemed alive, and the sense of life about me had upheld me. Then suddenly a change, the passing of something—I knew not what—and then a stillness that could be felt. Nothing but this gaunt quiet.

London about me gazed at me spectrally. The windows in the white houses were like the eye-sockets of skulls. About me my imag-ination found a thousand noiseless enemies moving. Terror seized me, a horror of my temerity. In front of me the road became pitchy black as though it was tarred, and I saw a contorted shape lying across the pathway. I could not bring myself to go on. I turned down St John's Wood Road, and ran headlong from this unendur-able stillness towards Kilburn. I hid from the night and the silence, until long after midnight, in a cabmen's shelter in the Harrow Road. But before the dawn my courage returned, and while the stars were still in the sky, I turned once more towards Regent's Park. I missed my way among the streets, and presently saw, down a long avenue, in the half-light of the early dawn, the curve of Primrose Hill. On the summit, towering up to the fading stars, was a third Martian, erect and motionless like the others.

An insane resolve possessed me. I would die and end it. And I would save myself even the trouble of killing myself. I marched on recklessly towards this Titan, and then, as I drew nearer and the light grew, I saw that a multitude of black birds was circling and clustering about the hood. At that my heart gave a bound, and I began running along the road.

I hurried through the Red Weed that choked St Edmund's Ter-race (I waded breast-high across a torrent of water that was rushing down from the waterworks towards the Albert Road), and emerged upon the grass before the rising of the sun. Great mounds had been heaped about the crest of the hill, making a huge redoubt[4] of it—it was the final and largest place the Martians made—and from behind these heaps there rose a thin smoke against the sky. Against the skyline an eager dog ran and disappeared. The thought that had flashed into my mind grew real, grew credible. I felt no fear, only a wild trembling exultation, as I ran up the hill towards the motionless monster. Out of the hood hung lank shreds of brown at which the hungry birds pecked and tore.

In another moment I had scrambled up the earthen rampart and stood upon its crest, and the interior of the redoubt was below me. A mighty space it was, with gigantic machines here and there within it, huge mounds of material and strange shelter-places. And, scattered about it, some in their overturned war machines, some in the now rigid Handling Machines, and a dozen of them stark and silent and laid in a row, were the Martians—*dead!*—slain by the putrefactive[5] and disease bacteria against which their systems were unprepared; slain as the Red Weed was being slain; slain, after all man's devices had failed, by the humblest things that God, in His wisdom, has put upon the earth.

For so it had come about, as, indeed, I and many men might have foreseen had not terror and disaster blinded our minds. These germs of disease have taken toll of humanity since the beginning of things —taken toll of our pre-human ancestors since life began here. But by virtue of this natural selection of our kind we have developed resisting-power; to no germs do we succumb without a struggle, and to many—those that cause putrefaction in dead matter, for instance —our living frames are altogether immune. But there are no bacteria on Mars, and directly these invaders arrived, directly they drank and fed, our microscopic allies began to work their overthrow. Already when I watched them they were irrevocably doomed, dying and rotting even as they went to and fro. It was in-

4. Fortification.
5. Causing decay or rottenness.

evitable. By the toll of a billion deaths, man has bought his birth-right of the earth, and it is his against all comers; it would still be his were the Martians ten times as mighty as they are. For neither do men live nor die in vain.

Here and there they were scattered, nearly fifty altogether in that great gulf they had made, overtaken by a death that must have seemed to them as incomprehensible as any death could be. To me also at that time this death was incomprehensible. All I knew was that these things that had been alive and so terrible to men were dead. For a moment I believed that the destruction of Sennacherib[6] had been repeated, that God had repented, that the Angel of Death had slain them in the night.

I stood staring into the pit, and my heart lightened gloriously, even as the rising sun struck the world to fire about me with his rays. The pit was still in darkness; the mighty engines, so great and wonderful in their power and complexity, so unearthly in their tor-tuous forms, rose weird and vague and strange out of the shadows towards the light. A multitude of dogs, I could hear, fought over the bodies that lay darkly in the depth of the pit, far below me. Across the pit on its farther lip, flat and vast and strange, lay the great fly-ing machine with which they had been experimenting upon our denser atmosphere when decay and death arrested them. Death had come not a day too soon. At the sound of a cawing overhead I looked up at the huge Fighting Machine, that would fight no more for ever.[7]

6. "The Destruction of Sennacherib" is the title of one of the most famous poems of Lord Byron (1788-1824). In II Kings: 19 it is related how the Assyrian King Sennacherib brought a great army to war against the Israelites; but, thanks to the prayers of the Israelites, the Lord killed Sennacherib's whole army in a single night. The legend has an obvious relevance to the sudden, total, and unhoped-for obliteration of the Martian invaders.

7. A last, and very curious, invocation of the sub-theme of colonial warfare and exploitation. In 1877 Chief Joseph of the Nez Percé Indians had surrendered to the United States Army in a noble and widely-reported speech: "I am tired of fighting. Our chiefs are killed. . . . Hear me, my chiefs, I am tired. My heart is sick and sad. From where the sun now

I turned and looked down the slope of the hill to where, enhaloed now in birds, stood those other two Martians that I had seen overnight, just as death had overtaken them. The one had died, even as it had been crying to its companions; perhaps it was the last to die, and its voice had gone on perpetually until the force of its machinery was exhausted. They glittered now, harmless tripod towers of shining metal, in the brightness of the rising sun. . . .

All about the pit, and saved as by a miracle from everlasting destruction, stretched the great Mother of Cities. Those who have only seen London veiled in her sombre robes of smoke can scarcely imagine the naked clearness and beauty of the silent wilderness of houses.

Eastward, over the blackened ruins of the Albert Terrace and the splintered spire of the church, the sun blazed dazzling in a clear sky, and here and there some facet in the great wilderness of roofs caught the light and glared with a white intensity. It touched even that round store place for wines by the Chalk Farm Station, and the vast railway yards, marked once with graining of black rails, but red-lined now with the quick rusting of a fortnight's disuse, with something of the mystery of beauty.

Northward were Kilburn and Hampstead, blue and crowded with houses; westward the great city was dimmed; and southward, beyond the Martians, the green waves of Regent's Park, the Langham Hotel, the dome of the Albert Hall, the Imperial Institute, and the giant mansions of the Brompton Road, came out clear and little in the sunrise, the jagged ruins of Westminster rising hazily beyond. Far away and blue were the Surrey hills, and the towers of the Crystal Palace glittered like two silver rods. The dome of St Paul's was dark against the sunrise, and injured, I saw for the first time, by a huge gaping cavity on its western side.

---

stands I will fight no more forever." Wells, by associating the tragic dignity of Chief Joseph's language with the now-defeated Martian invader, achieves a striking reversal of emotion. For we now understand that it is the Martians, pathetically overspecialized prisoners of their own technology, who are the truly pitiable, foredoomed losers of this war of worlds, of ecologies, of relationships to Nature.

And as I looked at this wide expanse of houses and factories and churches, silent and abandoned; as I thought of the multitudinous hopes and efforts, the innumerable hosts of lives that had gone to build this human reef, and of the swift and ruthless destruction that had hung over it all; when I realized that the shadow had been rolled back, and that men might still live in the streets, and this dear vast dead city of mine be once more alive and powerful, I felt a wave of emotion that was near akin to tears.

The torment was over. Even that day the healing would begin. The survivors of the people scattered over the country—leaderless, lawless, foodless, like sheep without a shepherd—the thousands who had fled by sea, would begin to return; the pulse of life, growing stronger and stronger, would beat again in the empty streets, and pour across the vacant squares. Whatever destruction was done, the hand of the destroyer was stayed. All the gaunt wrecks, the blackened skeletons of houses that stared so dismally at the sunlit grass of the hill, would presently be echoing with the hammers of the restorers and ringing with the tapping of the trowels. At the thought I extended my hands towards the sky and began thanking God. In a year, thought I—in a year. . . .

And then, with overwhelming force, came the thought of myself, of my wife, and the old life of hope and tender helpfulness that had ceased for ever.

CHAPTER IX

WRECKAGE

And now comes the strangest thing in my story. And yet, perhaps, it is not altogether strange. I remember, clearly and coldly and vividly, all that I did that day until the time that I stood weeping and praising God upon the summit of Primrose Hill. And then I forget. . . .

Of the next three days I know nothing. I have learnt since that, so far from my being the first discoverer of the Martian overthrow, several such wanderers as myself had already discovered this on the previous night. One man—the first—had gone to St Martin's-le-Grand, and, while I sheltered in the cabmen's hut, had contrived to telegraph to Paris. Thence the joyful news had flashed all over the world; a thousand cities, chilled by ghastly apprehensions, suddenly flashed into frantic illumination; they knew of it in Dublin, Edinburgh, Manchester, Birmingham, at the time when I stood upon the verge of the pit. Already men, weeping with joy, as I have heard, shouting and staying their work to shake hands and shout, were making up trains, even as near as Crewe, to descend upon London. The church bells that had ceased a fortnight since suddenly caught the news, until all England was bell-ringing. Men on cycles, lean-faced, unkempt, scorched along every country lane, shouting of un-hoped deliverance, shouting to gaunt, staring figures of despair. And for the food! Across the Channel, across the Irish Sea, across the Atlantic, corn, bread and meat were tearing to our relief. All the shipping in the world seemed going Londonward in those days. But of all this I have no memory. I drifted—a demented man. I found myself in the house of kindly people who had found me on the third day, wandering, weeping and raving, through the streets of St John's Wood. They have told me since that I was singing some inane doggerel about 'The Last Man Left Alive, Hurrah! The Last Man Left Alive.' Troubled as they were with their own affairs, these people, whose name, much as I would like to express my gratitude to them, I may not even give here, nevertheless cumbered themselves with me, sheltered me and protected me from myself. Apparently they had learnt something of my story from me during the days of my lapse.

Very gently, when my mind was assured again, did they break to me what they had learnt of the fate of Leatherhead. Two days after I was imprisoned it had been destroyed, with every soul in it, by a Martian. He had swept it out of existence, as it seemed, without any provocation, as a boy might crush an anthill, in the mere wantonness of power.

I was a lonely man, and they were very kind to me. I was a lonely man and a sad one, and they bore with me. I remained with them four days after my recovery. All that time I felt a vague, a growing craving to look once more on whatever remained of the little life that seemed so happy and bright in my past. It was a mere hopeless desire to feast upon my misery. They dissuaded me. They did all they could to divert me from this morbidity. But at last I could resist the impulse no longer, and promising faithfully to return to them, and parting, as I will confess, from those four-day friends with tears, I went out again into the streets that had lately been so dark and strange and empty.

Already they were busy with returning people, in places even there were shops open, and I saw a drinking-fountain running water.

I remember how mockingly bright the day seemed as I went back on my melancholy pilgrimage to the little house at Woking, how busy the streets and vivid the moving life about me. So many people were abroad everywhere, busied in a thousand activities, that it seemed incredible that any great proportion of the population could have been slain. But then I noticed how yellow were the skins of the people I met, how shaggy the hair of the men, how large and bright their eyes, and that every other man still wore his dirty rags. The faces seemed all with one of two expressions—a leaping exultation and energy, or a grim resolution. Save for the expression of the faces, London seemed a city of tramps. The vestries were indiscriminately distributing bread sent us by the French Government. The ribs of the few horses showed dismally. Haggard special constables with white badges stood at the corners of every street. I saw little of the mischief wrought by the Martians until I reached Wellington Street, and there I saw the Red Weed clambering over the buttresses of Waterloo Bridge.

At the corner of the bridge, too, I saw one of the common contrasts of that grotesque time: a sheet of paper flaunting against a thicket of the Red Weed, transfixed by a stick that kept it in place.

It was the placard of the first newspaper to resume publication—the *Daily Mail*.[1] I bought a copy for a blackened shilling I found in my pocket. Most of it was in blank, but the solitary compositor who did the thing had amused himself by making a grotesque scheme of advertisement stereo[2] on the back page. The matter he printed was emotional; the news organization had not as yet found its way back. I learnt nothing fresh except that already in one week the examination of the Martian mechanisms had yielded astonishing results. Among other things, the article assured me what I did not believe at the time: that the 'Secret of Flying' was discovered. At Waterloo I found the free trains that were taking people to their homes. The first rush was already over. There were few people in the train, and I was in no mood for casual conversation. I got a compartment to myself, and sat with folded arms, looking greyly at the sunlit devastation that flowed past the windows. And just outside the terminus the train jolted over temporary rails, and on either side of the railway the houses were blackened ruins. To Clapham Junction the face of London was grimy with powder of the Black Smoke, in spite of two days of thunderstorms and rain, and at Clapham Junction the line had been wrecked again; there were hundreds of out-of-work clerks and shopmen working side by side with the customary navvies, and we were jolted over a hasty relaying.

All down the line from there the aspect of the country was gaunt and unfamiliar; Wimbledon particularly had suffered. Walton, by virtue of its unburnt pine-woods, seemed the least hurt of any place along the line. The Wandle, the Mole, every little stream, was a heaped mass of Red Weed, in appearance between butcher's meat and pickled cabbage. The Surrey pine-woods were too dry, however, for the festoons of the red climber. Beyond Wimbledon, within sight of the line, in certain nursery grounds, were the heaped masses of earth about the sixth cylinder. A number of people were standing

1. Founded in 1896, one of foremost practitioners of the sensationalistic, "new journalism"; an immense success in the early twentieth century.
2. Short for stereotype, a metal block on which a company's advertising information is permanently typeset for easy reproduction in newspapers.

about it, and some sappers were busy in the midst of it. Over it flaunted a Union Jack,[3] flapping cheerfully in the morning breeze. The nursery grounds were everywhere crimson with the weed, a wide expanse of livid colour cut with purple shadows, and very painful to the eye. One's gaze went with infinite relief from the scorched greys and sullen reds of the foreground to the blue-green softness of the eastward hills.

The line on the London side of Woking Station was still undergoing repair, so I descended at Byfleet Station and took the road to Maybury, past the place where I and the artilleryman had talked to the hussars, and on by the spot where the Martian had appeared to me in the thunderstorm. Here, moved by curiosity, I turned aside to find, among a tangle of red fronds, the warped and broken dog-cart with the whitened bones of the horse, scattered and gnawed. For a time I stood regarding these vestiges. . . .

Then I returned through the pine-wood, neck-high with Red Weed here and there, to find the landlord of the Spotted Dog had already found burial; and so came home past the College Arms. A man standing at an open cottage door greeted me by name as I passed.

I looked at my house with a quick flash of hope that faded immediately. The door had been forced; it was unfastened, and was opening slowly as I approached.

It slammed again. The curtains of my study fluttered out of the open window from which I and the artilleryman had watched the dawn. No one had closed that window since. The smashed bushes were just as I had left them nearly four weeks ago. I stumbled into the hall, and the house felt empty. The stair-carpet was ruffled and discoloured where I had crouched soaked to the skin from the thunderstorm, the night of the catastrophe. Our muddy footsteps I saw still went up the stairs.

I followed them to my study, and found lying on my writing-table still, with the selenite[4] paper-weight upon it, the sheet of work I had

3. The British Flag.
4. Common hydrated calcium sulfate, a variety of gypsum.

left on the afternoon of the opening of the cylinder. For a space I stood reading over my abandoned arguments. It was a paper on the probable development of Moral Ideas with the development of the civilizing process; and the last sentence was the opening of a prophecy: 'In about two hundred years,' I had written, 'we may expect—'[5] The sentence ended abruptly. I remembered my inability to fix my mind that morning, scarcely a month gone by, and how I had broken off to get my *Daily Chronicle* from the newsboy. I remembered how I went down to the garden gate as he came along, and how I had listened to his odd story of the 'Men from Mars'.

I came down and went into the dining-room. There were the mutton and the bread, both far gone now in decay, and a beer bottle overturned, just as I and the artilleryman had left them. My home was desolate. I perceived the folly of the faint hope I had cherished so long. And then a strange thing occurred. 'It is no use,' said a voice. 'The house is deserted. No one has been here these ten days. Do not stay here to torment yourself. No one escaped but you.'

I was startled. Had I spoken my thought aloud? I turned, and the french window was open behind me. I made a step to it, and stood looking out.

And there, amazed and afraid, even as I stood amazed and afraid, were my cousin and my wife—my wife white and tearless. She gave a faint cry.

'I came,' she said. 'I knew—knew—'

She put her hand to her throat—swayed. I made a step forward, and caught her in my arms.

---

5. See Book I, Chapter Three, note 5. This is the "work" the narrator interrupted to go see the first Martian cylinder. The whole tale, of course, has been a grim vision of what "we may expect" from one, at least possible, future.

CHAPTER X
THE EPILOGUE

I cannot but regret, now that I am concluding my story, how little I am able to contribute to the discussion of the many debatable questions which are still unsettled. In one respect I shall certainly provoke criticism. My particular province is speculative philosophy. My knowledge of comparative physiology is confined to a book or two, but it seems to me that Carver's suggestions as to the reason of the rapid death of the Martians is so probable as to be regarded almost as a proven conclusion. I have assumed that in the body of my narrative.

At any rate, in all the bodies of the Martians that were examined after the war, no bacteria except those already known as terrestrial species were found. That they did not bury any of their dead, and the reckless slaughter they perpetrated, point also to an entire ignorance of the putrefactive process. But probable as this seems, it is by no means a proven conclusion.

Neither is the composition of the Black Smoke known, which the Martians used with such deadly effect, and the generator of the Heat-Ray remains a puzzle. The terrible disasters at the Ealing and South Kensington laboratories have disinclined analysts for further investigations upon the latter. Spectrum analysis of the black powder points unmistakably to the presence of an unknown element with a brilliant group of three lines in the green,[1] and it is possible that it combines with argon to form a compound which acts at once with deadly effect upon some constituent in the blood. But such unproven speculations will scarcely be of interest to the general reader, to whom this story is addressed. None of the brown scum that drifted down the Thames after the destruction of Shepperton was examined at the time, and now none is forthcoming.

1. A contradiction. In Book I, Chapter Fifteen, the black smoke is said to produce unusual lines in the blue of the spectrum.

The results of an anatomical examination of the Martians, so far as the prowling dogs had left such an examination possible, I have already given. But everyone is familiar with the magnificent and almost complete specimen in spirits at the Natural History Museum, and the countless drawings that have been made from it; and beyond that the interest of the physiology and structure is purely scientific.

A question of graver and universal interest is the possibility of another attack from the Martians. I do not think that nearly enough attention is being given to this aspect of the matter. At present the planet Mars is in conjunction, but with every return to opposition I, for one, anticipate a renewal of their adventure.[2] In any case, we should be prepared. It seems to me that it should be possible to define the position of the gun from which the shots are discharged, to keep a sustained watch upon this part of the planet, and to anticipate the arrival of the next attack.

In that case the cylinder might be destroyed with dynamite or artillery before it was sufficiently cool for the Martians to emerge, or they might be butchered by means of guns so soon as the screw opened. It seems to me that they have lost a vast advantage in the failure of their first surprise. Possibly they see it in the same light.

Lessing had advanced excellent reasons for supposing that the Martians have actually succeeded in effecting a landing on the planet Venus. Seven months ago now, Venus and Mars were in alignment with the sun; that is to say, Mars was in opposition from the point of view of an observer on Venus. Subsequently a peculiar luminous and sinuous marking appeared on the unillumined half of the inner planet, and almost simultaneously a faint dark mark of a similar sinuous character was detected upon a photograph of the Martian disc. One needs to see the drawings of these appearances in order to appreciate fully their remarkable resemblance in character.

At any rate, whether we expect another invasion or not, our views of the human future must be greatly modified by these events. We have learned now that we cannot regard this planet as being fenced

2. At conjunction, the Earth and Mars are on opposite sides of the Sun.

in and a secure abiding-place for Man; we can never anticipate the unseen good or evil that may come upon us suddenly out of space. It may be that in the larger design of the universe this invasion from Mars is not without its ultimate benefit for men; it has robbed us of that serene confidence in the future which is the most fruitful source of decadence, the gifts to human science it has brought are enormous, and it has done much to promote the conception of the commonweal of mankind. It may be that across the immensity of space the Martians have watched the fate of these pioneers of theirs and learned their lesson, and that on the planet Venus they have found a securer settlement. Be that as it may, for many years yet there will certainly be no relaxation of the eager scrutiny of the Martian disc, and those fiery darts of the sky, the shooting stars, will bring with them as they fall an unavoidable apprehension to all the sons of men.

The broadening of men's views that has resulted can scarcely be exaggerated. Before the cylinder fell there was a general persuasion that through all the deep of space no life existed beyond the petty surface of our minute sphere. Now we see further. If the Martians can reach Venus, there is no reason to suppose that the thing is impossible for men, and when the slow cooling of the sun makes this earth uninhabitable, as at last it must do, it may be that the thread of life that has begun here will have streamed out and caught our sister planet within its toils. Should we conquer?

Dim and wonderful is the vision I have conjured up in my mind of life spreading slowly from this little seed-bed of the solar system throughout the inanimate vastness of sidereal space. But that is a remote dream. It may be, on the other hand, that the destruction of the Martians is only a reprieve. To them, and not to us, perhaps, is the future ordained.

I must confess the stress and danger of the time have left an abiding sense of doubt and insecurity in my mind. I sit in my study writing by lamplight, and suddenly I see again the healing valley below set with writhing flames, and feel the house behind and about me empty and desolate. I go out into the Byfleet Road, and vehicles pass me, a butcher-boy in a cart, a cabful of visitors, a workman on a bicycle, children going to school, and suddenly they become vague and unreal, and I hurry again with the artilleryman through the hot, brooding silence. Of a night I see the black powder darkening the silent streets, and the contorted bodies shrouded in that layer; they rise upon me, tattered and dog-bitten. They gibber and grow fiercer, paler, uglier, mad distortions of humanity at last, and I wake, cold and wretched, in the darkness of the night.

I go to London and see the busy multitudes in Fleet Street and the Strand, and it comes across my mind that they are but the ghosts of the past, haunting the streets that I have seen silent and wretched, going to and fro, phantasms in a dead city, the mockery of life in a galvanized body. And strange, too, it is to stand on Primrose Hill, as I did but a day before writing this last chapter, to see the great province of houses, dim and blue through the haze of the smoke and mist, vanishing at last into the vague lower sky, to see the people walking to and fro among the flower-beds on the hill, to see the sightseers about the Martian machine that stands there still, to hear the tumult of playing children, and to recall the time when I saw it all bright and clear-cut, hard and silent, under the dawn of that last great day. . . .

And strangest of all is it to hold my wife's hand again, and to think that I have counted her, and that she has counted me, among the dead.

APPENDIX

The Landings of the Cylinders

In Chapter One, observers witness the launching of the cylinders as ten massive explosions on the planet Mars, on ten successive evenings. However, *The War of the Worlds* tells us where only seven of the cylinders land, in Surrey and London:

1. On Horsell Common, Thursday night (discovered Friday morning)
2. The pinewoods northwest of Woking, Friday midnight
3. Near Addlestone, Saturday night
4. Bushey Park, Sunday night
5. Near Kew, Monday night (this is the one that lands behind the house where the narrator and the Curate are hiding)
6. Wimbledon, Monday night
7. Primrose Hill, Tuesday night.

It is somewhat surprising that an invasion fleet from another world should concentrate seventy percent of its force within an area smaller than Rhode Island. But here, again, Wells sets an important precedent for later science fiction. His English readers in 1898 were startled and excited by just this audacious introduction of the unearthly and the apocalyptic into the most familiar, most everyday of landscapes. And innumerable stories of extra-terrestrial invasion since *The War of the Worlds*—in literature and in film—have begun with the axiom that when the aliens land, they always choose a small town or a peaceful country road for their first beachhead.

THE CONTEXT OF THE NOVELS

His books were sent to me, and I have read them. It is very curious, and, I will add, very English. But I do not see the possibility of comparison between his work and mine. We do not proceed in the same manner. It occurs to me that his stories do not repose on very scientific bases. No, there is no *rapport* between his work and mine. I make use of physics. He invents.

JULES VERNE

From a Review of The Time Machine in the Spectator, 13 July 1895

. . . This is, we take it, the warning which Mr. Wells intends to give:—'Above all things avoid sinking into a condition of satisfied ease; avoid a soft and languid serenity; even evil passions which involve continuous effort, are not so absolutely deadly as the temperament of languid and harmless playfulness.' We have no doubt that, so far as Mr. Wells goes, his warning is wise. But we have little fear that the languid, ease-loving, and serene temperament will ever paralyse the human race after the manner he supposes, even though there may be at present some temporary signs of the growth of the appetite for mere amusement.

In the first place, Mr. Wells assumes, what is well-nigh impossible, that the growth of the pleasure-loving temperament would not itself prevent that victory over physical obstacles to enjoyment on which he founds his dream. The pleasure-loving temperament soon becomes both selfish and fretful. And selfishness no less than fretfulness poisons all enjoyment. Before our race had reached anything like the languid grace and frivolity of the Eloi (the surface population), it would have fallen a prey to the many competing and conflicting energies of Nature which are always on the watch to crush out weak and languid organisations, to say nothing of the un-

By R. H. Hutton, literary editor of the Spectator.

canny Morlocks (the envious subterranean population), who would soon have invented spectacles shutting out from their sensitive eyes the glare of either moon or sun. If the doctrines as to evolution have any truth in them at all, nothing is more certain than that the superiority of man to Nature will never endure beyond the endurance of his fighting strength. The physical condition of the Eloi is supposed, for instance, so to have accommodated itself to external circumstances as to extinguish that continual growth of population which renders the mere competition for food so serious a factor in the history of the globe. But even supposing such a change to have taken place, of which we see no trace at all in history or civilisation, what is there in the nature of frivolity and love of ease, to diminish, and not rather to increase, that craving to accumulate sources of enjoyment at the expense of others, which seems to be *most* visible in the nations whose populations are of the slowest growth, and which so reintroduces rivalries and war. Let any race find the pressure of population on its energies diminishing, and the mutual jealousy amongst those who are thus placed in a position of advantage for securing wealth and ease, will advance with giant strides. The hardest-pressed populations are not the most, but on the whole the least, selfish.

In the next place Mr. Wells's fancy ignores the conspicuous fact that man's nature needs a great deal of hard work to keep it in order at all, and that no class of men or women are so dissatisfied with their own internal condition as those who are least disciplined by the necessity for industry. Find the idlest class of a nation and you certainly find the most miserable class. There would be no tranquillity or serenity at all in any population for which there were not hard tasks and great duties. The Eloi of this fanciful story would have become even more eager for the satisfaction of selfish desires than the Morlocks themselves. The nature of man must have altered not merely accidentally, but essentially, if the devotion to ease and amusement had left it sweet and serene. Matthew Arnold wrote in his unreal mood of agnosticism:—

> We, in some unknown Power's employ,
> Move on a rigorous line;
> Can neither, when we will, enjoy,
> Nor, when we will, resign.

But it is not in some 'unknown Power's employ' that we move on this 'rigorous line.' On the contrary, it is in the employ of a Power which has revealed itself in the Incarnation and the Cross. And we may expect with the utmost confidence that if the earth is still in existence in the year 802,701 A.D., either the A.D. will mean a great deal more than it means now, or else its inhabitants will be neither Eloi nor Morlocks. For in that case evil passions will by that time have led to the extinction of races spurred and pricked on by conscience and yet so frivolous or so malignant. Yet Mr. Wells's fanciful and lively dream is well worth reading, if only because it will draw attention to the great moral and religious factors in human nature which he appears to ignore.

From a **Review of** The Time Machine **in the** Daily Chronicle, **27 July 1895**

No two books could well be more unlike than *The Time Machine* and *The Strange Case of Dr. Jekyll and Mr. Hyde,* but since the appearance of Stevenson's creepy romance we have had nothing in the domain of pure fantasy so bizarre as this 'invention' by Mr. H. G. Wells. For his central idea Mr. Wells may be indebted to some previously published narrative suggestion, but if so we must confess ourselves entirely unacquainted with it, and so far as our knowledge goes he has produced in fiction that rarity which Solomon declared to be not merely rare but non-existent—a 'new thing under the sun.'

The narrative opens in the dining-room of the man who is known to us throughout simply as the Time Traveller, and who is expounding to his guests a somewhat remarkable theory in esoteric mathematics. . . . By this Poe-like ingenuity of whimsical reasoning the Time Traveller leads up to his great invention—nothing less than a machine which shall convey him through time, that fourth dimension of space, with even greater facility than men are conveyed through the other three dimensions by bicycle or balloon. He can go back either to the days of his grandsires or to the days of creation; he can go forward to the days of his grandsons, or still further to that last *fin de siècle*, when earth is moribund and man has ceased to be. The one journey of which we have a record is a voyage into far futurity, and when after a wild flight through the centuries the Time Traveller stops the machine the dial register tells him that he is in or about the year 802,000 A.D. Man is still existent, but a remarkable change has passed upon him. The fissure of cleavage between the classes and the masses instead of being bridged over or filled up has become a great gulf. In centuries of centuries the environment of the more favoured has become so exquisitely adapted to all their needs, and indeed to all their desires, that the necessity for physical or mental activity is so many generations behind them that it does not survive even as a memory; the powers of body and mind which are distinctively manly have perished in ages of disuse, and they have become frail, listless, pleasure-loving children. The workers, on the other hand, have become brutalised, bleached, ape-like creatures, who live underground and toil for their effeminate lords, taking their pay, when they can, by living upon them literally in a horrible cannibalistic fashion. The adventures of the Time Traveller among the Eloi and the Morlocks are conceived in the true spirit of fantasy—the effect of remoteness being achieved much more successfully than in such a book, for example, as Lord Lytton's *The Coming Race*. Still more weird are the further wanderings in a future when man has gone, and even nature is not what it was, because sun, moon, stars, and earth are tottering to their doom. The description of the seacoast of the dying ocean, still embracing a dying world, and of the huge, hideous creeping things which are the last remains of life on a worn-out planet has real impressiveness—it grips the imagination as it is only gripped by genuinely imaginative work. It is in what may be described literally as the 'machinery' of the story that Mr. Wells's imagination plays least freely and convincingly. He constantly forgets—or seems to forget—that his Traveller is journeying simply through *time,* and records effects which inevitably suggest travel through *space*. Why, for example, should the model of the machine vanish from sight when in the second chapter it is set in motion?[1]

---

1. Evidently the anonymous reviewer has not read the novel carefully enough. In the first chapter the Time Traveller explains that, while the machine travels through time, it is *present* at successive instants, but below the threshold of perception.

Why, in the last chapter, should the machine itself disappear when the Traveller has set out on his final journey; why on his progress through the centuries should it jar and sway as if it were moving through the air; why should he write of 'slipping like a vapour through the interstices of intervening substance,' or anticipate sudden contact with some physical obstacle? To these questions Mr. Wells will probably reply that it is unfair to blame an artist for not surmounting difficulties which are practically insurmountable; but the obvious rejoinder is that it is unwise to choose a scheme from which such difficulties are inseparable. Still, when all deductions are made *The Time Machine* remains a strikingly original performance.

H. G. WELLS
Writing The Time Machine

[Wells and Amy Catherine (Jane) Robbins had eloped in 1894, but were not to be married till 1895. At the time narrated in this excerpt, Wells was writing feverishly to support both the household of his first wife and his illicit—and, for the period, deeply scandalous—*ménage* with Jane.]

It seemed rather useless to go on writing articles. All the periodicals to which I contributed were holding stuff of mine in proof and it might be indiscreet to pour in fresh matter to such a point that the tanks overflowed and returned it. But I had one thing in the back of my mind. Henley had told me that it was just possible he would presently find backing for a monthly. If so, he thought I might rewrite the *Time Traveller* articles as a serial story. Anyhow that was something to do and I set to work on the *Time Machine* and rewrote it from end to end.

I still remember writing that part of the story in which the *Time Traveller* returns to find his machine removed and his retreat cut off. I sat alone at the round table downstairs writing steadily in the luminous circle cast by a shaded paraffin lamp. Jane had gone to bed and her mother had been ill in bed all day. It was a very warm

From H. G. Wells, Experiment in Autobiography (New York: Macmillan, 1934), pp. 436-437. Copyright 1934 by Herbert George (H.G.) Wells, copyright © renewed 1962 by George Philip Wells and Francis Richard Wells. Reprinted by permission of J. B. Lippincott Company.

blue August night and the window was wide open. The best part of my mind fled through the story in a state of concentration before the Morlocks but some outlying regions of my brain were recording other things. Moths were fluttering in ever and again and though I was unconscious of them at the time, one must have flopped near me and left some trace in my marginal consciousness that became a short story I presently wrote, *A Moth, Genus Novo*. And outside in the summer night a voice went on and on, a feminine voice that rose and fell. It was Mrs.—— I forget her name—our landlady in open rebellion at last, talking to a sympathetic neighbour in the next garden and talking through the window at me. I was aware of her and heeded her not, and she lacked the courage to beard me in my parlour. "Would I *never* go to bed? How could she lock up with that window staring open? Never had she had such people in her house before,—never. A nice lot if everything was known about them. Often when you didn't actually know about things you could feel them. What she let her rooms to was summer visitors who walked about all day and went to bed at night. And she hated meanness and there were some who could be mean about sixpences. People with lodgings to let in Sevenoaks ought to know the sort of people who might take them. . . ."

It went on and on. I wrote on grimly to that accompaniment. I wrote her out and she made her last comment with the front door well and truly slammed. I finished my chapter before I shut the window and turned down and blew out the lamp. And somehow amidst the gathering disturbance of those days the *Time Machine* got itself finished. Jane kept up a valiant front and fended off from me as much as she could of the trouble that was assailing her on both sides. But a certain gay elasticity disappeared. It was a disagreeable time for her. She went and looked at other apartments and was asked unusual questions.

It was a retreat rather than a return we made to London, with the tart reproaches of the social system echoing in our ears. But before our ultimate flight I had had a letter from Henley telling me it was all right about that monthly of his. He was to start *The New Review* in January and he would pay me £100 for the *Time Machine* as his first serial story. One hundred pounds! And at the same time the mills of the *Pall Mall Gazette* began to go round and consume my work again. Mrs. Robbins went back to stay with friends in North London and Jane and I found our old rooms with our Scotch landlady at 12, Mornington Road, still free for us.

JEAN-PIERRE VERNIER

The Time Machine **and Its Context**

The Time Machine has remained one of Wells's most popular books, and one of the most often reprinted. The circumstances of its publication are, in general, well enough known that here we need only recall them briefly. The Time Traveller appeared for the first time in the *Science Schools Journal*, in a story entitled "The Chronic Argonauts"; following are the principal transformations undergone by that original tale:[1]

A. "The Chronic Argonauts," published in the *Science Schools Journal*, 1881.

B. Two different versions of the same story, written in 1889 and 1892. The texts were never published, and Geoffrey West is the only authority attesting to their existence.

C. In 1893, another version was written by Wells and published in series form in *The National Observer* during the spring of 1894. This is actually the earliest form of *The Time Machine*.

1. This information is provided in Geoffrey West, *H. G. Wells: A Sketch for a Portrait* (London, 1930), pp. 287-296. A more detailed examination of the problem is found in the article of Bernard Bergonzi, "The Publication of *The Time Machine*, 1894-1895," *Review of English Studies* XI, 41 (February 1960): 42-51.

From Jean-Pierre Vernier, H. G. Wells et son temps (Publications de l'Université de Rouen, Etudes Anglaises 38, 1971). Translated by F. McConnell. Reprinted by permission of the Université de Rouen.

D. In 1894 Wells took up the story again, producing a new version serialized in *The New Review* beginning in January 1895. Except for a few details, this is the version Heinemann published in book form in June 1895. Preparing it for book form, Wells contented himself with rewriting the opening, making it more dramatic and less didactic, and excising a few episodes that unnecessarily slowed the plot development. But one highly interesting variation appears between the 1893 text and the 1894. In *The National Observer*, the last vision of a world where life has gradually disappeared due to the cooling of the sun is introduced only as a brief speculation within the final episode, while in *The New Review* this vision has been enlarged to the dimensions of the definitive version. We are dealing, then, with a slowly elaborated work, and one upon which Wells placed high hopes. In December 1894 he wrote to Miss Healey:

> You may be interested to know that our ancient *Chronic Argonauts* of the *Science Schools Journal* has at last become a complete story and will appear as a serial in the *New Review* for January. It's my trump card and if it does not come off very much I shall know my place for the rest of my career.[2]

To be sure, there is some exaggeration in this. We can hardly imagine Wells abandoning his writing career because of the failure of one book. On those rare occasions when an editor did reject his work, he simply revised, often restating the same ideas in altered form. But no such problem arose with *The Time Machine,* which was accorded a reception that must have surpassed even Wells's own hopes. In the *Review of Reviews,* W. T. Stead called him "a man of genius."[3] The sentiment was echoed by a number of reviewers, and indicates quite well the quality of praise lavished on Wells at the time. Unknown till then, he rapidly became one of the fore-

2. West, p. 102. Elizabeth Healey, a friend of Wells's at the Normal School of Science, remained his correspondent for nearly fifty years.
3. *Review of Reviews* XI (1895): 263. Stead, third editor of the sensationalist and widely-read *Pall Mall Gazette,* was one of the most important literary sponsors of his time.

most literary figures of his age—an age when young talent was relatively rare. We may ask what allowed him to achieve such success. Should we assume that Wells, in 1894, expressed the preoccupations of his age so clearly that his readers saw in his work an illustration of their own confusing problems? Or should we, on the other hand, assume that *The Time Machine* offered them an escape from those problems?

Many critics have claimed to find in the adventures of the Time Traveller a satire against the age, a warning from Wells to his contemporaries. . . . Indeed, it is possible—though not certain—that Wells meant to apprise his contemporaries of the dangers of science and show them the faults inherent in their social organization. But this does not appear to have been the essential motive of the work. Wells himself, of course, came to subscribe to this reading and, in hindsight, located *The Time Machine* in the line of his propagandistic works which provided the ideological basis of the Open Conspiracy.[4] In *All Aboard for Ararat* (1940) Noah Lammock—one of Wells's numerous incarnations—is arguing with the Lord:

> "I never wrote The Time Machine," said Noah.
> "Why pretend?" said the Lord. "The same idea is the framework of your *Work, Wealth and Happiness of Mankind*. It is *World Brain*. It crops up more and more frequently in your books as you get older and repeat yourself more and more—"[5]

But this is merely one of Wells's constant attempts to impose upon his lifework a unity which is not, in fact, there. In 1894 the realm of pure ideas scarcely attracted him. And like most of his stories from the same period, *The Time Machine* rests upon a fundamental ambiguity—an ambiguity, moreover, as fecund as the ambiguity of poetry, revealing meaning upon meaning at levels at once parallel to each other and superimposed upon one another.

4. The phrase for Wells's theory, maintained during his later years, that the intellectuals and scientists of the world should assume a benevolent dictatorship in order to introduce some measure of sanity into the counsels of international politics.
5. *All Aboard for Ararat* (London, 1940), p. 54.

As Bernard Bergonzi brilliantly indicates, the book's central episode is a metaphor for an extremely complex reality:

> The opposition of Eloi and Morlocks can be interpreted in terms of the late nineteenth-century class-struggle, but it also reflects an opposition between aestheticism and utilitarianism, pastoralism and technology, contemplation and action, and ultimately, and least specifically, between beauty and ugliness, and light and darkness. The book not only embodies the tensions and dilemmas of its time, but others peculiar to Wells himself, which a few years later were to make him cease to be an artist and become a propagandist.[6]

Certainly, despite Wells's own simplistic explanation of them, the Eloi and the Morlocks awaken archetypal responses in the reader. But that is not their only function.

The theme itself of time travel is called into play in a manner very characteristic of the period. Long before the book appeared, people had been discussing the plausibility of the hypothesis; and serious physicists had demonstrated that time travel is physically impossible. But that is a different problem from Wells's. Insofar as the reader is induced, by the narrative technique, to believe in the reality of the voyage, we have to admit that the writer has achieved his goal. What is significant—and what Paul Valéry saw splendidly—is that the "time" through which Wells's hero travels is wholly different from "time" as conceived by contemporary physics:

> Even Wells, in his famous story *The Time Machine,* employs and explores time *as it was,* old time, the time which was believed in *before* him. . . .[7]

It is no surprise, then, that the reader finds in the book characters who, fantastic as they may be, nevertheless betray familiar traits.

> The Eloi, with their childlike and sexually ambiguous appearance, and their consumptive type of beauty, are clear reflections of *fin de siècle* visual taste.[8]

6. Bernard Bergonzi, *The Early H. G. Wells* (Manchester, 1961), p. 61.
7. Paul Valéry, "Literature and Our Destiny," in *Remarks on the Modern World* (Paris, 1962), p. 252.
8. Bergonzi, pp. 48-49.

Apparently, for the contemporary reader, the identification of these frail creatures with the aesthetes of the Decadent Movement was inevitable. And over against the Eloi, the Morlocks may illustrate the same process of identification even more clearly. They evoke the demons of popular tradition, descended from the Middle Ages through the period of the Gothic Novel. And their origin, as explained by Wells, makes them descendents of the working class of the end of the nineteenth century. And it matters little what kind of workers. Their appearance and habitat inevitably suggest the miners. And the miners, we know, represented for both the upper and the middle classes of the time a barely human species—a species requiring constant surveillance if one did not wish to fall prey to their natural savagery. We may assert that, for the middle class of the late nineteenth century, the existence of the miner represented a constant and ominous annoyance, an image of potential revolution very like the "terrorist with a knife" of the period between the two World Wars.

So that Wells presents to his predominantly middle class audience a society composed of two other classes, with neither of whom they can identify: on the one hand the descendents of the capitalists, a collection of dilettantes at the margin of society; and on the other the Morlocks descended from the proletarians, traditional enemies of the middle class. Furthermore, Wells shows no sympathy for either class: and the reader thus finds himself a pure spectator. This is so much the case, indeed, that the reader feels no indignation when the hero fights the Morlocks with fire: he can regard it only as man's affirmation of his superiority over creatures with whom he has nothing in common. The world from which these creatures come is not the reader's. And, doubtless, this is one reason why *The Time Machine* has no value as propaganda. The original Chapter Seven was titled, simply, *Explanation*. We are in the realm of fantasy, and there is no conscious urge to instruct or warn us. As Kingsley Amis correctly observes:

When the Time Traveller finds that mankind will have become separated into two races, the gentle ineffectual Eloi and the savage

Morlocks, the idea that these are descended respectively from our own leisured classes and manual workers comes as a mere explanation, a solution to the puzzle; it is not transformed, as it inevitably would be in a modern writer, into a warning about some current trend in society.[9]

The book, rather, is a series of hypotheses based upon the theory of evolution—not as Darwin and Huxley expounded it, but as it was popularized among the reading public. The divorce between the real world and the imaginative universe is total: *The Time Machine* is above all a work of art, and is typical of its age only to the extent that all art is a re-creation of the world of the moment within the artist's own vision. It appears, besides, that Wells himself is more concerned to make his reader admit the plausibility of his hypothesis—more concerned, that is, with problems of literary technique— than with the actual validity of such hypotheses. As he himself later said:

> It was still possible in *The Time Machine* to imagine humanity on the verge of extinction and differentiated into two decadent species, the Eloi and the Morlocks, without the slightest reflection upon everyday life. Quite a lot of people thought that idea was very clever in its sphere, very clever indeed, and no one minded in the least. It seemed to have no sort of relation whatever to normal existence.[10]

Perhaps it is just because *The Time Machine* seemed to be a game that readers and critics gave it such an enthusiastic welcome. They found there a new, original world, which was, nevertheless, not disturbing since it could not conceivably come into existence. But the game is far from being simply frivolous; and behind the descriptions of fantastic beings and worlds, there is manifested a peculiar disquiet. To be sure, we do not find a concerted attack on this or that aspect of the modern world: but the violence itself, which is such an essential element in all the stories of this period, clearly illustrates Wells's unrest. But *The Time Machine,* finally, is not one of those numerous works in which he acerbically criti-

9. Kingsley Amis, *New Maps of Hell* (London, 1961), p. 33.
10. *The Fate of Man* (New York, 1939), p. 67.

cized his society and eventually elaborated a complex social philosophy. It is a youthful work that owe its triumph above all to its literary genius and its exuberance. . . .

Doubtless, there is a typical *fin de siècle* attitude in Wells's obvious pleasure in imagining the end of our world, and in the evocative power of his description of the planet dying under a sun that grows more and more cold. But these achievements do not in any way surpass the limitations of an aesthetic game founded upon an intellectual hypothesis. We can scarcely argue that this hypothesis was ahead of its time. For it is only a point of departure, a pretext for a dream which, disturbing as it may be, remains nevertheless a dream.

A Review of The War of the Worlds in Nature, 10 February 1898

Many writers of fiction have gathered material from the fairy-land of science, and have used it in the construction of literary fabrics, but none have done it more successfully than Mr. H. G. Wells. It is often easy to understand the cause of failure. The material may be used in such a way that there appears no connection between it and the background upon which it is seen; it may be so prominent that the threads with which it ought to harmonise are thrown into obscurity; or (and this is the worst of all) it may be employed by a writer whose knowledge of natural phenomena is not sufficient to justify his working with scientific colour. Mr. Wells makes none of these mistakes. Upon a groundwork of scientific fact, his vivid imagination and exceptional powers of description enable him to erect a structure which intellectual readers can find pleasure in contemplating.

The Time Machine—considered by the majority of scientific readers to be Mr. Wells's best work—showed at once that a writer had arisen who was not only familiar with scientific facts, but who knew them intimately enough to present a view of the future. *The Island of Doctor Moreau,* though decried by some critics, is a distinctly

By Sir Richard Gregory (1864-1952), a classmate of Wells at the Normal School of Science, editor of Nature from 1919 to 1939, and a brilliant scientific writer in his own right.

powerful work, and the worst that can be said of it is that the pabu-
lum it provides is too strong for the mental digestion of sentimental
readers. But in several respects *The War of the Worlds* is even better than either of these contributions to scientific romance, and
there are parts of it which are more stimulating to thought than
anything that the author has yet written.

The invasion of the earth by inhabitants of Mars is the idea
around which the present story is constructed. The planet is, as Mr.
Percival Lowell puts it, older in age if not in years than the earth;
and it is not unreasonable to suppose that if sentient beings exist
upon it they would regard our world as a desirable place for occu-
pation after their own globe had gone so far in the secular cooling
as to be unable to support life. Mr. Wells bring the Martians to the
earth in ten cylinders discharged from the planet and precipitated
in Surrey. The immigrants are as much unlike men as it is possible
to imagine, and only a writer familiar with the lines of biological
development could conceive them. The greater part of their structure was brain, which sent enormous nerves to a pair of large eyes,
an auditory organ, and sixteen long tactile tentacles arranged about
the mouth; they had none of our complex apparatus of digestion,
nor did they require it, for instead of eating they injected into their
veins the fresh living blood of other creatures. Their organisms did
not sleep any more than the heart of man sleeps; they multiplied
by budding; and no bacteria entered into the scheme of their life.
When they came to the earth they brought with them a means of
producing a ray of intense heat which was used in connection with
a heavy vapour to exterminate the inhabitants of London and the
neighbourhood.

This bald outline does not, however, convey a good idea of the
narrative, which must be read before the ingenuity which the author displays in manipulating scientific material can be appreciated.
The manner in which the Martians are disposed of is undoubtedly
the best instance of this skill. As the Martians had eliminated micro-
organisms from their planet, when they came to the earth their
bodies were besieged by our microscopic allies, and they were

destroyed by germs to which natural selection has rendered us immune. This is a distinctly clever idea, and it is introduced in a way which will allay the fears of those who may be led by the verisimilitude of the narrative to expect an invasion from Mars. Of course, outside fiction such an event is hardly worth consideration; but that the possibility of it can be convincingly stated, will be conceded after reading Mr. Wells' story. A remarkable case of the fulfilment of fiction is furnished by the history of the satellites of Mars. When Dean Swift wrote *Gulliver's Travels* (published in 1726), he made the astronomers on the island of Laputa not only observe two satellites, but caused one of these to move round the planet in less time than the planet itself takes to rotate on its axis. As every student of astronomy knows, the satellites were not discovered until 1877, and one of them actually does revolve around Mars three times while the planet makes a rotation. The coincidence is remarkable; but it is to be hoped, for the sake of the peace of mind of terrestrial inhabitants, that Mr. Wells does not possess the prophetic insight vouchsafed to Swift.

In conclusion, it is worth remark that scientific romances are not without a value in furthering scientific interests; they attract attention to work that is being done in the realm of natural knowledge, and so create sympathy with the aims and observations of men of science.

I. F. CLARKE

Tales of Invasion: The Background of
The War of the Worlds

[In 1871 Sir George Tomkyns Chesney published *The Battle of Dorking*, a fictionalized account of an invasion of England by Germany in which the Germans routed the helplessly disorganized and unprepared English Army. In the following excerpt I. F. Clarke discusses the massive vogue of invasion stories and future-war fantasies to which Chesney's story gave rise: a vogue which found its most lasting and most brilliant expression in *The War of the Worlds*.]

There had never been anything to compare with this in English fiction before Chesney wrote the *Battle of Dorking*—neither in method nor in quality. For Chesney has the unusual distinction that his success helped to launch a new type of purposive fiction in which the whole aim was either to terrify the reader by a clear and merciless demonstration of the consequences to be expected from a country's shortcomings, or to prove the rightness of national policy by describing the course of a victorious war in the near future. The strong or weak points of a situation—moral, or political, or naval, or military—were presented in a triumphant or in a catastrophic manner according to the needs of the propaganda. This technique was well suited to a period of increasing nationalism and

From I. F. Clarke, Voices Prophesying War, 1763-1984 (London: Oxford University Press, 1966), pp. 38-48. Copyright © 1966 by Oxford University Press. Reprinted by permission of the publisher.

unending change in armaments. In consequence the *Battle of Dorking,* as handled by Chesney, gave rise to a European device. French, German, British, and a few Italian writers applied the Chesney formula of defeat and disaster to their own versions of an imaginary war of the future in which they sought to show that a national defeat was the result of a national failure to adopt the military, or naval, or political measures favoured by the authors. Before the *Battle of Dorking* there was little effective method in the few tales of imaginary warfare that had appeared. After Chesney there were few of these tales that did not apply the techniques that had alarmed a nation, annoyed a Prime Minister, and amazed a continent.

Gladstone had good grounds for feeling annoyed at the upheaval created by the *Battle of Dorking.* Hitherto it had always been the crisis that had been responsible for the flood of pamphlets on the state of the Fleet or of the national defences; but in 1871 it was the publication of the *Battle of Dorking* in the form of a pamphlet that had caused the commotion. To a politician like Gladstone, who had begrudged money for ships and fortresses, it must have seemed decidedly improper and unjust that a colonel of engineers should have caused a political sensation with a short story in a respectable middle-class monthly magazine. He paid unwilling tribute to Chesney's skill as a writer and to the effectiveness of his story when he felt it was necessary to warn the nation against the dangers of alarmism. In a speech at Whitby, on 2nd September 1871, he attacked the *Battle of Dorking* and all whom it had aroused. It was a heart-cry from the Treasury:

In *Blackwood's Magazine* there has lately been a famous article called 'The Battle of Dorking'. I should not mind this 'Battle of Dorking', if we could keep it to ourselves, if we could take care that nobody belonging to any other country should know that such follies could find currency or even favour with portions of the British public; but unfortunately these things go abroad, and they make us ridiculous in the eyes of the whole world. I do not say that the writers of them are not sincere—that is another matter—but I do say that the result of these things is practically the spending of more and more of your money. Be on your guard against alarmism. Depend upon it that there is not this astounding disposition on the part of all mankind to make us the objects of hatred.[1]

Gladstone could talk with some heat about the effects of Chesney's story, since it had set in motion a series of counter-attacks that lasted from May until September, when the success of the autumn manœuvres showed that an invading force had little hope of leaving its beach-head. During those five months the episode attracted international attention. Coming so soon after the German victories in 1870, and appearing in the midst of the greatest maritime power on earth, it was taken seriously outside the country. An indication of what the *Battle of Dorking* meant abroad can be seen in the editions immediately printed in Australia, Canada, New Zealand, and the United States, in the numerous translations, and in the thirty-six pages Charles Yriarte wrote for his preface to the French edition. If there was amazement abroad, at home the feeling ranged from satisfaction to alarm and indignation. Kinglake, the historian of the Crimean War, wrote to congratulate John Blackwood and hoped that the story would prove 'a really effective mode of conveying a much-needed warning'. From the Carlton it was reported that no one could take up *Blackwood's* for five minutes without a waiter coming to ask if he had finished with it. By June the story had been reprinted as a sixpenny pamphlet and in a month over 80,000 copies had been sold, mostly to readers for whom it had never been intended. This fact impressed foreign observers. They regarded the appearance of the story in bookshops and on railway bookstalls as an indication that the whole nation was involved in the alarm, and not simply the readers of the select monthlies. In fact, the Press became a battlefield, as the counter-attacks and the anti-Chesney articles appeared in the papers and in the book-shops. Most of these began as short stories or articles in dailies like *The Times* and *St. James's Gazette*. All of them employed Chesney's methods against him in their attempts to prove there had never been a German victory at Dorking, or that after

1. *Annual Register,* 1871, Part I, p. 108.

the initial disaster the Fleet had returned from overseas and had routed the enemy. The number of these pamphlets and tracts, and the fact that they attacked Chesney's theme, are a remarkable sign of the alarm and indignation the *Battle of Dorking* had caused. They appeared by the week and by the month with their stories of victory: *After the Battle of Dorking or What Became of the Invaders?*, *The Battle of Dorking: a Myth*, *The Battle of the Ironclads*, *The Cruise of the Anti-torpedo*, *The Second Armada*, *What Happened after the Battle of Dorking*, *The Other Side at the Battle of Dorking*, *Chapters from Future History*. For Chesney's tale of defeat they substitute victories; they show how the Volunteers, who had failed so signally in Chesney's story, prove to be as good as the best regulars. For example, in *What Happened after the Battle of Dorking* the anonymous author dwells on the good discipline and the excellent training of the Volunteer forces. On several occasions he goes out of his way to describe how regular officers marvelled at the efficiency of the Volunteers. When a battalion carries out a difficult flanking movement the regulars stand by: 'The old general and his staff had watched the admirable coolness with which this manoeuvre was executed. "Gad, colonel," he said to our commanding officer, "the smartest regiment of the Line couldn't have done that movement better." ' Not even the veterans of Sedan could hope to conquer troops like these.

These counter-attacks produced some extraordinary pamphlets. One army officer, Lieutenant-Colonel William Hunter, published an *Army Speech dedicated to those who have been frightened by the Battle of Dorking*. He wrote 'to revive the drooping courage, to calm the shattered nerves of those who have been too lightly alarmed by the predicted woeful results of the phantom *Battle of Dorking*'. He attacked 'the extraordinary invasion panics' and showed that the British people were well able to take care of themselves. Anything could have happened during this period when the excitement was still running high. One enterprising publisher produced a faked issue of the *London Gazette*, which set out 'The official despatches and correspondence relative to the Battle of

Dorking, as moved for in the House of Commons. 21st July 1920.'
But by the time Chesney's story had been set to music, it was clear
that the panic had begun to subside, for the music halls were
singing:

> England invaded, what a strange idea!
> She, the invincible, has nought to fear.
> John Bull in his sleep one day got talking,
> And dreamt about a battle fought at Dorking.

And then in September there was the first of what subsequently
became the annual army manœuvres. They were a considerable
novelty, for the German successes in the war of 1870 had been attributed in part to their practice of training troops in fire discipline
and large-scale operations by means of annual manœuvres designed
to test both staff and troops. In 1871 Cardwell, who had done so
much for Britain as Secretary for War, introduced a Bill to make it
permissible for troops to be assembled in large numbers for the purposes of manœuvres. The first of these began in September, and
the innovation was closely watched by Press and public, since the
aim of the exercise was to test the co-operation between regulars,
militia, and volunteers. The scheme was for the home forces to en-
gage and repel an invading enemy. The results were felt to be very
encouraging. The Press gave signs of satisfaction and *Punch* celebrated the success of the manœuvers with a full-page drawing of
Mr. Punch reviewing members of the Army, the Militia, and the
Volunteers. The caption was *All's (Pretty) Well!* That summed up
the feeling of a country recovering from the alarms of the *Battle of
Dorking* episode. As the *Daily News* wrote: 'If the supposition on
which these manœuvres were planned should ever become reality—
if the fleet should be dispersed, the Channel crossed by an invading
force, the armies along the coast defeated and scattered, and the
enemy should have penetrated to the neighbourhood of the Hog's
Back, on his way to London—some Sir Hope Grant of the time will
render a very admirable account of himself.'[2] That was the end of
the *Battle of Dorking* episode for 1871. The last state of the affair

2. *Daily News*, 23 September 1871.

was that it became a stock joke to ask anyone with a trifling injury: 'Weren't you wounded at the Battle of Dorking?' The country had decided there was little danger of an invasion; and Chesney could now look forward to fame, reputation, and eventually a seat in the House of Commons. In the January of 1872 he was writing to Blackwood asking for a higher rate of pay; in the February he was asking Blackwood to use his good offices in his election to the Athenaeum; and in the April he sent Blackwood his grateful thanks for the sum of £279.8s. 10d. in final settlement for the *Battle of Dorking.*

The colonel of engineers had earned his money. Chesney had revealed the workings of a new literary device, which was admirably adapted to the mood and methods of the new epoch of belligerent nationalism. But he had not won a military victory, since there is no evidence that his story had any influence on the reorganization of the Army. Chesney had gained a great literary success, since his story established the pattern for a predictive epic on the victory or defeat of a nation-species in the international struggle to survive. It was a narrow and limited form of fiction; but it could be effective to the point of causing a national panic, if an earnest patriot could describe telling incidents in the Chesney manner, making actions speak with far greater force than lengthy arguments about the state of the nation's defences. It was for this reason that the form of the *Battle of Dorking* became dominant in its field throughout Europe and its influence lasted until the oubreak of the First World War. As late as the year 1900 that astute publisher, Grant Richards, calculated that the reputation of Chesney's story was still powerful enough to sell a book for him. His project was *The New Battle of Dorking,* an account of a successful French invasion, which he had commissioned from Colonel Maude 'in the hope that it might have the same kind of success that its predecessor had had three or four decades earlier'. Then, there was the American publisher, George Putnam, who paid a visit to England shortly before the outbreak of war in 1914. He went over the site of Chesney's battle with a copy of the story in his hand, and was amazed to find how closely Chesney had kept to the topography of the area. Finally, in 1940 the Nazis brought out a special edition under the menacing title of *Was England erwartet!*

There was the same interest in France. In the August of 1871 Charles Yriarte wrote his long preface to the translation, *Bataille de Dorking,* in which he made a detailed study of the reasons for the effectiveness of Chesney's story. He was so impressed by the vigour and ingenuity of the narrative that he wondered 'if such a book, published here in 1869, might not have had an influence on our future'. And, again in 1871, another Frenchman produced the first foreign imitation of Chesney when he recounted his comforting vision of a defeated Germany in *La Bataille de Berlin en 1875,* the first of many French fantasies of a war of national revenge for the humiliations of 1870. The author, Édouard Dangin, found considerable satisfaction in the hope that the burden of conscription and the indemnity paid by France would lead to the swift decline of Germany. His desire to make the Germans suffer for what they had done to France shapes the course of his imaginary war, which comes to a brisk finish with a proclamation designed for French readers rather than a conquered enemy: 'Germans! We do not come to conquer you. It is not you on whom we make war, but on your ruler who for four years has kept Europe in a state of war and troubled the peace of nations. Our sole desire is to break those iron fetters that oppress you and set you free.' The First World War, it would seem, had been desired and described long before it took place.

From 1871 onwards Chesney's story showed Europe how to manipulate the new literature of anxiety and belligerent nationalism. Between 1871 and 1914 it was unusual to find a single year without some tale of future warfare appearing in some European country; for, wherever certain conditions existed, there would also be these tales of coming war. The conditions were that a nation should be actively concerned in the international manœuvring of the time. Big power—or nearly big power—status alone qualified for entry into the new club. Spain and Serbia, for instance, are innocent of the new fiction; and Ireland only appears when Irish patriots from North or South are involved in the internal political struggles of their great power neighbour. The other conditions were that a nation should be troubled by naval or military problems; and that that nation should permit a free Press to operate. Thus, the United States (at the start) and Russia (for most of the time) are outside the conflict of the imaginary wars for different reasons. The United States lacked the strong and permanent sense of a foreign menace required to touch off tales of future wars, and Russia lacked the free Press and the free play of opinion that alone could produce private solutions for public perils.

Wherever these factors operated, then the name and the method of Chesney were remembered. Both Italy and Germany offer an excellent illustration of this connexion between the *Battle of Dorking* technique and the problems of a nation. About the end of the nineteenth century these two powers were both taken up with the question of their navies. On the Italian side it was a brief history of sharp decline, since the Italian fleet had failed to maintain its place at a time of rapid naval expansion. This was the characteristic Chesney situation; and in order to emphasize the danger to Italy the Lega Navale Italiana in 1899 published a story of future naval defeat, *La Guerra del 190–*. The story reveals the influence of the Chesney tradition. The author explains that he has taken for his model the *Racconto di un Guardiano di Spiaggia,* which was the *Battle of Dorking* translated and transposed to an Italian setting in 1872. The introduction indicates both the tradition and the intention behind the story: 'At a distance of thirty years the *Racconto di un Guardiano di Spiaggia* lives again in *La Guerra del 190–*. They are two signals of alarm, two cries of dismay, two invocations to the sea, to the nation, and to all who still believe in the Fatherland.' The author certainly carries out his promise of alarm and dismay, since he foretells how the French are able to destroy the Italian fleet, bombard La Spezia with impunity, and land in force at Viareggio.

There was a comparable propaganda situation in Germany at this time, when Tirpitz had called for a further expansion of the navy. The enabling bill was passed by the Reichstag in the June of 1900, after the Centre Party had forced the Government to cut the number of cruisers. Whilst the argument about the size of the fleet was in progress a German patriot, Gustav Erdmann, wrote his warning to the nation, *Wehrlos zur See*. The story was composed in the mood of the statement by von Bülow, the Foreign Minister, that 'in the coming century the German people must be either the hammer or the anvil'. For the purpose of his propaganda Erdmann chose to show that an inadequate navy accounted for the fact that 'Germany's sons rested with their ships at the bottom of the sea'. He describes a future war in which Russia, France, and Italy attack Germany, Austro-Hungary, and Turkey. Like Chesney before him, he relates in detail such moments of national humiliation as the destruction of the Baltic fleet, and a naval blockade that leads to starvation, typhus epidemics, and mass suicides. The responsibility for this disaster rests with the guilty party in the Reichstag: 'Through the fault of the Reichstag Germany has fallen inexcusably behind other maritime nations in the expansion of her fleet.' And, again like Chesney, he ends the long tale of disaster by describing how Germany would be reduced to the level of a small power: 'British and American industry seized the Germany markets throughout the world for themselves; and once their rival had been overthrown, they were strong enough to keep him down. That German industry, which a few weeks earlier had a dominant position in the world, to which Germany owed its wealth, saw itself suddenly reduced to the level of a small-state economy.'

From all that has been said so far it will be evident that Chesney's ability as a writer was in part responsible for the continental success that made the *Battle of Dorking* a model to be copied by all who had something to say about the state of a nation. But this is a literary explanation that does not answer the far more important question: Why does the mass production of this type of fiction begin in 1871 and why does it become a standard device for many writers in Britain, France, and Germany? Part of the answer would seem to begin from the fact that the publication of the *Battle of Dorking* had coincided with the coming of a new mood throughout Europe. In one way this appeared as a general realization that the German victories in 1870 had altered the European power system and that in consequence, as Matthew Arnold wrote in the January of 1871, 'one may look anxiously to see what is in the future for the changed Europe that we shall have'. One result of the change was that in France after 1871, for example, a succession of tales about future wars began. They appeared almost every year, growing in detail and in length, until they reached a climax in the large-scale epic forecasts of French victories written by Capitaine Danrit during the eighteen-nineties. The authors generally described how the enemy of the day—Germany, or sometimes Britain—was soundly defeated by the superior abilities and resources of the French troops.

Another reason for the rapid growth of the new literature of imaginary future wars was the extraordinary development in every type of armament that took place during the last quarter of the nineteenth century. The frequent changes in military equipment and the often spectacular advances in the design of quite new naval craft posed questions about the conduct of the next war which at times could cause considerable anxiety. Further, with the coming of universal literacy and the emergence of the popular Press towards the end of the century, it became a general practice in the major European countries for writers to appeal directly to the mass of the people in order to win support for the military or naval measures they advocated.

The practice undoubtedly dates from the success won by the *Battle of Dorking,* since Chesney had by chance introduced a new device in the communications between a specialist group and a nation. As an engineer, he belonged to the then still small group of well-educated officers to be found in the British Army of the period: he could move from the direction of a large engineering college to a seat in the Commons, and he was as much at home with a staff paper as he was with writing an article for *Blackwood's.* He was in touch with the political and military thinking of his time; and when he suggested to John Blackwood that his idea for a tale about an imaginary invasion might be 'a useful way of bringing home to the country the necessity for a thorough reorganization', he was looking for a suitable medium through which he could communicate the convictions of a professional to an influential section of the community represented by readers of a monthly like *Blackwood's*.

Thereafter, once the tale of imaginary warfare had established itself as a natural propaganda device for the period before the First World War, it quickly became a favourite instrument with eminent persons, whether they could write effectively or not. Admirals, generals, and politicians turned naturally to telling the tale of the war-to-come, since it so conveniently allowed them to draw attention to whatever they thought was wrong with the armed forces. The rate of development in this field can be gauged from the fact that in 1871 an unknown colonel considered the middle-class *Blackwood's Magazine* to be a suitable channel for his ideas. By 1906 all the varied effects of the new mass dailies, universal literacy, the growth of armaments and the ending of British isolation came together in the episode of the *Invasion of 1910*. With the agreement and active encouragement of Lord Northcliffe, Field-Marshal Lord Roberts worked in close association with the popular journalist, William Le Queux, in preparing a story about a German invasion of Britain in 1910 for serialization in the *Daily Mail*. Lord Roberts saw it was an opportunity to spread his conviction that Britain must be better prepared for a modern war. As he wrote in his commendation of the *Invasion of 1910:* 'The catastrophe that may happen if we still remain in our present state of unpreparedness is vividly and forcibly illustrated in Mr. Le Queux's new book which I recommend to the perusal of every one who has the welfare of the British Empire at heart.'

H. G. WELLS

The Rediscovery of the Unique

["The Rediscovery of the Unique" appeared in the *Fortnightly Review* in 1891. It is one of a number of meditative essays on science and the condition of modern man which had made Wells a widely known journalist by the time he began *The Time Machine* in 1893. Throughout his life, Wells remained pleased with this early piece; it articulates powerfully the "Wellsian pessimism" which so many commentators have found in his scientific romances of the nineties.]

The original title of this paper was "The Fallacy of the Common Noun." This was subsequently altered to the present superscription, which the author considers to be equally expressive and far preferable on account of its quiet grandeur. Either will convey the suggestion of our intent to most of our readers, but there are possibly a few, here and there, to whom both are unmeaning. To these we may perhaps, by way of introductory advertisement, or prospectus, address a few remarks on the scope, value, and necessity of our matter.

The Rediscovery of the Unique is the rediscovery of a quite obvious and altogether neglected common fact. It is of wide—almost universal—interest, and of quite universal application. To altogether practical people it is of value as showing the criminal injustice of cab regulations and an inspection of weights and measures; to those who love the subtle subjective rather than objective crudities, and who find it impossible to repeat facts, it is an inestimably precious justification; while to scientists it is important as destroying the atomic theory. It startles the philosopher dwelling in pure reason by giving logic such a twist as tall towers sometimes get from lively yet conservative earthquakes. It should, it will, decimate every thoughtful man's views as a pestilence thins a city. Among other things, after half a century of destructive criticism, it reinstates miracles and prophecy on their old footings. It shows that those scientific writers who have talked so glibly of the reign of inflexible law have been under a serious misconception. It restores special providences and unverified assertions to the stock of credible things, and liberty to the human imagination. To clergymen, forced to controversy in urban parishes; to classical scholars who as schoolmasters find *Spencer's Education*[1] a curse and a threat, to the softer and illogical sex everywhere, this rediscovery comes as a special boon and blessing. Properly financed it might be established as a cult; and those refuges for the feeble refined from vulgar and militant scepticism, the congregations of Theosophical Buddhism and mystic Catholicism, have a third rival. A new saying might be, and as a matter of fact is, being started in the marketplace: "Let us be unique"—in shoals; for the ambition of our young men and maidens to be at any sacrifice "lively and eccentric," is the unconscious moral aspect of this great rediscovery.[2]

The bare thing itself, like the theory of gravitation, may be expressed in a sentence, though like that theory it is the outcome of many centuries of thought. In a sentence it is, *All being is unique,*

1. The English philosopher Herbert Spencer (1820-1903) based his thinking upon an evolutionary, Darwinian view of the universe. In his *Education* (1860), he defended the training of the young in science as opposed to the traditional classical subjects.
2. In part, this is simply the conventional and perennial jibe of writers at the unconventionality of the younger generation. But it is also a not-so-veiled reference to the deliberate outrageousness of the *Yellow Book* asthetes and decadents of the period—who were to be even more crushingly characterized as the Eloi of *The Time Machine.*

or, nothing is strictly like anything else. It implies, therefore, that we only arrive at the idea of similar beings by an unconscious or deliberate disregard of an infinity of small differences. No two animals, for instance, are alike, as any bird or dog-fancier or shepherd can tell. Any two bricks, or coins, or marbles, will be fuond on examination to differ in size, shape, surface, hue—in endless details as you make your investigation more searching and minute. "As like as two peas in one pod," is a proverb which, like most proverbs, embalms a misconception: one can easily see for oneself when peas are in season. And so in the smallest clod of earth and in the meanest things of life there is, if we care to see it, the unprecedented and unique. As we are taught in the vision of Saint Peter,[3] and more dimly by Wordsworth, there is really nothing around us common and negligible. Thus, with a brief paragraph and a minute's thought, the scales drop from the reader's eyes and he makes the rediscovery of the unique.

Its logical consequences are so enormous that we would beg his patience for a moment to make sure of our position before proceeding to them. We may imagine some objections to what we have said. The case of two bullets following each other from a mould might perhaps be raised by an unscientific person, but actually the same mould never turns out two bullets alike: it has gained or lost heat and expanded or contracted; there is just a little more wear since the last bullet was cast; the lead itself is rising or falling in temperature and its impurities vary. Again, the little crystals of a precipitate seem identically alike till we test them with micrometer, microscope, polarizer, and micro-chemical tests; then we find quite acceptable individualisms of size, imperfection, strain, and so on. The stars of heaven and the sands of the sea are not evidently unique beings only on account of distance and size respectively.

3. In 1 Peter 2: 4-6, the saint urges the faithful to reclaim themselves in Christ and, in so doing, reclaim even the most common features of the everyday world: "Come to him, as to a living stone rejected by men, but chosen and prized in the sight of God, and build yourselves up as living stones into a spiritual house for a consecrated priesthood, so as to offer spiritual sacrifices that through Jesus Christ will be acceptable to God."

Everywhere repetition disappears and the unique is revealed as sense and analysis grow keener. And since adjectives are abstracted from nouns, it follows that uniqueness goes beyond things and reaches properties. The red of one rose petal seems the same as the red of another, because the man who sees them is blinded through optical insufficiency and mental habit. Put them side by side, is the shade the same? If you think so, take counsel with some artist who can really paint flowers. All learning nowadays tends to become practical, and we may yet see schools of metaphysicians in the fields, engaged severally in plucking daisy petals apart.

Hence the *common noun* is really the verbal link of a more or less arbitrarily determined group of uniques. When we take the term distributively the boundaries grow suddenly vague. It is the constant refrain in the teaching of one of the most eminent of living geologists[4] that everything passes into everything else by "insensible gradations." He holds up to his students a picture of the universe not unlike a water-colour sketch that has fallen into a water-butt and "run." The noun "chair," for instance, is definite enough to the reader—till he thinks; then behold a borderland of dubiety! Rocking chairs, lounge chairs, settees; what is this nondescript—chair or ottoman? and this—chair or stool? Here, again, have we a garden chair or seat, or a *cheval-de-frise?*[5] and where do you draw the line between chair and firewood? But the ordinary person, when he speaks of a number of chairs, never feels the imminence of this difficulty. He imagines one particular unique sitting apparatus with which he is familiar, and, taking a kind of vicious multiple mental squint at it, sees what is utterly impossible in the real world—so many others identical with it.

For, on the theory of our rediscovery, *number* is a purely subjective and illusory reduplication of uniques.

It is extremely interesting to trace the genesis of this human

4. John Wesley Judd, Wells's geology teacher at the Normal School of Science.
5. A four-legged wooden obstacle, like a sawhorse, used primarily in building military blockades or barriers.

delusion of number. It has grown with the growth of the mind, and is, we are quite prepared to concede, a necessary feature of thought. We may here remark, parenthetically, that we make no proposal to supersede ordinary thinking by a new method. We are, in harmony with modern biology, simply stating a plain fact about it. Human reason, in the light of what is being advanced, appears as a convenient organic process based on a fundamental happy misconception, and it may—though the presumption is against such a view—take us away from, rather than towards, the absolute truth of things. The *raison d'etre* of a man's mind is to avoid danger and get food—so the naturalists tell us. His reasoning powers are about as much a truth-seeking tool as the snout of a pig, and he may as well try to get to the bottom of things by them as a mole might by burrowing. This, however, is outside the scope of the present paper, and altogether premature.

The first substantives of primitive man were almost certainly not ordinary common nouns. They were single terms expressive of certain special relationships between him as the centre of the universe and that universe. There was "Father," who fed him; "Home," where he sheltered; and "Man," the adversary he hated and plotted against. Similarly, in the recapitulatory phases of a child's development, it uses "Pa," "Ma," "Pussy," strictly as proper nouns. Such simple terms become common as experience widens and analogies appear. Man soon exhausted his primitive stock of grunts, weird mouthings, and snorts; his phonetic, in fact his general, memory was weak, and his capacity of differentiation therefore slight; he was in consequence obliged to slur over uniqueness, and lump similar-looking things together under what was, for practical purposes, the same sound. Then followed the easy step of muddling repeated substantives into dual and plural forms. And then, out of a jumble of broken-down substantives and demonstratives grew up the numbers—grew and blossomed like a grove of mental upas trees.

They stupify people. When we teach a child to count, we poison its mind almost irrevocably. When a man speaks of a thousand of bricks, he never dreams that he means a unique collection of uniques that his mind cannot grasp individually. When he speaks of a thousand years, the suspicion never crosses his mind that he is referring to a unique series of unique gyrations on the part of the earth we inhabit; and yet, if he is an educated man, he knows perfectly well that the shape of the earth's orbit and the earth's velocity are things constantly changing! He is inoculated with the arithmetical virus; he lets a watch and a calendar blind him to the fact that every moment of his life is a miracle and a mystery.

All that is said of common nouns and number here has an obvious application to terms in logic. It is scarcely necessary to say more to strictly logical people, to convince them of the absurdity of being strictly logical. They fancy the words they work with are reliable tools, instruments of steel, while they are rather like a saw or axe of ice when the thermometer fluctuates about zero centigrade.[6]

The most indisputable corollary of the rediscovery is the destruction of the atomic theory. There is absolutely no ground in human experience for a presumption of similar atoms, the mental entanglement that created one being now unravelled, and similarly the certainty of all the so-called laws of physics and chemistry is now assailable.

Here a most excusable objection may be anticipated and met. "I grant," the scientist will say—in fact, does say—"that any presumption in favour of identically similar atoms disappears upon analysis; I grant that our original suspicion of such atoms arose from a mental imperfection; yet I still keep my theories intact with—experimental verification." Thus the whirligig of time brings round its revenges; here is science taking up the cast-off armour of religion and resting its claims on prophecy! The scientist predicts a planet, an element, or a formula, and the thing either comes almost as he said, or—he makes a discovery. Now the unique fact of averages explains the whole matter.

It is a well-known fact that at any theatre during the run of a

6. Such ice tools would be constantly melting or refreezing into new shapes.

fairly successful piece, on every recurring Monday, Tuesday, or other day in the week, almost exactly the same number of people will come nightly and distribute themselves in almost exactly the same way through the house. So many will go to the pit, so many to the dress circle, so many to the boxes, so much "paper" stuffing[7] will be required to give a cheerful plumpness to the whole. The manager can give all these numbers beforehand within a very small fraction of the total. Yet not one of these spectators is exactly the same as another; each one has his individual cares and sorrows, desires and motives, and comes and goes in accordance with the necessities of his unique life. Now and then there is a break in the even succession of attendances; a madman, perhaps, comes to the theatre, fires off a pistol and clears out the gallery; but take a sufficiently large theatre, a sufficiently large number of times, and it becomes impossible[8] to define the result of average attendance from the sum of the actions of a number of imagined indistinguishably similar persons. So with atoms—it is possible to think of them as unique things each with its idiosyncrasies, and yet regard the so-called verification of the atomic theory with tranquillity. But when the mad atom comes along, the believer in the unique remains tranquil, while the ears of the chemist get hot, his manner becomes nervous and touchy, and he mumbles certain unreasonable things about "experimental error." Or possibly, as occurred lately with an antic atom on a sensitive plate, he fancies jealous or curious spooks are upsetting his experiments.

We may here call attention to the unreasonable width of "margin of experimental error" allowed to scientists. They assert, for instance, in illustration of this atomic theory of theirs, that in water, hydrogen and oxygen invariably exist in the definite and integral ratio of one to eight. Any truthful chemist, if the reader can get one and "heckle" him, will confess that the most elaborate and accurate

7. Padded or falsified attendance figures, to enhance the "popularity" of a given show. Wells's irony is that even such falsifications of fact are predictable.
8. An obvious misprint for "possible."

analyses of water have given fractional and variant results; the ratio of the compounds gets wrong, theoretically speaking, sometimes to the left of the decimal place. The chemist gets results most satisfactory to himself by taking large quantities and neglecting fractions. The discrepancies so often noted by beginners in practical physics and chemistry between experimental and theoretical results are frequently extremely startling and instructive in this connection. At the beginning a student is naïve—honest; but presently he gets into the way of manipulating his apparatus—a laboratory euphemism.

Leaving the scattered atoms of the ordinary chemist, we may next allude briefly to the bearings of the rediscovery on morality. Here we are on ground where we modestly fear almost to tread. There is the dire possibility of awakening the wrath and encountering the rushing denunciations of certain literary men who have taken public morality under their protection. We may, however, point out that beings are unique, circumstances are unique, and that therefore we cannot think of regulating our conduct by wholesale dicta. A strict regard for truth compels us to add that principles are wholesale dicta: they are substitutes of more than doubtful value for an individual study of cases. A philanthropist in a hurry might clap a thousand poor souls into ready-made suits all of a size, but if he really wanted the people properly clothed he would send them one by one to a tailor.

There is no reason why a man who has hitherto held and felt honestly proud of high principles should be ashamed of sharing a common error, provided he is prepared for a frank abandonment; but though a principle, like a fetich, may be still convenient as a missile weapon, or entertaining as a curiosity, its supposed value and honourableness in human life vanishes with our rediscovery.

Finally we may turn away from proofs and consequences and note briefly how this great rediscovery grew to a head. The period of darkest ignorance, when men turned their backs on nature and believed in mystic numbers, has long passed away; even the skulls of the schoolmen have rotted to dust by this time, and their books are in tatters. The work of Darwin and Wallace[9] was the clear assertion of the uniqueness of living things; and physicists and chemists are now trying the next step forward in a hesitating way—they must take it sooner or later. We are on the eve of man's final emancipation from rigid reasonableness, from the last trace of the trim clockwork thought of the seventeenth and eighteenth centuries. The common chemist is a Rip Van Winkle from these buried times. His grave awaits his earliest convenience, yawning.

The neat little picture of a universe of souls made up of passions and principles in bodies made of atoms, all put together so neatly and wound up at the creation, fades in the series of dissolving views that we call the march of human thought. We no longer believe, whatever creed we may affect, in a Deity whose design is so foolish and little that even a theological bishop can trace it and detect a kindred soul. Some of the most pious can hardly keep from scoffing at Milton's world—balanced just in the middle of those crystalline spheres that hung by a golden chain from the battlements of heaven.[10] We no longer speculate

"What varied being peoples ev'ry star,"[11]

because we have no reason at all to expect life beyond this planet. We are a century in front of that Nuremberg cosmos,[12] and in the place of it there looms a dim suggestion of the fathomlessness of the unique mystery of life. The figure of a roaring loom with unique threads flying and interweaving beyond all human following, working out a pattern beyond all human interpretation, we owe to Goethe,[13] the intellectual father of the nineteenth century. Num-

9. Darwin, in *The Origin of Species,* based his theory of evolution through "natural selection" upon the transmission of small, but decisive, differences between the individual members of a species. Alfred Russell Wallace (1823-1913) was a brilliant naturalist who, independently of Darwin and at almost the same time, arrived at the theory of evolution through natural selection.
10. This image is from *Paradise Lost* II, 1047-1053.
11. Alexander Pope, *An Essay on Man,* Epistle I, 1. 27.
12. That is, a medieval, Germanic, superstitious view of the universe.
13. This famous image is from *Faust Part One,* "Night," 11. 501-509.

ber—Order, seems now the least law in the universe; in the days of our great-grandfathers it was heaven's first law.

So spins the squirrel's cage of human philosophy.

Science is a match that man has just got alight. He thought he was in a room—in moments of devotion, a temple—and that his light would be reflected from and display walls inscribed with wonderful secrets and pillars carved with philosophical systems wrought into harmony. It is a curious sensation, now that the preliminary splutter is over and the flame burns up clear, to see his hands lit and just a glimpse of himself and the patch he stands on visible, and around him, in place of all that human comfort and beauty he anticipated—darkness still.

SAMUEL L. HYNES
FRANK D. McCONNELL

The Time Machine **and** The War of the Worlds:

Parable and Possibility in H. G. Wells

H. G. Wells is sometimes called the "father of science fiction," and the two novels included in this volume are often referred to as the first (and, so far, perhaps the only) masterpieces of the genre. But the labels can be confusing. If "science fiction" is a literature that celebrates the infinite vistas and unlimited possibilities offered us by the growth of technology, then Wells was not a writer of science fiction, at least not in these two early novels. *The Time Machine* and *The War of the Worlds* may even be described as anti-science fiction, or at least anti-*scientific* fiction. By temperament and by education, Wells was a man caught in a crucial historical and ideological crisis: the crisis of late Victorian thought, in which the conventional pieties of romantic Christianity seemed on the verge of being finally destroyed by the overwhelming evidence for Darwinian materialism. And both of his most famous tales, the story of the traveler into the future and the story of the invasion of earth by ghastly aliens who *may be* our future, are not so much celebrations of, as reactions against, the implications of that grim and empty universe.

The two tales are very different, of course. *The Time Machine,* the earlier one, is an unrelievedly bleak examination of the chances for human survival in a cosmos governed by entropy; while *The*

War of the Worlds seeks to salvage, even from the entropic world-view, some marginal and bitter hope for man's survival. The crucial point, though, is that Wells, as the "father" of science fiction, was writing not celebrations of the technological future, but cautious warnings about that future; was concerned not with writing predictions, but with writing parables whose most immediate relevance was to the world of the present. And in this sense, as a creator of *parables,* Wells may be even more important for the later history of science fiction than most historians of the form have suggested.

I

Parable is not a term that has been much used in twentieth-century literary discourse (though Kafka used it, and so did W. H. Auden); but the kind of story that *parable* identifies is as common in our time as it has ever been—like love songs and elegies and fairy tales and tragedies, parables are a permanent form of the human imagination.

The common meaning of *parable* derives from its use in the New Testament: a parable is a fictional narrative through which a moral meaning is expressed, a way of teaching. Defined in this way, as a moral lesson in the form of a story, parable seems a simple and immediate form, like Aesop's fables. But Christ explained to his disciples that this was not the case. In the account of the parable of the sower given in the Gospel according to Saint Mark, after Christ has told the story, "they that were about him with the twelve asked of him the parable." Christ replies:

Unto you it is given to know the mystery of God: but unto them that are without, all these things are done in parables:

That seeing they may see, and not perceive; and hearing they may hear, and not understand; lest at any time they should be converted, and their sins should be forgiven them.   (Mark 4:11-12)

The point seems clear: parable is not simple, it resists immediate understanding, and it reveals its meaning only to those who are prepared to perceive and understand. Like every serious art form, it uses its complexity to exclude the unworthy.

This sense of the difficulty of parable remains a defining element. If you look up the term in the Oxford English Dictionary, you will find this point in both medieval and Renaissance usages. In 1340 Hampole writes in the *Prose Psalter:* "Lerand me to speke in parabils, that is, in likyngis that all men kan noght vnderstand"; in 1420, Lydgate: "Hit sownyd to me as a parable, Derke as a myste, or a feynyd fable"; and in 1589, Puttenham: "Whensoeuer by your similitude ye will seeme to teach any moralitie or good lesson by speeches misticall and darke, or farre fette, vnder a sence metaphoricall applying one naturall thing to another, . . . the Greekes call it *Parabola,* which terme is also by custome accepted of vs. . . ." And in our own time, Kafka, in his own ironic way, made a similar point, in his short piece "On Parables":

Many complain that the words of the wise are always merely parables and of no use in daily life, which is the only life we have. When the sage says: "Go over," he does not mean that we should cross to some actual place, which we could do anyhow if the labor were worth it; he means some fabulous yonder, something unknown to us, something too that he cannot designate more precisely, and therefore cannot help us here in the very least. All these parables really set out to say merely that the incomprehensible is incomprehensible, and we know that already.   (from *Parables and Paradoxes*)

We seem, then, to have arrived at a curious paradox in the definition of the term: parable is a method of teaching, but a method that actively withholds its meaning, a story-with-a-message in which the message is kept dark, "derke as a myste." But the point is not really as paradoxical as it sounds. Not all "messages" are simple; the central moral meanings of human existence cannot be learned by rules and propositions, as a child learns to cross the road, but only through felt experience. And that is what a parable is, meanings that are felt, because they are embodied in fictions.

II

And what about Wells? If he wrote parables, what were the feelings that he put into them? And what were the central moral meanings? The answer seems clear—feelings and meanings about *science;* it is in this sense, and only in this sense, that his stories are "science fictions"—though it would be more precise to call them "science parables," for they are essentially stories that embody moral judgments and dark, anxious feelings about the nature of science and about the human consequences of the scientific vision of reality.

Wells was peculiarly well suited to write such parables. He was, first of all, trained as a scientist; he had studied biology under T. H. Huxley, the great Victorian biologist, and he had taught science and had written scientific articles. He might have become another Huxley, teaching and preaching the doctrines of science to a world ruled by those doctrines. There were, however, two aspects of Wells's situation that made this course unlikely for him. First, Wells came of age at the end of the great Victorian period of scientific optimism. The nineteenth century had been a time of rapid scientific advances, and it is not surprising that Victorian scientists assumed that scientific advancement was progress, and that progress was moral. The theory of evolution, which to Darwin was morally neutral, as science was, came to be applied to social change, and to be taken as implying a process of inevitable moral improvement: man and his society would go on getting better and better, and science would be the instrument of the change.

But by the end of the century this optimistic view of science had become difficult to sustain—there was too much accumulated evidence that Victorian science had created more evil than good—industrial slums, instruments of war, class-divisions, irresponsible wealth were too insistently visible to be ignored. And Wells came along at just this point.

He came along from a particular class background, and this too is important. Wells came from the very lowest level of the lower middle class. His parents were not quite workers—his father kept an unsuccessful shop and made a little extra money as a professional cricket-player, and his mother was a housekeeper for a wealthy county family, but they were not quite bourgeois either. That level of society is peculiarly rootless, belonging neither to the lower nor to the middle class, but scrambling in between, lacking any tradition or fixed place in the world. In Wells's case even a significant geographical location was lacking—the part of Kent where he grew up was in the process of becoming a suburb of London, and was neither country nor city. So Wells came to maturity without roots, without the support of an inherited place in the world; nor did he have either religious belief or a traditional humanistic education to fall back on.

Such a young man, exposed to late-Victorian science, would respond to it not as a set of working theories for dealing with matter, but as a faith, an account of reality as comprehensive and as fulfilling as a religion; and because he knew no alternative, he would take it as *truth*. But because Wells was imaginative, and an artist, he felt the inadequacy of that truth; he was shaken and depressed by the dark spaces between the stars, and the Nothingness on the other side of Nothing, and he experienced the Second Law of Thermodynamics as a kind of nightmare. Out of that nightmare he made his scientific parables. They are, all of them, expressions of the feeling of living in a world in which science is all there is.

The Time Machine is a parable of this late-Victorian state of mind—a parable in which science is used as the vehicle for meanings that are profoundly anti-scientific. But it is the state of mind, the *feelings* about science, that Wells is concerned with, and not science itself; there is no credible science involved in the story, and Wells seems to have made the Time Traveller's machine intentionally ridiculous—a sort of stationary bicycle—in order that his reader should not be distracted from the moral issues by technology. The Traveller himself enters the story as a typical scientist, "expounding a recondite matter." In the opening scene he behaves in a strictly scientific manner, speaking of nothing but his theories, and giving no thought to goals, values, or consequences. Like any good experimental scientist, he is only interested in the future; he never considers turning his machine back into the past—for him what has already existed is uninteresting. Only one sentence prepares us for the changes that the Traveller will undergo in his travels; he had, says the narrator, "more than a touch of whim among his elements, and we distrusted him." Whim is not an appropriate quality in a scientist, and distrust is not an appropriate response to one. There will be more than science in this story, then, because there is from the beginning this additional element.

There are actually *two* parables in *The Time Machine,* corresponding to the Traveller's two journeys. The first, the journey to the Golden Age of the Eloi, is a parable of the social consequences of science, though that parabolic meaning emerges only gradually, as the Traveller discovers the nature of the society he has entered. At the beginning, he responds to his new experience like a scientist; he observes the Eloi and forms a hypothesis to account for them:

It seemed to me that I had happened upon humanity upon the wane. The ruddy sunset set me thinking of the sunset of mankind. For the first time I began to realize an odd consequence of the social effort in which we are at present engaged. And yet, come to think, it is a logical consequence enough. Strength is the outcome of need; security sets a premium on feebleness. The work of ameliorating the conditions of life—the true civilizing process that makes life more and more secure— had gone steadily on to a climax. One triumph of a united humanity over Nature had followed another. Things that are now mere dreams had become projects deliberately put in hand and carried forward. And the harvest was what I saw!

The Eloi—soft, passive, beautiful, and helpless—are simply what the unexamined goals of science imply; if man masters his environment, he deprives himself of the stimuli that make him energetic and human.

This is the Traveller's first hypothesis; but it is, as he later realizes, inadequate. For labor and strenuousness have not been eliminated from life—they have simply been thrust underground, into the hands of the Morlocks, a race of technological creatures that runs the world's underground machines. In this Golden Age, the human species has diverged biologically into two species—one idle and living above ground, the other industrious and subterranean. But Wells's point is not a biological one, and it is not prophetic. His text makes it clear that his attention remains fixed on the present.

At first, proceeding from the problems of our own age, it seemed clear as daylight to me that the gradual widening of the present merely temporary and social difference between the Capitalist and the Labourer, was the key to the whole position. No doubt it will seem grotesque enough to you—and wildly incredible!—and yet even now there are existing circumstances to point that way. There is a tendency to utilize underground space for the less ornamental purposes of civilization; there is the Metropolitan Railway in London, for instance, there are new electric railways, there are subways, there are underground workrooms and restaurants, and they increase and multiply. Evidently, I thought, this tendency had increased till Industry had gradually lost its birthright in the sky. I mean that it had gone deeper and deeper into larger and ever larger underground factories, spending a still-increasing amount of its time therein, till, in the end—! Even now, does not an East-end worker live in such artificial conditions as practically to be cut off from the natural surface of the earth?

So the Eloi and the Morlocks offer a parable of the class structure in a capitalist society—the workers thrust underground and deprived of light and the natural world, the rich living idly and softly on the surface, on the profits of the workers' labor.

This is a parable such as any socialist might tell; but Wells adds a further point that is not political: the Morlocks are cannibals, they feed on the flesh of the Eloi. There is no way that this fact can be assimilated into a socialist parable; Wells is saying something more fundamental and more pessimistic, that those to whom evil is done do evil in return, that exploitation makes monsters, that cruelty is an inevitable product of a cruel system, and inhuman conduct an inevitable product of inhumanity. The Traveller tries to see even this horror in an objective, scientific spirit. Man's preju-

dice against eating human flesh, he thinks, is no deep-seated instinct, and he tries to moralize upon it; perhaps the devouring of
the Eloi should be considered "as a rigorous punishment of human
selfishness." But he fails. The Eloi are human and sympathetic, and
the Morlocks are "inhuman and malign." Yet *both* are his descendants; like King Lear, he must acknowledge his evil offspring as well
as his good ones.

As a social parable, the Golden Age treats the social reality
created by nineteenth-century industrialism—that is, by science—
in a way that is both anti-Darwinian and anti-Marxist. There has
been no upward moral evolution, nor a survival of the fittest, and
the proletariat has not evolved into a classless society. Evil, aggres-
sion, class divisions, and fear still exist; humanity has in fact degenerated. "We are kept keen," the Traveller thinks, "on the grindstone of pain and necessity." Science, in Wells's parable, is the
enemy of human keenness.

The parable of the Golden Age ends on a somber note: man will
not evolve upward, science will hinder his moral growth, there will
always be the Haves and the Have Nots, the human carnivores and
their prey. But there is a still bleaker parable beyond this. The
Traveller, when he once more mounts his machine, travels still
further in a vast leap to the end of time, thirty million years hence.
That final vision of a dead earth, hanging motionless and unturning
in a black sky, is brilliant and horrible, and it is the ultimate scientific vision. For it is the inevitable consequence of living entirely in
scientific, material time that one must accept the end of a recognizable material world. In the face of this final darkness, the despairing vision of the future set forth in the Golden Age of the Eloi
no longer matters; the Second Law of Thermodynamics cancels out
mere questions of politics and society.

The Time Machine ends with an epilogue spoken by the narrator. As we know from his earlier appearances, this narrator has
reacted to the Traveller's theories and tales with ordinary doubt—
he is simply the ordinary man refusing to acknowledge what his
imagination cannot endure. So at the end he offers his own hearty

but ill-founded hopes: "I, for my own part, cannot think that these latter days of weak experiment, fragmentary theory, and mutual discord are indeed man's culminating time!" And he offers, as reasons for comfort, the flowers that the Traveller brought back from the Golden Age, "to witness that even when mind and strength had gone, gratitude and a mutual tenderness still lived on in the heart of man." But the reader who had read the story must feel the bitter irony of that foolish comfort; for mind and strength had indeed gone, but fear had not, and the preying of man upon man had not, and where is the comfort in *that?* And the last account of the Traveller that the narrator gives supports the necessity of pessimism: "He, I know . . . thought but cheerlessly of the Advancement of Mankind, and saw in the growing pile of civilization only a foolish heaping that must inevitably fall back upon and destroy its makers in the end." If that is what Wells thought, then he was a poor Victorian scientist. But he was a great maker of parables—pessimistic, despairing parables, but valid and instructive ones, parables that reveal the feelings, and the moral reactions, of a scientist who had gone to the end of science, and had found there a great darkness.

III

But that great darkness, mocking all man's science and passion, did not remain Wells's most characteristic vision. The cosmic pessimism of *The Time Machine* is, to be sure, present in all of his voluminous later writing; but it is subtly qualified, and increasingly countered, by a faith and an enthusiasm for science and technology that are bound to surprise readers who know only his early work. Indeed, it is difficult to reconcile the Wells we value most highly today, the Wells of the darkly brilliant scientific romances of the nineties, with the Wells who was such a pugnacious and tireless participant in the intellectual debates of the twentieth century, and whose prophecies run to self-assured titles like *The Outline of History* (1920), *The Salvaging of Civilization* (1921), and *The Fate of Homo Sapiens* (1939). The scruffy, underweight young man who described himself as "writing away for dear life" (on *The Time Machine*) while in the grip of what appeared to be a fatal lung ailment was replaced, sometime around the turn of the century, by another figure: the pudgy, best-selling pundit of science and culture we see in the later photographs, willing to dispense a seemingly endless series of firm opinions on almost any subject of importance. And it is *this* H. G. Wells who, throughout the century, is hailed by his supporters as a major philosopher of the coming technological era, and attacked or satirized by his adversaries as a genteel fascist, a ludicrous writer of hymns to the spiritual benefits of better plumbing.

The easy explanation—and the wrong one—would argue that he simply burned his talent out; that the writer of bitter parables on the Void of nineteenth-century science *did* die, to all intents, sometime before the First World War, and that what was left was only the windy, immensely well-read and remarkably unsubtle retailer of facts and middle-class self-confidence. But such an argument would distort, not only the real complexity of the early tales, but the merits of the later work. (It was Henry James, that most mandarin of literary men, who first advanced this explanation of his sometime friend's career: a kind of reverse metamorphosis, with the butterfly-spirit of the novelist transformed again into the lumpish, Science School-caterpillar.) Wells, to the very end of his life, heroically refused to be a stupid man. And while we can, perhaps must, find his later faith in technology misplaced, we cannot find it silly. There are moments of sweep and perception in *The Outline of History, The Fate of Homo Sapiens,* and especially his last, grim book, *Mind at the End of Its Tether* (1942) that show that his gift of visionary imagery had by no means been diminished. It had rather been *deflected;* and the process through which it was deflected is perhaps the most important story in Wells's life, as well as an important aspect of the early romances.

We have already quoted the passage at the end of *The Time Machine* where the narrator reports the Time Traveller's pessimistic view of nature and of civilization as something that "must inevitably fall back upon and destroy its makers in the end." But now we must take note of the narrator's immediate, famous response to that view: "If that is so, it remains for us to live as though it were not so." The narrator is, indeed, a less dynamic, less intelligent man than the Time Traveller, and his final words—about the survival of "mutual tenderness . . . in the heart of man"—when balanced against the awesome and negative visions of the Time Traveller, are bound to strike us as a late-Victorian excrescence, a pathetic grasping at straws (or at flowers) in the midst of the wreckage of all things. But in the simple dignity and resonance of the line, "If that is so, it remains for us to live as though it were not so," he really does rise above himself, and suggests to us one bit of wisdom—an almost existential courage against the Void—that the Time Traveller himself has *not* gleaned from his journey. The book offers us no resolution to this subtle disagreement between its characters. But it is a debate which occurred at a very deep level of Wells's imagination. And we can say that his later career, his evolution into an apologist of technology, was a deliberate choice to give fuller utterance to one of his two voices, the voice of the narrator, the first-person speaker (never very far from Wells himself) who draws lessons of solace and encouragement from the storytelling, parabolic, negating voice of the traveler through time and space. And if that choice meant that ultimately the parables, the stories themselves would have to cease, replaced now by only the first-person, moralizing speaker, Wells never tires of informing us that it is a sacrifice he does not mind making.

In fact, we probably owe the brilliance of the scientific romances to a historical moment, a fortuitous balance of ideas and motivations, which could not have lasted in any case. We have already observed that Wells owed his view of nature and of scientific truth largely to his study under T. H. Huxley and his reading of Huxley's own master, Charles Darwin. And the very impulse toward the kind of fiction he wrote in the scientific romances, toward parable, that is, was deeply imbedded in him by the Bible-centered Protestantism of his upbringing. But, by the time Wells began writing,

European culture had for a century been discovering a subtle and finally destructive tension between the scientific world-view and the possibilities of parable, allegory, and other morally symbolic modes of narrative.

Briefly, the problem is this: parabolic writing, using ordinary objects or at least objects from the "real" world, presents us with a hidden, symbolic moral meaning that does not so much *belong to* the "real world" as it is *imposed* upon that world by the stronger, more spiritually-informed vision of the parabolist. But this means that parable, like allegory and like liturgical drama, assumes an already-existing correspondence between the ordinary world and the world of moral values. A parable is not only an illustration of morality; it is, in the very fact of its utterance, a confirmation of a moral universe in which human action has meaning because it is related to an idea of "Nature" that is *already* humanized and moralized.

The intellectual and imaginative movement called romanticism, though, involves a discovery that this preestablished harmony does not exist—or exists only in highly complicated, attenuated forms. The literature of the romantic era and the science of the same era, so often imagined as at odds with each other, are better thought of as parallel and complementary developments. For if science from Laplace through Darwin to Einstein has increasingly informed us that the world out there is irretrievably *other,* unrelated to our own innate ideas of rational proportion or causality, so have poetry and fiction from Wordsworth through Conrad to Joyce informed us how isolated the world is *in here,* in the human mind, from any "Nature" that might putatively support or illustrate its passions or its deepest longings.

Not only, then, was the science that Wells inherited tending toward a world-view we might well describe as the "death of the parabolic," so too was the literary tradition. Goethe, who was not only a great poet but also an important scientist (his evolutionary thought anticipates Darwin), could still, in 1832, be expansively confident about the coming change in human thought. In the famous last chorus of *Faust* (*Part Two*) he writes:

> *Alles Vergängliche*
> *Ist nur ein Gleichnis . . .*

"All things destructible / Are but a parable. . . ." These are the opening lines of what is surely one of the most exalted moments of transcendence in European literature. But—*nur ein Gleichnis, only* a parable! If *all* things are the signs of something else, then nothing is the sign of anything, and the ancient resonance between man and the world that makes parables possible is on the verge of disintegration. Goethe's word, *Alles,* is important, for it helps us realize what a short step it is from the cosmic embrace of his optimism to the bitterly reductive, self-annihilating study of "meaning" of another great German, Ludwig Wittgenstein, in the *Tractatus Logico-Philosophicus* (1918), which begins with the celebrated formula: *Die Welt ist alles, was der Fall ist* (The world is everything that is the case). It is perhaps in this larger quarrel, between these two greater voices, that we can find the fullest meaning of Wells's own dark parables, and his own attempts to overcome their darkness.

We know that the young Wells, while staying at Up Park where his mother was in domestic service, read voraciously if unselectively, and that one of his favorite poets was Shelley—another great romantic who was also an ardent scientific experimenter. One passage from Shelley, especially, is deeply suggestive for the Wells of *The Time Machine* or *The War of the Worlds*—for the work, that is, of a young man raised in a penurious and conservative religious piety and struggling to assimilate the implications for that piety of the vast, chilling dimensions in space and time of modern science. In the *Hymn to Intellectual Beauty,* Shelley asks what we have seen other writers asking, why it is that the physical universe fails to sustain our perceptions of human dignity or permanent moral value; and, too wise to attempt an answer to the question, Shelley instead reflects upon our persistent, suicidal *repetition* of the question—our bad habit, that is, of making parables in a universe which will not tolerate them:

> No voice from some sublimer world hath ever
>> To sage or poet these responses given—
>> Therefore the names of Demon, Ghost, and Heaven,
> Remain the records of their vain endeavour,
> Frail spells—whose uttered charm might not avail to sever,
>> From all we hear and all we see,
>> Doubt, chance, and mutability.

"Frail spells" is Shelley's judgment upon the whole tradition of mythmaking. But even more fascinating for us is the set of terms that, for him, enforce such a judgment, the three great negatives uttered by nature against all man's attempts to construct parabolic value systems: "Doubt, chance, and mutability." The last two terms, at any rate, were within forty years of Shelley's poem to become the mainspring forces, absolutely irresistible and absolutely unconscious, of the most powerful and most anti-mythic work of nineteenth-century thought—which was, by the way, the most formative single influence on all of Wells's thought. We refer, of course, to Darwin's *Origin of Species* (1859).

One common misconception about romanticism is that it is a celebration of the healing powers of nature—or "Nature," as the romantics called it. But as our references to Goethe and Shelley suggest, and as much contemporary reevaluation of the romantics abundantly bears out, this is simply not the case. The romantic obsession with "Nature" is not the expression of a passionate at-homeness in the natural world, but quite the reverse: a profound nostalgia, at first loving but very rapidly becoming bitter, for a "Nature" that once seemed to support the imposition of moral values, but that resists more and more such imposition. And along these lines it is not really capricious to call Charles Darwin one of the most important romantic poets of the century. He was a widely cultured and sensitive, almost obsessively shy man; and he seems to have been more adequately aware of the truly revolutionary implications of his thought than many of his supporters, although he did his best to escape the intellectual shockwaves he himself generated. For our purposes, one of his most important passages is a remarkable aside in the crucial Fourth Chapter of *The Origin of Species,* the chapter discussing "Natural Selection; Or the Survival of the Fittest" (this chapter is, of course, the ultimate basis of the struggle between Eloi and Morlocks in *The Time Machine*). There he answers critics who accuse him of treating the blind mechanism of evolution as a kind of God:

> It has been said that I speak of natural selection as an active power or Deity; but who objects to an author speaking of the attraction of gravity as ruling the movements of the planets? Every one knows what is meant and is implied by such metaphorical expressions; and they are almost necessary for brevity. So again it is difficult to avoid personifying the word Nature; but I mean by Nature, only the aggregate action and product of many natural laws, and by laws the sequence of events as ascertained by us. With a little familiarity such superficial objections will be forgotten.

It is hard not to read the last sentence as one of the more ponderous jokes of the last few hundred years. The "superficial objections" to Darwin's redefinition of Nature not only have not been forgotten, they have remained the central imaginative problem of modern literature. In this passage the destructuring of Nature as the ground of human mythmaking is completed. And if Goethe, with heroic confidence, could describe all things as "only" a parable, the parable has by now evanesced in the corrosive atmosphere of all things in their inhuman factuality. For Darwin the metaphor is grimmer: all things—Nature—are "only" laws; and the laws themselves are only "the sequence of events *as ascertained by us"*— not a resonant and harmonic counterpoint to our own moral values, that is, but at best a factitious imposition of our own ideas of proportion and reason upon a process that neither understands nor contains such elegant, tidy concepts. Indeed, for Darwin metaphor itself is merely an undesirable though perhaps inevitable shorthand of scientific discourse. But without metaphor, how could we have parables? Or, to put the matter more seriously, how could we have human (and humane) life, as the last three thousand years of Western civilization have understood it? This is the question Darwin, Shelley, Goethe, and the other giants of romantic thought and science bequeath to the twentieth century. And while later writers (Kafka, Joyce, Mann) may have understood the question more self-consciously than did H. G. Wells, none *lived* it more dramatically than he.

IV

We can now perhaps say, in the context of the previous discussion, that the shift in Wells's vision, from writer of "anti-scientific" parables to defender of technology and would-be architect of the future, is the outcome of a psychic struggle implicit in his own identity and that of his age. For Wells to insist, like the narrator of *The Time Machine,* that despite the doom of entropy we must "live as though it were not so," it was necessary for him to accept the full implications of Darwinian science, which is to say the full impossibility of parabolic literature in the mode of his first triumphs. This is paradoxical, but not incomprehensibly so: to continue to write, he had to surrender his ability to write as a novelist; to locate a faith in something beyond the Nothing of science, he had to accept completely the anti-metaphoric, anti-parabolic "nature" *of* modern science. For the truly artistic impulse, as he richly possessed it, was bound to lead him again and again to create chilling exercises in the meaninglessness of meaning like *The Time Machine* (and like *Death in Venice, Metamorphosis,* and *Ulysses*—to invoke later writers who did not make Wells's choice of hope over art). But Wells needed a faith, in *something* at any rate, and it was probably his ability to reflect this need, more than any of his specific pronouncements, that made him so important for so many people in his later years. And if his faith in the scientific world-view could not cohabit in his imagination with the artistic, visionary impulse that constantly criticized and diminished that world-view, then the choice between the two voices was an evident if not an easy one. The remarkable thing about him, then, is not that he "sacrificed" his artistic talents for the sake of technological proselytizing, but rather that, in the midst of his capitulations to the technological view of reality, he managed for as long as he did to maintain an insight that we must call, in every sense, artistic.

Of all the scientific romances and tales Wells wrote between 1895 and 1906 (the date of his most argumentative and unsuccessful early book, *In the Days of the Comet*), none has been more widely read or more influential than *The War of the Worlds*. Only three years intervene between *The Time Machine* and *The War of the Worlds*, but they are separated by a very large shift in their creator's attitude. So much so, in fact, that it is possible to read *The War* as Wells's most characteristic narrative: written just before his final conversion to scientism, when the forces of anti-scientific parable and technological optimism were in a delicate balance in his mind. *The War*, indeed, is not so much a defense of the specific (and, therefore, always ludicrously delimited) benefits of technology, but rather an attempt to assimilate and, in the language of the new secularized universe, to mythologize the Darwinian view of nature itself.

Wells never commented on the relationship between *The Time Machine* and *The War of the Worlds* (in his remarks on his work, predictably, he always deemphasized rather than overemphasized his role as conscious artist); but the two books provide some fascinating contrasts. *The Time Machine*, as its title insists, is "about" time—time of geological immensity—and quite deliberately compresses, therefore, the other dimension of experience, space: the Time Traveller himself never journeys more than the distance of a comfortable Sunday walk away from his home in Richmond, and his Machine, for all the eons it travels, never moves more than a few feet from its original position (Wells is at pains to emphasize this paradox in the book). *The War of the Worlds* is "about" space, both "space" as a good Cartesian mathematician would have understood it in 1898 and "space" as the twentieth century has learned to interpret that originally neutral term—as in "spaceship," "space opera," and "outer space." Not only does the novel invoke, with precision, the interplanetary distances between the Earth and Mars, it also involves space as a real component of dramatic action: few novels are as riddled with specific, real place-names, or depend as much for their total effect upon a comprehension (rudimentary at least) of the geography and possibilities of transit in Sussex, Surrey, and London at the time of writing. But if the book emphasizes space, sheer distance, it correspondingly compresses time: the invasion of the Martians, shattering as it is, begins and ends with incredible rapidity. "The Work of Fifteen Days," Chapter Six of Part Two informs us, is all it takes for the Martian invasion absolutely to upset all previous assumptions about the centrality of human beings in their hegemony over the Earth. And it is a sign of Wells's great talent as a storyteller that the incredible speed of the Martian victory and defeat does not interfere with, but actually enhances, our sense of the uncanny "realism" of this first of all tales of extraterrestrial invaders.

There is another and deeper reason, though, why *The War of the Worlds,* after nearly a century and after many hundreds of imitations in literature and film, retains so much of its original conviction and power. It is a tale, not simply of extraterrestrial invaders, but of apocalypse, of the end of the world—as is *The Time Machine* in its great closing pages. But unlike *The Time Machine* it is an apocalypse that does not take man to his final end, but rather, more violently and more dramatically, takes the final end to man *as he is now: The War* is, in the most complete way, a rewriting of the parable of *The Time Machine* from the viewpoint of a changed, and perhaps more optimistic, sense of life.

We have already spoken of the "two voices" of Wells as manifested in the earlier book: how the Time Traveller, romantic adventurer and man of action, journeys into the future only to relate his journey to the more reflective, and more philosophically hopeful, first-person narrator. In *The War,* significantly, the same formal relationship is present, but reversed, between the two major witnesses of the action. The anonymous narrator, a very Wells-like writer on philosophical and scientific subjects, is here the center of our interest and the truly authoritative voice on the moral implications of the invasion; while the adventurous, romantic "other self," has dwindled into the figure of the narrator's brother, whose experience fills only the last four chapters of Part One—the bleakest, most pessimistic hours of the Martian triumph.

This is an important and revealing aspect of Wells's development as a thinker and writer of fiction, and deserves dwelling on. Instead of the Time Traveller's shattering experience of mankind's future in the mutually antithetical forms of Eloi and Morlocks, *The War of the Worlds* presents us with the same opposition of possibilities in the forms of the Curate and the artilleryman. But—and this is a measure of Wells's development in the four years separating the two books—the opposition in the later book is both more pronounced and less terminally discouraging. Eloi and Morlocks, dreamers and cannibalistic workers, are after all involved in a particularly disgusting symbiosis. But the Curate and the artilleryman never even meet each other in *The War*. Rather, they are characters, or better still potential states of mind, whom the narrator encounters in his own journey toward Primrose Hill and toward a rebirth of hope. Those two central forces behind the early Wells parables, his Bible-centered religious heritage and his education as Darwinian evolutionist and technologue, are in fact projected and redefined in these equally failed characters; and between their extremes lies, at the end of the book, not the negative vision of the Time Traveller but the measured optimism and heroic rationality of the narrator himself. It is this voice, tested and refined by the alternatives of passive superstition and feckless revolutionism, that utters the epitaph for the last, dying Martian war machine—surely one of the most eloquent passages in all of Wells:

> For so it had come about, as, indeed, I and many men might have foreseen had not terror and disaster blinded our minds. These germs of disease have taken toll of humanity since the beginning of things—taken toll of our pre-human ancestors since life began here. . . . By the toll

of a billion deaths, man has bought his birthright of the earth, and it is his against all comers; it would still be his were the Martians ten times as mighty as they are. For neither do men live nor die in vain.

The last sentence, a resounding commonplace of Victorian and post-Victorian sentimentality, is here redeemed from its banality by the context of the whole book in which it occurs. For *The War of the Worlds* demonstrates that it is *literally* true, not in terms of an abstract and outmoded spirituality, but in terms of the "hard" science of bacteriology and immunology. The story of the Martian invasion, in other words, works finally because it is a tough-minded and careful attempt to reclaim the Darwinian demythologizing of Nature, to turn even that most anti-mythic of visions into the stuff of myth. It is a reversal not only of the narrative technique, but of the basic attitudes of *The Time Machine*.

The Martians are a possible future of man. At many points in the novel, the narrator reminds us that for all their monstrosity the Martians must once have been humanoid, but that their advanced technology has mutated them to their present disgusting form. Wells's own early sketch, "The Man of the Year Million," in which the man of the future is presented as a revoltingly intellectual creature, all head and no body, suggests that the Martians are a vision not so much of aliens as of possible nightmare extensions of ourselves. So their invasion of the Earth is literally a time-machine story in reverse, where the future implodes upon the present. Thus it is brilliantly appropriate that the Martians are vampires: ghosts, this time not of the undead past, but of the yet-to-be-born, sucking the blood of life and joy from our own world.

The fact that the vampires do not succeeed in their ghastly work is a mark of Wells's own growing faith that the scientific worldview itself may not entail the dissolution of all traditional values. For the Martians are only a *possible* future, which the myth of *The War of the Worlds* seeks to prove an impossible one. The narrator informs us, in the last pages of the book, that he had been at work upon a project very much like the writing of *The Time Machine*. Returning to his home after the great and unexpected defeat of the

Martians, he enters his study and looks over the manuscript he had left to go examine the first cylinder, the cylinder on Horsell Common:

It was a paper on the probable development of Moral Ideas with the development of the civilizing process; and the last sentence was the opening of a prophecy: 'In about two hundred years,' I had written, 'we may expect————' The sentence ended abruptly.

The sentence ends abruptly because at that point in his work the narrator breaks off to buy his *Daily Chronicle,* and to wander down to Horsell Common for a look at the men from Mars. But as every sensitive reader of *The War of the Worlds* will note, the sentence is not really fragmented. For the whole book, the whole story of the Martian invasion and its inevitable, predestined defeat, is the completion of the phrase "we may expect." The book is a massive reclamation of the future from despair, on the principles of man's own natural tendency to rationality, and more importantly on the basis of the tendency toward rationality of nature itself, of the permanence and beneficence of the Earth, even imagined as a Darwinian ecosystem.

Some readers have faulted the novel for the seemingly arbitrary and *ex machina* ending. But to fault the novel this way is to misunderstand its very title. "The War of the Worlds" is, of course, the war between Martians and Earthmen (a war that, the artilleryman says, is no war at all); it is also, as we have been pointing out, a war between the world of the comfortable present, a present defined in terms of suburban English complacency, and the world of the chilling future, a future of horrifying technologization and inhumanity. But it is also, and most importantly, a war literally of *worlds*—of Earth, the planet, and Mars, the planet. And it is *Earth* that wins the war, not because of the superior intelligence of men over Martians, but because of the superior complexity of its ecology, the greater energy of its endemic struggle for existence. The bacteria that kill the Martians, actually, are not *ex machina* at all. They have been present from the opening paragraph of the novel, where the narrator tells us that the Martians have studied us "almost as narrowly as a man with a microscope might scrutinize the transient creatures that swarm and multiply in a drop of water." They have only waited, throughout the narrative of the Martian invasion, for their chance to make the transition from metaphor to reality, and to reestablish, in their violent, mindless teeming and breeding, the bases of life: bases that Wells, in the years after *The War of the Worlds,* more and more held to be the only principles upon which a truly humane culture could be based.

Technology will not, cannot defeat us or turn us into the mutant shapes of the nightmare future, as long as we recognize and hold fast to the realities of the Earth and the biological energy underlying even the most abstract of human theories. This is the ultimate meaning of the parable that is *The War of the Worlds;* a meaning that does not so much refute as energetically oppose and attempt to negate the meaning of the entropic *Time Machine.* Against the terrifying discovery, in the earlier work, of the Second Law of Thermodynamics, Wells now poses the hope that consciousness itself, reason liberated from the twin traps of terror and disaster, might be able to circumvent entropy and the frozen doom of all created things. To do that, he had to imagine a myth that could make even of the Darwinian struggle for survival, godless and eyeless as it is, the stuff of a prophecy; and to maintain that attitude in his later work, he had even to sacrifice the genius that makes *The War of the Worlds* and *The Time Machine* such triumphs of the modern parabolic imagination. But whatever later changes Wells endured, the writer, his moment, and his intellectual heritage produced at least these two central fictions: fictions whose antithetical voices continue to carry on an argument—on man, on nature, and on human fate—that a century of imaginative writing inside and outside science fiction has elaborated and expanded, but never more graphically articulated than these two tales of 1895 and 1898.

THE SPIRIT OF H. G. WELLS

BERNARD BERGONZI

The Early Wells and the Fin de Siècle

1

H. G. Wells died in 1946 at the age of eighty. He was so much a man of the twentieth century that it is hard to believe that he started his literary career in the middle of the eighteen-nineties. The author of the *Outline of History* and *The Shape of Things to Come* appears, at first sight, to have nothing in common with the world of *The Green Carnation* and *The Yellow Book*. Wells, the tireless designer of scientific utopias, rather despised art, while the men of the nineties lived for it. The robust creator of Kipps and Mr Polly manifestly does not belong in the shadowy gallery peopled by such exotic and attenuated figures as Dorian Gray, Aubrey Beardsley, Enoch Soames and Ernest Dowson (with the passing of time the real and the fictitious names become strangely confused). Nevertheless, Wells did begin life as a writer in, if not quite of, the eighteen-nineties. If, like his friend Stephen Crane, he had died in 1900 he would already have been established as the author of more than a dozen short novels and collections of stories or essays. Had Wells's career been truncated in this fashion he would be remembered primarily as a literary artist and hardly at all as a publicist

From Bernard Bergonzi, The Early H. G. Wells (Manchester: Manchester University Press, 1961), pp. 1-22. Reprinted by permission of Manchester University Press.

and pamphleteer. In 1900 Wells had scarcely embarked on the self-appointed task of educating humanity that was to take up most of his time and energy during the next four decades.

In the course of this study I hope to show why Wells could be considered an artist in the first few years of his career. It must be admitted that he was temperamentally alien to the self-conscious aestheticism that is thought of as a characteristically *fin de siècle* phenomenon, and which is inevitably associated with the names of Oscar Wilde and Aubrey Beardsley, despite the personal antipathy that existed between the two men. There were, however, occasional points of contact between the young Wells and the aesthetic *milieu*. In 1897 Wilde, writing to Robert Ross from Reading Gaol, remarked, 'you mentioned Henley had a protegé':[1] this was Wells, whose first novel, *The Time Machine,* had been serialized by W. E. Henley in *The New Review.* In a letter of October 1896, Beardsley referred to *The Island of Dr Moreau* as 'certainly a horrible affair and very well set forth'.[2] Wells himself contributed a short story to *The Yellow Book,* though admittedly to one of the more respectable numbers that appeared after Beardsley had severed his connection with it. He was sufficiently aware of the excesses of contemporary aestheticism to be able to satirize them. In a sketch called 'A Misunderstood Artist', first printed in 1894 and then included in his collection of essays, *Select Conversations with an Uncle* (1895), he describes an imaginary encounter with a cook who is an extreme devotee of *l'art pour l'art:*

Then I produced some Nocturnes in imitation of Mr Whistler, with mushrooms, truffles, grilled meat, pickled walnuts, black pudding, French plums, porter—a dinner in soft velvety black, eaten in a starlight of small scattered candles. That, too, led to a resignation: Art will ever demand its martyrs.

Here we have a remarkable though presumably inadvertent echo of the famous all-black banquet given by the Duc Jean des Esseintes in that bible of the aesthetic movement, Huysmans' *A Rebours.*

1. *The Works of Oscar Wilde* (ed. G. F. Maine), 1948, p. 895.
2. *Last Letters of Aubrey Beardsley* (ed. John Gray), 1904, p. 26.

The cook continues, insisting on the absolute separation of art from all practical or moral considerations, in a way which is uncomfortably close to some of the exchanges at Wilde's trials:

> *My* dinners stick in the memory. I cannot study these people—my genius is all too imperative. If I needed a flavour of almonds and had nothing else to hand, I would use prussic acid. Do right, I say, as your art instinct commands, and take no heed of the consequences. Our function is to make the beautiful gastronomic thing, not to pander to gluttony, not to be the Jesuits of hygiene. My friend, you should see some of my compositions. At home I have books and books in manuscript, Symphonies, Picnics, Fantasies, *Etudes* . . .[3]

Yet if Wells—as these extracts suggest—found the contemporary aesthetic ideal amusing rather than inspiring, it must be remembered that *Yellow Book* aestheticism was only one element in the complex of cultural manifestations and attitudes known as the *fin de siècle*. I would claim that the young Wells, though not an aesthete, was, in essentials, a *fin de siècle* writer.

2

One of the earliest uses of the phrase in English occurs in Chapter XV of *The Picture of Dorian Gray:*

> *'Fin de siècle,'* murmured Lord Henry.
> *'Fin du globe,'* answered his hostess.
> 'I wish it were *fin du globe,'* said Dorian with a sigh. 'Life is a great disappointment.'

In its widest sense *fin de siècle* was simply the expression of a prevalent mood: the feeling that the nineteenth century—which had contained more events, more history than any other—had gone on too long, and that sensitive souls were growing weary of it. In England this mood was heightened by the feeling that Queen Victoria's reign had also lasted excessively long. But at the same time, no one knew what the coming twentieth century was going to bring, though there was no lack of speculation. The result could be described as a certain loss of nerve, weariness with the past combined

3. Ibid., pp. 107–8.

with foreboding about the future. The *fin de siècle* mood produced, in turn, the feeling of *fin du globe,* the sense that the whole elaborate intellectual and social order of the nineteenth century was trembling on the brink of dissolution. *Fin de siècle* was not confined to art or aesthetics; its wider implications affected moral and social and even political attitudes and behaviour.

The fullest contemporary account of the phenomenon can be found in Max Nordau's massive work of destructive criticism, *Degeneration.* Nordau was ostensibly a scientist, a disciple of Lombroso, to whom his book is dedicated, but his tone and manner—as a contemproray reviewer observed—are rather those of the old-fashioned mad-house keeper complete with whip. Nordau's contention was that virtually all forms of late nineteenth century European art and literature—whether represented by Wagner, Ibsen, Zola, or the French symbolists—were the products of mental and physical degeneration. In his single-minded reduction of his subject to the demands of his conceptual apparatus, Nordau anticipates the rigours of twentieth century Freudian or Marxist criticism; and in general his book remains a curious but informative chapter of cultural history rather than the scientific document he intended it to be. *Degeneration* is, in fact, as much symptomatic as diagnostic: there is something decidedly *fin de siècle* about the way in which Nordau unfailingly discovers evidence of a pathological decline whenever he wants to. The English translation of *Degeneration* which appeared in 1895, was an immediate *succès de scandale*—seven impressions appeared between February and August—no doubt because it coincided with the trials of Wilde. Nordau's work appeared most opportunely as the culmination of the bourgeois and philistine counter-attack against the aesthetes, which had been prepared for by the constant sniping of *Punch* throughout 1894 at Beardsley and *The Yellow Book.*[4]

The first section of *Degeneration* is entitled 'Fin de Siècle', and

4. A number of refutations of Nordau subsequently appeared, the most celebrated being an extended review by Bernard Shaw (published in book form in 1908 as *The Sanity of Art*).

though characteristically intemperate in tone, it offers some useful evidence of the way in which the wider implications of the phenomenon could be regarded in the early nineties. Nordau describes its French origins—he exhibits a constant gallophobia—and shows how it has spread to Germany and other countries, though he has little to say about the English scene. He contends that the term has no objective validity, and that it illustrates a tendency of humanity to objectify its own subjective states: the French, in particular, 'ascribe their own senility to the century, and speak of *fin de siècle* when they ought correctly to say *fin de race'*. Nordau continues, in a significant passage:

But however silly a term *fin de siècle* may be, the mental constitution which it indicates is actually present in influential circles. The disposition of the times is curiously confused, a compound of feverish restlessness and blunted discouragement, of fearful presage and hang-dog renunciation. The prevalent feeling is that of imminent perdition and extinction. *Fin de siècle* is at once a confession and a complaint. The old Northern faith contained the fearsome doctrine of the Dusk of the Gods. In our days there have arisen in more highly developed minds vague qualms of a Dusk of the Nations, in which all suns and all stars are gradually waning, and mankind with all its institutions and creations is perishing in the midst of a dying world.[5]

Here Nordau is describing the *fin du globe* myth, which, as we shall see, was a dominant element in Wells's early work. He goes on to give a list of *fin de siècle* characters or events, taken from contemporary newspapers. A king who abdicates but retains by agreement certain political rights, which he afterwards sells to his country to provide means for the liquidation of debts contracted by gambling in Paris, is a *fin de siècle* king. The police official who removes a piece of the skin of a murderer after execution and has it tanned and made into a cigar-case is a *fin de siècle* official. An American wedding ceremony held in a gasworks and the subsequent honeymoon in a balloon is a *fin de siècle* wedding. A schoolboy who, on passing the gaol where his father is imprisoned for

5. *Degeneration*, 1895, p. 2.

embezzlement, remarks to a friend, 'Look, that's the governor's school,' is a *fin de siècle* son. These cases do not, at first sight, seem to have a great deal in common, but Nordau remarks:

All these *fin de siècle* cases have, nevertheless, a common feature, to wit, a contempt for traditional views of custom and morality.

Such is the notion underlying the word *fin de siècle*. It means a practical emancipation from traditional discipline, which theoretically is still in force. To the voluptuary this means unbridled lewdness, the unchaining of the beast in man; to the withered heart of the egoist, disdain of all consideration for his fellow-men, the trampling under foot of all barriers which enclose brutal greed of lucre and lust of pleasure; to the contemner of the world it means the shameless ascendency of base impulses and motives, which were, if not virtuously suppressed, at least hypocritically hidden; to the believer it means the repudiation of dogma, the negation of a super-sensuous world, the descent into flat phenomenalism; to the sensitive nature yearning for aesthetic thrills, it means the vanishing of ideals in art, and no more power in its accepted forms to arouse emotion. And to all it means the end of an established order, which for thousands of years has satisfied logic, fettered depravity, and in every art matured something of beauty.

One epoch of history is unmistakeably in its decline, and another is announcing its approach. There is a sound of rending in every tradition, and it is as though the morrow would not link itself with today. Things as they are totter and plunge, and they are suffered to reel and fall, because man is weary, and there is no faith that it is worth an effort to uphold them. Views that have hitherto governed minds are dead or driven hence like disenthroned kings, and for their inheritance they that hold the titles and they that would usurp are locked in struggle.[6]

If we discount the excesses of Nordau's rhetoric, we see in his analysis some of the essential elements of *fin de siècle:* the disappearance of old and familiar forms—whether in art or behaviour or intellectual attitudes—and their replacement by forms which are new and strange and even bizarre. This differs from the normal processes of development and change by being conscious and more or less *voulu.* The cult of the artificial as against the natural, which is evident *passim* in *The Picture of Dorian Gray,* is an obvious in-

6. Nordau, op. cit., pp. 5–6.

stance of this deliberate replacement, usually accompanied by an implicit or explicit desire to *épater le bourgeois.* Max Beerbohm's essay 'In Praise of Cosmetics', which appeared in the first number of *The Yellow Book,* is an ironical and urbane example, and the theme appears in much of the poetry of the period. But the most systematic abandonment of all previous forms of behaviour and modes of feeling is to be found in *A Rebours,* a work which is symptomatic of the whole *fin de siècle* state of mind, and not merely its aesthetic aspects. Des Esseintes leads a mode of life totally opposed to normal human standards; he turns night into day, abhors company, and even attempts to go without eating, being fed instead by enemas. He personifies the cult of the artificial and the unnatural far more thoroughly than Dorian Gray, his somewhat pallid imitation. He expresses the *fin de siècle* mood at its most negative, for he can only regard with blank despair the unknown manifestations of the future, as we see in the final sentences of the novel:

'Well, it is all over now. Like a tide-race, the waves of human mediocrity are rising to the heavens and will engulf this refuge, for I am opening the flood-gates myself, against my will. Ah! but my courage fails me, and my heart is sick within me!—Lord, take pity on the Christian who doubts, on the unbeliever who would fain believe, on the galley-slave of life who puts out to sea alone, in the night, beneath a firmament no longer lit by the consoling beacon-fires of the ancient hope!'[7]

3

A more positive, and perhaps more disturbing, attitude is apparent in Ibsen, who was a major target for Nordau's abuse. Bernard Shaw, in *The Quintessence of Ibsenism* (1891), described the almost hysterical hostility that greeted the early performances of Ibsen's plays in England. Throughout the nineties the bourgeois was being constantly *épaté,* by both the aesthetic and the realistic manifestations of the *fin de siècle:* following the outcry against

7. Translated by Robert Baldick (Penguin Classics), 1959, pp. 219–20.

Ibsen, comparable dismay was aroused by George Moore's *Esther Waters,* Grant Allen's *The Woman Who Did,* Beardsley's drawings, and *The Yellow Book.* With the conviction of Wilde the bourgeoisie appeared to have mounted a successful counter-attack. Yet they were still to be shocked by Hardy's *Jude the Obscure* in 1896, and in the same year Wells's *The Island of Dr Moreau* received a generally hostile reception, even though there was no suggestion of sexual impropriety in its violent pages. In Ibsen, as Shaw insisted, the likely forms of the future became painfully precise. Ibsen was that uncompromising kind of reformer who not only asserted that it was wrong to do things which no-one had previously objected to, but who also claimed that it was right to do things hitherto regarded as infamous. With Ibsen we are in the realm of the transvaluing of values, particularly where sexual morality is concerned. Shaw claimed that just as theology and the rule of a transcendent God had given way to rationalism and the concept of 'duty' as a guide to conduct, so rationalism must now be replaced by the Will to Live, and duty, in the abstract, by a man's duty to himself—or, as Ibsen had abundantly illustrated, by a woman's duty to herself. Self-realization was to be the paramount good, not the fulfilment of a transcendent or altruistic morality. Ibsen, in his very different fashion, was expressing a *fin de siècle* mood no less than Huysmans or Wilde; his demand for moral emancipation and the untrammelled realization of the personality was echoed, in another key, by the paradoxes of Dorian Gray, which were themselves to acquire a tragic significance a few years later at the Old Bailey. But, as I have said, Ibsen was the more positive figure; many of his revolutionary attitudes have come to form the basic assumptions of contemporary humanist morality.

However, it is to another of Nordau's victims that we must turn in order to find the writer who can be considered the dominant intellectual figure of the *fin de siècle,* and whose work embodies all its various strands: Friedrich Nietzsche. His writings had been known and discussed in Germany through the eighties, but it was several years before they received any attention in England. Apart from a few brief quotations in John Davidson's *Sentences and Paragraphs* (1893) and Nordau's denunciatory chapter in *Degeneration,* the first sustained account of Nietzsche in English was a long essay by Havelock Ellis published in *The Savoy* in 1896, which concluded that 'the nineteenth century has produced no more revolutionary and aboriginal force'. In the same year there appeared the first two volumes of a projected English translation of all Nietzsche's works (though the series was not completed for several more years). These included *Thus Spake Zarathustra, The Twilight of the Idols,* and *The Antichrist,* works which contain most of the essential aspects of Nietzsche's thought: the 'death of God' and the transvaluing of values; the glad acceptance of the break-up of the traditional order, and the advent of the *Übermensch.* The true philosophical significance of Nietzsche's thought, whether he is a precursor of Nazism, or whether, even, he is a philosopher at all, are questions which lie far beyond the scope of this study. What is more important for my immediate purpose is to see what was made of Nietzsche's ideas when they were first received in England; Nietzsche, like Machiavelli or Freud, is one of those thinkers whose work tends to become influential at second or third hand, with all the inevitable distortions and misinterpretations that this involves. Thus, Alexander Tille, Nietzsche's first English editor, associated Nietszche with the Darwinian assertion of the primacy of struggle in the natural order. He remarked that the word 'higher' was used in two different senses with respect to the animal world and to man:

In the first case the 'higher' being among a species is that which leaves the stronger and more numerous progeny, in the latter case the 'higher' being is that which does a larger number of such acts as are believed to serve certain ends particularly esteemed by a certain portion of the community to which it belongs.[8]

For Tille, this was an unreal distinction: man was part of the animal world, and the same criteria should apply to him as to the rest of it. Tille rejected both Spencer's attempt to show that moral

8. *The Works of Friedrich Nietzsche,* 1895, XI, xiii.

progress was implicit in evolutionary development, and Huxley's assertion that the cosmic process must be opposed in the interests of ethics. Tille argued that as Darwin had demonstrated the inevitability of struggle, we should adjust our values so as to admit the dominance of the 'physiological'. And this, he claimed, was precisely what Nietzsche had done: 'it is worthy of a great thinker to undertake thus the task of transvaluing the intellectual currency of our time'. Tille, it seems to me, made Nietzsche into a less complex and interesting writer than he in fact is: Nietzsche's attitude to Darwin was ambiguous and not particularly respectful, and it is not at all clear that the *Übermensch* can be identified with some ultimate product of human evolution.[9]

Nevertheless, Tille's interpretation of Nietzsche can be called plausible in its historical context, and it makes a convenient point to return to the subject of this study, the young H. G. Wells. Wells would have received the full impact of Darwin during his studies at the Royal College of Science in the late eighties, and the presence of Darwin is apparent in a number of ways in his so-called scientific romances of the next decade. Whether or not he read the English translations of Nietzsche and Tille's introduction, when they appeared in 1896, is not certain and not particularly relevant. Yet it is significant that in *The Island of Dr Moreau,* which was drafted and written the previous year, we find in the chapter called 'Dr Moreau Explains' something very like Tille's attempt to assimilate Nietzsche and Darwin. (It is interesting that in October 1896 Aubrey Beardsley, in addition to *The Island of Dr Moreau,* was also reading the new translation of Nietzsche.) In Wells's later books Nietzsche's influence may be more explicit: Ostrog, in *When the Sleeper Wakes,* claims that the coming of the 'Overman' is inevitable, while the Samurai of *A Modern Utopia,* and Wells's later versions of an élite, may be attempts to give a sociological embodiment to the *Übermensch.* Yet I am not primarily concerned with tracing influences; it is sufficient to show that both Nietzsche and

9. Nevertheless, we also find this identification in Shaw, particularly in *Man and Superman.*

Wells drew on ideas and attitudes which can, I think, be called *fin de siècle*. Both *The Island of Dr Moreau* and *The Time Machine,* as I hope to demonstrate, make substantially the same claim as Tille in his interpretation of Nietzsche: that the traditional view of man's place in the universe, and the morality appropriate to that place, is no longer supportable.

4

The *fin du globe* motif recurs constantly in Nietzsche's work: for specific instances one may point to the section called 'Nihilism' in *The Will to Power.* And a similar preoccupation can be found in much popular literature of the time. During the final three decades of the century there appeared a large number of novels or pamphlets describing catastrophic future wars, including, in many cases, the invasion of England followed by the partial or total defeat of the nation. These works will be referred to again in Chapter V; representative examples include Sir George Chesney's *The Battle of Dorking* (1871), Sir William Butler's *The Invasion of England* (1882), William Le Quex's *The Great War in England in 1897* (1894) and F. N. Maude's *The New Battle of Dorking* (1900). In M. P. Shiel's *The Yellow Danger* (1898) we see Western civilization overrun and almost destroyed by the Chinese hordes; and in the same author's *The Purple Cloud* (1902) human society is destroyed by a natural catastrophe. It is true that many of these works were written with a homiletic purpose, to encourage the nation to a greater state of military efficiency, but this does not prevent them being, at the same time, expressions of the prevalent mood, whatever their authors' stated intentions. It was felt that the normal life of society had continued too long in its predictable and everyday fashion, and that some radical transformation was overdue, whether by war or natural disaster (in 1901 the Nietzschean magazine *The Eagle and the Serpent* published an article entitled 'Why England must be Invaded'). These novels, with their images of physical destruction, showing the fair face of England desecrated by foreign troops, afford an obvious parallel to the moral and intellectual shocks administered to bourgeois complacency and self-confidence by Ibsen and the aesthetes. Indeed, it is hard to resist the conclusion that a certain collective death-wish pervaded the national consciousness at the time, despite its superficial assertiveness and brash jingoism. The willingness to be shocked was at least as significant as the readiness of others to administer the shocks. As Shaw had remarked of the type of reformer who declares that it is right to do something previously regarded as infamous: 'They call him all manner of opprobrious names; grudge him his bare bread and water; and secretly adore him as their saviour from utter despair.'[10]

Nordau had complained that 'the prevalent feeling is that of imminent perdition and extinction', and this is apparent not only in the neurasthenic rejections of a des Esseintes, and the violence of the *fin du globe* novels, but in rather less expected places. In Hardy's *Jude the Obscure,* published in 1896, Jude's precociously aged small son, 'Father Time', is an almost archetypal *fin de siècle* figure. When the boy has murdered Jude's other children, and killed himself, Jude observes:

It was in his nature to do it. The doctor says there are such boys springing up amongst us—boys unknown in the last generation—the outcome of new views of life. They seem to see all its terrors before they are old enough to have staying power to resist them. He says it is the beginning of the coming universal wish not to live (Part 6, Chapter 2).

Nevertheless, despite the prevalence of the negative aspects of the *fin de siècle,* they were not, in fact, universal. Just as Nietzsche had welcomed the end of the old order and had looked for the coming of the *Übermensch,* so speculations about the future went beyond the terrors of the *fin du globe.* (As a student, Wells had taken a wholly farcical view of the possibilities of the coming era in his short story, 'A Tale of the Twentieth Century'.) Works of utopian fiction such as Edward Bellamy's *Looking Backward* (1888) and

10. *The Quintessence of Ibsenism,* 1891, p. 2.

William Morris's *News from Nowhere* (1891) are important examples of the *fin de siècle* desire to discover new forms, embodied in images of a transformed society. One might also mention Richard Jefferies' *After London* (1885), a work which seems to embody the *fin du globe* motif, since it shows an England in which urban civilization has been overthrown by some unknown catastrophe, and where the whole country has reverted to a natural state (described by Jefferies in passages of great power and beauty). Yet since it also conveys Jefferies' positive conviction that human dignity is only possible in a pastoral society it can be seen as presenting a 'new form', if of a somewhat primitivistic kind. Even a war novel such as Sir William Butler's *The Invasion of England* ends on a positive and faintly utopian note: after the long years of misery and defeat, when London has almost fallen into decay, there appears 'a smaller and a cleaner city growing, as it were, amid the ruins of the old metropolis', while elsewhere the country shows healthy signs of reverting to a peasant economy. Butler, Jefferies and Morris appear agreed in their rejection of industrialism.

5

So far I have attempted to indicate, in outline, some of the intellectual components of the *fin de siècle;* they can be found equally in the writings of Nietzsche or Nordau, and in the minor imaginative works of the period, many of which have little or no literary merit. As will be seen, they dominate Wells's novels and stories of the nineties. The preoccupation with the future first appears in *The Chronic Argonauts,* a fragment of a novel Wells wrote at the age of twenty-one, and is sustained in *The Time Machine* and, less interestingly, in *When the Sleeper Wakes.* The transvaluation of values is evident in *The Island of Dr Moreau* and *The Invisible Man,* while the *fin du globe* motif is predominant in *The War of the Worlds* and several short stories. Yet, since I am concerned with Wells as an imaginative writer rather than as a purveyor of ideas, this sketch of the intellectual background of his early work must be supplemented by some account of the literary context in which it takes its place. The eighties and nineties in England were marked by an unusual variety of prose fiction. Dickens had been able more or less successfully to combine in his novels the two distinct elements of realism and romance (or fantasy). But in the final decades of the century there was an increasing tendency for the two types of fiction to assume distinct literary forms. So, on the one hand we have writers of strictly realistic fiction, such as George Moore, George Gissing and Arthur Morrison (and Wells himself, in *Love and Mr Lewisham*), and on the other many authors of fictional romances; in addition to Wilde and Stevenson, there were such secondary but immensely popular figures as Anthony Hope, Stanley Weyman and Conan Doyle. Among specific kinds of romance the ghost story was very popular, and perhaps the greatest example of the *genre* is Henry James's *Turn of the Screw*. Nordau remarked sourly on the popularity of ghost stories, and added, 'but they must come on in scientific disguise as hypnotism, telepathy, somnambulism'.[11] The classical example of the semi-supernatural, semi-scientific romance is certainly Stevenson's *Strange Case of Dr Jekyll and Mr Hyde*, which was published in 1886 and exerted a considerable influence throughout the following decade, on Wells and various of his contemporaries. In the mid-nineties, at about the time Wells's first books were published, there appeared several collections of stories which made excursions into the weird and the marvellous, sometimes employing would-be scientific elements, sometimes relying on the more traditional elements of magic and the supernatural; the influence of Stevenson, and sometimes of Poe, is often evident. As examples, one may mention Arthur Machen's *The Great God Pan* (1894) and *The Three Imposters* (1895), M. P. Shiel's *Shapes in the Fire* (1896) and Vincent O'Sullivan's *A Book of Bargains* (1896). That they are now largely forgotten, whereas Wells's work in a similar vein is still read and kept in print, can, I think, be taken as a sign of his considerable literary superiority.

11. Nordau, op. cit., p. 14.

6

Nevertheless, Wells has not, on the whole, been taken very seriously as a literary artist; partly, perhaps, because he was at such pains in later years to deny that he was one. As one of his earliest critics, J. D. Beresford, remarked: 'The later works have been so defensive and, in one sense, didactic that one is apt to forget that many of the earlier books, and all the short stories, must have originated in the effervescence of creative imagination.'[12]

I want to suggest that Wells's romances are something more than the simple entertaining yarns they are generally taken to be—though without, of course, wishing to deny that they *are* admirably entertaining. I refer to them as 'romances' rather than 'scientific romances', since, apart from anything else, the adjective is not always appropriate. There are no 'scientific' elements, for instance, in a novel such as *The Wonderful Visit* or in stories like 'The Country of the Blind' and 'The Door in the Wall'. Wells's early novels and tales are romances in the traditional sense, insofar as they contain an element of the marvellous, which may have a scientific—or pseudo-scientific—explanation, but which may equally originate in a supernatural happening, or in some disturbance of the individual consciousness. To stress the scientific component to the exclusion of the other qualities may give a distorted picture. It is true that Wells had had a scientific education, and frequently employed scientific language as a kind of rhetoric to ensure the plausibility of his situations; but these situations themselves may have only a tenuous, or even non-existent, connection with the actual possibilities of science. Thus, in *The Invisible Man,* Wells uses the folklore motif of invisibility, and apparently gives it a rational justification in terms of modern optics; nevertheless, in a letter to Arnold Bennett of October 1897 he admitted the fundamental impossibility of the notion.[13] At this point one may consider the differences between Wells and Jules Verne, who is so often considered to be his

13. *Arnold Bennett and H. G. Wells* (ed. Harris Wilson), 1960, p. 34.
12. *H. G. Wells,* 1915, p. 18.

predecessor in the manufacture of scientific romances. There can be no doubt that Wells's romances are a good deal better written than those of the excessively prolific Verne, but there is a much more fundamental difference, which Wells himself has indicated. In the preface to a collected edition of his romances, published in 1933, he wrote:

These tales have been compared with the work of Jules Verne and there was a disposition on the part of literary journalists at one time to call me the English Jules Verne. As a matter of fact there is no literary resemblance whatever between the anticipatory inventions of the great Frenchman and these fantasies. His work dealt almost always with actual possibilities of invention and discovery, and he made some re- markable forecasts. The interest he invoked was a practical one; he wrote and believed and told that this or that thing could be done, which was not at that time done. He helped his reader to imagine it done and to realize what fun, excitement or mischief would ensue. Most of his inventions have 'come true'. But these stories of mine col- lected here do not pretend to deal with possible things; they are exer- cises of the imagination in a quite different field. They belong to a class of writing which includes the *Golden Ass of Apuleius,* the *True Histories of Lucian, Peter Schlemil,* and the story of *Frankenstein.*

As Wells insists, many of Verne's inventions have materialized since his time. Submarine travel is a commonplace, and the circum- navigation of the moon is more than a possibility. Wells's imag- inings, however, remain as unattainable now as when he wrote: no one has yet contrived to travel through time, or spend several days in the Fourth Dimension of space; we are still unable to make our- selves invisible, nor can we transform animals into men by surgical means. Whereas for Verne there is a scientific element in the very conception of his story, for Wells it is merely present rhetorically. This opinion, as will be seen in Chapter VI, was shared by Verne himself, who, in old age, read certain of Wells's romances and com- plained of their lack of scientific foundation.

It is, I think, more helpful to compare Wells not with Verne but with such masters of the romance and the imaginative fable as Hawthorne—whose influence on his earliest work he acknowledged

—or Kafka. Romance is more likely to be symbolic—even if not specifically allegorical—than realistic fiction, and this is true of Wells. Some of his critics have already hinted at the symbolic quality of his romances. V. S. Pritchett, for instance, has remarked of *The Time Machine*, 'Like all excellent works it has meanings within its meaning . . .'[14] while as long ago as 1923 Edward Shanks observed of Wells's romances, 'They are, in their degree, myths; and Mr. Wells is a myth-maker.'[15] Shanks's use of the word 'myth' is particularly suggestive; it has, of course, become a fashionable term in recent criticism, but it has a peculiar applicability to Wells's romances. The word is easier to use than to define accurately, but one can, I suggest, distinguish between major and minor myths as they occur in works of literature. The former are centred on such archetypal figures as Prometheus, Don Quixote, Faust, and Don Juan, whose significance is universal and not confined to a specific phase of cultural development (though in a sense they can be both: Faust *is* Renaissance man, but he also stands for the general human tendency towards 'overreaching', which can occur in individuals in any kind of society and at any period). The major myths, one might say, give a generalized cultural form to certain abiding elements in the pattern of human experience. The minor myths, on the other hand, possess a wide relevance but nevertheless have a particular historical point of departure. A celebrated example is *Robinson Crusoe*, which, as Ian Watt has shown, is a myth embodying certain essential themes of modern civilization; they can be briefly described as 'Back to Nature', 'The Dignity of Labour', and 'Economic Man'.[16]

Wells's early romances are minor myths of this kind. As I have suggested, they reflect some of the dominant preoccupations of the *fin de siècle* period; and it is important to remember that this significance is more than simply historical. If the *fin de siècle* expressed the final convulsions of the nineteenth century, it also

14. *The Living Novel*, 1946, p. 120.
15. *First Essays on Literature*, 1923, p. 158.
16. In *The Rise of the Novel*, 1957, pp. 60–92.

marked the birth pangs of the twentieth, and many of the issues that concern mid-twentieth century man first appeared during that period. For that reason its literary myths still have a contemporary relevance. In *A Rebours*, for instance, we find an anticipation of the extreme eclecticism of our culture, and the rootlessness and mental and emotional fragmentation of the modern intellectual. *Dr Jekyll and Mr Hyde* vividly dramatizes the discovery of the unconscious mind, with all its revolutionary implications; we may, if we wish, go on to interpret it in Freudian terms as symbolizing the conflict between Super-ego and Id, or in a Jungian sense as illustrating the encounter between Consciousness and the Shadow.

In addition to their objective *fin de siècle* elements, Wells's romances also contain themes personal to himself, and one could, no doubt, subject them to a fairly detailed search for psychological symbolism: I have resisted the temptation to do so, except in the case of one or two short stories, where such symbolism seems unusually obtrusive. Certainly, the longer romances abound in suggestions of archetypal imagery; this is most apparent, perhaps, in *The Time Machine*, with its division between paradisal and demonic imagery, seeming to symbolize the conflict between a precarious consciousness and the increasingly menacing pressures of the unconscious. Similarly, *The Island of Dr Moreau* has various complex implications, but one can see Moreau as a manifestation of the Super-ego, eventually succumbing to the dark forces he is trying to control. Griffin, in *The Invisible Man*, has affinities with Stevenson's Dr Jekyll, and, like him, suggests the Jungian Shadow or Dark Self. *The War of the Worlds* can be read as an expression of the traditional eschatological preoccupation with the end of the world, which has been the source of so much religious imagery; equally, it expresses the myth of things or creatures falling from the skies, most recently manifested in the form of 'flying saucers'.[17]

However, my interpretation will, in general, be inclined towards

17. See, for instance, Jolande Jacobi, *The Psychology of C. G. Jung,* 1951, p. 127; C. G. Jung, *Flying Saucers,* 1959.

history rather than psychology. Apart from certain short stories, this study will not go beyond 1901. In that year Wells published *The First Men in the Moon*, which I consider his last genuine novel-length romance, and *Anticipations*, his first major non-fictional work, where we see him ceasing to be an artist and beginning his long career as publicist and pamphleteer. It is true that the following year there appeared *The Sea Lady*, which can be considered a romance; but though it is a *jeu d'esprit* of some charm it is, I think, essentially an expression of certain recurring themes in Wells's realistic fiction, which had first appeared in *Love and Mr Lewisham*, and were to be more fully explored in *The New Machiavelli* and later novels. While the early romances originated in what J. D. Beresford called 'the effervescence of creative imagination', Wells's later attempts at the form all had a didactic aim, and suffered an according loss of imaginative power. They are no longer myths, merely illustrations of an argument. This is true of *The Food of the Gods* (1904); although the first part of the book contains a good deal of Wells's customary imaginative exuberance, his homiletic purpose becomes fatally obtrusive in the later chapters (Wells remarked in his autobiography that the novel was based on a Fabian paper called *The Questions of Scientific Administrative Areas*).[18] And this applies still more to such later works as *In the Days of the Comet* (1906), *The World Set Free* (1914), *Men Like Gods* (1923) and *The Dream* (1924).

The War in the Air (1908) is a rather different case. It is less immediately didactic than these works, and correspondingly more entertaining. Its hero, the ebullient Bert Smallways, has a recognizable affinity with the heroes of Wells's realistic fiction, such as Kipps or Mr Polly. Insofar as it is a romance, it is of a more strictly 'scientific' kind, in the Verne sense, than any of Wells's works of the nineties. It is partly a vivid prophecy of the military possibilities of aeronautics, and partly an apocalyptic reflection on the growing likelihood of a major war, inspired by the increasing power of Im-

18. *Experiment in Autobiography*, 1934, II, 654.

perial Germany. In some ways it is a return to Wells's *fin du globe* note of the nineties, and is a by no means negligible work, but it lacks the depth and complexity of the earlier romances.

Wells, at the beginning of his career, was a genuine and original imaginative artist, who wrote several books of considerable literary importance, before dissipating his talents in directions which now seem more or less irrelevant. In considering these works, it will be necessary to modify the customary view of Wells as an optimist, a utopian and a passionate believer in human progress. The dominant note of his early years was rather a kind of fatalistic pessimism, combined with intellectual scepticism, and it is this which the early romances reflect. It is, one need hardly add, a typically *fin de siècle* note.

VAN WYCK BROOKS

The Wellsian Mind

[Brooks was one of the earliest academic critics to appreciate and cele-
brate Wells's talent. His appraisal of the "Wells spirit," though written
in 1915, some time after the triumph of Wells's first novels and some
time before his final statements on the human condition, is nevertheless still one of the most perceptive and valuable essays on the man's
significance in the history of English literature.]

In order to understand Wells at all one must grasp the fact that he
belongs to a type of mind which has long existed in European literature but which is comparatively new in the English-speaking
world, the type of mind of the so-called "intellectual." He is an "intellectual" rather than an artist; that is to say, he naturally grasps
and interprets life in the light of ideas rather than in the light of
experience.

To pass from a definition to an example, let me compare Wells
in this respect with the greatest and most typical figure of the opposite camp in contemporary English fiction; I mean Joseph Conrad.
This comparison is all the more apt because just as much as Wells
Conrad typifies the spirit of "unrest" (a word he has almost made
his own, so often does he use it) which is the note of our age. Both
of these novelists have endeavored to express the spirit of unrest;

From Van Wyck Brooks, The World of H. G. Wells (Kennerley, 1915).

both have suggested a way of making it contributory to the attainment of an ideal. But how different is their method, how different is their ideal! And roughly the difference is this: that to Conrad the spirit of unrest is a personal mood, a thing, as people used to say, between man and his Maker; whereas to Wells the spirit of unrest is not a mood but a rationally explicable frame of mind, a sense of restricted function, an issue to be fought out not between man and nature but between man and society. In other words, where Conrad's point of view is moral, Wells's point of view is social; and whereas in Conrad the spirit of unrest can only be appeased by holding fast to certain simple instinctive moral principles, integrity, honor, loyalty, etc., contributing in this way to the ideal of personal character, the spirit of unrest in Wells is to be appeased by working through the established fact, by altering the environment in which man lives, contributing in this way to the ideal of a great society of which personal character is at once the essence and the product.

In the end, of course, both these views of life come to the same thing, for you cannot have a great society which is not composed of greatly living individuals, or vice versa. But practically there is a world of difference between them, according as any given mind emphasizes the one or the other. This difference, I say, is the difference between life approached through experience and life approached through ideas. And when we penetrate behind these points of view we find that they are determined very largely by the characters and modes of living of the men who hold them. That explains the vital importance in literary criticism of knowing something about the man one is discussing, as distinguished from the work of his brain pure and simple. There is a reason why the intellectualist point of view occurs as a rule in men who have habitually lived the delocalized, detached, and comparatively depersonalized life of cities, while men of the soil, of the sea, of the elements, men, so to speak, of intensive experience, novelists like Conrad or Tolstoy or Hardy, are fundamentally non-intellectual, pessimistic, and moral.

And this explains the natural opposition between Conrad and Wells. Aside from the original bent of his mind, the intensive quality of Conrad's experience—an experience of ships and the minute, simple, personal, tragic life of ships, set off against the impersonal, appalling sea and an always indifferent universe, a life remote from change, in which the relations of things are in a peculiar sense abiding and in which only one problem exists, the problem of character, imminent nature being kept at bay only through the loyalty, integrity and grit of men—the intensive quality of this experience, I say, acting upon an artistic mind, would naturally tend to produce not only a bitterly profound wisdom, but an equally profound contempt for the play of ideas, so irresponsible in comparison, and for a view of the world based upon ideas the real cost of which has never been counted in the face of hunger, icy winds, storm and shipwreck, and the abysmal forces of nature. Men who go down to the sea in ships have a right to say for themselves (tempering the credulity of those who have remained at home) that the intellectualist view of life is altogether too easy and too glib. It is they who throw into relief the deep, obscure conviction of the "plain man"—commonly the good man—that to endeavor to make life conform with ideas is in some way to deprive the world of just those elements which create character and to strike at an ideal forged through immemorial suffering and effort.

Merely to dismiss as dumb folly an all but universal contention of this kind (no doubt in the back of people's minds when they say that socialism, for instance, is "against human nature") is to beg the whole question of intellectualism itself. For, if it could be conclusively shown that any view of life not incidentally but by its nature emasculated life and destroyed the roots of character, then of course, no matter how rationally self-evident it might be and how much confusion and suffering it might avert, it would never even justify its own reason for being—it would never *succeed,* the best part of human nature would oppose it to the end of time and the intelligence itself would be discredited. And indeed to the man of experience rather than the man of ideas, just because of his rich humanity, just because he never passes out of the personal range, belong the ideal things, morality, philosophy, art. Like charity, these things "begin at home"; and whenever (as in pragmatism, when pragmatism ceases to be a method and claims to be an interpretation of life) they are approached not from the side of experience but from the side of ideas they cease to have any real substance. Morality has no substance when it springs from the mind instead of the conscience, art when it appeals to the mind instead of the perceptions; and as to philosophy, what is any scheme of things that springs out of the head of a man who is not himself wise? It is a certain condemnation of Bergson, for example, that he would never pass muster in a group of old fishermen smoking their pipes on the end of a pier. Not that they would be expected in any case to know what he was talking about, but that his fibre so plainly is the fibre not of a wise but of a clever man and that in everything, as Emerson said, you must have a source higher than your tap.

That is why, as it seems to me, Wells ought not to be considered from any of these absolute standpoints. He has put before us not so much a well-wrought body of artistic work, or a moral programme, or an explanation of life—words quite out of place in connection with him—as a certain new spirit, filled with all sorts of puzzled intimations of a new beauty and even a new religion to be generated out of a new order of things that is only glimpsed at present. And the point I should like to make about this spirit is that it is entirely irrelevant to the values of life as we know them, but that it may in the end prove to have contributed to an altogether fresh basis for human values. . . .

Intellectualism, in fact, the view that life can be determined by ideas (and of this socialism is the essence) if it can be justified at all has to be justified in the face of all current human values. It is based on an assumption, a grand and generous assumption, I maintain, and one that has to take what is called a sporting chance with all the odds against it. This assumption is, that on the whole human nature can be trusted to take care of itself while the surplus energy of life, commonly absorbed in the struggle against incapacity, sloth, perversity, and disorder ("original sin," to sum it all up), is released for the organization of a better scheme for mankind; and further, that this better scheme, acting on a race naturally capable of a richer and fuller life, will have the effect on men as a whole that re-environing has on any cramped, ill-nourished, unventilated organism, and that art, religion, morals (all that makes up the substance and meaning of life) instead of being checked and blighted in the process will in the end, strong enough to bear transplantation, be re-engendered on a finer and freer basis. This, in a word, is the contention of the intellectual, a splendid gambler's chance, on which the future rests, and to which people have committed themselves more than they know. It is a bridge thrown out across the void, resting at one end on the good intentions of mankind and relying at the other upon mankind's fulfilling those good intentions. It is based like every great enterprise of the modern world upon credit, and its only security is the fact that men thus far and on the whole have measured up to each enlargement of their freedom and responsibility.

To feel the force of this one has to think of the world as a world. Just here has been the office of socialism, to show that society is a colossal machine of which we are all parts and that men in the most exact sense are members one of another. In the intellectualist scheme of things that mathematical proof has to come first, it has to take root and bury itself and become the second nature of humankind before the new world of instinct can spring out of it and come to blossom.

That has been the office of socialism, and just so far as that proof has been established socialism has played its part. Now the point I want to make about Wells is that in him one sees already in an almost precocious form the second stage of this process. In him this new world of intelligence is already exuberant with instinct; the social machine has become a personality; that cold abstraction the world has become in his hands a throbbing, breathing, living thing, as alive, awake, aware of itself, as engaging, adventurous, free, critical, well-primed, continent, and all-of-a-piece as a strong man running a race. People never felt nature as a personality before Wordsworth showed them that it was, or a locomotive before Kipling wrote *McAndrew's Hymn;* and it seems to me that Wells has done for the social organisms very much that Wordsworth did for nature, discovering in a thing previously felt to be inanimate a matter for art and a basis for religious emotion.

But if the world is a personality it is a very stupid, sluggish, unawakened personality, differing from nature in this respect, that we ourselves compose the whole of it and have it in our hands to do what we will with it. It has always been out of joint, a great slipshod Leviathan, at sixes and sevens, invertebrate and fungusbrained. Just so is the average man, sunk in routine, oppressed with microscopic tasks that give birth one to another, his stomach at war with his head, his legs unwilling to exercise him, resentful of his own capacity not to be dull. But certain happier moments bring him an exuberant quickened life in which routine tasks fall nimbly from his fingers and he is aware of a wide, humorous, generous, enlightened vision of things; he pulls himself together, his parts reinforce one another, his mind wakens, his heart opens, his fancy stirs, he is all generosity and happiness, capable of anything that is disinterested, fine, and becoming to a free man. It is in these moments that individual men have done all the things which make up the real history of this planet.

If individual men are capable of this amazing experience, then why not the world? That is the spirited question Wells has propounded in a hundred different forms, in his earlier, more theoretical, and more optimistic writings suggesting that society as a whole should turn over a new leaf, and even picturing it as doing so, in his later work, more experienced and less hopeful but with a compensating fervor, picturing the attempt of delegated individuals to act on society's behalf. I do not wish at this point to become pious and solemn in tone; that would be inept in connection with Wells. But I do wish to make it plain that if he is devoid of those grander traits which spring from the sense of being "ten-on'd and mortised upon something beyond change, if his strength lies wholly in his intelligence, the intelligence itself in Wells is an amazing organ, a troubled and rapturous organ, an organ as visionary and sensitive as the soul of a Christian saint. That is why I have said that in him the new world, governed by the intelligence, is already exuberant with instinct; and anyone who doubts that he has lavished a very genuine religious instinct upon the social process itself and in the dream of a society free, magnanimous and seemly, should turn to the passage where he describes Machiavelli, after the heat and pettiness of the day, retiring into his chamber alone, putting on his dress of ceremony and sitting down before his table in the presence of that magnificent thought.[1]

The mass of men have acted more consistently than they know on the principle that the whole world is nothing in comparison with one soul, for their politics and economic science, solemn as they appear, are as frivolous and secondary as if they actually did believe fervently that heaven is their true home and the world a bad business of little account. In all that concerns private virtue and the private life, in religion, poetry, their lawyer, their doctor, their broker, they exact the last degree of excellence and efficiency, but they trust to the blind enterprise of individual men to push mankind chaotically forward little by little. We are in fact so wonderfully made that if our grocer tells us in the morning that he has no fresh eggs he throws us into a deeper despondency than six readings of the *Inferno* could ever do. And that explains why so few people can extend themselves imaginatively into the greater circles that surround them, why, on the social plane, we never think of demanding wisdom from politicians, why we never dream of remembering that they should belong to the august family of Plutarch, why it is not the profound views of wise men and the brilliant discoveries of science that fill the newspapers, but the incredibly banal remarks of this president and that prime minister, why presidents and prime ministers in a society that lives from hand to mouth are so much more important than poets and prophets, and

1. In *The New Machiavelli,* 1911.

why statesmanship has gathered about itself a literature so incomparably trivial and dull. Socialists, indeed, just because they alone are serious about the world, are apt to be the least mundane in spirit; they are, as Wells has himself said, "other-worldly" about the world itself.

JACK WILLIAMSON

Wells and the Limits of Progress

1. Defining the Limits

"It is surely significant," writes Norman Nicholson,

> that the man who preached progress more eloquently than anyone else should be the one who had the most vivid vision of cosmic accident, and who realized . . . that the destiny of the whole earth . . . hangs by a thread.[1]

The significance is that Wells preached progress not out of confident hope, but out of cold desperation. Uniquely gifted both with the analytic brain that might have served a great scientist and with the creative imagination of a great artist, he saw the probable shape of the future more vividly, by the testimony of his work, than any other man of his time. Distressed by his own visions of the world to come, he strove for many years to change it, with dramatic warnings, impatient exhortations, and attempts at mass education. As Nicholson says,

> Wells was aware from the first that the development of scientific knowledge was not in itself any guarantee of progress, and many of his

1. *H. G. Wells* (London, 1957), pp. 37-38.

From Jack Williamson, H. G. Wells: Critic of Progress **(Baltimore: Mirage Press, 1973), pp. 47-62. Reprinted by permission of the author.**

romances were based on the idea that science, divorced from humanity, . . . may bring disaster to mankind.[2]

But we exist in double jeopardy, from within ourselves and from without. Though the deadliest danger may be our own heritage, we also inhabit a hostile cosmos. Lecturing in 1902, Wells reviewed a whole series of possible external perils. He speculated that some great unsuspected mass of matter might swirl out of space and destroy all life upon earth. He suggested that some unknown disease might end the human race, "some trailing cometary poison, some great emanation of vapor from the interior of the earth." He warned that "there may arise new animals to prey upon us by land and sea, and there may come some drug or wrecking madness into the minds of men." He considered the "reasonable certainty" that the solar system will continue to run down "until some day this earth of ours, tideless and slow moving, will be dead and frozen and all that has lived upon it will be frozen out and done with."[3]

In *The Discovery of the Future,* he writes that

I do not believe in these things, because I have come to believe in certain other things, in the coherence and purpose in the world and in the greatness of human destiny.[4]

Earlier, however, during the last years of the century, the years of doubt and discovery which produced the best of the scientific romances and most of the short stories, he was still very much aware of the cosmic indifference to our survival. His studies of science, especially of biology, had given him a view of the probable future that he could neither accept nor ignore. Such thinkers as Malthus had led him to look at humanity in the emotionless light of biology. "Probably no more shattering book than the *Essay on Population* has ever been written, or ever will be written," he comments in *Anticipations.*[5]

2. *Ibid.,* p. 37.
3. *The Discovery of the Future: A Discourse Delivered to the Royal Institution on January 24, 1902* (London, 1902), pp. 86-87.
4. Pp. 312-313.
5. *Anticipations of the Reaction of Mechanical and Scientific Progress upon Human Life and Thought* (New York, 1902).

It was aimed at the facile liberalism of the deists and the atheists of the eighteenth century; it made clear as daylight that all forms of social reconstruction, all dreams of earthly golden ages, must be either futile or insincere or both, until the problems of human increase were manfully faced. . . . It aimed simply to wither the rationalistic utopias of the time, and, by anticipation, all the communisms, socialisms, and earthly paradise movements that have since been so abundantly audible in the world.

The writer of those words was hardly a preacher of inevitable and automatic progress! The earlier Wells, as his fiction shows, seems rather to have been fascinated with his imaginative exploration of the darkest aspects of the cosmos. At the very beginning of his writing career, as Anthony West observes, he had broken with Herbert Spencer's sort of progressive optimism. In "The Rediscovery of the Unique,"[6] he rejects the whole idea of evolutionary progress, "which depends on a picture of the universe in which mind is increasingly valuable."[7] He accepts in its stead the mechanistic view that the world is "nothing but a mere heap of dust, fortuitously agitated." West comments that

it is impossible to be an optimist believing in inevitable progress if you also believe in a universe in which mind figures only as a local accident. There is also considerable difficulty in reconciling the idea of progress with a universe which by its essential nature cannot support a permanent world order. That Wells should have dealt with the ideological basis of pessimism in his first serious piece of writing throws some light on the real cast of his mind.

The prominence of the idea of progress in the early fiction does not mean that Wells was writing tracts for it or against it. The tracts came later. His major aim, during those beginning years, was more probably to find himself as a creative writer, to discover and perfect his own means of expression. He writes in *Experiment in Autobiography* that in the years 1893-1894, under the influence of his friend Walter Low, "I was beginning to write again in any

6. Reprinted elsewhere in this edition.—Ed.
7. Anthony West, "The Dark World of H. G. Wells," *Harper's Magazine,* CCXIV (May, 1957), 68.

scraps of time I could snatch from direct money-earning. I was resuming my criticism of life."[8] The life that he criticized most searchingly, it would seem, was his own. The autobiography, as well as the fiction, reveals the clash of discordant attitudes and emotions in his mind. He was his mother's son, no less than his father's. He had learned contempt for a useless aristocracy, but he had also been taught to fear the raw proletariat. He had trained his mind to the disciplines of science, but he had forgotten neither the traditional culture nor the desperate emotions of his youth. He hoped for a better world, but his idealism clashed with a bitter knowledge of real human life.

The idea of progress in his early work may best be regarded as a metaphor, perhaps, around which he was striving to organize all these discrepant attitudes and emotions. The early science fiction may be examined as a laboratory in which Wells was seeking to find and test his own attitudes. A study of the fiction from this viewpoint will clarify the processes by which the tension between unreconciled attitudes gives life and form; it will often reveal the sources of the validity and intensity and depth evident in the early fiction but lacking from much of what Wells wrote after this tension had begun to subside.

As biologist, Wells sees us as only one more species swept along by the flow of evolution, commonly blind to our nature and our future. As human being, he longs to help us discover and guide our destiny, but he finds small room for hope that intelligence can free us from the cosmic laws and control all life. His early fiction often dramatizes this conflict of hope and fear for the future of man. His troubled emotions clothe themselves in troubled characters; even the details of setting are frequently revealing.

Weather phenomena symbolize the hostile or indifferent nature of the cosmos. A hailstorm greets the Time Traveller with a symbolic chill when he arrives in the future world where even the elements seem generally to have been tamed (Ch. 3), and an icy wind and showering snowflakes in the more remote future warn him of

8. New York, 1934, p. 293.

the nearing death of the planet (Ch. 11). The Martians, in *The War of the Worlds*, have been spurred to their high progress by "the secular cooling" of Mars (Bk. I, Ch. 1), and the narrator himself, at the peak of his suffering under the Martians, is beaten with "a thin hail." In *When the Sleeper Wakes,* the snow on the city roofs is in symbolic contrast with the sheltered warmth within, showing the human victory over the cosmos to be narrow or illusory (Ch. 8). In *First Men in the Moon,* the freezing atmosphere represents the stern cosmic forces which have driven the Selenites to their ultimate degree of evolutionary adaptation, and which now menace Bedford himself (Ch. 18).

The early science fiction is first of all good fiction, the characters engaging and the invention bright and the narrative absorbing. Beneath the surface story, however, the main thematic emphasis is on the hazards to continued human progress: on the cosmic limits that promise to cut it short, on the human flaws that threaten to spoil it. Even when Wells admits the occasional short-term success of adaptive change, his evaluation of its fruits is seldom enthusiastic. In this chapter and those following, we shall consider in some detail first his imaginative exploration of the cosmic limits, next his study of the human limits, and finally his usually pessimistic evaluations of progress achieved.

Any separation of the novels and stories into such categories is, of course, arbitrary. The scheme is imposed upon the fiction, not discovered in it. At this point in his career, Wells was not writing a thesis on progress; he was striving instead to give objective form and aesthetic distance to some of the gravest conflicts within his own personality. The idea of progress is simply one important metaphor. He does not set out to discuss first the external and then the internal limits upon progress and then to examine the consequences of progress beyond these limits. Often, in a single story, he does all these things. *The Time Machine,* for example, concludes with a dramatic emphasis upon the cosmic limits, when the vividly realized collapse of the solar system precludes further progress. But there is an earlier emphasis upon the human limits, when the human race is shown differentiating into the dainty cattle of the upper world and the gray troglodytes that eat them. There is also a sardonic evaluation of the consequences of progress, in the revelation that normal evolutionary adaptation has produced these two new breeds of not-quite men. Here, however, *The Time Machine* will be classified as dealing with the external or cosmic limits. *The War of the Worlds,* in which human survival is threatened by invasion from Mars, seems logically to belong in the same group. So do a number of the short stories which deal with astronomical or biological hazards to the indefinite advancement of mankind.

2. The Time Machine

If the early fiction of Wells owes its form and life to the tension between incompatible attitudes, the nature of that inner conflict is easiest to see, perhaps, in *The Time Machine,*[9] his first major work and perhaps his most brilliant. Though much of his later writing was done hastily and inadequately revised, he labored painstakingly through at least seven versions of *The Time Machine,* of which five survive.[10] The earliest is the unfinished serial, "The Chronic Argonauts," published in the *Science Schools Journal*— of which Wells himself had been a founder and the first editor—for April, May, and June, 1888. By 1892, Wells had made two revisions of the story. Though these have been lost, Wells read parts of them to a college friend. A. Morley Davies, whose description is quoted by Geoffrey West.[11] The fourth version consists of seven unsigned articles published in the *National Observer* between

9. First edition, 1895; included in *Seven Famous Novels by H. G. Wells* (Garden City, New York, 1934).

10. Bernard Bergonzi discusses and compares the texts of the known versions of *The Time Machine* in "The Publication of *The Time Machine* 1894-95," *The Review of English Studies,* New Series, XI (1960), 42-51; he reprints the first version in *The Early H. G. Wells: A Study of the Scientific Romances* (Manchester, 1961), pp. 187-214; the history of *The Time Machine* in Sam Moskowitz's *Explorers of the Infinite* (Cleveland, 1963), is inaccurate.

11. *H. G. Wells* (New York, 1930), pp. 262-264.

March and June, 1894, while W. E. Henley was editor; this series has no sustained narrative, and it was broken off when Henley left the *Observer.* When he became editor of the *New Review,* he accepted a narrative version and ran it in five parts, January through May, 1895. Two different book versions were published the same year, by Heinemann in London and Holt in New York. All these careful revisions show that Wells, in the beginning, was a literary artist almost as conscientious as Henry James.

Comparing the first attempt with the finished novel, we can clearly see Wells' conflicting attitudes giving form and dramatic life to his materials. "The Chronic Argonauts" is melodramatic, wordy, derivative, and conventional. Wells himself wrote of it in the autobiography:

The prose was over-elaborate. . . . And the story is clumsily invented, and loaded with irrelevant sham significance. The time traveller, for example, is called Nebo-gipfel, though manifestly Mount Nebo had no business whatever in the story. There was no Promised Land ahead.[12]

A striking difference between the first version and the finished novel is in the treatment of the idea of progress. "The Chronic Argonauts" merely hints at the idea. A few symbols of progress do appear, in the name Nebogipfel, in the invention and explanation of the time machine, in the statement that it has been used to secure "valuable medical, social, and physiographical data for all time."[13] We never learn, however, exactly what those data are. The symbols of progress are completely submerged beneath contrasting metaphors of decay, terror, and death. A figure of fear, not of hope, Nebogipfel is the scientist as destroyer. The most vividly presented part of the setting is a decaying Manse where foul murder has been done. The action, so far as it goes in the three installments Wells wrote, is conventional gothic melodrama with overtones of "unearthly noises and inexplicable phenomena."[14] Instead of the peo-

12. *Experiment,* pp. 253-254.
13. Bergonzi, *The Early H. G. Wells,* p. 203.
14. *Ibid.,* p. 196.

ple of the future, Wells introduces a mob of degenerate Welsh villagers.

"A cleansing course of Swift and Sterne intervened before the idea was written again for Henley's *National Observer*," as Wells confesses in his preface to the Atlantic Edition.[15] The final version takes its shape from Wells' intention to explore the possible future history of mankind. The satanic scientist and the haunted Manse and the angry villagers are gone. The new Time Traveller is an amiable and rather ordinary man, who explains his extraordinary machine to a group of completely ordinary skeptics in a setting of commonplace detail carefully selected to contrast with the wonder of travel in time. The time machine itself is made real by means of a convincing laboratory demonstration which is followed by ingeniously created and vividly given sense impressions of the actual flight through time, with night following day "like the flapping of a black wing," and the trees on the hillside "growing and changing like puffs of vapor, now brown, now green" (Ch. 3). Since Wells was an ardent cyclist at the time he wrote, he borrowed sensations and experiences from his familiar sport. The time machine itself is apparently very much like a bicycle; it turns over and stuns the Time Traveller when he stops too suddenly in the year 802,701 A.D.

The chief plot interest of the middle section of the novel comes from the effort of the Time Traveller to learn the real nature of his future world, to trace out the results of eight hundred thousand years of change. Enormous but crumbling buildings around him are evidence both of long progress and of subsequent decay. Tiny, childlike men and women flock around him: they are the Eloi, idle vegetarians whose lives of aimless play are passed in weedless parks and great communal halls. The time machine is stolen; in attempting to recover it he discovers an underground world of vast mysterious machines and finds that the Eloi are fed and cared for by a race of hideous albino creatures like small apes. At length he understands that the parasitic Eloi are descendents of the Victorian upper classes, and that the little underground apes, the Morlocks,

15. *Atlantic Edition of the Works of H. G. Wells* (New York, 1924), I, xxi.

are the children of the proletariat. Now the masters, the Morlocks breed the Eloi for food.

Escaping on the recovered time machine into the infinite future, he finds mankind extinct and the solar system itself near death, the earth spiraling inward toward the dying sun. Yet life persists: bright green moss grows on the sunward faces of the rocks, and enormous crab-like things crawl along the shore of an oily, tideless sea. The Time Traveller is appalled by

the red eastern sky, the northward blackness, the salt Dead Sea, the stony beach crawling with these foul, slow-stirring monsters, the uniform poisonous-looking green of the lichenous plants, the thin air that hurts one's lungs (Ch. 11).

Attacked by the gigantic crabs, he ventures even further into the future, testing an ultimate frontier of possible progress. An icy night falls, as the red sun is eclipsed. Ill and shivering, he sees a moving creature.

It was a round thing . . . black against the weltering blood-red water, and it was hopping fitfully about. . . . A terrible dread of lying helpless in that remote and awful twilight sustained me while I clambered upon the saddle (Ch. 11).

So, from this vision of a time when the last chance of progress on earth has ended in "abominable desolation," the Time Traveller returns to the nineteenth century.

Some few flaws from the earlier drafts are left in this final version of the novel, but Wells has generally been able to redeem them with his emerging narrative genius. The story of Weena, the little Eloi girl who falls in love with the Time Traveller after he has saved her from drowning, is an unconvincing vestige of Victorian sentimental romance. The entire plot is manipulated to add dramatic interest to the imaginative tour of the future which is Wells' main concern. Sometimes this manipulation has awkward results, especially in the double climax of the escape from the Morlocks and the vision of the end of the world, and in the improbable readiness of the exhausted Time Traveller to talk for most of the night after his return. The ending, in which he does not come back from a second expedition, is a purely arbitrary device, implying little of either theme or character. But for the reader under the spell of Wells' paradoxical ideas, prophetic speculations, and persuasive narrative magic, such faults scarcely matter.

In this first and most sweeping survey of our imagined future, Wells evaluates the idea of progress from many angles. The human limits upon progress appear most strikingly in the conservative guests who greet the Time Traveller's discoveries with varied attitudes of stupidity, bewilderment, and doubt. "It sounds plausible enough tonight," says the Medical Man. "But wait until tomorrow. Wait for the common sense of the morning" (Ch. 1). The future world is filled with evidence of long progressive ages: the magnificent buildings and surviving works of art, the elimination of weeds and insects and germs of disease, the apparently complete subjugation of nature. Yet the Time Traveller not only finds that this age-long march of progress has been in vain; he finds that it has been in fact the cause of the later decay. This law of nature, that progress itself results in degeneration, is a cosmic limit that shapes the body of the novel. A second cosmic limit, which shapes the concluding section and provides the second climax, appears in the final collapse of the solar system, the planets falling one by one into the dying sun.

This particular catastrophe, incidentally, no longer seems so near as it did when Wells was writing. The accepted theories of his day held that the sun's energy, being chiefly gravitational, could last only a few million years. More recent theories, offering atomic sources for solar energy, have extended the probable life of the solar system a thousand times. In spite of such sweeping revisions, however, the physical limits upon human progress seem as implacable now as they did to Wells. In the new light of the exploding atom, human life looks no more secure.

The other limit, the law that progress sets its own bounds, is worth a closer look. Wells, at least in the early fiction, is no utopian setting up an ideal world as the goal of all progress. A scientist instead, he sees the world as a dynamic train of cause and effect. Progress, conceivably, may lead to some sort of perfection, but even perfection in turn must result in something else. "What," the Time Traveller asks, "is the cause of human intelligence and vigor?" He answers himself: "Hardship and freedom: conditions under which the active, strong, and subtle survive and the weaker go to the wall." He points out that

physical courage and the love of battle . . . are no great help—may even be hindrances—to a civilised man. And in a state of physical balance and security, power, intellectual as well as physical, would be out of place (Ch. 4).

The Time Traveller grieves for the suicide of the human intellect.

It had set itself steadfastly toward comfort and ease, a balanced society with security and permanency as its watchword, it had attained its hopes—to come to this at last. . . . There is no intelligence where there is no change and no need of change (Ch. 10).

Thus the Time Traveller discovers that progress limits itself. This fact he sees as natural law, an aspect of the cosmos as deadly to the dream of unlimited perfection as are the physical laws of mass and energy that decree the death of planets.

The Time Machine, in summary, is a profoundly pessimistic assessment of progress. Anthony West has stressed its gloomy theme. The machine carries the Time Traveller to a point in the future

from which it is obvious that a cosmic event is impending which will destroy the whole frame of reference in which mind, consciousness and experience have any meaning. . . . Wells is saying that the universe, like Kali, gives birth only to destroy, and that the scientific apparatus for examining reality can only bring home to man that everything he can do, think, or feel is finally futile. The end for the environment, as for the race and the individual, is extinction.[16]

The Time Traveller himself holds no brief for progress. In the epilogue, added for a later edition, the narrator says of him,

16. West, p. 68.

He, I know—for the question had been discussed among us long before the Time Machine was made—thought but cheerlessly of the Advancement of Mankind, and saw in the growing pile of civilisation only a foolish heaping that must inevitably fall back upon and destroy its makers in the end.

3. The War of the Worlds

The War of the Worlds[17] takes its shape from another aspect of the cosmic limits upon progress, one merely hinted at in *The Time Machine*. In the major climax of *The Time Machine,* Wells shows the future of man eclipsed by the physical nature of the universe. In *The War of the Worlds* he explores a more immediate limit, one set by the laws of life. A biologist, Wells views mankind not as the completed achievement of creation, but simply as one species evolving in competition with others, adapting to the same environmental pressures, making the same hard fight for survival. In *The War of the Worlds,* as in a group of short stories written during the same early years, he shows mankind clashing with an alien biology.

The novel is constructed with a classic simplicity. The alien biology is introduced in the opening sentence, with this world "being watched keenly and closely by intelligences greater than man's and yet as mortal as his own" (Bk. I, Ch. 1). The Martians,

minds that are to our minds as ours are to the beasts that perish, intellects vast and cool and unsympathetic, regarded this earth with envious eyes, and slowly and surely drew their plans against us.

Their planet is dying, and "the immediate pressure of necessity has brightened their intellects, enlarged their powers, and hardened

17. First published as a serial in 1897, *The War of the Worlds* is included in *Seven Famous Novels;* the theme is foreshadowed in Wells' essay, "The Extinction of Man," *Pall Mall Gazette* (September 23, 1894), reprinted in *Certain Personal Matters* (London, 1898), pp. 172-179; Wells's brother Frank suggested the idea of interplanetary invasion; for a critical text, based upon unpublished matter in the University of Illinois Archive, see David Yerkes Hughes, *An Edition and a Survey of H. G. Wells'* The War of the Worlds (doctoral dissertation, the University of Illinois, 1962).

their hearts." The invaders reach the earth in ten immense missiles, fired at intervals of twenty-four hours. Night after night, they fall near London. The Martians emerge to subjugate the earth. Men, curious and friendly at first, are stung into armed resistance by the unprovoked Martian attacks, and finally driven out of London in dazed and helpless panic. Although two or three Martians are killed, their superior weapons easily crush the best human defenses. Their victory seems secure——when suddenly they die, rotted by the micro-organisms of decay.

Telling his strange tale with immense gusto and skill, Wells avoids most of the defects that flaw *The Time Machine*. Fittingly, since men are such helpless victims of the cosmic struggle for survival, there is no human hero. The narrator is simply an observer of the action; writing after the war is over, he is able to fill out his account with scientific explanations, summaries of the wider action, and philosophic interpretation. Documentary in style, the narrative is so appallingly convincing that Orson Welles was able to create an actual panic in New Jersey on an October evening of 1938, with a radio version of it.[18, 19] The technique is Defoesque: precisely pictured fact is mixed with ingenious invention. The Martians are invented, but their targets are overwhelmingly convincing: the English countryside, the towns, the victims. In the autobiography, Wells has written how he "wheeled about the district marking down suitable places and people for destruction."[20] The writing is economical and objective, the details tellingly selected.

Then we crept out of the house, and ran as quickly as we could down the ill-made road by which I had come overnight. The houses seemed deserted. In the road lay a group of three charred bodies close together,

18. L. Sprague de Camp, *Science-Fiction Handbook* (New York, 1953), pp. 15-17.
19. Marjorie Hope Nicolson, *Voyages to the Moon* (New York, 1948), pp. 1 f.
20. P. 458; Wells remarks in the preface to the third volume of the Atlantic Edition that the incidents were so vividly imagined "that now when he passes through that country these events recur to him as though they were actual memories."

struck dead by the Heat-Ray; and here and there were things that people had dropped—a clock, a slipper, a silver spoon (Bk. I, Ch. 12).

Now and then Wells trips over his impressionistic method of using bits of trivial detail to cover vagueness in more important matters. At one point he writes of the Black Smoke, a Martian poison gas:

Save that an unknown element giving a group of four lines in the blue of the spectrum is concerned, we are still entirely ignorant of the nature of this substance (Bk. I, Ch. 15).

Later he forgets the detail, but not the method. "Spectrum analysis of the black powder points unmistakably to the presence of an unknown element with a brilliant group of three lines in the green" (Bk. II, Ch. 10). Generally, however, he is far more successful; one of the first comments, a long and favorable review in the *Spectator,* compared the novel with Defoe's *Journal of the Plague Year.*[21] The story as a whole creates an unforgettable impression of reality; the descriptions of devastation and panic might almost have been based upon actual observation of twentieth-century war.

Traces of the Victorian sentimental romance appear in a few chapters about the narrator's younger brother, a medical student in London, who rescues a conventional romantic heroine from robbers and sees her and her companion safely through the invasion and across the channel to France. But even these chapters are written in an objective style, with the emphasis not upon the love story but upon the convincing particulars that suggest the disintegration of a great city.

It was a stampede—a stampede gigantic and terrible—without order and without goal, six million people, unarmed and unprovisioned, driving headlong. It was the beginning of the rout of civilisation, of the massacre of mankind (Bk. I, Ch. 17).

The ending of the story, at first glance a flaw, is actually a tellingly ironic restatement of the main theme. The ending does violate the dramatic rule that the central plot problem must be solved by

21. Bergonzi, *The Early H. G. Wells,* p. 123.

the action or the nature of the protagonist, with no interference from coincidence. The germs that kill the Martians appear at first glimpse to be coincidental, simply a convenient *deus ex machina* invented by the author to bring about a pleasing conclusion. A second glance, however, shows this solution arising logically from the theme that progress is controlled by biological laws—which bind Martians, no less than men. Meeting a competing species of life against which they have no biological defenses, the Martians are eliminated. Ironically, their lack of defenses is probably the result of their own past progress. "Micro-organisms . . . have either never appeared upon Mars or Martian sanitary science eliminated them ages ago" (Bk. II, Ch. 2). Again, as in *The Time Machine,* Wells shows the culmination of progress leading to decline.

The War of the Worlds, like *The Time Machine,* draws its vital dramatic tension from the clash of Wells' own contradictory attitudes toward progress. The novel is artistically successful because Wells has found effective metaphors and has placed them in a plot which reveals their meaning through dramatic action. The Martians stand for progress, continued almost to infinity. The human characters represent attitudes toward progress which range from blind ignorance to insane terror. Risking the error of identifying Wells' own attitudes with those of his characters, and allowing for the fact that in plot construction the need for powerful antagonistic forces can betray the uncommitted writer into a sort of accidental pessimism, we can hardly avoid feeling that the early Wells regards the future with a fascinated dread. He seems to relish contemplating "the extinction of man";[22] in the midst of *The War of the Worlds,* he writes Elizabeth Healey,

I'm doing the dearest little serial for Pearson's new magazine, in which I completely wreck and destroy Woking—killing my neighbors in painful and eccentric ways—then proceed via Kingston and Richmond to London, which I sack, selecting South Kensington for feats of peculiar atrocity.[23]

22. See *Certain Personal Matters,* pp. 172-179.
23. Quoted by Geoffrey West, *H. G. Wells,* p. 108.

A scientist, Wells knows that adaptive change is inevitable; he has even developed a rational technique for studying the shape of things to come.[24] A humanist, he loves the values of the past and the people he knows. He is appalled by the future he foresees—yet he lingers almost lovingly over each new figure of terror and death.

Such ambivalent attitudes shape the novel in many ways. In the body of the story, the suspense is intensified by hints of human decline. Writing from his viewpoint in the time after the end of the war, the narrator implies that progress has been reversed. Recalling the white cloth and the silver and glass on his dining table at home, he comments that "in those days even philosophical writers had many little luxuries" (Bk. I, Ch. 7). At the end of the novel, however, there has been no apparent harm inflicted on earth outside a small area of England; even the greater part of London has escaped. A study of the derelict Martian machines has given "an enormous impetus to terrestial invention" (Bk. II, Ch. 2).

The narrator—the "philosophical writer"—is unusual among the human characters in that he accepts the fact of progress. Looking back at the days of peace and plenty before the Martian invasion, he writes, "For my own part, I was much occupied in learning to ride the bicycle, and busy upon a series of papers discussing the probable development of moral ideas as civilisation progressed" (Bk. I, Ch. 1). At the end of the stories he returns to his unfinished papers with a changed attitude. He writes that

our views of the human future must be greatly modified by these events. We have learned now that we cannot regard this planet as being fenced in and a secure abiding-place for Man; we can never anticipate the unseen good or evil that may come upon us suddenly out of space (Bk. II, Ch. 10).

Yet his progressive optimism is not entirely gone; he suggests that men may later reach new planets too.

Dim and wonderful is the vision I have conjured up in my mind of life spreading slowly from this little seed-bed of the solar system

24. In *Anticipations;* see above, pp. 36-39.

throughout the inanimate vastness of sidereal space. But that is a remote dream. It may be, on the other hand, that the destruction of the
Martians is only a reprieve. To them, and not to us, perhaps, is the
future ordained (Bk. II, Ch. 10).

The pitiless Martian onslaught has convinced the narrator that
progress does not increase goodness. Despite the fitful gleams of
optimism with which he relieves the ending of the story, he writes
that "I must confess the stress and danger of the time have left an
abiding sense of doubt and insecurity in my mind." Dark visions
haunt him.

Of a night I see the black powder darkening the silent streets, and the
contorted bodies shrouded in that layer; they rise upon me tattered
and dog-bitten . . . mad distortions of humanity (Bk. II, Ch. 10).

Two minor characters, the curate and the artilleryman, represent
two opposed attitudes toward progress, neither of which Wells himself seems to admire. The narrator, emerging from the scalding
water into which he has dived to escape the Heat-Ray, becomes
aware of the curate as "a seated figure in soot-smudged shirt-
sleeves," inquiring, "Why are these things permitted? What sins
have we done?" (Bk. I, Ch. 13). When the Martians struck, the
curate had been walking after the morning service to clear his
brain; dazed, now, he cannot accept the fact of change. The narrator soon learns to hate his "trick of helpless exclamation, his stupid rigidity of mind" (Bk. II, Ch. 3). When the two men are
trapped in a ruined house from which they can watch the Martians
emerging from their missile, the curate slowly breaks under the
pressure of terror. When he will not keep silent, the narrator kills
him. His body is dragged away by the Martians that his raving has
alarmed. His inflexible resistance to change, the attitude of conventional religion, has led only to death.

If the curate can be taken to symbolize the traditional culture
with its pessimistic resistance to progress, the artilleryman seems
to stand for the optimistic and progressive culture of the technolo-
gist. He lacks traditional education, but he shows a surprising tal-

ent for survival. A practical man, he is quick to accept and take advantage of the changes in his environment. He is immediately prepared to fight for survival in a world where

there won't be any more blessed concerts for a million years or so; there won't be any Royal Academy of Arts, and no nice little feeds at restaurants (Bk. II, Ch. 7).

Shrewdly, he has turned back from the fugitive mobs, to seek his food and shelter under the feet of the Martians. A cosmic pessimist in his own right, he observes that

it's just men and ants. There's the ants builds their cities, live their lives, have wars, revolutions, until the men want them out of the way, and then they go out of the way. That's what we are now—just ants.

And, he adds, "We're eatable ants." Under the new order of things, "Cities, nations, civilisation, progress—that's all over. That game's up. We're beat."

Yet, with something of the desperate optimism of the later Wells himself, the artilleryman is laying plans for survival—even for continued human progress. Scornfully, he condemns the fearful, conformist majority of mankind.

They'll come and be caught cheerful. They'll be quite glad after a bit. They'll wonder what people did before there were Martians to take care of them (Bk. II, Ch. 7).

Declaring that "we have to invent a sort of life where man can live and breed, and be sufficiently secure to bring the children up," he outlines a bold scheme for survival underground, in drains and subways and tunnels. He has even begun digging. When the narrator joins him, however, he proves to be easily distracted from his vast progressive schemes, by the temptations of looted food and drink and cigars and cards. Disillusioned, the narrator resolves "to leave this strange undisciplined dreamer of great things to his drink and gluttony, and go on into London." Thus, finally, the artilleryman becomes no more than a satiric thrust at the optimist planners of progress. The technological is no better than the traditional culture.

Although such symbolic figures sometimes debate Wells' quarrel with himself, his own attitudes toward progress appear more strikingly in his treatment of the invaders. For the Martians are not merely an alien species competing with men for control of the earth. Symbolically, they are also a final stage in the evolution of mankind. However sleepless, sexless, and monstrous they may be, the Martians are perhaps "descended from beings not unlike ourselves, by a gradual development of brain and hands" (Bk. II, Ch. 2). The narrator mentions "a certain speculative writer of quasi-scientific repute, writing long before the Martian invasion," who "forecast for man a final structure not unlike the actual Martian condition." This writer was Wells himself.[25] Attempting to forecast the tendency of natural selection, he had suggested that machines and chemical devices would gradually replace most of the parts and functions of the human body.

But the fact that Wells the scientist foresaw such evolutionary adaptations of mankind does not mean that Wells the human being approved them. Quite the contrary: he presents the Martians as vampire-like figures of horror. The first one emerging from the missile is "a big greyish rounded bulk, the size, perhaps, of a bear," glistening "like wet leather" (Bk. I, Ch. 4). The narrator, even before he sees the Martians feeding themselves by injecting human blood directly into their veins, is "overcome with disgust and dread" by the

peculiar V-shaped mouth with its pointed upper lip . . . the incessant quivering of this mouth, the Gorgon groups of tentacles . . . the extraordinary intensity of the immense eyes . . . vital, intense, inhuman, crippled and monstrous . . . something fungoid in the oily brown skin, something in the clumsy deliberation of the tedious movements unspeakably nasty (Bk. I, Ch. 4).

25. The article is "The Man of the Year Million," *Pall Mall Budget,* November 16, 1893. See Bergonzi, *The Early H. G. Wells,* pp. 36-38, and Geoffrey West, *H. G. Wells,* p. 105. The article is reprinted in *Certain Personal Matters,* pp. 161-171, under the title, "Of a Book Unwritten."

If the Martians represented an ultimate projection of the consequences of human progress, all the benign possibilities are ignored. Wells, instead, places his heaviest emphasis on improvements in the art of war. Writing at Woking in 1896, he was able to outline future military developments in remarkable detail. His Martians, in their armored vehicles, advance against mankind with the panzer tactics of World War II. Their Black Smoke is a poison gas, dispersed in cannisters fired from rockets, and they are developing military aircraft for use in the heavier air of earth. They are waging total war. The scenes of destruction by the Heat-Ray suggest Hiroshima, and the chapter in which the refugees from the vicinity of London are ferried across the Channel to France by "the most amazing crowd of shipping of all sorts that it is possible to imagine" (Bk. I, Ch. 17) reminds one of Dunkerque.

Finally, it is the great past progress of the Martians, rather than any act of their intended human victims, that leads to their destruction. Having lost their immunity to the germs of decay, they are "overtaken by a death that must have seemed as incomprehensible to them as any death could be" (Bk. II, Ch. 8). As painfully as mankind, they have encountered the cosmic limits upon progress. The ultimate creation of evolutionary adaptation has been eliminated by the simplest. Progress, following cosmic law, has limited itself.

MARK R. HILLEGAS
Wells and Later Science Fiction

I

It is a truism that one of the most revealing indexes to the anxieties of our age is the great flood of works like Zamyatin's *We,* Huxley's *Brave New World,* and Orwell's *Nineteen Eighty-four.* Appalling in their similarity, they describe nightmare states where men are conditioned to obedience, freedom is eliminated, and individuality crushed; where the past is systematically destroyed and men are isolated from nature; where science and technology are employed, not to enrich human life, but to maintain the state's surveillance and control of its slave citizens. Although sometimes given such names as *dystopias* or *cacotopias,* they have most often been called *anti-utopias* because they seem a sad, last farewell to man's age-old dream of a planned, ideal, and perfected society, a dream which appeared so noble in Plato's *Republic,* More's *Utopia,* Andreae's *Christianopolis,* and Bellamy's *Looking Backward.* In recent years, we are told, writers have seen the possibility of utopia approaching, but in the form of dictatorships, welfare states, planned economies, and all manner of bureaucracies, and they have become disillusioned. Thus the anti-utopias seem a phenomenon of our contem-

From Mark R. Hillegas, The Future as Nightmare: H. G. Wells and the Anti-Utopians (New York: Oxford University Press, 1967), pp. 3-15. Reprinted by permission of the author.

porary world, no older perhaps than the governments of Hitler, Stalin, or Roosevelt.

The explanation of the anti-utopian phenomenon in these familiar cultural and political terms is only partially correct, however, for it leaves out of consideration the fact that the modern anti-utopian tradition was shaped by an earlier and somewhat different world, that of the period from the 1890's to World War I. Overwhelmingly, the most important influences of this period in creating the modern anti-utopias were the scientific romances, utopias, and future histories of H. G. Wells, which, even when occasionally written after World War I, are still the unique product of this period.

There is nothing new, of course, in the idea that a relationship exists between H. G. Wells and the anti-utopias of the twentieth century. It can be found, for example, in G. Lowes Dicksinson's praise in 1928 of Forster's "The Machine Stops" for turning the Shaw-Wells prophecies inside out, in George Orwell's praise in 1937 of Huxley's *Brave New World* for parodying Wells's vision of utopia, in Wyndham Lewis's description in 1952 of *Nineteen Eighty-four* as a Wellsian prophetic nightmare.[1] But none of those who have commented on this relationship have done more than note that certain anti-utopias are counter-Wellsian or that their general scheme is foreshadowed by Wells's complementary stories, *When the Sleeper Wakes* and "A Story of the Days To Come." Actually, it is a much more complex relationship, without whose exploration both H. G. Wells and the twentieth-century anti-utopian phenomenon go only partially understood. In discussing it, I will follow three main lines of approach.

The first is that the great anti-utopias of the twentieth century constitute, with Wells's scientific romances, future histories, and, to some extent, utopias, a single kind of fiction, for which there is no other name than science fiction. Although Wells's work had various ancestors, it is from him that the writers of anti-utopias

---

1. Dickinson is quoted in Forster, *Goldsworthy Lowes Dickinson* (London, 1934), p. 217; Orwell, *Road to Wigan Pier* (London, 1937), p. 225; and Lewis, *The Writer and the Absolute* (London, 1952), p. 154.

learned the uses of this form. Second, many of the central as well as peripheral images in the anti-utopias were first generated in Wells's early scientific romances, chiefly those written in the 1890's. Third, the relationship between Wells's writings and the major anti-utopias extends beyond images and form. To an extraordinary degree the great anti-utopias are both continuations of the imagination of H. G. Wells and reactions against that imagination. At the same time they often attack ideas that Wells championed, in many cases ideas which were in turn a protest against the decaying Victorian order of things. Altogether, it is doubtful that without Wells the anti-utopian phenomenon would ever have taken the shape it has.

Wells had this impact on anti-utopias because of his enormous popularity with the generation reaching maturity in the first decades of the twentieth century. All the major anti-utopians fall roughly into this generation: E. M. Forster was born in 1879, Evgenii Zamyatin in 1884, Aldous Huxley in 1894, C. S. Lewis in 1898, and George Orwell in 1903.

To many young people today, who have been taught that Wells lost the argument with Henry James about the "Novel," and escaped, as Mark Shorer put it, "from literature into the annals of an era," it may seem unlikely that Wells had any influence at all.[2] But an older generation would remember that from 1900 to 1920, and perhaps even to 1930, Wells was an angry young man fighting against taboos and conventions, fighting against the whole of a planless, greedy society. His impact was enormous, as dozens of men, among them H. L. Mencken, Sinclair Lewis, André Maurois, Eric Goldman, and Joseph Wood Krutch, have testified. Thus Orwell wrote in 1945:

Thinking people who were born about the beginning of this century are in some sense Wells's own creation. How much influence any mere writer has, and especially a "popular" writer whose work takes effect quickly, is questionable, but I doubt whether anyone who was writing

2. "Technique as Discovery," in William Van O'Connor (ed.), *Forms of Modern Fiction* (Minneapolis, 1948), p. 15.

books between 1900 and 1920, at any rate in the English language, influenced the young so much. The minds of all of us, and therefore the physical world, would be perceptibly different if Wells never existed.[3]

Wells was, said *The New York Times* in an editorial on the occasion of his death in 1946, "the voice of the rising generation of the Nineteen Hundreds" and the "greatest public teacher of his time."[4] Or as J. I. M. Stewart has recently written, "Upon youth—not literary youth merely, but youth substantially and at large—no writer was to have a comparable influence until George Orwell."[5]

But most intellectuals have long since rebelled against Wells and the ideas he represented, so that F. R. Leavis rather naturally used the phrase "crass Wellsianism" in attacking C. P. Snow. Leavis rightly linked Snow with Wells, but, as Martin Green remarked, whether one condemns Snow and Wells depends upon where one stands with regard to two major but antithetical movements in the intellectual life of England in the twentieth century. The spirit of the first, said Green, "was summed up in Wells's three huge compilations, *An Outline of History, The Science of Life,* and *The Work, Wealth, and Happiness of Mankind;* a spirit of broad general knowledge, national and international planning, optimism about (or at least cheerful businesslike engagement with) the powers of contemporary science and technology, and a philistinism about the more esoteric manifestations of art and religion." The second movement, which began its ascendancy in the 1920's, insists on narrow intense knowledge (insights), on the need for personal freedom within the best-planned society, on the dangers of modern science and technology, on the irreducibility of artistic and religious modes."[6] The paradigm of the confrontation between these two movements, as Green aptly pointed out, is the quarrel between Henry James and H. G. Wells. But anyone who has read the full

3. "Wells, Hitler and the World State" in *Dickens, Dali and Others* (New York, 1946), p. 121.
4. "Passing of a Utopian," August 14, 1946, p. 24.
5. *Eight Modern Writers* (Oxford, 1963), pp. 11–12.
6. *Science and the Shabby Curate of Poetry* (New York, 1965), p. 4.

record of that quarrel in Gordon Ray and Leon Edel's *Henry James and H. G. Wells* would have to agree that wisdom and humanity are hardly the exclusive possession of either side.

II

Since the great anti-utopias, along with many of Wells's writings, are what we have called "science fiction," we need to define it and explain the relationship of Wells's work to other examples of the form. Admittedly in talking about this subject one runs the risk of not being taken seriously, in large part because of the connotations of the term itself. Coined in 1929 by the pulp publisher Hugo Gernsback, it has come for many educated people to mean the supposed worst excesses of the pulp magazines: creaking plots and cheap sensationalism, characters of cardboard and glue, a prose style to set one's teeth on edge, perhaps a degrading obsession with gadgets and machines. And so most people have dismissed science fiction as fit at best for what T. S. Eliot once called the "pre-adolescent imagination," though a few others, like J. O. Bailey in *Pilgrims Through Space and Time,* Sam Moskowitz in *Seekers of Tomorrow,* and Kingsley Amis in *New Maps of Hell,* have found much to praise. Often, though by no means always, science fiction's bad reputation has been deserved, particularly so in the early novels and stories in the magazines. But deserved or not, this reputation has had one very unfortunate consequence: it has prevented recognition of the fact that there exist novels and stories similar to pulp science fiction in their conventions and themes but greatly superior in their literary quality and significance of comment on human life. It is this superior science fiction with which this book is concerned and which at the moment we are trying to define.

Here Amis's definition makes a very good beginning. "Science fiction," he wrote, "is that class of prose narrative treating of a situation that could not arise in the world we know, but which is hypothesised on the basis of some innovation in science or technology, or pseudo-science or pseudo-technology."[7] It is distin-

7. New York, 1960, p. 18.

guished from pure fantasy by its need to achieve verisimilitude and win the "willing suspension of disbelief" through scientific plausibility. To this definition Amis adds two codicils, kinds of narratives which he includes because they appear to the same set of interests or are written and read by the same writers and readers. The first category—stories about prehistoric man—is important for our discussion because it includes William Golding's *The Inheritors.* The second category, of little interest to us, consists of stories "based on some change or disturbance or local anomaly in physical conditions," very often the threatened destruction of earthly life in a worldwide or cosmic disaster.

To Amis's definition we must make certain additions. The first is the extremely important one—that "quality" science fiction, such as is represented by the great anti-utopias, always makes a significant comment on human life: usually it is a vehicle for social criticism and satire. Then we must discriminate between science fiction and satiric utopia. While science fiction can be satiric and borrows techniques from the satiric utopia, as it does in the case of *Brave New World,* the pure satiric utopia, such as *Erewhon,* is not science fiction. In the satiric utopia, the author assumes a more ironic attitude toward his subject and is not as consistently serious about achieving verisimilitude, whether scientific or otherwise. Or put another way, the writer of science fiction presents what he intends to be taken as actual possibilities, whereas the satiric utopist can be more tongue in cheek about what he presents, at least once he gets his reader to his imaginary world. What the satiric utopist usually offers in this other world are inversions, parodies, or grotesque variations of things in our world—thus Butler's Musical Banks or his College of Unreason, thus Swift's Lilliputian courtiers who dance under ribbons or walk tightropes to win preferment. In science fiction, on the other hand, the fundamental principle is prediction or extrapolation, from existing knowledge and conditions, of things to come. But, of course, mixture of the two forms can occur; and occasionally science fiction (such as some of the work of Frederik Pohl) seems to be almost pure satiric utopia.

As we have defined science fiction (chiefly following Amis), it is pre-eminently a modern phenomenon, but works which more or less fit our formula exist at least as early as the seventeenth century, so that the whole tradition needs to be related to our discussion. This kind of literature had its beginning under the stimulus of the first scientific revolution: Bacon's *New Atlantis* (1624), with its House of Salomon and its various prophecies of scientific marvels, such as submarines and aircraft, is surely in part science fiction. More important than the *New Atlantis* in the seventeenth century as science fiction are the cosmic voyages, which Marjorie Nicolson discussed in her *Voyages to the Moon* and which she showed to be the response of the literary imagination to the new astronomy—works like Kepler's *Somnium* (1634), Godwin's *The Man in the Moone* (1638), and Cyrano de Bergerac's *Voyages to the Sun and Moon* (1650). In the eighteenth century, cosmic voyages continued to be written, though most are trivial, and in this connection one should note that probably only the "Voyage to Laputa" in *Gulliver's Travels* is significant as science fiction (as Professor Nicolson shows, it is actually a moon voyage in reverse).

But in the nineteenth century, a period of astonishingly fertile scientific activity and of technological developments which completely changed the conditions of human life, science fiction really began to flourish. Under the impact of Herschel's new descriptive astronomy, and the discoveries about the limits of the atmosphere that resulted from the invention of the balloon, cosmic voyages proliferated and became much more realistic. Meanwhile there also appeared many other varieties of science fiction, represented by such varied works as Hawthorne's "The Birthmark," Poe's "The Facts in the Case of M. Valdemar," Mary Shelley's *Frankenstein,* and Robert Louis Stevenson's "Dr. Jekyll and Mr. Hyde." Some utopias, particularly late in the century, contained science-fiction elements: thus Bellamy's *Looking Backward* and Hertzka's *Freeland,* but especially the German "technological utopias," such as Lasswitz' *Auf Zwei Planeten* (also a variety of the cosmic voyage, the "Martian romance"). But by far the most important development of science fiction appeared in the writings of Jules Verne. In a sense, Verne prepared the way for Wells, whose science fiction in turn molded the anti-utopias of the twentieth century.

The sheer volume of Verne's output—usually one or two books a year from 1863 to 1905—and his extraordinary popularity explain his influence. Not all of his "Voyages extraordinaires," of course, are science fiction, for many are tales of adventure, appealing to the romantic interests of the nineteenth century—stories of journeys on rafts up the Amazon, of castaways marooned like Crusoe on desert islands, of expeditions to the pole, of journeys around the world in eighty days or into the heart of unexplored Africa. Nor was Verne a great writer in terms of characterization or sophistication of style, but at times he rose to a poetry, if not of expression, at least of imaginative conception. As far as his science fiction is concerned, he did this most notably at the beginning of his career, in *A Journey to the Center of the Earth* (1864), *From the Earth to the Moon* (1865) and *Around the Moon* (1870), and *Twenty Thousand Leagues Under the Sea* (1870). In these books he was, as Kenneth Allott has shown, the almost archetypal expression of nineteenth-century romantic interest in science and technology.[8] In this respect his greatest contribution was to establish in the public consciousness science fiction as a distinct mode of writing. Although he had only slight direct influence on Wells, his writings helped to create the readership for the much more important scientific romances and stories which Wells began writing in the 1890's.

Wells's early scientific romances, which launched his career as writer and prophet, not only sold well and were read widely, but they reached a much more sophisticated audience than the books which Verne created. Verne never received the kind of attention from serious writers that was given to Wells. Thus the master, Henry James, filled with "wonder and admiration" for Wells's early stories and scientific romances, spoke of reading *The First Men in the Moon* "à petites doses* as one sips (I suppose) old Tokay," and of allowing *Twelve Stories and a Dream* "to melt lolli-

8. *Jules Verne* (London, 1940).

popwise, upon my imaginative tongue."[9] Joseph Conrad wrote to Wells how much he liked his work, particularly *The Invisible Man:* "Impressed is *the* word, O Realist of the Fantastic!" Of *The Invisible Man,* he added, "It is masterly—it is ironic—it is very relentless—and it is very true."[10] In the 1890's and in the first years of the twentieth century, other writers—Bennett, Shaw, Gissing, Galsworthy—similarly admired the gifts of storytelling and the vitality of imagination displayed in Wells's early stories and scientific romances. The reviewers—when they chose to notice—were generally favorably disposed. W. T. Stead, editor of the powerful *Review of Reviews,* welcomed *The Time Machine*—Wells's first major publication—as the work of a man of genius, and the *Spectator,* reviewing *The War of the Worlds,* concluded that Wells, at least in the writing of scientific romances, was Poe's superior.[11]

And so it is that because of the power and immediacy of his ideas, because of the quality and sophistication of his imagination, because of his skill as a writer, Wells's scientific romances and stories have exerted a powerful influence on the development of science fiction in our century. In passing I should also note, although it is not the subject of this book, that Wells had great impact on the lower reaches of science fiction, beginning with the first issues of Hugo Gernsback's *Amazing* in 1926. For years pulp writers, at first interested in adventure and sensational effects, took ideas from Wells, who had developed or invented such themes as time travel, the destruction of earth by cosmic accident, the return of mankind to barbarism after the collapse of civilization, the journey to another world in space, the invasion from space, all to comment on life in a mechanical and scientific age. (His influence was also felt indirectly through the writings of Olaf Stapledon, whose *Last and First Men* (1930) and *The Star Maker* (1937), both

9. Leon Edel and Gordon Ray (eds.), *Henry James and H. G. Wells* (Urbana, 1958), p. 80.

10. G. Jean-Aubry (ed.), *Joseph Conrad: Life and Letters* (New York, 1927), I, 259.

11. *Review of Reviews,* XI (1895), 263; *Spectator,* January 29, 1898, p. 168.

heavily indebted to Wells, became a mine of ideas for pulp stories.) But for us his most important impact is not only on such works as *We, Brave New World,* and *Nineteen Eighty-four,* but also on others, like Forster's "The Machine Stops" and C. S. Lewis's "cosmic trilogy," as well as occasional works of quality by professional science-fiction writers, such as Ray Bradbury's *Fahrenheit 451,* Kurt Vonnegut, Jr.'s *Player Piano,* and Walter Miller, Jr.'s *A Canticle for Leibowitz.*

III

Wells turned naturally and easily to the writing of science fiction because he possessed what demands to be called "the Wellsian imagination." This Wellsian imagination is the key to his science fiction as well as to the nature of its impact, and I shall attempt to describe it briefly.

Wells is, of course, closely identified with a particular vision of a utopian World State, a vision which is important in explaining his relationship to the anti-utopians and which I will discuss at length in a subsequent chapter devoted largely to his utopias. What I am dealing with now, however, is a quality, a way of looking at things, which was first described at length by Van Wyck Brooks in 1915.[12] This quality, which must surely be a chief characteristic of the mind scientifically educated, is detachment. As Brooks remarked about Wells's fiction in general, and as we would say particularly about his scientific romances, future histories, and utopias, Wells saw men chemically and anatomically, the world astronomically. Brooks also put it another way: it is the distinction between the intellectual, who views life in terms of ideas, and the artist, who views life in terms of experience. Generally speaking, the intellectual dominated Wells's writings, though sometimes— most continuously in *Tono-Bungay, Kipps,* and *Mr. Polly*—the artist took over. But it must be emphasized that this distinction between "intellectual" and "artistic" refers to the angle at which reality is viewed, not to the quality of writing. Even at his most "intel-

12. *The World of H. G. Wells* (New York, 1915).

lectual," as in, say, *The Time Machine,* Wells was capable of vividness in both conception and expression. *The Time Machine,* though
it differs greatly from ordinary fiction, has some right to the title of
"art."

Surely the single most spectacular manifestation of this detached
quality of the Wellsian imagination is its preoccupation with the
future. This preoccupation, which is central to many of Wells's
writings, is most enthusiastically explained in "The Discovery of
the Future," a lecture Wells delivered at the Royal Institution in
January 1902, which was published in *Nature* the next month. In
this lecture, Wells distinguished between two kinds of minds. The
first, oriented to the past, regards the future "as sort of black non-
existence upon which the advancing present will presently write
events." It is the legal mind, always referring to precedents. The
second kind of mind, oriented to the future, is constructive, creative, organizing. "It sees the world as one great workshop, and the
present is no more than material for the future, for the thing that is
yet destined to be."[13] Finally, Wells predicted what might be accomplished if the future-oriented mind were given freedom to express itself:

All this world is heavy with the promise of greater things, and a day
will come, one day in the unending succession of days, when beings
who are now latent in our thoughts and hidden in our loins, shall
stand upon this earth as one stands upon a footstool and shall laugh
and reach out their hands amidst the stars."[14]

(In the context of that entire lecture, this passage is not, incidentally, the expression of simple optimism it can easily be taken to
be.)

Along with the detached imagination and its preoccupation with
the future go certain clearly defined and inevitable values and interests. Wells—not surprisingly for a former student and admirer of
T. H. Huxley—was a supreme rationalist and believer in science

13. *Nature,* LXV, 326.
14. Ibid. 331.

and the scientific method, a Francis Bacon reborn. And so for Wells, as for one of his Utopians in *Men Like Gods,* there was no way out of the cages of life but by knowledge—knowledge of man himself and of man in relation to the things about him. Naturally the Wellsian imagination is drawn to certain characteristic subjects. It is fascinated by the revelations of man's place in time and space given to us by science, fascinated by the vistas of astronomy, particularly the death of the world and the vastness of interstellar space, fascinated by the vision of geological epochs, the evolution of life, and the early history of man vouchsafed by geology, paleontology, and archaeology.

The first, brilliant fruit of this Wellsian imagination were the scientific romances and stories written in the 1890's which led, in their turn, by a complicated process which also involved reaction against the Wellsian utopias, to the major anti-utopias of the twentieth century.

V. S. PRITCHETT
Wells and the English Novel

A cloud of dust travels down the flinty road and chokes the glossy
Kentish greenery. From the middle of the moving cloud come the
ejaculations of an unhandy driver; the clopper of horses' hoofs, the
rumble of a wagonette or trap. One catches the flash of a top-hat
or a boater. One smells horse manure and beer. And one hears that
peculiar English spoken by the lower middle class, a language in
which the syllable "-ing" either becomes "-ink" or loses its final
"g," and which is enlivened by cries of "Crikey" and "Golly." The
accent is despairing, narrow-voweled yet truculent, with something
of the cheap-jack and Sunday League in it, and it is broken by a
voice, not quite so common, which says things like, "We're not
the finished thing. We're jest one of Nature's experiments, see.
We're jest the beginning." And then—I don't quite know why—
there is a crash. Over goes the wagonette, the party inside hit out
with their fists, noses bleed, eyes are blackened. Most surprising, a
nearby house catches fire. Do not be alarmed. The time is the late
'nineties and you have simply been watching the outing of a group
of early H. G. Wells characters who have become suddenly aware
that science is radically changing the human environment. No

From V. S. Pritchett, The Living Novel (New York: Reynal & Hitchcock, 1947), pp.
122-129. Copyright 1947, renewed 1974 by V. S. Pritchett. Reprinted by permission of
Harold Matson Co. Inc.

Frenchified or Russianized fiction this, but plain, cheerful, vulgar, stoic, stupid and hopelessly romantic English. It is as English as the hoardings.[1]

There are always fist-fights and fires in the early Wells. Above all, there are fires. They occur, as far as I remember, in all the scientific romances except *The Island of Dr. Moreau*—a very pessimistic book—and are an ingredient of the Wellsian optimism, an optimism whose other name, I fear, is ruthlessness. I have lately read all those scientific books from *The Time Machine* to *The War in the Air* and it has been a refreshing experience. There was a time, one realizes, when science was fun. For the food of the gods is more entertaining than the prosaic efficacy of vitamins; the tripods of the Martians are more engaging than tanks. And then, here you have Wells at his best, eagerly displaying the inventive imagination, first with the news and at play, with an artist's innocence. Here you see his intoxicated response—a response that was lacking in his contemporaries—to the front-page situation of his time, and here you meet his mastery of the art of story-telling, the bounce and resource of it. Above all, in these early books, you catch Wells in the act, his very characteristic act, of breaking down mean barriers and setting you free. He has burst out himself and he wants everyone else to do the same. "Why," cries the engineer in *The Food of the Gods*—the poorest of these books—"Why don't we do what we want to do?"

For that matter, I have never read any book by H. G. Wells, early or late, which did not start off by giving me an exhilarating sense of personal freedom. Every inhibition I ever had faded from me as I read. Of course, after such a high, hard bounce one comes down again. The answer to the engineer's question is that we do not do what we want to do because we want to do opposite things at the same time. Yet that infectious Wellsian sense of freedom was not all anarchy, romantic ebullience or Utopian uplift. That freedom was a new fact in our environment; one pays for everything— that is all. I do not know what date is given to the second scientific

1. *Hoardings* is the British term for billboards.

revolution, but one has to go back to the great centuries of geographical discovery for a comparable enlargement of our world;
and it is a suggestive fact that we have to go back to Swift, the
Swift of Lilliput and Laputa, before we find another English novelist going to science for his data and material as Wells has done.
(The influence of science, in the one hunderd fifty years that lie
between those two writers, is philosophical, not factual.) Wells's
eager recognition of the new environment is one of the sources of
the sense of freedom we get from him. I make no comparison of the
merist of Wells and Swift—though the Beast-Men of *The Island of
Dr. Moreau* are derivatives of the Yahoos and are observed with
Swift's care for biological detail—but in his best narratives Wells
does go back to the literary traditions of the early eighteenth century, the highest traditions of our narrative literature. The ascendancy of Swift is a question of imaginative range and style; above
all it is due to a humanity which is denied to Wells because he
arrived at the beginning, the crude beginning, of a new enlargement, whereas Swift arrived toward the end of one. None of Wells's
narrators, whether they are South Kensington scientists or people,
like the awful Bert, who appear to be suffering from an emotional
and linguistic toothache, is capable of the philosophical simplicity
and sanity of Gulliver; for Wells has only just spotted this new
world of agitating chemicals, peculiar glands, and obliterating machines. The sense of wonder has not grown far beyond a sense of
copy. He is topical and unstable, swept by eagerness yet visited by
nausea sudden and horrifying. Suppose we evolve into futility or
revert to the beast from which we have arisen? Such speculations
are alien to the orthodox eyes which were set in Swift's mad head;
he had no eye to the future; the eighteenth century believed in a
static world. The things Swift sees *have happened.* To Wells—and
how typical of an expanding age—the things he sees have *not* happened. They are possibilities. In these scientific romances one
catches occasionally the humane and settled note: in *The Time
Machine,* in *The Island of Dr. Moreau* and in *The War of the
Worlds,* which are the most imaginative stories of the group and

are free of the comic Edwardian horseplay. The practical experiment has been detached from the practical joke; the idea is untainted by the wheeze. The opening sentence of *The War of the Worlds* suggests a settled view of humanity, besides being an excellent example of Wells's mastery of the art of bouncing us into belief in anything he likes to tell us:

No one would have believed in the last years of the nineteenth century that human affairs were being watched keenly and closely by intelligences greater than man's and yet as mortal as his own.

It is not surprising that the passages of low comedy, which elsewhere are Wells's excellence, should be a failure in the scientific romances. Naturally they break the spell of the illusion with their clumsy realism. And if love is born, Wells is Walt Disney at his worst. The love scenes between the giants in *The Food of the Gods* are the most embarrassing in English fiction, and one wonders that the picture of the awful Princess, goggling in enormous close-up and fanning herself with half a chestnut tree, did not destroy the feminist movement. But except for faint squirms of idyllic petting in *The Time Machine,* none of these aberrations misdirects the narratives of the three books I have mentioned. I cannot include *The War in the Air* among the best; it *is* an astonishing piece of short-term prophecy and judgment. One remembers the bombing of battleships and the note on the untroubled mind of those who bomb one another's cities; but the book is below Wells's highest level. So, too, is *The Invisible Man,* which is a good thriller, but it develops jerkily and is held up by horseplay and low comedy. Without question *The Time Machine* is the best piece of writing. It will take its place among the great stories of our language. Like all excellent works it has meanings within its meaning and no one who has read the story will forget the dramatic effect of the change of scene in the middle of the book, when the story alters its key, and the Time Traveler reveals the foundation of slime and horror on which the pretty life of his Arcadians is precariously and fearfully resting. I think it is fair to accuse the later Wells of escaping into a dream world of plans, of using science as a magic staircase out of essential social problems. I think the best Wells is the destructive, ruthless, black-eye-dealing and house-burning Wells who foresaw the violence and not the order of our time. However this may be, the early Wells of *The Time Machine* did not escape. The Arcadians had become as prettty as flowers in their pursuit of personal happiness. They had dwindled and would be devoured because of that. Their happiness itself was haunted. Here Wells's images of horror are curious. The slimy, the viscous, the fetal reappear; one sees the sticky, shapeless messes of pond life, preposterous in instinct and frighteningly without mind. One would like to hear a psychologist on these shapes which recall certain surrealist paintings; but perhaps the biologist fishing among the algæ, and not the unconscious, is responsible for them. In *The Time Machine*—and also in the other two books—Wells is aware of pain. None of his investigators returns without wounds and bruises to the mind as well as the body, and Dr. Moreau is, of course, a sadist. *The Island* is hard on the nerves and displays a horror more definite and calculated than anything in Wells's other books. Where *The Time Machine* relieves us by its poetic social allegory, *The Island of Dr. Moreau* takes us into an abyss of human nature. We are left naked at the end of the shocking report, looking with apprehension at the bodies of our friends, imagining the tell-tale short legs, the eyes that shine green in the dark, the reversion to the wolf, the hyena, the monkey and the dog. This book is a superb piece of story-telling from our first sight of the unpleasant ship and its stinking, mangy menagerie, to the last malign episode where the narrator is left alone on the island with the Beast-Men. Neither Dr. Moreau nor his drunken assistant is a lay figure and, in that last episode, the Beast-Men become creatures of Swiftian malignance:

The Monkey Man bored me, however. He assumed, on the strength of his five digits, that he was my equal, and was forever jabbering at me, jabbering the most arrant nonsense. One thing about him entertained me a little: he had a fantastic trick of coining new words. He had an idea, I believe, that to gabble about names that meant nothing was the proper use of speech. He called it "big thinks," to distinguish it from "little thinks"—the sane everyday interests of life. If ever I made a remark he did not understand, he would praise it very much, ask me to say it again, learn it by heart, and go off repeating it, with a word wrong here and there, to all the wider of the Beast People. He thought nothing of what was plain and comprehensible. I invented some very curious "big thinks" for his especial use.

The description of the gradual break in the morale of the Beast-Men is a wonderful piece of documented guesswork. It is easy enough to be sensational. It is quite another matter to domesticate the sensational. One notices, too, how Wells's idea comes full circle in his best thrillers. There is the optimistic outward journey, there is the chastened return.

It would be interesting to know more about the origins of *The Island of Dr. Moreau,* for they must instruct us on the pessimism and the anarchy which lie at the heart of Wells's ebullient nature. This is the book of a wounded man who has had a sight of sadism and death. The novelist who believed in the cheerful necessity of evolution is halted by the thought of its disasters and losses. Perhaps man is unteachable. It is exciting and emancipating to believe we are one of nature's latest experiments, but what if the experiment is unsuccessful? What if it is unsurmountably unpleasant? Suppose the monkey drives the machine, the gullible, mischievous, riotous and irresponsible monkey? It is an interesting fact that none of Wells's optimistic contemporaries considered such a possibility. Shaw certainly did not. Evil, in Shaw, is curable. He believes in the Protestant effort. He believes that men *argue* their way along the path of evolution, and that the life force is always on the side of the cleverest mind and the liveliest conscience. When he reflects on the original monkey, Shaw cannot resist the thought that the monkey was a shrewd animal going up in the world, and Shaw feels a patronizing pride in him which the self-made man may feel about the humble ancestor who gave him his start in life. There is certainly no suggestion that he will ever lose his capital, which is civilization, and revert. There is no thought, in this quintessential

Irish Protestant, that the original monkey may be original sin. Nor could there be: the doctrine of original sin is a device of the emotions, and about our emotions Shaw knows absolutely nothing at all. But to the emotional Wells, the possibility of original sin in the form of the original monkey is always present. The price of progress may be perversion and horror, and Wells is honest enough to accept that. Shaw appears to think we can evade all painful issues by a joke, just as Chesterton, the Catholic optimist of his generation, resolved serious questions by a series of puns.

Wells can be wounded. It is one of his virtues. One is reminded of Kipling, another wounded writer—was Wells satirizing Kipling in that chapter of *The Island of Dr. Moreau* where the Beast-Men are seen mumbling their pathetic Law?—and Kipling and Wells are obviously divergent branches of the same tree. Wells the Utopian, Kipling the patriot—they represent the day-dream of the lower middle class which will either turn to socialism or fascism. Opposed in tendency, Wells and Kipling both have the vision of artists; they foresee the conditions of our time. They both foretell the violence with a certain appetite. Crudity appeals to them. They are indifferent or badhearted, in human relations. They understand only personal independence which, from time to time, in their work is swallowed up in mass relationships. In the final count, Kipling—like Wells's man in the sewer in *The War of the Worlds*—falls back on animal cunning. It is the knowing, tricky, crafty animal that survives by lying low and saying nothing. Kipling, for all his admiration of power, believes in the neurotic, the morbid and defeated mind. This strain is in Wells also, but he has more private stoicism than Kipling has, a stoicism which blossoms from time to time into a belief in miracles and huge strokes of luck. Impatient of detail, mysteriously reticent about the immediate practical steps we must take to ensure any of his policies, Wells believes—like Kipling—in magic: a magic induced by impudence or rebellion. Wells and Kipling—these two are light and shadow to each other.

Wells's achievement was that he installed the paraphernalia of our new environment in our imagination; and life does not become visible or tolerable to us until artists have assimilated it. We do not need to read beyond these early scientific works of his to realize what he left out. The recent war, whose conditions, he so spryly foresaw has made that deficiency clear. When we read those prophetic accounts of mechanized warfare and especially of air bombardment, we must be struck by one stupendous misreading of the future. It occurs where we should expect it to occur: in the field of *morale*. Wells imagined cities destroyed and the inhabitants flying in terror. He imagined the soldiers called out to keep order and the conditions of martial law and total anarchy. He imagined mass terror and riot. He did not reckon with the nature, the moral resources, the habits of civilized man. Irresponsible himself, he did not attribute anything but an obstructive value to human responsibility. That is a serious deficiency, for it indicates an ignorance of the rooted, inner life of men and women, a jejune belief that we live by events and programs; but how, in the heyday of a great enlargement of the human environment, could he believe otherwise? We turn back to our Swift and there we see a mad world also; but it is a mad world dominated by the sober figure of the great Gulliver, that plain, humane figure. Not a man of exquisite nor adventurous spirituality; not a great soul; not a man straining all his higher faculties to produce some new mutation; not a man trying to blow himself out like the frog of the fable to the importunate dimensions of his program; but, quite simply, a man. Endowed with curiosity, indeed, but empowered by reserve. Anarchists like Wells, Kipling, Shaw and the pseudo-orthodox Chesterton, had no conception of such a creature. They were too fascinated by their own bombs.

ANTHONY WEST

H. G. Wells

I find it difficult to write dispassionately of H. G. Wells. One of my
earliest memories of him, too early for me to date, is of the occasion on which I first discovered the physical aspect of death. It
was at a time when I had a treasure box, a small cigarette tin I
believe, with a hinged lid. In it I kept some of the old-fashioned
glass marbles, a button with a coat-of-arms upon it, and a few
things of that kind which had taken my fancy. To these I one day
added a few heads of snapdragon. I hoped that I would find them
there in their bright prettiness whenever I wanted to look at them.
But when I opened the box again after several days had gone by
it held corruption and green moulds, and I screamed with dismay.
I do not remember all the details of what followed, but I remember
taking refuge from H. G.'s incomprehension under a gate-legged
table, and I remember his lifting the edge of the table-cloth to peer
in at me where I crouched, still screaming in grief and fear, and
muttering "I just don't understand you."

It was a phrase he repeated, and with the same bewilderment, to
me during his last illness. He was sitting with a light rug over his
knees on a chair which had been placed where he could catch the
sun on the grassed-in balcony at the back of his house in Hanover

Terrace. We were sharing silences rather than talking. He was already extremely weak, and he husbanded his energies through long drowsy periods in which he seemed almost comatose, surfacing, so to speak, only occasionally when he wished to give his full attention to something or somebody. I would go to see him, in the hope of catching his interest and drawing him up to the surface. I wanted to drive out of his mind an impression—I do not care, even now, to think how he had been given it—that I had been "got hold of" by a pro-Nazi conspiracy somehow entrenched in the British Broadcasting Corporation which was then employing me in its News division. These conspirators were, he had been told, blackmailing me in some way and forcing me into some mysteriously discreditable line of conduct for an arcane ulterior purpose, the nature of which I have never been able to discover. This nightmare cobweb of misunderstanding had fallen between myself and my father in the first stages of the V-1 attack on London; it remained upon our faces through all the time the attack lasted, through the stranger time of V-2, until the war receded into the Pacific and left London in shocked and stunned silence. At first my father seemed too ill to be bothered with the necessary explanations. Then he made a partial recovery and I was able to hope. I sat with him often, when I was not on duty in the newsroom at the B.B.C., longing for the moment when he would open his mind to me. But the occasion never came, and at last I became aware that it never would. Sitting beside him one day, at once in the closest proximity to him and utterly remote from him, and, thinking him asleep, I fell into a passion of misery and buried my face in my hands. How long this spasm of pain lasted I don't know, but when its intensity slackened I suddenly became conscious that I was being watched. I looked up to find his eyes fixed upon me with all the clarity of his fully-conscious mind behind them. We stared at each other for an instant before he said, once again, "I just don't understand you." Then the light left his face. He had, as it were, turned himself off, and had relapsed into his dozing state on the frontier between sleep and death. The last chance of communication had gone, and there was never to be another. Rather more than a year later I chartered a boat named the *Deirdre* owned by a Captain Miller of Poole in Dorset, my half-brother came down from London bringing with him H. G.'s ashes, and we went out to scatter them on the sea at a point on a line between Alum Bay on the Isle of Wight and St. Alban's Head on the mainland. As we returned I found myself surprised at the extent of my bitterness. That I should have preferred my father to realize that I had been going through a sufficiently banal marital crisis, rather than to believe that I was falling into the hands of blackmailers who had been using me as a tool for treasonable purposes, was easy enough to understand. But that I should feel so violently about the matter when he was no longer in a position to believe anything at all shocked me, as it still does.

It will be realized why in those circumstances a self-protective device told me that Wells's mind was clouded by illness at a much earlier stage than it probably was to any significant extent. For some years after his death I reacted angrily to the criticisms of the quality of his thought which made so much of the extreme pessimism of his last writings and utterances. These were, and still are, being represented as an abandonment of a superficial optimism in the face of those realities of which his coming death was a part. The suggestion is made that they were some kind of final admission that he had been wrong about the nature of things for the greater part of his life. I felt at one time that this was a wilful exploitation of the auto-intoxication of a very sick man who no longer enjoyed full command of himself. But since sifting my recollections of his talk, and doing a great deal of preparatory work on his biography, I incline to another view. I cannot now agree that his final phase of scolding and complaining at human folly represented any essential change in his views at all. What happened as his powers declined from 1940 onwards was that he reverted to his original profoundly-felt beliefs about the realities of the human situation. He was by nature a pessimist, and he was doing violence to his intuitions and his rational perceptions alike when he asserted in his middle period that mankind could make a better world for itself by an effort of will.

This contention may seem grotesque to those who have a picture of him firmly entrenched in their minds as a kindly, avuncular figure promising men a birthday with lavish presents every week if the scientists were only given control of society. Last year Dr. Bronowski took time off from his duties as Director of the Coal Research Establishment to tell Section L of the British Association:

H. G. Wells used to write stories in which tall, elegant engineers administered with perfect justice a society in which other people had nothing to do but be happy: the Houyhnhnms administering the Yahoos. Wells used to think this a very fine world; but it was only 1984. . . .

This represents the received view. Mr. St. John Ervine in his life of Shaw asserts that Wells believed that infinite social progress was inevitable unless there were some global catastrophe; and George Orwell attributed his final despair to a belated realization that science was just as effective on the side of evil as on the side of good. And only the other day Mr. Geoffrey Barraclough, Professor Arnold Toynbee's successor in the Stevenson Research Chair of International History in London, was telling us that the evolutionary conception of society found its supreme expression in Wells' *Outline of History*. According to him this postulates that

the development of intelligence is the work of 'natural selection,' and that inexorable laws of natural selection will result in the replacement of the present imperfect society by one in which a finer humanity will inhabit a more perfect world.

The diffuseness and looseness of much of Wells' writing, and the tone of a great deal of his occasional journalism, lends itself to this distortion of his basic ideas. But the fact remains that the body of work which bears his name contradicts these assumptions about his views, and the reader who undertakes to examine all of his writing scrupulously is in for a number of surprises. Wells received a scientific education and he never fell into the fallacy of confusing the Darwinian conception of evolution with the idea of progress. The idea of progress depends fundamentally on a picture of the universe in which mind is increasingly valuable, and which is also increasingly orderly. Wells' first serious piece of writing was a paper called "The Rediscovery of the Unique" of which he remained proud throughout his career. Though it does not reach a standard which would be acceptable to professional philosophers and logicians, it restates with clarity and force the idea which Hobbes put forward in *Leviathan* (I, iv) when he says that there is "nothing in the World Universal but Names, for the things named are every one of them Individual and Singular."

This is the foundation stone of the mechanistic view according to which the whole world is "nothing but a mere heap of dust, fortuitously agitated" and the universe a similar aggregation. It is impossible to believe in progress if you believe in a universe in which mind figures as a local accident, and which by its nature cannot support any permanent moral order or indeed any permanent thing.

That Wells was deeply committed to this view is evident from his first novel, *The Time Machine,* which has its climactic scene at a point some thirty million years in the future. The planet has ceased to revolve. It no longer supports human life, and it is evident that the time is rapidly approaching when it will no longer support life at all. A cosmic catastrophe is impending which will finally obliterate the material context in which such concepts as mind, consciousness, and value can possess any meaning. The possibility of such a situation is irreconcilable with the idea of progress, and Wells states his disbelief in it in this book without ambiguity. The questions which the Time Traveller asks himself on the first phase of his journey into the future are interesting, and revealing:

What might not have happened to men? What if cruelty had grown to be a common passion? What if in this interval the race had lost its manliness, and had developed into something inhuman, unsympathetic, and overwhelmingly powerful? I might seem some old-world savage animal, only the more dreadful and disgusting for our common likeness —a foul creature to be incontinently slain.

What is implicit in these questions is the idea that an evolutionary trend that would make a man a more intellectual animal might also make him a much less humane one. This not only questions the idea of progress, but also suggests that virtue is not innate in the intellect as Victorian moralists were inclined to believe. I stress this point because it seems to me to be an important one if one wants to understand Wells' thinking. The conventional picture then was, and still to a considerable extent is, of a conflict between mind and man's animal nature, with the virtues seated in the intellect and the defects in the instincts and the animal behaviour patterns. Wells suggests that morals and ethics have their basis in man's behaviour as a social animal. That is to say that disinterested behaviour develops from a hunting animal's practice of bringing food back to its lair for its mate and its young; and that humanitarianism, and the sympathies that make life endurable, develop from the animal habit of snuggling in a huggermugger, as puppies or kittens do, for warmth. The intellect on the other hand is amoral and ultimately recognizes the single value of efficiency, so that a continuation of the line of development that had made man a reasoning animal might ultimately make him more callous, indifferent, and cruel, and not more moral. This nagging fear of the liberated intellect as something inhumane was to play an important part in Wells' later work, but he raised in it *The Time Machine* only to drop it in favour of an explicit statement about natural selection. The premise is that the nineteenth century layered class society constituted an artificial environment to which man was adapting himself. The donnée for the purpose of *The Time Machine* was that it was going to endure; so the Time Traveller finds, in the year A.D. 802701 that adaptation has divided the human race into two distinct subspecies. The descendants of the old ruling and propertied classes live above ground and fear the dark, those of the workers and managers subterraneously in fear of the light. Both are hopelessly degenerate, and neither considers the Time Traveller to be an old-world savage, because neither group is capable of sufficient sustained thought to frame so elaborate a concept. It is with something of a shock that one finds that what has brought about their debasement is precisely the complete success of mankind in establishing a technological society and world order of the kind to which Wells is supposed to have given his unqualified endorsement. At some point during the eight hundred thousand year interval men completely mastered their environment and solved all the social problems. When they were comfortable they stopped thinking, and then degenerated along the lines of their own inherent weaknesses.

One of the difficulties of writing about Wells is that his mind was undisciplined, and that on any given point he can be found either to contradict himself, or to appear to do so. *The Time Machine* was immediately followed by *The Island of Dr. Moreau,* which Wells discussed much later, in the twenties, as if he had accepted a dualistic picture of human nature while he was writing it: "Humanity is but animal rough-hewn to a reasonable shape and in perpetual internal conflict between instinct and injunction.

This would give innate virtue a refuge in the intellect, and would allow for optimism as a possibility. But what happens in *The Island of Dr. Moreau* is a disaster, the liberated intellect in the person of a Darwinian humanitarian arrives on the island and disintegrates its theocratic moral order by making an appeal to reason which assumes that Dr. Moreau's victims are moral creatures with better natures. When they are set free from the Hobbesian régime of terror under which they have been living it is revealed that they are, beneath Dr. Moreau's scar tissue, brutes interested only in the satisfaction of their appetites. So far as a conflict between instinct and injunction goes, it is no contest; order and law are imposed on the brutish inhabitants of the island by an exterior force, and as soon as that is removed the system collapses. What the book in fact expresses is a profound mistrust of human nature, and a doubt about the intellect's ability to contain it. There is even a doubt about the intellect as a possible containing force, since its role in the story is a purely destructive one.

The Island of Dr. Moreau relates closely to two other stories, a short novel and a short story, which deal with the same theme of the liberated intellect as a destructive element. *The Invisible Man* is a parable about the amoral aspects of the scientific outlook, and invisibility figures in it as a symbol of intellectual isolation. "The Country of the Blind" is a much more mature version of the same parable, in which the symbolic situation of the sighted man in the community of the blind is even more harrowing. In both stories men are cut off from normal human feeling and corrupted by the sense that their special knowledge gives them a right to power over the unenlightened. They both end by running amok in the same lonely terror which overtakes the visitor to Dr. Moreau's Island. The theme is carried further in *The War of the Worlds* and in *The First Men in the Moon*. The Martians, like the ruling class on the moon, are brain cases with the merest of vestigial bodies, symbols of the intellect triumphant over the animal. The point that technological mastery has given the Martians a sense that they are free from moral responsibility is obscured by the surface action in *The War of the Worlds*. Most readers do not see beyond the fact that the Martians arrive, and treat Europeans as Europeans had been treating native populations and animals in the hey-day of colonialism, to the deeper argument. But there is no possibility of misunderstanding the description of lunar society which appears towards the end of *The First Men in the Moon*. The unfettered intellect rules, and respect for efficiency stands in the place of morality. What has come into being is the worst kind of slave state. It has reduced most of its members to simple automata. Many of them are actually deformed physically to fit them more precisely for specific social functions. When the labourers of various types are not required they are laid aside in induced coma until they are needed. Wells' scientist, Cavor, reports on this society with naïve approval, so that there can be no doubt about what he is getting at. The clear implication is that a further extension of human intellectual powers in the post-renaissance direction of abstract rational thinking will lead to the growth of cruel and inhuman planned societies which will be utterly indifferent to human values and individual happiness. Human sympathies will be stifled, and endless cruelties perpetrated in the name of an abstract common good, because logical analysis finds that human sympathies have no basis in the sort of reality that it can recognize. The scientific apparatus for examining reality is hostile to values in so far as it shows that any system of values is purely arbitrary. In the end, what Wells is saying in *The First Men in the Moon,* is that the basis of operations which Huxley recommended in his famous Romanes lecture, and which he had himself adopted and stated in the concluding paragraphs of *The Time Machine,* is not viable. Because if a mechanistic view of the universe is constructed by the right hand the left will inevitably loose its grip on any ethical system it may have decided to grasp.

It may seem that this is reading something into *The First Men in the Moon* which is not there, but Wells went out of his way to state it in a mundane context in *When the Sleeper Wakes.* Many people recall this novel of 1899 as a description of the triumph of gadgetry with its descriptions of flying machines, television, public address systems, and air-conditioned roofed-in cities. It stands as the optimistic and naïvely uncritical forerunner of Aldous Huxley's *Brave New World,* and Orwell's *1984.* In fact Wells' society of 3002 includes many of the worst features of both these later constructions. It "features" a deliberately debased and systematically misinformed proletariat, constant surveillance and thought control, and an amoral brutality; and these things are described as evils. The difference between Wells' horrors and those described by Huxley and Orwell reside mainly in points of detail. Wells was writing before the two great wars and the dictatorships had made the State as dangerous an engine as it now seems. For Wells the enemy was monopoly capitalism as it presented itself in the form of the great corporations. But his business State is just as monstrous as the police State of Orwell's imagination, and is perhaps worse in that it does not bother to persecute individuals as individuals, but simply treats people in terms of social categories and utility. Wells' equivalent of Big Brother, Ostrog, the head of the super-corporation's governing body says:

"I can imagine how this great world of ours seems to a Victorian Englishman. You regret all the old forms of representative government . . . the voting councils and Parliaments and all that eighteenth-century tomfoolery. You feel moved against our pleasure cities. I might have thought of that—had I not been busy. But you will learn better . . . the pleasure cities are the excretory organs of the State, attractive places that year after year draw together all that is weak and vicious, all that is lascivious and lazy, all the easy roguery of the world, to a graceful destruction. They go there, they have their time, they die childless, and mankind is the better. . . . And you would emancipate the silly brainless workers that we have enslaved, and try to make their lives easy and pleasant again. Just as they have sunk to what they are fit for . . . I know these ideas; in my boyhood I read your Shelley and dreamt of liberty. There is no liberty save wisdom and self-control. Liberty is within, not without . . . suppose that these swarming yelping fools in blue [the proles wear blue uniforms] got the upper hand of us, what then? They will only fall to other masters. So long as there are sheep Nature will insist on beasts of prey. It would mean but a few hundred years' delay. The coming of the aristocrat is fatal and assured. The end will be the Overman—for all the mad protests of humanity. Let them revolt, let them win and kill me and my like. Others will arise—other masters. The end will be the same."

From this viewpoint in 1899 Wells was able to see that the growth of a technological society would throw up régimes much worse than those of such simple-minded tyrants as Napoleon III. Ostrog is more like Hitler than anything which had then been seen, he was probably conceived as a criticism of Carlyle's hero worship, while the society he presides over is a criticism of the structural aspects of Plato's Republic.

I have dwelt on these early books of Wells' because they seem to me to show how foreign to his thought the ideas that either evolution or technical development would inevitably produce a moral order, or even a better order, were. I think, too, that the view of human nature taken in these early books accounts for the flaw in the later ones which now makes them seem ill-considered and confused. These are forced in so far as they say things which Wells wishes to believe, and in which he, ultimately, does not believe. What he ultimately does not believe in is the ability of the human animal to live up to its ideals. *The Time Machine, The Island of Dr. Moreau,* and *When the Sleeper Wakes,* all state this idea quite bluntly. In mid-career Wells stopped saying this and adopted the progressive line, stating a body of ideas which can be called Wellsian.

These can be summarized roughly as follows. Education and the liberal tradition have produced a disinterested group of men of good will capable of taking hold of the drift of modern life and of giving it coherent direction. Cheap paper and mechanized printing together with the prosperity and leisure produced by industrialization have made universal education a practical possibility. An educated community (as distinct from a merely literate one) would be able to establish rational relationships with other communities. Improved communications would bring these educated communities into increasingly close contact with each other and a world community would develop. A sense of kinship would grow up among all men, and instead of squandering their creative potential in pointless and destructive wars they would learn to settle their differences by negotiation and agreement. A world order would take shape in which racial, regional, and national frictions would have no place. Men would work happily together to bring each other a fair share of the world's abundant wealth. There are no logical objections to this as a plausible future course of development for human society if the romantic view of human nature is once accepted, and man is taken to be a creature of infinite possibility. If man is such a creature, it is then just a matter of adopting this rational aim and making a great collective effort to secure it. Wells wished to proceed, and to persuade other people to proceed, on this basis. But he knew that in the long run all human effort was futile and that man was base. The world was Dr. Moreau's Island and the men of goodwill were building on sand with obdurate material which by its essence excluded any possibility of success. Wells' "progressive" writing represents an attempt to straddle irreconcilable positions, and it involved a perpetual conflict of a wasteful character. In all too much of his work he is engaged in shouting down his own better judgment.

The change of front from an explicit pessimism to an apparent optimism dates roughly from 1901 and the publication of *Anticipations*. It coincides with Wells' entry into the sphere of influence of the Fabian society in political matters and of that of William James in philosophy. James' name shows up in a list of men recognized as great by the business State described in *When the Sleeper Wakes*. This may suggest that Wells may have had some doubts about his ideas at first but the reference is misleading. Wells admired James greatly and gave Pragmatism his very emphatically expressed approval. It is easy enough to see why, since James' main positions are designed to plug the holes in Huxley's Romanes lecture. Huxley's straddle involved mental compartmentation. One part of the mind accepted the mechanistic view of the universe and one kind of truth, the other accepted the idea of amoral order and another kind of truth to which the first was hostile and destructive. James invented the idea of operative truth which is supposed to cover the difficulty:

. . . ideas (which themselves are but parts of our experience) become true just in so far as they help us to get into satisfactory relations with other parts of our experience.

True ideas are those we can assimilate, validate, corroborate, and verify. False ideas are those we cannot.

The true, to put it very briefly, is only the expedient in the way of our thinking, just as "the right" is only the expedient in the way of our behaving.

The two first of these propositions dispose of the mechanistic view of the universe much as a lazy housemaid disposes of dust by sweeping it under the rug. The truth about the universe which it states neither helps us to get into satisfactory relations with other parts of our experience nor is subject to verification. (It is possible to postulate conditions in which mind, consciousness, and experience would have no meaning, but not to verify or experience them.) The basis for pessimism therefore loses its status as truth. The last proposition deals with any realistic appreciation of human nature: it is inexpedient to consider man base, at any rate when one is trying to construct a better world, so that the idea may be dismissed as untrue.

However much these propositions may have appealed to Wells' humanitarian feelings, they grated on his æsthetic sense and his intelligence fought with them, so that it became an increasing effort to pretend that they "worked." The doubts emerge as early as 1904, in *The Food of The Gods*. This is a progressive parable about the way in which human undertakings have outgrown petty national States and their parochial administrative units. It had its genesis in a talk on Areas of Administration given at the Students' Union in the Grosvenor Road in March 1903—with Beatrice Webb in the chair. It is rounded out with a pep-talk for the new order. But, and the but is a large one, the scientists who produce the food of the Gods have no idea of what they have done. The Skinners, who put it into use in the world, are monstrous parodies of the average man, and the food produces super-rats as well as supermen and super-chickens as a result of their sloppiness and carelessness. The book is very convincing as long as it is describing how things go wrong and hardly convincing at all when it attempts to say how they will go right. What it effectively describes is the frustration and destruction of a great possibility by inferior human material. The optimism of the conclusion rests on a trick. The food of the Gods has produced a new, larger, nobler breed of human being adequate to the technological possibilities open to it, and the future rests with them. The device is transparent, and it is hard not to feel that the evasion of the real problem, of what can be done with human nature as it is, is not a conscious one. It is the first of a series of such calculated evasions. They are less apparent in the books about people than elsewhere, but they emerge from these too: *Kipps, Tono-Bungay, Ann Veronica, The History of Mr. Polly, The New Machiavelli, Marriage, The Passionate Friends,* and *The Wife of Sir Isaac Harman,* all superficially suggest that Wells is asking the question "what shall we do with our lives" as if the answer could be "whatever we wish." But the line of development followed in the books shows an underlying doubt about this answer. They show a steadily diminishing confidence in the possibility of individual solutions. What emerges at the end of the chain is the idea of the Mind of the Race, a group intellect which will be freed from individual weaknesses, and which will save humanity from its instincts. This group intellect is to be served by semi-religious orders of devotees, the Samurai, who are to surrender their lives to it. But at the back of this conception is an awareness that it is not consistent with human nature that such a surrender should in fact take place. This recognition led to Wells writing a series of catastrophe books, stories in which he imagines that human nature undergoes some fundamental change that will permit the construction of a Utopian society. The ideas of Hobbes play a large part in these fantasies. Fear, generated by a cosmic disaster as *In the Days of the Comet,* or by atomic war in *The World Set Free* (1914), leads men to submit to some kind of central world government modelled on the Common Power described in *Leviathan.* But the idea of a change in human nature itself is the *sine qua non* of his utopias, and in the end Wells conceded that such a change was not within the realm of possibility. His much-parodied *Men Like Gods* is the point of concession, and it is odd that those who have criticized the book as representing the unpracticality and unreality of his idealism in its extreme form have not noticed the fact. The ideal beings which inhabit its Utopia exist in a free zone which is not within the realm of human reality. They are special creations like the giant children in *The Food of The Gods* and like them they are designed to evade the truth about human nature. They live in another universe outside the earth's spatial scheme altogether, which is part of a very elaborate construction indeed:

> Wonder took possession of Mr. Barnstaple's mind. That dear world of honesty and health was beyond the utmost boundaries of our space, utterly inaccessible to him now for evermore; and yet, as he had been told, it was but one of countless universes that move together in time, that lie against one another, endlessly like the leaves of a book. And all of them are as nothing in the endless multitudes of systems and dimensions that surround them. "Could I but rotate my arm out of the limits set to it," one of the Utopians had said to him. "I could thrust it into a thousand universes."

This is optimism at the last ditch, an allowance of the cold comfort of an eternal moral order somewhere in a system of plural universes wholly inaccessible to human experience. And beyond that, the construction has the effect of making the book not a debate between man-as-he-might-be and man-as-he-is, but an essentially sterile clash between reality and an unattainable ideal. At best it is a cry of distress, a plea for things to be other than they are. *Men Like Gods* is in reality an altogether pessimistic book. Read in conjunction with *The Undying Fire,* which prepared the way for it, and which is a violently expressed hymn of loathing of things as they are, it leaves no doubt that in his last writings Wells was only giving a new form to beliefs which he had held all along. *The Undying Fire* is particularly moving, to those who have any sympathy with Wells at all. It shows the pendulum of his mind swinging away from its natural despairing bent over to the side of determination to construct something better out of human opportunities and back, again and again. Men are good enough to do something better than this, he says, gesticulating at the mess of the horrible world of 1919; and something better would be worth building however briefly it were to endure—and then he swings back:

> I talk . . . I talk . . . and then a desolating sense of reality blows like a destroying gust through my mind, and my little lamp of hope blows out. . . .

These words were written when he was fifty-one, and they cannot be attributed to the loss of powers which are held to account for the tone of his writing from 1942 onwards. The difference between the two phases is that in 1919 his physical buoyancy and vitality supported his will to reject what he knew in his bones. In 1919, in *The Undying Fire,* he wrote:

> I can see nothing to redeem the waste and destruction of the last four years and the still greater waste and spiritless disorder and poverty and disease ahead of us. You will tell me that the world has learnt a lesson it could learn no other way, that we shall set up a League of Nations now and put an end to war. But on what will you set up your world League of Nations? What common foundations have you made in the last four years but ruins? Is there any common idea, any common understanding yet in the minds of men?

The utterance is a despairing one. But Wells reacted to it by setting himself the task of attempting to fabricate the necessary common idea. *The Outline of History* was designed to provide a universal history which would serve as the basis for a patriotism of humanity, as national histories serve as a basis for national patriotism. What the book states is, not that progress is inevitable, but that mankind has a common historical background, not a racial or a regional one. It goes on to say that given the will mankind might, by a tremendous concerted effort, establish a world order in which all its energy could be consumed in constructive and creative enterprises, physical, æsthetic, and intellectual. The pendulum swung from one extreme to the other between 1919 and 1920; with the publication of *Men Like Gods* in 1923 it had swung right back.

If I appear to be saying that Wells was inconsistent, it cannot be helped, inconsistency is the natural consequence of an unresolved conflict in a writer's work or thought. Wells' inconsistencies could be quite dazzling at times. I remember receiving a kind of marriage sermon from him when I was first married in which he made a great point of monogamy and fidelity as being an essential to true happiness. Later on I received a number of tongue-lashings on the subject of divorce: when I told him that I had always thought of him as a man who had saved himself much unhappiness by divorce, he objected that this had no bearing on the fundamental principle. Later on we had some violent arguments on the question of pacifism. I had read a substantial part of *The Autocracy of Mr. Parham* in the light of a case for pacifism, and I still find it very hard not to do so. But in 1939 I was surprised to find that Wells took the line that once the country was at war it was the citizen's job to do what he was told to do without argument. We had many heated discussions about this which generally became a great deal more heated whenever I began to defend myself with the phrase "but you said, in Mr. Parham, that . . ." *"That* has nothing to do with it, nothing at all. . . ." During the extremely bitter internal dispute among the Fabians in the early nineteen-hundreds Shaw attacked Wells on these grounds, attributing his lack of intellectual discipline to the fact that he had such tremendous facility and rapidity of mind that he had never had really to face any practical or intellectual difficulty, he had always been able to dodge. This may be so. But I am inclined to trace the trouble to the central dilemma, and to think that inconsistency and evasion became a habit of mind because he could never bring himself to deal with it. He comes out with it in *Boon:*

> "And that is where I want to take you up," said Wilkins. "I want to suggest that the mind of the race may be just a gleam of conscious realization that passes from darkness to darkness. . . ."
> "No," said Boon.
> "Why not?"
> "Because I will not have it so," said Boon.

Wells was Wilkins and Boon at once, and also Hallery, the intensely serious exponent of moral values who introduces an almost

Calvinist note into the book. It was, of course, *Boon* with its parody of Henry James, and its harsh criticism of æsthetic values, which finally established his reputation as a Philistine. From *Boon* onwards he made increasingly strident attacks on literary values which are, in my view, only partially explicable by his sense that in the state in which the world found itself æsthetics were a luxury for which there was not enough time. It is my view that these attacks, which went along with his reiterated statements that his own work had no literary value, that it was merely journalism, attached to contemporary issues; which would become meaningless inside a couple of decades, reflected a troubled inner sense that there was something profoundly wrong about his own course of development. In the end I believe, on the strength of conversations which I had with him on the particular subject of what he meant by Dr. Moreau, and on some related topics, that he came to feel that a realization of the truth of the human situation, in all its ultimate hopelessness, was much more likely to stir men to present effort to make life more tolerable than any pretence. He felt, or so I think, that he had made a mistake in not quashing *Boon's* easy sentimentality. He knew in his bones that the æsthetes were right, and that the writer's sole duty is to state the truth which he knows. At the close of his life, from *The Croquet Player* onwards, he was trying to recapture the spirit in which he had written *The Island of Dr. Moreau,* and what haunted him, and made him exceedingly unhappy, was a tragic sense that he had returned to the real source of what could have been his strength too late.

All this is, of course, about the inward centre of his work. Few people have brought so much buoyant vitality to the business of living, or have exercised so stimulating an effect on their friends. He spread a spirit of pleasure about him, and he made every kind of mental activity seem to be the best of sport. Although he made a number of enemies through impatience and lack of tact he made many more friends whose friendship endured through episodes which would not have been forgiven in a lesser man, and who when all was said and done rejoiced in having known him. Beyond that close circle of people who knew him there was the larger army whose hearts were warmed by the abundant spirit and courage which emanate from his writing and which make it easy to miss the intensity of his internal struggle with his demon.

1st sentence
Tasmanians — 125
Darwin — 124
Mars — star of war — 126